A Place in th

— 4 |

A Place in the Sun

*Africa in Italian Colonial Culture from
Post-Unification to the Present*

EDITED BY

Patrizia Palumbo

UNIVERSITY OF CALIFORNIA PRESS

Berkeley   Los Angeles   London

University of California Press
Berkeley and Los Angeles, California

University of California Press, Ltd.
London, England

© 2003 by the Regents of the University of California

Library of Congress Cataloging-in-Publication Data

A place in the sun : Africa in Italian colonial culture from post-
unification to the present / edited by Patrizia Palumbo.
    p.   cm.
    Includes bibliographical references and index.
    ISBN 0–520-23232-1 (alk. paper).—ISBN 0-520-23234-8 (pbk. :
alk. paper)
    1. Italy—Colonies—Africa.   2. Italy—Relations—Africa.
3. Africa—Relations—Italy.   4. Popular Culture—Italy—History.
I. Palumbo, Patrizia.

DT35 .P56 2003
303.48'24506—dc21   2003005685

Manufactured in the United States of America

12 11 10 09 08 07 06 05 04 03
10 9 8 7 6 5 4 3 2 1

The paper used in this publication meets the minimum
requirements of ANSI/NISO Z39.48-1992 (®1997) ⊚.

To Sofia

CONTENTS

Introduction

Italian Colonial Cultures

Patrizia Palumbo

Italian studies has only recently begun to dedicate its attention to Italian colonialism. Indeed, after decades of neglect, the subject of Italy's colonial exploits has reemerged as a topic of heated debate. In the decade following
the fall of the fascist regime, when Italian intellectuals were addressing issues related to national reconstruction, the colonial past was almost completely forgotten. During the following two decades, the economic boom,
internal and external migrations by Italian nationals, and domestic political
scandals garnered the lion's share of public attention.[1] Scholars' failure to
examine the Italian colonial past in this period, it has been noted, may be
partially justified by the difficulty of accessing national colonial archives.
The virtual inaccessibility of these archives made a probing, politically in-
flammatory investigation of the Italian colonial past impossible.[2] The isolation of Italian scholars from the growing number of postcolonial theorists
in the anglophone academy also contributed to the lack of serious discussion
on Italian expansionist politics in Africa. Indeed, because of Italian educational policies in the colonies, no postcolonial critics—that is, critics from
formerly colonized nations writing in Italian—emerged after Italy's departure from Africa.[3]

  Italian colonialism finally came under scrutiny in the late 1960s and early
1970s, when several scholars provided new interpretations of Italian expansionism.[4] It is only in the last two decades, nonetheless, that Italian colonialism has been given intense scholarly attention in Italy. The urgent need for
attention has become even more apparent since the 1980s, when immigration into the country from Northern and sub-Saharan Africa made the exploration of the Italian colonial past and its relation to national identity imperative. In this period, indeed, works on colonialism have proliferated in
Italy; they cover many aspects of Italian colonial culture, including, for ex-

ample, the financial, juridical, and racial politics of the expansionist era.[5] A further, controversial response to recent African immigration into Italy can be found in the autobiographical literature written by Italians settlers. This literature, produced by Italians who were born or resided in the colonies and published since the late 1980s, nostalgically recalls the privileges of colonial living.[6] Although Italy has not experienced anything on the scale of Great Britain's Raj revival, Italians have started to consume its colonial past in the form of documentaries broadcast by national television, videocassettes sold at newspaper stands, and the aforementioned settler literature.[7] The Italian colonial enterprise was certainly more limited geographically than the British and the French. In addition, Italian colonialism did not last as long as that of these two European powers, coming to an end after a few decades of often troubled domination.[8] The Italian colonial past, however, must also be a primary object of investigation since, in spite of its limits, it obviously has had huge repercussions in Italy and in the colonies, as well as in countries not directly involved in the Italian colonial effort. As William R. Scott argues in *The Sons of Sheba's Race: African-Americans and the Italo-Ethiopian War, 1935–1941,* the Italian invasion of Ethiopia in 1935 ignited solidarity among the world's peoples of color and helped to unify antifascist sentiment all over the world. The Italian attack on Haile Selassie's empire may be seen, then, as the catalyzing force not simply for the struggle against fascist expansionism, but perhaps more significantly for the wave of pan-African organization that contributed to the decolonization of Africa during the postwar period.[9] Furthermore, the growth of postcolonial studies in American institutions has inspired Italian studies scholars in the United States to explore Italian colonial and postcolonial culture in the light of theoretical perspectives that, in general, have not been elaborated by Italian scholarship in Italy. For example, Karen Pinkus has analyzed the impact of Italy's colonial politics on domestic advertising and consumption in her *Bodily Regimes: Italian Advertising under Fascism,* a study of the popular imagery of the fascist *ventennio.*[10] Significantly, *Revisioning Italy: National Identity and Global Culture,* a collection that aims at questioning the notion of a stable Italian national identity, devotes considerable attention to the historical and cultural reverberations of Italian colonialism in the volatile space of the nation.[11] Finally, in 1998 an interdisciplinary symposium on the centuries-long exchanges between Africa and Italy was held at Miami University and drew a remarkable number of scholars from African, Italian, and American institutions. These examples, among others, demonstrate the pressing need for an overview of the diverse fields of inquiry into Italian colonial culture.

This collection, *A Place in the Sun: Africa in Italian Colonial Culture from Post-Unification to the Present,* grows out of the increasing interest in Italian colonialism and its political, economic, and cultural legacies. Through the broad time span embraced by the articles it includes, this collection is intended to provide a panorama of Italian colonial culture and to illuminate the wealth of material that still needs to be addressed and debated by scholarship. However, the significant interventions made by each article into a wide variety of fields, as well as the synthetic quality of the volume as a whole, offer a significant contribution to the reexamination of Italian colonial history. We believe that such analysis is an imperative element of Italy's transformation into a multicultural, multiracial democracy.

The collective identity of the nation is, after all, constantly being reinvented. The fictive and multidimensional character of history has been emphasized by critics who in recent decades have embarked on a major effort to reconceptualize the discipline. In the 1970s, indeed, the traditional view of history as an "unproblematic, extra-textual and extra-discursive real" started to be dismantled.[12] New perceptions of history, emerging in the work of theorists such as Michel Foucault, Raymond Williams, and Edward Said, were distinguished by a disbelief in the objectivity of history and by an emphasis on the way the past is constructed or invented in the present. These academic debates take on particular salience in the context of the reconstructions of national identity that have followed the end of the Cold War and the consolidation of new political entities such as the European Union.

PART I: THE SHAPING OF ITALIAN COLONIAL HISTORY

The first section of this collection is clearly sustained by interrogations of national history. Indeed, this section illuminates the manner in which accepted versions of Italian colonial history have been nothing but a reflection of the hegemonic political interests that have shaped inquiry into the past for decades. This, indeed, is the subject of Angelo Del Boca's opening article, "The Myths, Suppressions, Denials, and Defaults of Italian Colonialism," in which the prominent historian highlights the efforts made by colonialist lobbies to provide an almost hagiographic picture of the Italian campaigns in Africa and to prevent access to the national archives of the colonial past. Del Boca also provides a valuable full account of the political exchanges to date between the Italian government and the former colonies. Dealing, for example, with the negotiations between the Italian and Ethiopian authorities for the restitution of the obelisk of Axum, a monument of great spiritual value to the Ethiopian people, Del Boca exposes the perpetuation of colonial abuses and the Italian government's reluctance to renounce a symbol of its colonial power. Del Boca also shows how the same dismissive attitude is manifested by Italian authorities toward Libya, where Italian domination was more fiercely repressive, as well as toward Eritrea, the ever-sentimentalized "firstborn" colony. Finally, disclosing the grievous shortcomings in Italy's postcolonial history, Del Boca underlines the failure of Italian trusteeship of Somalia and of successive political and economical interventions to prevent Somalia from falling into its present disastrous condition.[13] Italy's actions on the global stage today, then, are, inextricably linked to hegemonic articulations of national identity during the postcolonial period.

The essays included in this section also emphasize the need for scrutiny of Italy's colonial history by locating that history in the broader geographical and scientific context that contributed to its formation. Fascist colonialism and its relation to colonialism of the great powers, France and Britain, is at the core of Nicola Labanca's "Studies and Research on Fascist Colonialism, 1922–1935: Reflections on the State of the Art." In this article, Labanca deals with the scarcity of Italian historiography on the fascist colonial period before the formation of the empire and with the consequent perpetuation of misleading national narratives. Agreeing with Del Boca, Labanca argues that the insufficiency of historiographical work on fascist colonialism is a consequence of the fact that the "decolonization" of colonial historiography has been a very slow process in republican Italy. The enduring hold of apologetic versions of colonial history is, according to Labanca, linked to the retention of control of the Italian colonial archives by old colonial officials or, in general, philocolonialists, who certainly did not want to unveil their involvement in episodes of repressive colonial politics. Labanca observes that the dearth of studies on preimperial fascist colonialism has contributed to the magnification of the Ethiopian war as a triumphant success of Mussolini's regime, which has, in turn, precluded comprehension of fascist colonialism and of its relation to that of the liberal imperialist regimes of France and Britain.

The correlation of "scientific" disciplines and Italian colonial history and culture are discussed in the remaining two essays of this section. In "Italian Anthropology and the Africans: The Early Colonial Period," Barbara Sòrgoni shows how anthropology and colonialism benefited from one another in Italy. According to Sòrgoni, the government sought the advantages of anthropological "knowledge" for its colonial endeavors; anthropology in turn proffered its services to the colonial effort. The European context delineated by Sòrgoni, within which Italian anthropologists elaborated and located their theories, was one in which, in spite of individual theoretical variations, cultural aspects were blurring with the biological. Anthropological definitions of cultural difference, in other words, dovetailed all too neatly with the taxonomic theories of racial classification that underpinned social Darwinism. The main focus of Sòrgoni's chapter, however, is the theories of Italian anthropologists concerning the origins of Eastern African populations who would later become central to the Italian colonial project. Although Aldobrandino Mochi, Giuffrida Ruggieri, and Giuseppe Sergi assumed different positions concerning the origins of Eastern African populations, the common denominator that united their theories was the ultimate assertion of European superiority in relation to the autochthonous African peoples. For Sòrgoni, in other words, scientific theory ultimately legitimized the much-propagated idea of a European civilizing mission in Africa.

The last essay in this section, Giulia Barrera's "The Construction of Racial Hierarchies in Colonial Eritrea: The Liberal and Early Fascist Period (1897–1934)," describes the foundations of national colonial history through an analysis of documents from the colonial archives. Barrera's essay follows the growth in the field of history of alternative subjects of investigation, including women's history, oral history, and the postcolonial rewriting of Eurocentric viewpoints. These recent areas of scholarly interest, together with the more general blurring of disciplinary boundaries between historiography, sociology, anthropology, and cultural studies, have all cast doubt on the validity, relevance, and accessibility of historical facts. It is this new awareness of the limitations of truth claims of the traditional positivist historiography that leads Barrera to examine in her article a substantial but neglected issue of Italian colonialism: the interracial relationship. In doing so, she resorts to documents that traditionally have been marginalized in Italian colonial historiography, such as judiciary records and oral interviews. Avoiding a simplistic binary opposition between colonizers and colonized, Barrera delineates a historical profile of colonial life in Eritrea since the formation of the colony to 1934 that is complicated by issues of both gender and class. Although interracial relationships in the Eritrean colony were not free of colonial abuses and forms of racism, the intense intermingling between Italian settlers and the indigenous population can be understood, Barrera argues, only by taking into consideration the socioeconomic characteristics of the Italian community in the colony.

PART II: COLONIAL LITERATURE

Part II delineates changes in the textual representation of the colonial experience, from the formation and consolidation of a colonial imaginary to the creation of an empire. The wide variety of writings analyzed in this section demonstrate the extent to which the range of colonial texts produced in Italy grew together with Italian involvement and interests in Africa. A highly romanticized image of Africa in nineteenth-century literature, which circulated among a limited and prevalently male audience, was later flanked by and reelaborated into colonial fantasies for mass consumption, made available in new venues such as variety shows, popular novels, magazines, and comic books.

Although the nationalistic belief in Italy's civilizing mission that informed much of the later colonial discourse is deeply embedded in the Risorgimento, it was only in 1885 that the Italian government initiated its colonial campaigns in Africa, officially in order to revenge the death of Italian explorers slaughtered in Eastern Africa.[14] After unification, the Italian nation did not express much interest in the African continent, absorbed as it was in the building of the new state and in dealing with the economical and cultural disparities between North and South, the Roman question, and the creation of European alliances that would guarantee national autonomy. At that time, only scholars, travelers, missionaries, and financial speculators were intent on increasing knowledge of the African continent.[15] The governmental interference in their African exploits was minor and did not have much visibility within the nation.[16]

In this period travelers, free from political and bureaucratic obligations, were able to portray the encounter with Africans as an interactive experience, producing documents that were markedly different from the accounts of conquest written during the later period of actual colonial domination. Such a traveler was the Tuscan Carlo Piaggia, who spent two years among the Sudanese tribe of the Azande and who, according to the illustrious specialist on Zande history, Evans-Pritchard, was the earliest traveler in Zandeland.[17] The peculiarity of Piaggia's experience with the Azande is discussed by Cristina Lombardi-Diop in her essay, "Gifts, Sex, and Guns: Nineteenth-Century Italian Explorers in Africa." Relying upon theories of political economy elaborated by Karl Marx and subsequent renowned anthropologists such as Claude Levi-Strauss, Marcel Mauss, and Bronislav Malinowsky, Lombardi-Diop argues that Piaggia's narrative is immune from the evolutionary racism that informed later travel narratives such as those of Giovanni Miani and Gustavo Bianchi because of the precapitalistic mode within which the encounter between Piaggia and the Azande tribe took place. Miani and Bianchi's ethnocentric accounts, Lombardi-Diop suggests, are situated within an imperialist economy in which "guns, rather than gifts, are the primary object of exchange."

Although nineteenth-century Italian travelers, such as those discussed by Lombardi-Diop, journeyed to Africa to satisfy a great variety of interests not closely related to national causes, they would later be invoked as precursors of the Italian colonial enterprise. Africanists like Cesare Cesari, who in 1928 praised the pioneering spirit of early explorers, certainly did so in order to provide Italian expansionistic philosophy with more ancient origins and more solid foundations.[18] Traditions are, in fact, often invented simply in order to legitimize recent practices. Terence Ranger and Eric Hobsbawm's concept of the invention of tradition is particularly apposite in the context of the colonial encounter. While Europeans often represented the zones of the earth to which they were journeying as history-less blank spaces on the world map, colonial projects were often fuelled by fictive narratives of cultural identity and continuity. This is certainly the case in Italy, where the history of imperial Rome was invoked to legitimate the expansionist aims of the recently formed nation-state.[19]

Although the early accounts of Italian explorers analogous to those analyzed by Lombardi-Diop did not clearly express literary aspirations, after Italy's interests in the African continent had consolidated, Italian intellectuals manifested the desire to define and regulate Italian colonial literature. In 1931, indeed, colonial literature was at the center of a debate among several Italian intellectuals concerned with both defining and envisioning the present and future state of Italian colonial literature. The positions adopted by the futurist Filippo Tommaso Marinetti—who enthusiastically participated in this debate—are analyzed by Cinzia Sartini-Blum in "Incorporating the Exotic: From Futurist Excess to Postmodern Impasse." Focusing on the elaboration of the fundamental paradoxes of fascist-era culture in a colonial setting, Sartini-Blum examines a number of texts by Marinetti that embody a clash between orientalist nostalgia and futurist "modernolatria." The futurist primitivism that develops in Marinetti's colonial texts attempts to overcome this impasse by staging the exotic as a site of heroic self-fulfillment, where the sovereign individual can effect a fusion of savagery and progress denied in the standardized world of European modernity. Yet, as Sartini-Blum argues, while offering this imagined resolution, Africa is simultaneously a space of ambivalence and phobia. Seeking to mollify the melancholy feelings prompted by their belated travel through a land that reminds them of their lost youth, the characters in Marinetti's fictional works and travel narratives consume the picturesque sites of Northern Africa in a voracious manner, in one instance literally eating the pyramids whole. According to Sartini-Blum, the combination of incorporation and abjection to be found in Marinetti's African texts exposes the violent, split unconscious of orientalist discourse.

Orientalist discourse is the point of departure of the third essay in this section, Lucia Re's "Alexandria Revisited: Colonialism and the Egyptian Works of Enrico Pea and Giuseppe Ungaretti." Re's critique of Edward Said's interpretation of *Aida* as an oriental fantasy and product of European imperialism introduces her discussion of Pea's and Ungaretti's colonial texts.

According to Re, Said's interpretation of *Aida* neglects the political context from which Verdi's opera emerged, and therefore tends to homogenize all colonial productions as reflections of European imperialism. Actually, as Re illustrates, Egypt, which had hosted a consistent Italian colony since the nineteenth century, and Alexandria in particular are in Pea's and Ungaretti's texts symbolic sites that promote the authors' lucid meditation on colonialism in general. With its cultural and historical complexities, Alexandria was the ideal location to speculate on the failure of Western imperialism and on the alternative colonial model embodied by this multiethnic city.

Pea's and Ungaretti's writing, Re indicates, expresses the writers' awareness of how race, class, and gender problematize the colonial experience, thereby undermining the binary and oppositional view of colonial relationships embraced by Said, particularly in his early work.

In the 1930s, both before and after the creation of the Italian empire, radio, cinema, variety shows, and popular culture in general disseminated exotic colonialist fantasies for mass consumption that both promoted and reflected Italians' escapist acceptance of the national colonial politics of the day. The fabulous image of Africa circulating in Italian popular culture of the time was obviously susceptible to variations dictated by the gender of its audience and producers. In "Mass-Mediated Fantasies of Feminine Conquest, 1930–1940," Robin Pickering-Iazzi deals with the ways in which the women's press of the period educated women about Eastern Africa. For Pickering-Iazzi, these popular texts represented "Africa Orientale" as the land of professional opportunities as well as of regenerating and liberating adventures. Discussing three popular cultural sites for the articulation of these fantasies of upward and outward mobility, Pickering-Iazzi explores the ideological components of "demographic colonialism," the fascist project for Italian settlement abroad. Texts such as Pina Ballario's *La sposa bianca* mobilize gendered fantasies in which sexual and territorial conquest are aligned. Analysis of these colonial fantasies produced by and for women allows Pickering-Iazzi to discuss the crucial issue of women's complicity with and resistance to the colonial enterprise. Pickering-Iazzi responds, therefore, to recent scholarly work on Western women's ambivalent colonial perspectives. In fact, with the maturation of feminist theory, women's history, and women's studies, the role of Western women in the colonies has drawn a lot of attention from scholars in these fields. Anne McClintock, Vron Ware, N. Chaudhuri and M. Strobel, and Ann Stoler, to mention just a few, have challenged the traditional theorization of the colonial space as masculine and have emphasized the complexities of Western women's identification with colonial discourses and of their lives in the colonies.

In the 1930s, children were also consistently called on to relate enthusiastically to the national colonial enterprises. Immediately prior to and during the Ethiopian war, especially, imperialist propaganda directed toward the youngest Italians increased remarkably. Fascist schools and youth organizations of the period subjected children to a deluge of insistent depictions of Italy's civilizing mission in Africa and of the future economic and political opportunities provided by colonization. This propagandistic effort was also supported by complacent authors of children's literature, whose stories were quick to incorporate and support the Italian campaign in Ethiopia. As Patrizia Palumbo shows in her chapter, "Orphans for the Empire: Colonial Propaganda and Children's Literature during the Imperial Era," children's literature of the era replicated imperialistic governmental assumptions and perpetuated a traditionally nationalistic gendering of social roles. Palumbo argues, however, that the unenthusiastic reception found by this literature, ignored until this point by literary history, testifies to the failure of this orchestrated propagandistic effort. The ambiguities of the imperialist ethos that pervaded Italian children's literature of the imperial age and that inform colonial discourse in general could not be embraced by the youngest Italians. This editorial and political failure also points, according to Palumbo, to the possibility of some form of agency and resistance, an agency that is habitually denied to children. In addition to analyzing the role of colonial discourse in children's literature in the period, Palumbo brings attention to the cultural relevance of children's literature and other productions addressing the youngest in the formation of national identities. For Palumbo, children's literature takes on a particularly important role within the imperial projects of totalitarian regimes such as Mussolini's Italy.

PART III: THE COLONIAL PRODUCTION OF AFRICA AND THE SILENT SCENE OF DECOLONIZATION

The role of colonialism's uncertainties and "weaknesses" in Italian cinema is the subject of the third and concluding section of *A Place in the Sun*. More specifically, the three articles included in this section, highlight how Italian cinema went from constructing a strong Italian national identity in the interwar period to diverting public attention from the process of decolonization by focusing on a form of domestic expansionism promoted by the economic boom. Contributors argue that through three phases of Italian cinema, from the 1930s to the 1960s, film either failed to address the colonial subject or revealed significant anxieties about Italy's imperial identity.

The cultural superiority upon which the "civilizing" mission of Italian expansionism rested has been demonstrated since the post-unification period through the invocation of specious notions of modern Italy's continuity with imperial Rome. Nevertheless, tradition, in addition to being invoked to legitimate foreign politics, was also summoned in Italy to solidify national sentiment. It has been observed, indeed, that "the need for organic metaphors of identity or society implies a counter-sense of fragmentation and dispersion," a cultural condition that perfectly coincides with that of the newly formed Italian nation.[20] After national political unification had taken place, "Italian-ness" was nothing but a rhetorical trope, whose lack of meaning was made evident by the ever-unfinished project of a true cultural and economic homogenization. Indeed, within the peninsula, the metaphorical distance between the North and South in particular was still alarming, the South's condition being one of extreme economic "backwardness" with respect to the North.[21] In spite of this sharp national division, Italian culture was marked by a discourse of national unity and grandeur sustained through the resuscitation of Rome's glorious history and antiquity. Literature, cinema, arts, and popular culture all participated in this recovery of Roman civilization and superimposed it onto national uncertainties. The significant contribution made by Italian silent cinema to this cultural effort is the starting point of Giorgio Bertellini's "Colonial Autism: Whitened Heroes, Auditory Rhetoric, and National Identity in Interwar Italian Cinema." In the first part of his essay, Bertellini shows that at the time of the Libyan war, rather than dealing with colonial topics, Italian cinema was absorbed in the resurrection of ancient Roman grandeur and the contemplation of monumental heroisms. This cinema of imperial nostalgia gradually expelled the African, the racial other, from its screen. The genealogy of this expulsion is signified, as Bertellini shows, by the countless *Maciste* movies, in which the popular hero turns from a black African slave to a very domestic white hero. The exclusion of the African adversary continues, Bertellini argues, in the Italian films of the 1930s. However, although the Italian films of these years maintained their homosocial character, representations of Italian identity and national integrity were problematized by the introduction of sound. From the early 1930s, the fascist government engaged in a linguistic policing effort in order to guarantee the use of the standard Italian instead of numerous regional dialects in contemporary cultural productions. Although much of the cinema of the period complied with fascist linguistic dictates, some makers of colonial movies resisted this imposition of patriotic speech. Both *Lo squadrone bianco* and *Il grande appello,* Bertellini points out, exemplify the Italian colonial cinema's incapacity to identify with the fascist rhetoric of national oneness through their respective aphasia and linguistic fragmentation.

The much-celebrated Italian empire in Eastern Africa was not only short-lived, but also geographically limited and militarily insecure. Indeed, after the declaration of the Italian empire, two-thirds of the Ethiopian territory was still administered by Haile Selassie's officials, and indigenous patriots troubled the whole period of Italian domination in that country.[22] In those years, therefore, the total submission of the Ethiopians could only be a reassuring projection. In "Black Shirts / Black Skins: Fascist Italy's Colonial Anxieties and *Lo Squadrone Bianco,*" in fact, Cecilia Boggio shows that the "African" cinematic works made by Italian directors in the 1930s do not celebrate the contemporary colonization of the Ethiopian territory, which, as historians have pointed out, never really took place. Instead, as Boggio observes, both documentaries and narrative films manifest a remarkable crowd anxiety that they solve through different representations of the colonial encounter. *Maldafrica* and *Il cammino degli eroi,* two of the most illustrious "African" documentaries sponsored by the fascist regime at the time, present African crowds as mesmerized by the Italian technological power embodied in the camera. These documentaries emphasize, in addition, the huge physical potential of this innocuous African mass, destined to construct the empire's infrastructures. In the narrative films of the period, such as *Lo squadrone bianco,* the African populations are depicted, on the contrary, as an invisible threat that has to be erased. These cinematic representations of the African crowds are analyzed by Boggio, who relates them to the crowd theories and conceptualizations of space elaborated since the late nineteenth century. Relying upon this wide range of theoretical material, Boggio demonstrates that the narrative films of the 1930s betrayed an approach to colonial domination that was certainly less confident than that heralded by the regime's rhetoric.

The postwar historiographical neglect and obfuscation of the Italian colonial past is naturally matched by the blankness left by this past in the national culture. As Karen Pinkus observes in her essay, "Empty Spaces: Decolonization in Italy," in the postwar period there were no traces in Italy of the process of cultural decolonization that France, on the contrary, was undergoing. In the two decades that followed the loss of the colonies, rather than confronting its colonial history, Italy turned to a form of internal expansionism sustained by the new mobility allowed by the economic boom. In order to illustrate the spatial exploration and penetration going on in Italy in the postcolonial period, Pinkus engages in an original discussion of three landmarks of Italian cinema produced between 1960 and 1962: Michelangelo Antonioni's *L'eclisse,* Federico Fellini's *La dolce vita,* and Dino Risi's *Il sorpasso.* Pinkus shows that spatial motion into the desertlike outskirts of urban areas—prominent in these cinematic works—can be seen as a symbolic analogue of the colonization in Africa. In other words, although Italian cinema of the postcolonial period does not manifestly deal with the colonial past, this repressed past reemerges in the "recoding of urban and neobourgeois space" that this cinema visualizes.

Colonial discourse is an integral part of Italian culture. Indeed, this discourse goes back to the era before the expansionistic wars of the late nineteenth century in Africa and the unification of the nation. We find such discourse circulating in the period of discoveries and ventures in foreign territories that characterized the Age of Exploration. Colonial discourse may be found in latent forms that not only have not been analyzed, but have yet to be singled out. Even its manifest expressions, in the form, for example, of the cultural and military expansion into African lands, are some of the least-known aspects of Italian history. This vacuum was caused by discourses of an essentialized national benevolence and fantasies of an impermeable Italian national identity. In turn, such rhetoric helped foster insular and benign representations concerning Italy's past and present. The perilousness of these essentialist fantasies, source and fuel of contemporary nationalisms, has been extensively examined and foregrounded in recent theoretical discussions about multiculturalism and hybridity in the postnational European era.[23] It has been argued in this context that the concepts of both multiculturalism and hybridity are based on cultural essentialism, that is, on the idea, that prior to either the co-presence of cultures in multiculturalism or the mixing of them in hybridity, "there were two different cultures bounded and closed."[24]

Although this collection intends primarily to cast light on the specificity of Italian colonialism and its cultural and discursive articulations, it aims also to dismantle resilient notions of an impenetrable Italian national and cultural identity. Indeed, the locution *Italian colonial cultures* itself is intended to underline and thereby to undermine such reified and sanitized constructions of national identity. It is only by developing a full understanding of the historical conjunctions in which Italian colonial culture was produced and perpetuated that we may hope to decolonize national identity successfully.

NOTES

1. The Italians' repression of their colonial past is discussed in Angelo Del Boca's "Il mancato dibattito sul colonialismo," *L'Africa nella coscienza degli Italiani: Miti, memorie, errori, sconfitte* (Bari: Laterza, 1992), 111–27.

2. Ibid., 119.

3. On schooling in Eritrea, see Negash Tekeste, *Italian Colonialism in Eritrea, 1882–1941: Policies, Praxis, and Impact* (Uppsala, Sweden: Uppsala University, 1997), 66–91. For the Italian policy in *Africa Orientale Italiana*, see Del Boca, *Gli Italiani in Africa orientale*, vol. 3 (Milano: Mondadori, 1992), 240.

4. The most illustrious examples are the works of Rochat and Del Boca: Giorgio Rochat, *Il colonialismo italiano* (Torino: Loescher, 1974); Angelo Del Boca, *Gli italiani in Africa orientale*, 4 vols.

5. I am referring, for example, to Angelo Del Boca, ed., *Le guerre coloniali del fascismo* (Roma-Bari: Laterza, 1991); Gian Piero Brunetta, *L'ora d'Africa del cinema italiano 1911–1989* (Rovigo: Materiali di lavoro, 1990); Nicola Labanca, *In Marcia verso Adua* (Torino: Einaudi, 1993); *L'Africa in Vetrina: Storie di musei e di esposizioni coloniali in Italia* (Treviso: Pagus, 1992); Luigi Goglia, *Colonialismo e fotografia: Il caso italiano* (Messina: Sicania, 1989); Gian Luca Podesta, *Sviluppo industriale e colonialismo: Gli investimenti italiani in Africa orientale, 1869–1897* (Milano: Giuffré, 1996); Scovazzi Tullio, *Assab, Massaua, Adua: Gli strumenti giuridici del primo colonialismo italiano* (Torino: Giappichelli, 1996); and Paola Sòrgoni, *Parole e corpi: Antropologia, discorso giuridico e politiche sessuali interrazziali nella colonia Eritrea (1890–1941)* (Napoli: Liguori, 1998). Attention has recently also focused on authors coming from the former colonies, such as the Somali writer Nuruddin Farah, whose works deal with Italian colonialism and its cultural and political consequences. See, for example, Rossana Ruggiero, *Lo specchio infranto: L'opera di Nuruddin Farah* (Pasian di Prato: Campanotto, 1997); Itala Vivan, "Nurrudin Farah's Beautiful Mat and Its Italian Plot," *World*

Literature Today 72 (1998): 786–90; Claudio Gorlier, "Nuruddin Farah's Italian Domain," *World Literature Today* 72 (1998): 781–85.

6. Besides the now-renowned novels written by Erminia Dell'oro—*Asmara addio* (Pordenone: Edizione dello Zibaldone, 1988) and *L'abbandono: Una storia eritrea* (Torino: Einaudi, 1991)—another example of Italian autobiographical texts set in the colonies is Grazia Arnese Grimaldi's *I ragazzi della IV sponda* (Milano: Nuovi autori, 1990) and the self-aggrandizing work of Rodolfo Graziani, originally published in 1948 and recently reproposed to the Italian audience, *Una vita per l'Italia: "Ho difeso la patria"* (Milano: Mursia, 1994).

7. The Raj revival mode is excellently illustrated by Jenny Sharpe in "The Ruins of Time: The Jewel in the Crown," *Allegories of Empire: The Figure of Woman in the Colonial Context* (Minneapolis and London: University of Minnesota Press, 1993), 137–61. The Italian documentary *Maldafrica* was broadcast by Rai 3 in February 1998 as part of a series with the pompous title of *La grande storia*.

8. On the history of Italian colonialism in Northern and Eastern Africa, see the detailed and indispensable account given by Del Boca in *Gli italiani in Africa orientale*.

9. William R. Scott, *The Sons of Sheba's Race: African-Americans and the Italo-Ethiopian War, 1935–1941* (Bloomington: Indiana University Press, 1993). As Robin D. G. Kelley indicates, the invasion of Ethiopia also encouraged African-American participation against Spanish fascism. See his *Race Rebels: Culture, Politics, and the Black Working Class* (New York: Free Press, 1996), 123–58.

10. Karen Pinkus, *Bodily Regimes: Italian Advertising under Fascism* (Minneapolis: University of Minnesota Press, 1995).

11. Beverly Allen and Mary Russo, eds., *Revisioning Italy: National Identity and Global Culture* (Minneapolis: University of Minnesota Press, 1997).

12. Catherine Belsey, "Making Histories Then and Now: Shakespeare from Richard II to Henry V," in F. Barker, P. Hulme, and M. Iversen, eds., *Uses of History: Marxism, Postmodernism and the Renaissance* (Manchester: Manchester University Press, 1991), 26.

13. In addition to Del Boca's work, an important contribution on contemporary Somalia is that of Paolo Tripodi, *The Colonial Legacy in Somalia: Rome and Mogadishu, From Colonial Administration to Operation Restore Hope* (New York: St. Martin Press, 1999).

14. On twentieth-century Italian nationalism's reelaboration of Risorgimento theories of the nation, see Franco Gaeta, "Dalla nazionalità al nazionalismo," in *La cultura italiana tra '800 e '900 e le origini del nazionalismo* (Firenze: Olschki, 1981), 21–46.

15. On these "pioneers" see Del Boca's "Origini del colonialismo italiano," in *Gli italiani in Africa orientale*, vol. 1.

16. The Italian government's support of early colonial exploration is reported in the first seven chapters of Del Boca, *Gli italiani in Africa orientale*, vol. 1.

17. E. E. Evans-Pritchard, *The Azande: History and Political Institutions* (Oxford: Clarendon Press, 1971), 2.

18. Del Boca, *Gli Italiani in Africa orientale*, vol. 1, 4.

19. On the resort to the universal idea of Rome of which Italians were depositary as a legitimation of colonial expansion, see the still valuable and dense work by Federico Chabod, *Storia della politica estera italiana dal 1870 al 1896* (Bari: Laterza,

1951), 170–209. As Chabod indicates, after unification was achieved Giuseppe Mazzini, champion during the Risorgimento of the idea of the resurrection of Rome, expressed his hopes that the young nation would dominate the Mediterranean again.

20. Robert Young, *Colonial Desire: Hybridity in Theory, Culture and Race* (London and New York: Routledge, 1995), 4. On discourses on the nation, the obvious reference is Benedict Anderson, *Imagined Communities: Reflections on the Origin and Spread of Nationalism* (New York: Verso, 1983).

21. The failure of nation building in Italy is illustrated and discussed by John Dickie in "Imagined Italies," which is part of the groundbreaking *Italian Cultural Studies: An Introduction,* edited by David Forgacs and Robert Lumley (New York: Oxford University Press, 1996), 19–33.

22. The geographical limits of Italian control over Ethiopia after the declaration of the Italian empire are delineated by Harold G. Marcus in *A History of Ethiopia* (Berkeley: University of California Press, 1994), 147–51.

23. A valuable example of the theoretical debate on multiculturalism in a supranational Europe is Tariq Modood and Pnina Werbner, eds., *The Politics of Multiculturalism in the New Europe: Racism, Identity and Community* (London and New York: Zed Books, 1997).

24. Ibid.

PART I

The Shaping of
Italian Colonial History

Political Practices and Theoretical Legitimization

The Myths, Suppressions, Denials, and Defaults of Italian Colonialism

Angelo Del Boca

Twenty-five years ago, Giorgio Rochat wrote in his short but seminal book, *Il Colonialismo italiano:*

> For what we did in Africa from 1913 to 1943, that is, for the greatest part of the history of Italian colonialism, we have to be satisfied with often sentimental memories and documents of various and often casual origin, sometimes even purloined for lucrative publication in magazines with large distribution. It is enough to remember that not even a single organic study on the reconquest of Libya (1922–1932) exists, nor are any available that deal with the organization of this colony or the creation of the Italian empire of Ethiopia and its brief and tormented life. (Rochat 1973: 9)

Rochat's judgment is rigorously exact. With the exception of *La prima guerra d'Africa* by Roberto Battaglia, published by Einaudi in 1958, and of *La guerra libica (1911–1912)* by Francesco Malgeri, which came out in 1970, no works published in the first three postwar decades deserve any attention. In 1973, finally, Giorgio Rochat published his little volume on colonialism, a book that seems to have been written with few pretensions, intended for *licei* and university courses on contemporary history. But it turns out that this book constitutes an authentic turning point in studies of Italian colonialism. Both the text and the choice of documents reveal very clearly the will of the Waldensian historian not to compromise, to keep away from novelized and derivative interpretations, and to highlight the tremendous cost in human lives of the colonial enterprises without excusing the highest Italian political officials for the horrors of the colonial episode.

The study of Italian colonialism did not enjoy great favor in the postwar period, especially compared to other events of Italian national history that have attracted extraordinary, and in some cases even exaggerated, attention. The reasons for this lack of interest in a phenomenon that is certainly not marginal—it involved the nation for almost eighty years—are numerous and have not yet been deeply investigated.

The main reason for this neglect, in my opinion, is the behavior of the ruling class. Following the signing the Treaty of Paris on February 10, 1947, which deprived Italy of its colonies, this class refused to initiate a serious, organic, broad, and definitive debate on the phenomenon of colonialism in the country, one similar to that engaged in by other nations with a colonial history. This debate would have shed light on the positive and the negative aspects of the colonial period, the values to be preserved, and the myths and legends to be packed away in the attic. If this debate had been conducted with scientific rigor and had been disseminated by the media, it would have stimulated the historians to come forth with their irreplaceable contributions. It would also have ended the many useless and bothersome polemics, starting with the controversy concerning the use of gas in Ethiopia and ending with the myth of the good-hearted Italians *(Italiani brava gente).*

Nothing of the sort happened. The postwar Italian governments not only eluded their obligations to clarity but actively impeded the emergence of truth. It should suffice to mention the colossal, costly, and almost incredible effort of mystification promoted by the Ministry of Foreign Affairs with the publication, in fifty volumes, of *L'Italia in Africa.* The supporters of this corpus claimed to intend to provide an assessment of the Italian presence in the colonies of Eastern and Northern Africa. Instead, *L'Italia in Africa* is a coarsely and impudently falsified account that aims to exalt Italian colonialism and underline its "difference" from other contemporary colonialisms.

But then, what could be expected from the committee that managed this work? Fifteen of twenty members were former colonial governors or high officials of the dissolved Ministry of Italian Africa, while the others were scholars of sound colonialist faith. The work produced by this committee— paradoxically instituted by the antifascist Giuseppe Brusasca—could only be evasive on the one hand and hagiographic on the other. As Giorgio Rochat rightly pointed out, a good part of the fifty volumes lacks "any requisites of seriousness and scientific nature." The volumes by Vitale on the military aspects of the Italian conquest, for example, are characterized by total dependence on the extremist theses of the fascist era, by superficiality and vagueness in their reconstruction of events, by ignorance of non-Italian sources, and by renunciation of the use of the archives of the dissolved Ministry of Italian Africa, exclusive access to which the ministry arrogated to itself (Rochat 1973: 109).

The operation of the committee, conducted so arbitrarily, unavoidably led to the silencing or even to the confutation of the many mistakes and crimes committed during the wars of conquest, from the very high price paid by the subjected populations, to the attempt to deprive them of their own cultural and national identities, or even, as in Cirenaica, to their physical elimination. There are no traces, in fact, in any of the fifty volumes of *L'Italia in Africa* of the massive employment of chemical weapons in Ethiopia between 1935 and 1940, not a single reference to the lethal concentration camps in Libya, Somalia, and Eritrea. Absolute silence is maintained concerning the decimation of the Coptic Church after the attempt on Rodolfo Graziani's life on February 19, 1937—an operation led by General Maletti with such zeal and professionalism that it caused the death of 1,200 deans and priests—which has recently been proved by Ian L. Campbell and Degife Gabre-Tsadik (1997: 79–128).

The lack of debate on colonialism and the failure to condemn its most brutal aspects have promoted Italy's denial of its colonial faults. One hundred and fourteen years after the docking of Colonel Tancredi Saletta in Massawa, eighty-eight years after the invasion of Libya, and sixty-four years after the fascist attack on Ethiopia, republican and democratic Italy still hasn't been able to get rid of the myths and legends that took shape in the last century and in the first three decades of the twentieth century. Such myths are carefully cultivated and defended with obstinacy by a significant minority of former servicemen, nostalgists, and revisionists.

The persistent reading in an apologetic key of the African enterprises and, by reflex, the lack of condemnation of colonialism have also allowed all the Italians who stained themselves with colonial crimes to be acquitted. This group includes those who participated in the campaigns to reconquer Libya (1922–32), in the operations against the Somali guerrillas of Migiurtinia (1926–32), in the war against Ethiopia (1935–36), and in the failed attempt to crush the resistance movement of Ethiopian partisans (1936–41). From Mussolini to Badoglio, from Graziani to De Bono, from Lessona to Pirzio Biroli, from Geloso to Gallina, from Tracchia to Cortese, from Maletti to Belly, all those culpable for the African genocides have gone unpunished, and some obtained honors from republican Italy. Meanwhile, for some of them a process of rehabilitation is going on, thanks to some complaisant and factitious biographers.

In this general climate characterized by absolution of colonial faults and rehabilitation of the protagonists of the African enterprises, the main colonial diplomatic and military archives have been utilized for decades almost exclusively by the old colonialist lobby. This lobby is certainly not intent on denouncing the wrongdoings of Italian colonialism. The difficulties of getting access to the primary sources of colonial history alone help explain the extreme poverty of research at a scientific level. And, although there were plenty of memoirs and diaries produced in the same period, they generally tend to cultivate deformed and mythical visions of the colonial events.

Nevertheless, in spite of difficult and discontinuous access to the archives, the theft of documents from the deposits of Farnesina,[1] and the lack of encouragement from those state institutions that should have promoted a historical revision of Italian actions in Africa instead of sabotaging it, studies of Italian colonialism have made substantial progress in the last twenty years thanks to the research of Giorgio Rochat, Enrico Serra, Francesco Malgeri, Enzo Santarelli, Giuliano Procacci, Eric Salerno, Carlo Zaghi, Renato Mori, Gianluigi Rossi, Francesco Surdich, Giampaolo Calchi Novati, Nicola Labanca, and Alessandro Triulzi. Their works have inaugurated new research methods and offered new interpretations of Italian colonialism. They constitute, moreover, an initial, healthy antidote to the common repression of Italian colonial faults.

This innovative and restorative historiography—together with rare but effective state documentaries such as *L'Impero: Un'avventura africana,* directed by Massimo Sani, and *Mal d'Africa,* directed by Emanuele Valerio Marino, and the meritorious exhibitions of images such as those curated by Enrico Castelli—has undoubtedly tended to modify in a positive way the collective imaginary concerning Africa, the Africans, and the wars of conquest.

However, these are still partial results, even if they are noteworthy ones. It suffices to mention the obstinate survival of the legend of Italian colonialism as different, more tolerant, and more humane than other colonialisms. One needs only to recall the fact that the use of asphyxiating gases in Ethiopia was concealed for sixty years, stubbornly denied, and then finally admitted in 1996 by the Ministry of Defense, although not without reticence (Del Boca 1992: 111–27).[2]

Even if one looks with an indulgent eye at the seventy years of Italian presence in Africa, it needs to be said that the merits that have been celebrated are few and very modest, while the demerits are numerous. To begin, Italy did not lag behind any other colonial power in exercising violence against the indigenous populations. It should suffice to mention the 100,000 Libyans killed between 1911 and 1932, and the 3,000 to 4,000 Ethiopians who died between 1935 and 1941 while defending their motherland. It needs to be added that Italy was not particularly concerned about improving the living conditions of the administered populations. In 1945, indeed, they figured among the poorest of the continent and their education rates were close to zero.

It is difficult to believe that politicians at the level of De Gasperi, Sforza, Nenni, and Brusasca were not aware of what had really happened in Africa, yet for almost five years they fought in an attempt to recover the prefascist colonies. The relinquishment of the colonies, imposed by the Treaty of Paris, was challenged by almost everyone in the political class as iniquitous, unjustified, and unacceptable. As Benedetto Croce underlined, Italy's colonies had been "acquired with its blood, and administered and led toward

civil European life with its ingenuity and with the expenditure of its relatively meager finances" (Croce 1966: 209).

Never were such rhetoric, such hypocrisy, and such mystification employed as in those years. But in this sterile antihistorical battle, the politicians did not have the support of public opinion, nor certainly that of the
United Nations (Rossi 1980; Del Boca 1984: 3–75). Ethiopia immediately
reacquired its independence under Haile Selassie. Libya became a sovereign state in 1951 and had King Idris es-Senussi as its monarch. Eritrea obtained autonomy and was federated with Ethiopia in 1952. Only Somalia
was assigned to Italy with a ten-year trusteeship. This mandate was of very
little consolation to Italian politicians if one considers that Somalia was and
still is one of the poorest and most backward countries of the world, and
that the task of leading it toward self-government in such a short period of
time appeared extremely arduous and risky.

THE PURLOINED OBELISK

The relationships between Italy and its former colonies in the postwar period were not always easy and straightforward. This is especially true of relations with Ethiopia and Libya, both of which claimed a right to financial
reparations because of the war damages they had suffered at Italian hands.
Reconciliation was hindered by a ruling class that was pressured heavily by
the colonialist lobby and that, as I said, was promoting rather than preventing the repression of colonial faults. This attitude could only produce mis-
understandings, petty and endless negotiations, humiliating vetoes, and un-
fulfilled obligations.

But the peace accord of 1947 was clear. Regarding Ethiopia, article 37
stated, "Within eighteen months from the enforcement of this accord, Italy
will return all the works of art, archives, and objects of religious and historical value belonging to Ethiopia or to the Ethiopian citizens, which were
taken from Ethiopia to Italy after the third of October of 1935."[3] The Treaty
of Paris established, moreover, that Italy would pay 25 million dollars in war
reparations to Ethiopia "within seven years from the enforcement of this
treaty."[4]

The imperial Ethiopian government judged the amount of 25 million
dollars absolutely derisory and presented Rome with a bill of 184,746,023
pounds, equivalent, in 1945, to 326 million lira. Italy replied by arguing
that the bill was too high and failed to take into consideration the huge investments made in Ethiopia. The two countries negotiated for a decade and
ended up agreeing on the sum of ten and a half billion lira in 1956, the year
of the signing of the agreement on reparations (Del Boca 1984: vol. 4, 94–
110). The artworks and religious objects purloined between 1935 and 1941

were returned incompletely in dribs and drabs. In fact, only what was in possession of the Italian state was returned to Ethiopia, except for some goods I will deal with later. Not a single object of the huge booty taken by Badoglio, Graziani, Teruzzi, and other generals, governors, and party leaders was ever returned.

Among the objects seized by the Italian state and not yet returned to the Ethiopian people are the precious library of the Negus; the airplane belonging to one of the daughters of Haile Selassie, now exhibited in the *Museo Storico dell'Aeronautica* in Vigna di Valle; and, finally, a monument of inestimable value, the Axum obelisk.[5] The history of this theft is renowned. Stolen in March 1937 from the ecclesiastic quarter of Nefas by order of the minister Lessona and taken to Massawa on the steamship *Cafiero,* the obelisk was transported to Rome and erected on Porta Capena square to give luster to the celebration of the fifteenth anniversary of the fascist March on Rome.

From his exile in England, the emperor Haile Selassie immediately condemned the sacrilegious stealing of the "historical obelisk erected 1600 years ago" (Haile Selassie 1994: vol. 2, 27). Afterwards, after Ethiopia regained its freedom, the imperial government demanded the restitution of the monument in 1947, coinciding with the signing of the peace accord between Italy and the Allies. A second request was formulated in 1952 by the Ethiopian ambassador in Rome, Emanuel Abraham. In 1968 the Ethiopian parliament pressured the emperor to refuse an invitation to go to Italy before the restitution of the obelisk had taken place. Rome replied to all Ethiopian demands either by simply refusing them or by advancing unacceptable proposals, like that of transferring the monument to Naples, leaving to the Ethiopians the full cost of transporting it back to Axum.

In 1992, after the flight of Menghistu Hailemariam from Ethiopia, a group of five hundred Ethiopian intellectuals again asked Italy to pay its debt. The same demand was made by thousands of students from the University of Addis Ababa, while forty thousand spectators, gathered in the capital's stadium, repeatedly shouted *"Yimelles, yimelles!"* ("Return it, return it!") [6]

The restitution of the obelisk also was solicited by a growing number of Italians. After three scholars—Vincenzo Francavilla, Giuseppe Infranca, and Alberto Rossi—called for the obelisk's return, the deputies of the PDS, Ciabassi, Salvadori, and Trabacchini, urged the government to take the decisive step. The reply to the interpellation, signed by the undersecretary to foreign affairs, Carmelo Azzara, was a masterpiece of ambiguity and hypocrisy whose only goal was to temporize in the hope that the Ethiopians would one day get tired of asking for the restitution of the ill-gotten obelisk.[7]

In the fall of 1995 the story seemed finally to have come to a turning point. The Dini government put an end to all the obstacles and sent the undersecretary of foreign affairs, Michele Scammacca, to arrange the logistics of the restitution of the monument with the Ethiopian authorities. But

Figure 1. Inauguration of the Axum obelisk in Rome, 1937. Courtesy of Archivio Fotografico Istituto Luce, Roma.

Scammacca's mission aroused substantial criticism among the Italian right wing. The deputy of Alleanza Nazionale, Maurizio Gasparri, disapproved of Lamberto Dini's initiative and argued that the obelisk should stay where it was because it was "by now part of the urban landscape of Rome and recalled a precise historical period, however one wants to judge it."[8] The mayor of Rome, Rutelli, who feared that the limestone stele would shatter during the journey back to Ethiopia, expressed reservations. But it was also insinuated that Rutelli feared being smeared by the right as the "mayor who lost the stele."[9]

The process again came to a halt. Meanwhile in Ethiopia, where celebrations of the centennial of the Adwa victory over the Italians were about to begin, the new procrastination provoked sullenness and protests, so much so that on February 15, 1996, the Ethiopian parliament passed a resolution by which the restitution of the obelisk was asked for once again. On February 20, the Ethiopian minister of foreign affairs, Seyoum Mesfin, sent an urgent call, the second in three months, to the Italian minister of foreign affairs, Susanna Agnelli, requesting the stele's return.[10] Noting that the monument has "a great historical and spiritual value" for the Ethiopian people, Mesfin assured Agnelli that the restitution of the obelisk from Axum would be considered as "a gesture of deep friendship," to be remembered "for many generations."

In June 1996, the very inhabitants of Axum called for the restitution of the obelisk, which constitutes for them "a historical inheritance of inestimable value."[11] Around the same time, the patriarch of the Coptic Church, Paolo V, addressed a call to all the African churches and to the Vatican so that they would support his sorrowful request. Even some Italians were taking initiative. In an interrogation addressed to the ministers of foreign and cultural affairs, two parliamentarians of Rifondazione Comunista, Giovanni Russo Spena and Giovanni De Murtas, demanded to know what was preventing the enforcement of article 37 of the peace accord. The two appealed to the government to return to the Ethiopian people "a piece of their history . . . as a symbolic reparation of the many atrocities perpetrated by fascist Italy against those people."[12]

In November 1996, the president of the Republic, Oscar Luigi Scalfaro, intervened to break down the last resistance within Farnesina and to mollify Rome's mayor, Rutelli. Greeting the head of the Ethiopian state, Negasso Gidada, who was ending his visit in Italy, Scalfaro assured him that the obelisk would return to Ethiopia, and as soon as possible. In fact, the minister of foreign affairs, Lamberto Dini, was ordered to initiate the operational phase, and on March 3, 1997, the Italian and Ethiopian delegations met in Rome to "define the most appropriate techniques for the transfer of the work in absolute safety."[13] A few weeks later, on the occasion of the visit of the first Ethiopian minister, Meles Zenawi, the Italian government took the last step, declaring "its prompt willingness to return the obelisk of Axum, an operation to be carried through by the end of 1997."[14]

On November 22, 1997, having learned that President Scalfaro would leave the day after on a trip that would take him to Ethiopia and Eritrea, the *Corriere della Sera* urgently called the president to attend to the moral obligation to condemn the fascist adventure in Ethiopia once he arrived in Addis Ababa.[15] In the two brief speeches he delivered on November 24, Scalfaro fully satisfied the expectations of those who had been hoping for so long that Italy would atone for its colonial faults. Scalfaro described the fascist occupation of Ethiopia as "bloody pages." He confirmed that the obelisk of Axum would soon be returned and apologized for the delay of nearly sixty years. At the toast during that evening's banquet the president chose to address once more the problem of the colonial past, declaring "our Constitution proclaims the disavowal of war; we would like this 'no' to have the strength to purify the past."[16]

The commitment to return the obelisk by the end of 1997, however, was disregarded. We are now in the summer of 1999 and the monument is still towering in front of the United Nations Food and Agriculture Organization. What is the reason for this failure? Is there anybody in Rome who might provide a believable answer?

THE DISPUTE WITH LIBYA

Ethiopia is not the only country with which Italy has an ongoing dispute. In the last ten years, Libya too has been putting pressure on the Italians to recognize its right to reparations of some sort. Italy certainly owes a great debt, both moral and material, to the Libyan people, who have suffered the same wrongs as the Ethiopians. On the shelves of the former Casa del Mutilato in Tripoli there are about five thousand dossiers. Each of them tells the story of a political assassination, a summary hanging, a final deportation, a theft of land, a confiscation, a mutilation, or myriad other abuses. One hundred thousand tragic stories occurred between 1911 and 1943. They illustrate the calvary of a people who have been, without any justifiable reason, attacked, subdued, humiliated, and, in some regions, decimated.

After the inception of the Italian-Turkish war, in which the Turkish participated as allies of the Ottomans, the expeditionary force led by General Carlo Caneva distinguished itself by its ruthlessness. It responded to the Arab rebellion of Sciara Sciat with thousands of summary executions and massive deportations. Following the Peace of Ouchy (1912), with the Turkish out of the picture, the Libyans were left alone to oppose the Italian penetration of their country. The Arab resistance lasted twenty years. In order to crush it, the fascist regime employed the most deadly means of the time, including aerial bombardment and armored cars. It also resorted to forbidden weapons, including chemical weapons, and to "final solutions" such as the deportation of the entire population of Cirenaic Gebel and their internment in thirteen concentration camps, which proved to be lethal for almost half of their detainees. Finally, religious hatred was exploited when Italy employed the Christian Ascari, recruited in Eritrea and in Ethiopia, against the Muslim Libyans. When, on January 24, 1932, the governor of Libya, Marshal Pietro Badoglio, announced that the "rebellion had been completely and definitively crushed," at least 100,000 Libyans, soldiers and civilians, had lost their lives in defense of their country (Graziani 1932: 307). One needs to keep in mind, in order to fully evaluate the price paid in blood by the Libyan people, that the entire Libyan population numbered fewer than 800,000 inhabitants in the 1920s. This means that one-eighth of the population was exterminated. Having gained its independence in 1951, with Idris es-Senussi as a sovereign, Libya brought up the issue, as it was easy to foresee it would, of war damages and asked for fair compensation. The Italian government initially replied, during the period between 1935 and 1955, that war damages were not to be paid at all because Libya was part of the metropole in all respects during World War II. And paying for damages caused by thirty-two years of colonial occupation was out of the question, because no other European power had paid for them. In the end, a very modest amount was agreed upon: 2,750,000 Libyan sterlings, equal to 4,812,500,000 lira. Italy demanded, moreover, that no reference would be made in the text of the Accord of April 2, 1956, to damages caused during World War II, nor to those caused in the colonial period. The money was in fact officially described as a "contribution to the economic reconstruction of Libya." With this naive artifice, leaders of republican Italy decided to cover up the crimes of Giolittian and fascist Italy. This was a very incautious and dishonorable course of action that, above all, exposed Italy to the danger of future requests for reparations because of the lack of a specific quittance (Del Boca 1988: 443–45).

These requests were in fact unfailingly made, and in a much more peremptory manner once the old and hesitant king Idris was succeeded in 1969 by the very young and resolute colonel al-Qaddafi. And since Rome refused to consider the issue again, the Libyan government, in an unexpected move, confiscated all the property of the last twenty thousand Italians left in Libya in 1970 (ibid., 468–77). In spite of the enormous confiscation of assets (estimated at two thousand billion lira today), al-Qaddafi was not satisfied, arguing that all the properties seized were nothing other than Libyan estates that were being returned to their legitimate owners. This was certainly true of the huge farms that were acquired by Italians in a fraudulent manner, but not of the hundreds of small properties (houses, stores, artisan's shops) that represented the modest fruit of an entire working life.

Almost thirty years have passed since the forced exodus of the Italians of the *quarta sponda,* but the Italian-Libyan dispute has not moved forward. Al-Qaddafi periodically and sometimes in a threatening tone demands reparations. Farnesina, with similar obstinacy, replies that the Accord of October 2, 1956, erased every debt. In strictly legal terms, Italy would seem faultless, especially since it took upon itself the heavy burden of indemnifying the twenty thousand Italians expelled from Libya. But an accord is not always equipped to solve a difficult controversy such as the Italian-Libyan one. The Accord of October 2, 1956, in particular, is not only ambiguous but is also extremely ungenerous. If this were not the case Giulio Andreotti, at that time minister of foreign affairs, would not have made a proposal during a conversation with al-Qaddafi on February 4, 1984, saying he wanted to make a "concrete gesture toward the Libyan people." This gesture would later assume the form of the gift of the Cardiological Center, to be built in Tripoli (ibid., 515).

Andreotti's proposal to solve the dispute with a humanitarian gesture was at first appreciated by the Libyans, who in fact started to discuss the details of the plan with the Italian ambassador in Tripoli, Giorgio Reitano. But the plan was not carried out because, once more, Rome revealed a petty attitude. In January 1987 the number of beds was still being discussed. The Libyans were asking for 1,200; Farnesina would make a counteroffer of 100.

But there is a detail that very few people know and that transforms the humanitarian act into nothing more than a farce. The hospital promised by Andreotti in 1984, and presented by him as a gift and "a symbolic gesture," is an obligation that was never honored. In fact, Enclosure C of the Accord of October 2, 1956, reached with King Idris es-Senussi provided for the building in Tripoli of a hospital on an area of twenty-eight thousand square feet. Almost fifty years went by after the signing of the accord, but there is no trace yet of this hospital.

There is another, moral obligation that has been eluded: the obligation to recognize in a clear and unequivocal manner that Giolittian and fascist Italy stained itself with very serious crimes in Libya. In order to fulfill this obligation, a few words would suffice. But none of the Italian governments of the postwar period has found the moral courage to pronounce these words.

In a recent conversation with the head of the Libyan state, Colonel Mu'amar al-Qaddafi, I realized that the Libyans have higher expectations that Italy recognize their sufferings and their patriotic struggle, and that it condemns its history of colonialist oppression, than that Italy provides material compensation for the damages caused by the colonial occupation. To stay silent or not to stay silent? I hope that President Scalfaro, who pronounced words of understanding and condemnation in Ethiopia, will not forget Libya.[17]

THE LONG SILENCE ON ERITREA

Luckily, Italy does not have any open dispute with Eritrea, but one cannot say that Italy has had a fair and unambiguous attitude toward its former first-born colony in the postwar period. And yet Italy got its best indigenous troops from this land, troops with which it kept and enlarged its colonial dominions. Perhaps Eritrea deserves something more than silence since napalm incinerated many of its villages, and an entire generation of soldiers disappeared in the most willingly forgotten of the wars.

In 1945, faced with the prospect of losing Eritrea, Alcide De Gasperi pronounced these sorrowful words: "If Italy happened to be expelled from Eritrea, the measure would seem very serious to Italians; its annexation to Ethiopia, then, would take it back half a century."[18] Seven years later, however, Eritrea was federated with Ethiopia according to resolution 390/A/5 of the United Nations. Italy's plans, which since the beginning had been predicated on the recovery of full sovereignty over Eritrea and, short of this, on its administration as a trusteeship or on conducting the territory to independence, were thereby upset. The heavy diplomatic defeat suffered by Rome could not but leave traces, especially if one thinks that in the state apparatuses there were still many nostalgic for the past regime and the pomp of colonialism.

The first form of revenge was disinterest and then silence. Italy, which had the duty to ensure that the mechanisms of the federation of Eritrea and Ethiopia would work properly, instead distanced itself from its obligations, even when Eritrean autonomy was repeatedly and plainly violated, and even when, on November 14, 1962, Emperor Haile Selassie imperiously dissolved the federation and incorporated Eritrea as the fourteenth province of his empire.

The Ethiopian coup provoked a war that would last thirty years and that would develop subject to the total indifference of the United Nations and all the foreign ministries of the world. So indifferent was the world that Emperor Haile Selassie and then his successor, Colonel Menghistu Hailemariam, would have the advantage when arguing that the war in Eritrea was an internal Ethiopian affair and that any interference in favor of the Eritrean partisans would be considered intolerable. Italy accepted this point of view and, consequently, never exerted any pressure on the government of Addis Ababa, not even when, with the burden of its huge aid, it certainly could have uttered statements in favor of a people who had been bled dry for Italy's "greatness."

The genocide in Eritrea, however, pushed some Italian politicians to put pressure on the government to break the silence and assume a clear and responsible position. Placed on the spot by the Socialists, Communists, Radicals and Christian Democrats, the minister of foreign affairs, Giulio Andreotti, on July 6, 1988, authorized the dispatch to Ethiopia of a parliamentary delegation with the task of addressing the Eritrean issue. For the first time since 1962, the parliamentarians rejected the definition of "terrorists" applied to Eritrean partisans and invited the interlocutors "to look for the way toward an agreement, within a process of liberalization, in Ethiopia."[19] Some months later, in December of 1988, the Italian government subscribed to an agenda, approved by all the political forces, that argued for the necessity of "reproposing the Eritrean question in the appropriate international seats on the basis of the UN resolution 390/A/5."[20]

The problem finally had been put in the right terms, but the results of the Italian initiative turned out to be disappointing because the gap between the declaration of intention and the actual exercise of political will was still too large. In reality, Farnesina was persuaded that Eritrea would never be capable of gaining independence from Ethiopian domination by the force of its weapons, and, consequently, it was paying little attention to the calls sent to it by the Eritrean resistance and by an increasingly large segment of the Italian public.

Against all expectations, in the spring of 1991 Eritrea emerged as the winner from its thirty years of war with Ethiopia. Shortly afterward, Menghistu was forced to flee and the Tigrean leader Meles Zenawi took Addis Ababa. According to agreements already concluded between Meles Zenawi and the leader of the Eritrean resistance, Isaias Afeworki, Eritrea could choose through a referendum sponsored by the United Nations between independence and federation with Ethiopia. It was, however, taken for granted that the great majority of Eritreans would vote for the former solution.[21]

Eritrea was exhausted by this war, with 80,000 casualties, 90,000 invalids, and 50,000 orphans at its conclusion. In addition, 500,000 refugees were camping in neighboring Sudan; entire cities, such as Massawa and Nafka, were destroyed; and the annual grain deficit was more than 300,000 tons. According to the estimates of some international agencies, no less than two thousand billion dollars was necessary to rebuild the country. The moment had arrived for Italy to remember its former firstborn colony and to earn forgiveness for thirty years of total indifference.

A lot of promises were made; one year later, however, not a cent of the guaranteed aid had reached Asmara. Eritreans were surprised and embittered. Some were talking about betrayal, others about "negligent neglect." Then, slowly, the machine of aid to Eritrea was turned on. Within the Dipartimento per la Cooperazione allo Sviluppo, 106 billion lira were allocated between 1992 and 1995, and other 104 billion were allocated according to the Bridge Program of 1996–98. So far, of the assigned 210 billion lira, 140 have been delivered, a fact that places Italy at the top of the list of donating nations.

Italian aid is now supporting almost all sectors of the Eritrean economy and driving grand projects such as the reconstruction of Massawa's port, the installation of a high-tension line between Massawa and Asmara, and the improvement of health services. Now that the mechanism of aid has started to work again, it would be appropriate for Italy to remember the few hundred Ascaris who are still alive and who have not received a pension since 1993. Although they were fighting for an unjust cause, they served the Italian flag in years in which Italy obstinately carved out its ephemeral empire in Africa.

In the late spring of 1998, a conflict between Ethiopia and Eritrea ignited over territory and as a result of an old and never-appeased rancor. Italy immediately tried to mediate, but its efforts, like those of Organizzazaione dell'Unità Africana (OUA) and the United States, did not prevent the war from proceeding. On the contrary, this war has spread and become crueler since February 1999. In addition, the Italian government does not have what is necessary to bring back peace to the Horn of Africa. It should not be forgotten that in 1996 Italy sold five Aermacchi MB-339 combat planes to Eritrea. And those who sell weapons cannot expect them not to be used.

SOMALIA: HALF A CENTURY OF FAILURES

Still defaulting with Ethiopia and Libya, and half-generous with Eritrea, Italians have been prodigiously supportive of Somalia. The aid to Mogadishu reaches not simply hundreds but thousands of billions of lira, almost as if Somalia had become an extension of the Italian peninsula. This is a history yet to be written, one that explains, in addition, how and why the first republic ended the way it did.

With the assignation to Italy, in 1950, of the trusteeship of Somalia, the international community intended to administer to Italy, which had not showed great capabilities in Africa, a kind of remedial exam. The task, though, was complicated by the fact that, in fifty years of domination, Italy had invested little in Somalia; the few investments that had been made were intended to benefit the Italian community. When Giovanni Fornari took office in Mogadishu in April 1950 as first administrator of the Amministrazione Fiduciaria Italiana della Somalia (AFIS), a dark colonial night still hovered over Somalia. The illiteracy rate was 99.4 percent. Of the population of 1.242 billion inhabitants, only 20,000 had houses made of stone. There was one doctor for every 60,000 people and 1,254 beds in the ten small hospitals spread across a territory that was one and a half times the size of Italy. There were few if any people with the requisite level of education to whom power could be shifted. It was necessary to create a ruling class from zero, and this process could take no longer than ten years.[22]

At the start of the mission, Giuseppe Brusasca, the undersecretary for

foreign affairs, made Italy's intentions clear: "We were going back to demonstrate that we were able to inaugurate a new politics in Africa, not one of
exploitation anymore, but of collaboration."[23]

Brusasca's intentions, reiterated by De Gasperi and Sforza, were certainly
sincere and admirable. In reality, though, as Giorgio Assan correctly pointed
out, the mandate on Somalia was above all "desired by and imposed on the
government by the most obtusely fascist sector of the bureaucracy: the high
officials of the ministry of Italian Africa, supported by colonial agricultural
capitalists, who did not have any intention of giving up their ordinary and
extraordinary prebends."[24] With this poor and unreliable human material,
an absolutely plethoric bureaucratic-administrative organization was created in Somalia, which moreover reproduced all the defects of the metropolitan organization and included completely outmoded institutes and systems, which were, above all, disconnected from the Somali reality.

The state that was born on July 1, 1960, was characterized by very fragile
bureaucratic structures and was doomed to decades of dependency on international aid. In fact, although Italy had invested 200 billion lira in Somalia, it did not succeed in solving two of the fundamental problems of the
country: creating a vital economy and guaranteeing secure and precise borders. This failure would force the young state to build up its army, thereby
diverting huge amounts of money from productive investments. Furthermore, a disconcerting number of colonial and neocolonial debts burdened
the country, so much so that in 1969, just nine years after independence,
democracy in Somalia was nothing but a memory and a parody of multiple-
party politics. On October 21, 1969, the democratic state created by AFIS
was buried by the only efficient organism in the county, the army, within
which some forces had developed in a progressive direction before the
gradual degeneration of the first Somali republic.

After a promising beginning, in 1977 the revolutionary regime of Mohammed Siad Barre made the unforgivable mistake of attempting to annex
the province of Ogaden, primarily inhabited by Somalis. Beaten on the battlefield by the Ethiopians, whose forces were supported by the Cubans and
the Soviets, Siad Barre's army was forced to withdraw behind Somalia's borders. After the defeat, a second phase characterized by the renunciation of
the socialist option, by the intensification of the repression of any form of
dissent, and by a resurgence of tribalism began. Since the beginning of the
1980s, the involution of the Somali regime has been fully evident, and it is
surprising that, in that period, the disconcerting idyll between the Italian
Socialist Party and the regime in Mogadishu flourished, an idyll that lasted
virtually until the fall of the dictator.

The PSI not only offered its political support to an increasingly discred-
ited dictatorship for a decade, but it also engineered the transfer of huge
amounts of aid to Somalia (more than 2,000 billion lira) through the Fondo

Aiuti Italiani, presided over by Francesco Forte. In few cases did this aid benefit the extremely poor Somali population. Instead, the money gave life to white elephant projects such as desert cathedrals or ended up reinforcing the oppressive regime of Siad Barre. After the flight of the dictator from Mogadishu, Italy could have prevented Somalia from ending up in pieces and in chaos, if only it had demonstrated greater commitment, imagination, loyalty, and coherence in the task of mediating among the various tribal forces that had become players during the civil war. Instead, attempts at mediation of exemplary coarseness would fail one after the other. Then, in November 1991, Italy abandoned Somalia to its destiny, just when the country, devastated by tribal wars, was breaking into five zones and thereby being precipitated into the abyss of anarchy.

The world recognized the Somali tragedy only when the number of starving people reached 300,000 and the exodus from the country involved more than one million Somalis. At this point, near the end of 1992, in the wake of the American initiative Restore Hope, Italy went back into Somalia with a military contingent for the third time. How the mission ended is well known. Between February 27 and March 2, 1995, the last contingents of the United Nations were sent again by ship under the protection of the American Marines and of the Italian *marò*. Not only had the United Nations not been able to stop the civil war in Somalia, but they had even supported it through a perverse mechanism. The representative of Boutros Boutros-Ghali in Somalia, Victor Gbeho, confessed that indeed a good part of the five thousand billion lira that the United Nations Operation in Somalia (ONUSOM) had diffused in the country ended up in the pockets of warlords.[25]

It needs to be said that the Italian corps contributed significantly to the disastrousness of the humanitarian mission in Somalia. Persuaded that they were the only ones who knew Somali reality, military men and politicians claimed command of the operations but, not being able to obtain it, withdrew their contingent from Mogadishu and relocated it further north, along Uebi Scebeli. This pretension to always have the optimal solution has been a curse on Italy since the beginning of its colonial adventures, similar to its presumption of difference from the other colonial powers, that is, the presumption that it is more tolerant, more respectful, and more generous. Actually the history of the Italian presence in Africa is studded by unedifying episodes, of failures and of precipitous withdrawals. At the end of a sloppily run operation in Somalia, the minister of defense, Fabio Fabbri, pronounced these memorable words: "It is a little like the game of the match. The last to get it burns his fingers. It is for this reason that we will leave together with the Americans."[26]

Finally, to confirm the groundlessness of the presumed "difference" of the Italian army, in the spring of 1997 the scandal of the tortures practiced in Somalia by some soldiers of the Ibis mission erupted in Italy. After some pitiful attempts on the part of the army to divert the investigation through the denial or downplaying of these episodes of violence, the Prodi government was forced to nominate some inquiry committees, whose first conclusions confirm the trustworthiness of some of the most damaging accounts.[27]

MISSED OPPORTUNITIES

I believe that the preceding points illustrate clearly enough that the relationship between Italy and its former colonies has never been either easy or serene, much less constructive. In the beginning, as I have shown, it was the sense of frustration and resentment experienced by some sectors of the Italian administration that made the relationship with the former colonies difficult. Instead of constructive exchanges, forms of obstructionism, delays in execution, and the denial of proclaimed rights were the rule. And a badly concealed desire to punish Italy's former colonies hung over every initiative.

First to pay the expenses of this politics were Ethiopia and Libya, both of which experienced a remarkable delay in compensation for war damages. When compensation was finally meted out, it was so unsatisfactory that Tripoli has not accepted Italy's apologies, and Addis Ababa is still awaiting the restitution of the Axum obelisk as specified in article 37 of the Treaty of Paris. Even Eritrea was a victim of this myopic and spiteful politics. This nation was guilty of not having invoked the return of Italy as a sovereign power immediately after the end of World War II.

With the abolition of the Ministry of Italian Africa and the succession of a new generation of leaders, the colonialist lobby's influence has begun to wane, without, however, disappearing completely. Access to the colonial archives of Farnesina was still denied to many scholars labeled as progressive at the beginning of the 1970s, and even later there were vetoes and restrictions.[28] The influence of the colonialist lobby was heightened afterward by the governmental parties that, starting from the 1970s and even later, gave life to the never sufficiently deplored phenomenon of the apportionment. After the allotment of Africa realized in Berlin in 1884, a second and unrequested division took place among the Italian parties: Ethiopia, Kenya, and Egypt went to the Christian Democrats, while Somalia, Mozambique, Senegal, and Tunisia went to the Socialists. And if the stakes to be won by the first allotment had been raw materials and the search for new markets, those of the second were the right to administer the huge capital of the Cooperazione allo Sviluppo, which even in the 1980s exceeded thirty-seven billion lira.[29]

Noble purposes were obviously behind this allotment. It would allow Italy to exert a beneficial influence on some countries in a crisis. To provide an example, Farnesina had two ambitious objectives in the Horn of Africa:

shepherding the Ethiopian regime away from the influence of Moscow, and avoiding conflicts between Ethiopia and Somalia in addition to that over Ogaden. In both cases the weight of Italy proved inconsequential. Menghistu freed himself from the Soviet embrace only because Gorbachev decided to abandon him to his destiny. Siad Barre and Menghistu drafted a precarious peace accord only because both were in desperate straits because of the growing aggression of their respective armed opposition movements. Although Italy had delivered thousands of billions of lira to the Horn of Africa, it did not even succeed in stopping the genocide in Eritrea or in preventing Somalia from becoming a battlefield, leading to the country's disappearance from the list of sovereign nations.

The series of mistakes, delays, and defaults that I have listed is almost certainly a product of the total denial of colonial atrocities, the lack of debate on colonialism, and the survival, in the collective imaginary, of convictions and theories of justification. While other countries engaged in a serious reflection on the colonial past, in Italy, as I have shown, the falsification of historical truth was preferred through the renowned *L'Italia in Africa.* All this could not but influence the politics elaborated with respect to the former colonies, a politics that even managed its own aid programs badly—a petty politics, often coarse and sometimes punitive, without programs or imagination.

Italy lost a great opportunity. It could go back to Africa to repair its faults with generosity and to carry out a satisfactory collaboration with the capabilities that nobody denies to it. Instead, it has squandered large amounts of capital, has supported indecent dictatorships, has added new injustices to the old, and has not even finished honoring its debts. The politics inaugurated by Minister of Foreign Affairs Lamberto Dini, who for the first time has escaped the wake of Americans' politics, is a hopeful sign. This new politics, in conjunction with the trip to Eastern Africa of President Scalfaro and the explicit admission of colonial atrocities, can constitute a significant turning point and the beginning of a new way of cooperating with the countries of the "Third World."

NOTES

1. The Palazzo della Farnesina is the seat of the Ministry of Foreign Affairs in Rome.

2. On the same subject, see also my essay "I gas di Mussolini," in *Il fascismo e la guerra d'Etiopia* (Roma: Editori Riuniti, 1996).

3. *Gazzetta Ufficiale della Repubblica Italiana*, supplemento ordinario 295, Dec. 24, 1947, 47.

4. Ibid., 53.

5. The obelisk is described on page 62 of the *Catalogo del Museo.* It was pointed out to me by my friend Alberto Imperiali.

6. "Stadium Demonstration for Return of Axum Obelisk," *Ethiopian Herald,* June 3, 1992, 6.

7. Carmelo Azzara's letter to the deputy Vincenzo Ciabarri, dated Oct. 23, 1992.

8. *Corriere della Sera,* Oct. 18, 1995.

9. Andrea di Robilant, "Roma 'sequestra' l'obelisco," *La Stampa,* Dec. 12, 1996.

10. Minister Mesfin had written a first letter on Nov. 24, 1995.

11. The petition, signed in the first three weeks of June 1996 by more than thirteen thousand inhabitants of Axum for the immediate return of their obelisk, is now in Rome.

12. The interrogations were presented on May 15 and 16, 1996.

13. Agenzia Nazionale Stampa Associata, Roma, Mar. 4, 1997.

14. From the official document of the Italian Ministry of Foreign Affairs, "Declaration on the Return of the Axum Obelisk to Ethiopia."

15. Del Boca, "L'Italia chiede scusa alle ex-colonie," *Corriere della Sera,* Nov. 22, 1997.

16. On Scalfaro's trip to Eastern Africa, see Marzio Breda's "Scalfaro in Etiopia: Purifichiamo il passato," *Corriere della Sera,* Nov. 25, 1997; Toni Fontana's "Del Boca: Un gesto importante che fa finalmente giustizia," *L'Unità;* Paola Caridi, "Una svolta dopo colpevoli silenzi," *L'Unità.* I appreciate Caridi's perspective, but add "Ora tocca alla Libia," *Il Secolo XIX;* Renato Rizzo, "Scalfaro chiude la guerra coloniale," *La Stampa;* "Africa scusaci," *Liberazione.*

17. For a detailed examination of the Italian-Libyan relationship from 1969 to 1997, see Del Boca, *Gheddafi: Una sfida dal deserto* (Roma-Bari: Laterza, 1998).

18. Ministry of Foreign Affairs, *Inventario delle rappresentanze diplomatiche,* Francia e Russia, envelope 337, telegram of July 14, 1945, to the ambassadors Carandini and Tarchiani.

19. *La Repubblica,* Sept. 9, 1998. The words within quotation marks belong to Flaminio Piccoli, who led the parliamentary mission.

20. For a deeper examination of the Eritrean problem, see Stefano Poscia, *Eritrea, colonia tradita* (Roma: Edizioni Associate, 1989); Giovanni Moneta, *La questione eritrea* (Roma: Cablo, 1987); John Markakis, *National and Class Conflict in The Horn of Africa* (London: Zed Books, 1990); Giampaolo Calchi Novati, *Il corno d'Africa nella storia e nella politica* (Torino: Sei, 1994); Angelo Del Boca, "La questione dell'Eritrea nei rapporti fra Roma e Addis Ababa," *Studi Piacentini* 6 (1989): 35–64.

21. In the referendum of April 1993, 99 percent of Eritreans expressed their preference for independence.

22. Cf. Ministry of Foreign Affairs, *Rapport du Gouvernment italien à l'Assemblée Général des Nations Unies sur l'administration de la Somalie placée sous la tutelle de l'Italie, avril-décembre 1950* (Roma: Istituto Poligrafico dello Stato, 1951), 2, 288–90.

23. Author's interview with Giuseppe Brusasca.

24. *Rinascita,* Nov–Dec. 1958, 864.

25. *Corriere della Sera,* Feb. 25, 1995. On Italy's participation in the mission in Somalia see, Del Boca, *Una sconfitta dell'intelligenza: Italia e Somalia* (Roma-Bari: Laterza, 1993); Del Boca, *La trappola Somala: Dall'operazione Restore Hope al fallimento delle Nazioni Unite* (Roma-Bari: Laterza, 1994); Mario Sica, *Operazione Somalia* (Venezia: Marsilio, 1994); Claudio Pacifico, *Somalia: Ricordi di un mal d'Africa italiano* (Città di Castello: Edimond, 1996).

26. *La Repubblica,* Dec. 23, 1993.

27. On the tortures practiced in Somalia, see Mario Todeschini Lalli, "Somali torturati dagli italiani: Le foto choc di un ex-para," *La Repubblica,* June 6, 1997; Massimo Martinelli, "Prodi: l'Italia non tollera le torture," *Il Messaggero,* June 7, 1997; Giuliano Gallo, "Torture in Somalia, si rompe l'omertà," *Corriere della Sera,* June 8, 1997; Flavia Amabile, "Somalia, la caduta dei generali," *La Stampa,* June 25, 1997; Renato Rizzo, "Scalfaro: Punire gli atti inumani," *La Stampa,* June 29, 1997; Riccardo Luna, "Somalia: I servizi segreti sapevano," *La Repubblica,* June 26, 1997; Giovanni Porzio, "Somalia: Gli italiani torturavano i prigionieri, ecco le prove," *Panorama,* June 12, 1997.

28. The situation changed remarkably in the 1990s with the arrival of Professor Enrico Serra to the Servizio Storico e Documentazione; Serra is a former member of the partisan group Giustizia e Libertà and a historian of international repute.

29. In the beginning of the 1990s, the Cooperazione allo Sviluppo entered a crisis as a result of scandals that were revealed. In 1996, after three years of investigation, the investigating judge Vittorio Paraggio committed thirty-five prominent political figures for trial, including Bettino Craxi, Gianni De Michelis, and Mach of Palmestein. But on October 21, 1997, during the first phases of the trial, the court of Rome suspended proceedings because it believed the prosecution's case was too sketchy and, consequently, that it had to be redone. On this matter see the following articles: Daniele Mastrogiacono, "Le tangenti sui poveri del mondo," *La repubblica,* Oct. 10, 1996; Flavio Haver, "Scandalo Cooperazione, cancellata l'inchiesta," *Corriere della Sera,* Oct. 22, 1997; Daniele Mastrogiacono, "Silos sciolti al sole e strade inutili, cosi truffavano il Terzo mondo," *La Repubblica,* Oct. 22, 1997.

WORKS CITED

Battaglia, Romano. 1958. *La prima guerra d'Africa.* Torino: Einaudi.

Campbell Ian L., and Degife Gabre-Tsadik. 1997. "La repressione fascista in Etiopia: La riscostruzione del massacro di Debra Libanos." *Studi Piacentini* 21: 79–128.

Croce, Benedetto. 1966. *Discorsi parlamentari.* Roma: Bardi.

Del Boca, Angelo. 1984. *Gli italiani in Africa orientale: Nostalgia delle colonie.* Roma-Bari: Laterza.

———. 1988. *Gli italiani in Libia: Dal fascismo a Gheddafi.* Roma-Bari: Laterza.

———. 1992. "Il mancato dibattito sul colonialismo." In *L'Africa nella coscienza degli italiani: Miti, memorie, errori, sconfitte.* Bari: Laterza.

Graziani, Rodolfo. 1932. *Cirenaica pacificata.* Milano: Mondadori.

Haile Selassie. 1994. *My Life and Ethiopia's Progress.* 2 vols. East Lansing: Michigan State University Press.

Malgeri, Francesco. 1970. *La guerra libica (1911–1912).* Roma: Edizioni di storia e letteratura.

Rochat, Giorgio. *Il colonialismo italiano.* 1973. Torino: Loescher.

———. 1978. *Storia d'Italia,* vol. 1, *Colonialismo.* Firenze: La Nuova Italia.

Rossi, Gianluigi. 1980. *L'Africa italiana verso l'indipendenza (1941–49).* Milano: Giuffré.

Studies and Research on Fascist Colonialism, 1922–1935

Reflections on the State of the Art

Nicola Labanca

Within historical works on Italian colonialism, the study of the colonial expansion of the fascist regime seems to be marked by sharp limits. In every general work on fascism, reference is made to fascist expansionism and, in particular, to colonial imperialism. But these works' use of the category of "imperialism" is often vague, tending to blur into a generic "dynamism" on the terrain of foreign politics. Studies of fascist colonial imperialism have remained for a long time, according to a historiographical survey of about twenty years ago, "very rare."[1]

Since then, some relevant contributions have been made and important research has been conducted, but my dissatisfaction with the dearth of historical-colonial studies today, both in absolute terms and in relation to the progress made in general studies of the fascist period, can only be reiterated. And yet for fascism, both as a movement and as a regime, the dimension of the overseas, of the empire and the colonies, was of central relevance at multiple levels: foreign politics, military preparation, organization of consent in the motherland, and administration of power in the conquered African lands.

Examining the available studies more closely, then, one observes that their distribution is far from satisfactory and that they contribute very little to our understanding of the durability and the centrality of colonial politics throughout the entire fascist *ventennio*. Existing analysis, in fact, focuses mainly on the imperial period and, more precisely, on the military turning point of the Ethiopian campaign, which is not by chance well known today in its diplomatic, political, and military aspects and in terms of its organization of consent. Such a predominant focus, perhaps comprehensible to the foreign scholar, is less justifiable for the Italian. Undeniably, the rupturing of the international order caused by the war of 1935–36 remains the harshest deed of the regime's colonial politics. Yet an understanding of the empire's construction has been prevented by the paucity of studies on the period before 1935, almost as if the thematics and problematics that emerged between 1935 and 1936 had not had an incubation or a previous life. All this, finally, facilitated an interpretation of 1935–36 as a Mussolinian masterpiece and has lead scholars to dilute the peculiarity of the fascist colonial experience—notwithstanding its articulation into phases and moments—both before and after the Ethiopian campaign.[2]

Within studies of Italian colonialism, moreover, the few works available on the fascist period were sharply affected by the national reluctance to study this topic.[3] But if it is difficult to understand the first African war or the Libyan enterprise in isolation from the more general European "scramble for Africa," it is almost impossible to single out the peculiar, the novel, and even the dramatic aspects of fascist colonialism by abstracting it from the experience of global imperialism between the two wars. The other critical observations about Italian historical-colonial studies, such as their limitation to a narrow historical and diplomatic setting and their failure to examine cultural and ideological issues adequately, appear not so much as secondary but as a consequence of this national closure. Such closure does little to further our comprehension of fascist colonialism's peculiarities either in relation to the imperial designs of liberal powers such as Britain and France, or in relation to authoritarian or para-fascist regimes like those of Portugal and Spain.

The condition of these studies may be explained in several ways. At a general level, what has been defined as "the missed debate on Italian colonialism" has had remarkable weight.[4] From a more specific historical point of view, this lack of a discussion is responsible for the failure to challenge fundamental assumptions of traditional colonial studies. Thus the outlook of the "colonial historians" ended up prevailing, especially during the republic's first decades. The harmful consequences of this attitude have been reinforced by the politics that arose in relation to the archives, particularly in relation to the preparation of the "official" *Opera dell'Italia in Africa*. Even in the most rigorously documented volumes of the series there was not a single scholar occupied with the fascist period. In general, in other works a laudatory tone was prevalent, with frequent examples of the deliberate repression of the most scabrous aspects of colonialism and of the fascist regime in particular. The *Opera dell'Italia in Africa* was very disappointing not only because it was prepared through a "privatized" management of the colonial archives, but also because the committee in charge of its preparation amply tampered with the original order and state of the documents in a way that leaves little hope for further scholarship unless a very consistent cultural and archival investment is made, which today does not seem imminent.[5] The few scholars who dealt with fascist colonial history often turned to other archives, or hoped that in the future they would be able to make the most of the other colonial documents that have only recently begun to be deposited in the Archivio Centrale dello Stato.[6]

A critical evaluation of the state of colonial studies, whatever the causes of the current predicament are, should not obscure the fact that a literature has nonetheless accumulated.[7] In spite of the lacunae I have indicated, it is evident that some moments and aspects of fascist colonialism have by now been clarified. First of all, we owe a comprehensive reconstruction of this period to Angelo Del Boca, whose work has marked a remarkable advance in relation to the general text by Raffaele Ciasca (of 1938), and in relation to the even more abbreviated book by Jean-Louis Miege (1968).[8] In the second half of the 1960s, in addition to studies more strictly historical-diplomatic, some interesting research on fascist foreign politics was initiated and published.[9] The most advanced and organic example of such research is Giorgio Rochat's work, published before Del Boca's.[10] Some of the outcomes of this research were later reexamined and discussed by Renzo De Felice in his biography of Mussolini, but only as they related to the theme of the outbreak of the Ethiopian war (on which many scholars, including non-Italians, had already worked) or, later, to the Arab politics of the regime.[11] Other contributions worthy of being recalled are the introductions to the photographic volumes, bibliographic essays, and articles on military history written by Luigi Goglia; the research of Claudio Segre on agrarian politics in Libya and on Balbo; and Alberto Sbacchi's excavation of documents on the Ethiopian empire.[12] Some progress has also been made in the investigation of the organization of consent in the motherland and more recently on the construction of a racial system in the colonies.[13] The studies that followed have highlighted the weak and secondary, but no less dangerous, character of fascist imperialism on political, economic, and social levels.[14] Thanks to such recent investigations, the backwardness in the studies of the regime by the "colonial historians" and in the studies of the first decades of the republic has been overcome, and it has become possible to place the colonial events in the more general context of fascism's foreign politics.[15] But too many important aspects of colonialism under fascism are still waiting an adequate clarification. A problematic synthesis, made from a historiographically updated and comparative perspective rather than a nationalistic one, a synthesis that would highlight the centrality of the imperial myth in the fascist regime, and not only after 1935, is still due.[16]

AN INTERNATIONAL PERSPECTIVE

From an international perspective, it is useful to start again from some fundamental geographical, demographic, and political data. When the fascists took power, only four years after the end of the Great War, Italy ruled the colonial dominions of Eritrea, Somalia, Tripolitania, and Cirenaica in Africa. Eritrea, with the main centers of Massawa and Asmara, was the "first-born colony." The Italian colonial yearbook of the official Istituto Coloniale Italiano of Rome affirmed that Italian dominions extended to 120,000 square kilometers and had an indigenous population of roughly 300,000 people (a third more were reported, but the general unreliability of these official calculations must be recalled here). Forty years after the conquest, the colonial revenues consisted of less than 7 million in current lira, half of which was due to customs duties (mainly from Massawa's port). The colony exported, in descending order of value, coffee, dry skins, flaxseed, mother of pearl, and palm nuts: in short, little that could be considered industrial production. Among the imports were textiles and coffee, in addition to some iron tools for agriculture. Textiles, wines, flour, and pasta were exported from Italy to Eritrea in particularly large quantities. The whole volume of transactions of the main local credit bank (obviously consisting of discount operations, advances, and issues of stock) did not even add up to a billion lira in 1924.

The territory and the peoples of Somalia were of more substantial dimensions, but in general it was not possible to identify them with precision because of the lack of definition of the borders with Ethiopia and above all because of the very limited Italian control, which extended only to the main towns along the coast and the circumscribed irrigated lands of the interior. The figures provided by the yearbooks in the early 1920s (600,000 square kilometers and a million inhabitants) were therefore only a rough estimate. In spite of the extent of the colonial territories, in 1924 the colonial revenues were only eighteen million lira, fifteen million of which consisted of customs duties. Exports included dry skins, cotton oil, cotton, and kapok, the last two being typical of the Italian concessions. Imports were more traditional—cotton cloth and food products—since Somalia was unable even to take advantage of the consumer goods needed by Italian and other European colonists. Also for this reason the turnover of the sole institute of local credit was about a quarter of the Eritrean one.

Geographically, economically, and strategically more relevant were the two Mediterranean territories of Tripolitania and Cirenaica, later unified in the colony of Libya. Even here, as a result of the vastness of these desert territories and of the very limited colonial control that the Italians could brag about when the fascists took power, some figures in the yearbook are to be considered approximate. It was, however, significant that the geographical extent of Tripolitania and Cirenaica together was calculated as 1,640,000 square kilometers, with 850,000 inhabitants (although the tenuous control of the Italians and their consequent limited ethnological knowledge is made obvious by a very vague subdivision of this total figure into nomadic, seminomadic, and other populations). The diversification of the two territories was nonetheless evident even from the numbers related to the revenues of the two colonies, in 1924 fifty-four and fifteen million lira, respectively, while the extent of the customs duties was not more than nine and three million lira, data that confirm a still very backward state of colonial "exploitation." The presence of a growing colony of Italians, together with the expenses of maintaining a conspicuous backbone of necessary troops to combat resistance and maintain public order, explains instead a more interesting general movement of local credit banks (more than 6 billion lira). As far as colonial wealth and trade go, on the contrary, the Libyan colonies exported only dry skins and wool, while the imports (especially textiles, but later also flour, pasta, wine, tobacco, wood, marble, soap, and hay) would satisfy the needs of the urban communities, especially the Italian ones.

It is interesting to compare these first rough elements with other data. Demographically, for example, the population of the Italian peninsula was calculated at the beginning of the 1920s as slightly fewer than thirty-eight million, while the French population was thirty-nine million and the British more than forty-four million. It was not, therefore, an issue of Italian overpopulation, as the fascist propaganda had been thundering, but rather an issue of the density of the Italian population and its relation to the national wealth, both factors that would legitimate demographically the urge of the regime to find "a place in the sun." It is difficult, therefore, to sustain the demographic necessity of fascist expansionism.

At the beginning of the 1920s, annual production of steel was approximately more than 9 million tons in Great Britain and a little less than 3 million tons in France, while Italy could not produce more than 700,000 tons. (Perhaps steel production is not a sufficient index, but it reveals much about the strength of a power in the era of the second industrial revolution and of the first world conflict.) It is true that at the end of the following period (that is, at the eve of World War II), Italy's industrial production grew in absolute terms for the peninsula, almost doubling the country's productive capacity in relation to 1913 (although in the meantime Japan had quintupled its production). Slower to grow were Great Britain and France. Going back to the production of steel, in 1938 the Italian productive capacity was still half that of the French and a quarter that of the British. (Italy's capacity was also still less than a tenth of Germany's capacity, which was at the time subject to the frantic effort of Nazi rearmament.) [17]

From the point of view of the overseas dominions—whether they were calculated in demographic, geographic, or economic terms—Italy's international position, relative and absolute, was not much better. In 1915–16, Lenin, accumulating data for his *Imperialism: The Final Stage of Capitalism,* set down in his notebooks that London ruled about 400 million colonial subjects, Paris more than 56 million, The Hague about 38 million, and Lisbon 9 million, while Rome held power over little more than 1.3 million colonized people.[18] Analogous, if not worse, was the relationship between the different extension of the respective colonies. The rate of Italian colonial geographic extension was similarly anemic in relation to that of other European powers. This disparity had increased from 1914 to 1922, if one takes into account the disappearance of the German colonial empire and of the Turkish dominions in the Middle East, divided as they had been between Great Britain and France into forms of trusteeship. At the end of the fascist period, the modest border adjustments obtained in the meantime and especially the conquest of Ethiopia had certainly enlarged Italy's African booty, from the point of view of geographical expansion as well as in terms of subjects ruled and resources being exploited. This expansion did not, however, subvert the substantial limits of Italian colonial imperialism.

These quantitative data, although schematic and often ignored in discussions of diplomatic and political history, are nevertheless important when talking about the fascist regime and its imperial propaganda, and about the ambitions and the pretenses of its ruling class. This is particularly true with respect to Mussolini's ambitions (which even Renzo De Felice considers exaggerated) of seeing Italy as a power on a par with other European colonial powers such as the British and the French.[19] These data not only emphasize the discrepancy between reality and desire typical of fascist politicians in the colonial field, but above all they indicate how disconcerting Mussolini's perseverance in such ambitions and demands was for governmental offices and for the public in other countries. Fascist ambitions and demands, pretending to radically change the status quo, promised to subvert the international order of the day.

Nevertheless, the considerable quantitative modesty, from a global perspective, of Italy's liberal colonialism and of the fascist project that succeeded it should not induce us to underestimate either the national relevance of the overseas dimension for the history of the regime or, on the other hand, the peculiarity of fascist colonialism in relation to that of the other liberal powers and, in general, in relation to the colonial experience between the two world conflicts. I will return to these points often in the following pages. For now two observations on this matter will be enough.

The first and most obvious is that, even taking into account the overseas possessions of Salazar (since 1932) and the by then meager colonial dominions of fascist Spain (since 1936), Mussolini's empire was the longest and substantially the only experiment of colonialism in Africa by a fascist power.[20] Such uniqueness entailed the substantial peculiarity of the colonial fascist dominion. This fact is all too often forgotten, especially because of the nationalist mindset of the colonial historians of the regime and of the liberal government that followed in its wake. In order to understand this peculiarity it is, however, necessary to extend our analysis to the colonies of the other powers, as well as to the differences between the past age of the scramble for Africa (1875–1914) and the age between the world conflicts. Now, it is true that European imperialism and the white colonial oppression of Africa, Asia, and Oceania had, in the twenty years that followed the Great War, strong elements of continuity with the decades of the scramble. Something changed, however, especially after the two major colonial powers, Great Britain and France, imposed onerous requirements to participate in the Great War on a good part of their colonial dominions. The drain of resources and the cost in human lives, recruited in the colonies and sacrificed on the fields of the Western front, had undermined the relationship between the motherland and colonies from the economic, political, and ideological points of view. It is impossible not to think of the fact that the London delegates at the peace conference refused to define themselves as "English" but rather spoke of themselves as representing the British empire, creating a symbolic link with the 1.4 million Indians who found under the Union Jack between 1914 and 1918. Or how could one believe that Paris would not somehow have to transform, after the conflict, the administration of those Senegalese whose legions of *tirailleurs* (African soldiers who fought for France during World War I) had served and aroused such pride in the French empire?

It is not insignificant, therefore, that histories of decolonization, and not only the most updated, use 1918 as a point of departure.[21] The birth and growth, although slow and difficult, of the first modern national movements animated by the political and religious elites of the people subject to the white colonial dominions must be placed between the two wars, in spite of the evident diversity of chronologies, geographies, and local histories. Both the British and the French engaged in acts of brutal repression against these anticolonial movements, even between the two wars and in particular in the years immediately following the conclusion of the Great War, brutalities on the part of both the British and the French were not lacking. The massacre of Amritsar of 1919 and the war without quarter against Abd el-Krim in 1920 testify to that. But what such brutal episodes indicate is, crucially, the presence of indigenous political and religious opposition movements, which in some cases were crushed and in others were only temporarily sedated. It is thus possible to understand why, starting from the end of the Great War, for both London and Paris the basic political problems of the administration of their empires consisted of control of these indigenous movements as well as colonial exploitation. In other words, decolonization came after World War II, but it was rooted in the preceding twenty years.

Still, in order to understand the uniqueness of the colonial politics of the fascist regime, a further consideration, one of chronological order, is necessary. Throughout the *ventennio* two moments were particularly critical for the rulers of colonial empires. The first occurred immediately following the end of the First World War, when the memory of the sacrifices made for the war waged by the colonial oppressors was still fresh in the subject societies. A huge wave of unrest, riots, and revolutions swept through the colonial dominions, from Morocco to Algeria, from Libya to Egypt, from Persia to Afghanistan, from Iraq to South Africa, from the Congo to Indonesia, from India to Korea and China.[22] The movement, simultaneous but uncoordinated, very much alarmed the colonial administrators. Limited success was realized by various national movements (for example, the gaining of autonomy by the Egyptian Wafdist government) but, even when the revolutionary wave of 1918–23 was harshly repressed, it had lasting consequences. It was enough, for example, to induce London and Paris to grant concessions and even autonomy in some cases, reinforcing indirect rule; and it was enough to convince Moscow of the importance of constant attention to colonial peoples. Such concessions strengthened the thirst for national emancipation in the nationalist elites; such observations would not lack relevance even in view of a reexamination of the colonial politics of liberal Italy, which need to be discussed elsewhere.

The second critical moment in the relationship between colonial powers and overseas dominions came after 1929. Only a few years had gone by since the post-revolutionary adjustment recalled above, when the crash of the stock market put all the European economies in serious difficulties. In two or three years at the most, the colonial powers strengthened their economic links with their own dominions, intensifying their exploitation and raising the protectionist barriers that linked motherland to colonies. The necessity, imposed by the crisis, of having access to resources at prices lower than those of the international free markets, of enlarging outlet markets for national productions, of creating new opportunities to export capital (preferably under the protection of the flag), and of lifting the level of profits created contradictory political consequences. Among these were greater sensitivity of the bureaucracies concerning all that could involve the overseas dominions, the necessity for the bureaucracies to better control the indigenous middle classes, and the growth of the anticolonial nationalist movements. All this entailed a shifting of the axis of the great powers' imperial interests, in other words, a passage, between the two global conflicts, from the age of imperialism and the scramble for possessions to a phase of consolidation and exploitation. A phase characterized by bellicose inter-imperialistic contradictions was succeeded by another marked by the pre-eminence of pacific administrations and of economic exploitation.

Such a general picture as I have just sketched here will have to be kept in mind in the examination of fascist colonialism. In relation to the international trend, liberal Italy had been going against the grain in its last phase, with its insistent demand for "equal compensation" linked to the Treaty of London and with the beginning of the reconquest of Libya. But it was above all the colonial politics of fascism that marked a deep continuity in relation to the international picture. The characteristic traits of that politics were, therefore, an insistence on revision of the colonial configuration established in Versailles, the further push toward administrative centralization, military reconquest, scarce development of the overseas dominions, and, finally, the unleashing of an aggressive regime of racial discrimination.

The Ethiopian war has often been defined as anachronistic. But this characterization should be both extended to other sectors of colonial politics (one thinks of so-called "indigenous politics") and substantially anticipated, taking into consideration the totality of colonial politics of the regime, starting from 1922. If one did so, the genesis of the war of 1935–36 would seem much less "episodic" and incomprehensible than it currently does.

THE FOUNDATIONS OF FASCIST COLONIALISM

In addition to presenting the peculiarities, recalled above, in relation to contemporaneous colonialism projects, fascist colonialism highlights a discontinuity even in relation to that of liberal Italy. Among scholars, it is well known, there is no unanimity about such discontinuity. On the other hand, the serious backwardness of historical colonial studies, together with the fact that the studies on liberal colonialism are better developed in comparison with those of the fascist period, does not allow definitive conclusions.

Simply in discussing the economic foundations of Italian colonialism, one can observe the complex relationship between continuity and change. From Agostino Depretis's seizure of Massawa in 1885 to Giovanni Giolitti's decision to occupy Tripoli in 1911 to Mussolini's choice to attack Ethiopia, no one doubts the relevance of the political element and diplomatic calculations; that is, more generally put, of prestige and of power politics in crucial moments of the history of Italian colonialism. But, within this continuity, one cannot ignore some signs of a remarkable change from Francesco Crispi to Giolitti, and, later, in the passage from liberal Italy to fascism. In such a perspective, some structural elements need to be kept in mind.

The first element is that of state expenses for the overseas territories as one of the indexes of the relevance attached to colonial politics in its entirety.[23] The general situation was well illustrated by the bitter considerations of a convinced colonialist about "the scarce and ungrateful Italian colonial patrimony. None of the three colonies was self-sufficient, and all three together weighed not indifferently on the perennially meager budget of the motherland."[24] The fact is that, in spite of the absence of specific studies, it is difficult to deny that the colonial budgets of fascism were much more substantial than those of liberal Italy long before the conquest of Ethiopia. This is true in absolute terms as much as in relative terms, both in relation to the total of the state expenses and in relation to the overall national product. On the one hand, one could observe how, within this significant change, strong elements of continuity remain, for example, as far as the structure of the budgets is concerned (absolute prevalence of the military portion of the colonial budget, a strong increase in expenses for the staff, etc.). On the other hand, it would be misleading not to point out that, unlike what took place during the Crispi government, behind the solemn words of the fascist propaganda there was an effective and substantial financial commitment in the ordinary budgets of the regime, budgets perhaps never considered sufficient by colonialist circles, but not for this reason less real and consistent. Even in the extraordinary allocations, colonial expenses frequently represented a fourth consideration, after those of defense, public works, and financial services. It might be objected, to those who illuminate such discontinuities with liberal Italy, that explicitly colonial expenses remained only a tenth of the military expense of the regime. However one wants to judge such a ratio, it is evident that, while in Europe the first experiments in welfare were being carried out, fascist Italy continued to spend more on the colonies than on domestic charity and social welfare, more than on railroads and more than on justice. It is apparent, therefore, that if liberal Italy had invested ten times more in instruction than in the colonies, the fascist regime was spending only three times more for its schools than for its colonies. And this is true only until 1935; after that date, the "imperial plan" tipped increasingly toward the budgets of the regime.

A second and more important element, which reveals the relationship between the politics of expansion and its social rooting, seen always in terms of fascist colonialism's continuity with and change in relation to that of liberal Italy, can be seen in the quantity, in the direction, and in the cycles of foreign trade.[25] Some numbers, although limited by the studies available, are sufficient, however, to highlight the fact that, between liberal Italy and the fascist regime, the signs of discontinuity—in percentile as well as in absolute terms—were greater than those of continuity.

Even within this ambit it is necessary to keep in mind the exceptional perturbations caused by the Great War at the level of international trade and of the confused configurations of the immediate postwar period, a period characterized by harsh struggles caused by the search for new hierarchies of influence and by new commercial challenges. (As an example, one should think of the new value assumed by the Middle East after the decline of Turkish power and the confirmation of the dimensions of the region's oil fields.) Not later than 1925–26, however, the international colonial economy had stabilized and, as I have said, already by 1929 and no later than 1931 a dense protectionist net had fastened the large colonial markets to their motherlands.

How was Italy situated in this international picture?[26] It has to be recalled that the interchange between the peninsula and the colonial dominions had always been quite limited, to the extent of constituting a justified and powerful subject for the anticolonialist critics. More interesting, perhaps, was the Italian-Mediterranean interchange (that is, the Italian exchange with the English territories in Egypt, the French ones of Tunisia and of Algeria, and those in the Turkish empire) and the interchange between Italy and Africa in its whole. In any case, the global numbers had remained modest, and they were not showing any signs of dynamism. Something changed with the war and became especially evident in the postwar period. The reduction of international trade during the war and in the postwar period and the troubles linked to the reconstruction of the lines of traffic allowed industry, agriculture, and an enterprising class of Italian merchants, big and small, to glimpse the possibility of an expansion in this sector during and immediately after the conflict. They were, in fact, able to occupy more significant international positions. In addition, these positions were often totally new during the postwar period, and in particular in the years of expansion between 1922 and 1926, an important fact in the national perception and in the perception of foreign governments and economic centers. Such a phenomenon, so far not sufficiently highlighted by Italian historians, explains or at least enhances our understanding of the objective and constant strengthening of the colonialist environment between the Treaty of London and the Convegno Nazionale Coloniale of April 1917, and then from the Convegno Nazionale Coloniale in the colonies of January 1919 until the time Mussolini took power and later. In particular, it needs to be pointed out that if, until 1919–20, there were mixed demands and concrete interests linked to the traditional Italian tendencies toward imperialistic expansionism in the Balkans and Africa, starting with the end of the war, the Italian ambitions in Africa acquired definitive consistency and autonomy and therefore a certain self-sufficiency. It was with press organs visibly supported by these economic environments that Italy first tried to influence the Ministry of Foreign Affairs so that it would ask for some realizations of the agreements of the Treaty of London; later Italy started to hope, to no avail, for a revision of the configuration established in Versailles.

The positive Italian performance in the general commercial interchange with Africa (nearly half of which was accounted for by exchanges with Egypt) and more or less at the same time with the colonies was particularly evident around 1925. The Italian performance was particularly positive in the case of Libya, which was closer to Italy geographically and more densely populated by Italians, even if these settlers were still more often equipped with rifles for the control of the territory and the repression of anticolonial resistance than with spades and hoes for agrarian colonization. These exchanges thrived for international economic reasons not directly linked to the fascist regime's seizure of power, if not perhaps as a result of the free trade doctrines of the first Mussolini–De Stefani governments. It is legitimate to presume that this situation would strengthen or at least coincide with the nationalistic appeals of the minister of the colonies, Federzoni, for a revision of the colonial order established at Versailles.

The spaces left open between World War I and the period after World War I by the colonies (above all, the ones in Africa) of other powers to Italian exports of goods, which were often of low monetary value and therefore easily replaceable, were soon closed again. In the meantime, between the second half of the 1920s and the first few years of the 1930s, with the exception of some specific sectors (bananas, rubber, dry skins, etc.), the economies of the Italian colonies themselves had not been sufficiently developed and therefore could not satisfy the demand of the motherland, which was left unanswered because of the closure of other colonial markets. The protectionist policies implemented following the crisis of 1929 further marginalized colonial markets, multiplying the pressures on the government and the state.

In the meantime, specific conjunctural difficulties together with the more general alignment between fascist state and industry, between politics and economy, had transformed a good number of the actors involved in this area in the course of a few years. The companies and the individual enterprising merchants of the past, traditional figures of the Italian interchange with the Middle East, were heading with the regime toward a rationalization and integration. An explicit directive dated 1934, imparted by the Istituto per la Ricostruzione Industriale (IRI) and agreed upon by the Banca d'Italia, can be read as follows: "We have to establish as a general norm, except in case of specific examination of the demands of the individual foreign nations, that, where there are more credit banks dependent from Comit, from Credit, and from the Banco di Roma, such credit banks have to be reduced to one alone, both by dividing participation among the three credit banks and eventually through the disentanglement of one from the other."[27] It is difficult to determine how much such centralization of the Italian forces in Africa and the orient was linked to the diplomatic difficulties encountered by the regime in its attempts to procure the colonial compensation that the Treaty of London had suggested, or to the economic difficulties the regime experienced in penetrating other colonial markets while belatedly developing its own. What is certain is that a similar directive ended up linking the regime to economic groups interested in an expansionistic politics, prefiguring the exceptional relevance that the Italian colonial interchange (but it would be better to say Italian-Ethiopian) would assume in 1935–41.

Apart from such hypotheses, whose verification depends on the progress of the studies on the subject, everything that I have said up to this point about the direction and phases of the commerce between Italy and Africa (and between Italy and its colonies) was aimed at demonstrating that the period between the two wars constituted for Italy a significant discontinuity in the economic foundations of the colonial relationship, which meant, on a more general level, a discontinuity in the social basis of "consent" to the colonial designs of the regime.[28]

It is opportune to dwell upon a third element, finally, in order to be able to base the evaluation of the degree of continuity or change existing between liberal and fascist colonialism on foundations more solid than those of political diplomatic history alone: the demographic element.[29] It is necessary to talk about this element for several reasons: because within the ideology of Italian colonialism it represented a constant reference, because its peculiarity was theorized in relation to the imperialism of the Terza Roma, and because on this element in particular the fascist regime based a great part of its propaganda and founded the theoretical (and historiographic) legitimization of its own expansionistic politics. The demographic argument evolved quickly in the direction of myth.[30]

That Italy had a larger labor force than capital to export to Africa and in particular to its colonies was well known. But often the regime's propaganda occulted the fact that there were more Italians in the colonial territories subject to other powers than in the Italian colonies themselves. It has been noted, for example, that until the 1930s—and one could even say until the Ethiopian war—the most Italian colony, that is, Libya, was not hosting even half the number of Italians hosted by Tunisia.[31] In addition to this, the Italian colony in Libya was not quantitatively comparable to the French settlement in Algeria; and yet the Italian colonization of Libya remained, until the years of the Mussolinian empire in Ethiopia, the greatest demographic realization of fascism in Africa.

The numbers are not always univocal, given the embarrassment of the regime in having to exhibit what might have been construed as a failure of Italian colonization. Sometimes researchers themselves are induced by these numbers to make mistakes, for example when computing the military population, which was always a significant component as a result of the regime's tradition and politics, among the residing colonists.[32] The fact is that at the beginning of the 1930s, the Italians unequivocally indicated by the censuses as residents in Somalia totaled only in the hundreds, in Eritrea in the thousands, and in Libya approximately forty thousand. If one takes into account the number of French in Algeria or in Tunisia or even the number of the British in some of their African colonies, the definition of "demographic imperialism" espoused by an entire Italian tradition becomes acceptable only with many subtle distinctions.[33] As is well known, things changed radically with the Ethiopian war and, for Libya, with the two expeditions for which Alessandro Lessona argued. Ironically, Lessona did not take part in such expeditions because in the meantime he had been replaced by Attilio Teruzzi. Above all, the situation was changed by Italo Balbo of the "twenty thousand" (actually only fifteen thousand and twelve thousand, respectively, in 1938 and in 1939). But until then, if colonization really equaled "consent," the regime would have, as it really did, grounds to lament the "colonial conscience of the Italians."

It is not possible to conclude even such a summary panorama of the structural, economic, and demographic foundations of fascist colonialism univocally. Certainly, however, it is evident that the fascist seizure of power marked a radical structural change in relation to the politics of the liberal era. Notwithstanding this shift, Italian colonialism remained circumscribed and secondary. The analyses that have insisted, together with the debates on the passage from the foreign politics of liberal Italy to fascism, on a mere change of style in fascist colonialism therefore not only remain on the surface of a much more complex historical phenomenon, but they preclude comprehension of the specificities of colonial fascist imperialism between the 1920s and 1930s.

TOWARD ETHIOPIA

The celebration in 1932 of the decennium and, in general, the first years of the 1930s coincided with a radical reformulation of the spaces of action and of the character of the regime, by now on its way to totalization. This transformation found a reflection and at the same time a powerful accelerator in the terrain of colonial politics, which, from that moment on, started to head toward the Ethiopian adventure. With this enterprise, significant aspects of fascist imperialism surfaced, aspects that had operated in isolation in the 1920s and in the early years of the 1930s.

Various interlinking elements propelled fascism toward Ethiopia. At the international level, the distancing of the regime from the English and American orbits; the increasing significance assumed by Germany for Mussolini's political outlook; and the difficulties met in regard to the other traditional direction of Italian imperialism in the Balkans led the regime to give greater attention to Africa and therefore to colonial politics in the ambit of the foreign. That there were spaces for audacious action and that the League of Nations was unable to prevent them or to repress such actions became plain to il Duce at the time of the Japanese invasion of Manchuria in September 1931.

At the internal level, the different forces that the regime had in the meantime created or fueled and strengthened were pressing in on Mussolini, who from 1932 had assumed again the leading position in the Foreign Ministry. Primary among such forces were colonialist and expansionist political circles, which from the beginning of the 1930s found themselves with a role and a force that they had never had in the history of Italy. These circles were flanked by important diplomatic sectors that had earlier seen the Italian expansionism favorably, and by the army, both that fraction of the armed forces that was operating in the colonies and had led the reconquest and, more generally, the high ranks, which were threatened by the growing power of the fascists and which feared that they would lose control of important missions after Mussolini again took over the Ministry of War in 1933. One could add to such forces the Crown, although the influence of Vittorio Emanuele III over Mussolini was far inferior to that of Umberto I over Crispi during the first African war. Nevertheless, even if it seems that the king did not agree in 1932 to actions in Africa, it is impossible to deny that on more than one occasion—for example when Federzoni headed the Ministry of the Colonies—he had demonstrated great interest concerning the African prospects of fascism. Indeed, in the first half of the 1930s, the royal trips, among which were those to Eritrea, Somalia, and Egypt, had represented significant political initiatives and important opportunities for propaganda for the regime. But after 1929 an equally important but heretofore neglected role was probably played by Italian economic interests. Such interests included both those that were traditionally invested in Africa and the colonies and all those (from the shipping companies to the makers of vehicles, from the textile manufacturers to the agrarians) that the internal crisis was pushing to look for profits in whatever adventure as long as it was covered by state intervention.

The third level to be kept in mind is the economic. It has been repeatedly recalled that, after a decade of colonial propaganda, the regime had difficulty justifying the absence of an empire. But facts signified more than words, and the facts highlight all the difficulties of the Italian economy: unemployment had tripled from 1929 to 1931 (and quadrupled by 1932), and foreign trade had been cut in half between 1929 and 1932 (and by 1935 it would decline to a third). In the meantime, while in 1931 the Viennese Kredit Anstalt had collapsed, the crisis was opening huge gaps in some Italian financial pillars, a situation to which the regime replied with the politics of the great rescues that, it was observed later, would cost not less than the entire, very costly Ethiopian campaign. Relevant, from the point of view of expansionist politics and of the weight gained by Italian imperialism, was the fact that the dynamic of the crisis and the reply of the regime led to a drastic interpenetration of state and business, politics and economy, as is made evident by credit banks like IMI and IRI. It is true that the Italian economy had started to improve by 1933; however, in 1934 the specter of recession was anything but banished, and this proved sufficient to induce the economic actors—by then no longer isolated, if not completely intertwined with the state—to see the advantages of the expansionist politics opted for by Mussolini. The support of such forces was, in addition, indispensable since, as I will show, il Duce had in the meantime developed the idea of fighting not a limited colonial war for Ethiopia, but a real national and fascist war.

Seen in such a perspective, the colonial imperialism of the fascist regime

by the midpoint of the 1930s loses a little of its widespread image as an archaic or premodern imperialism aimed exclusively at demographic colonization, an image that, even if legitimate in the 1920s, is not adequate to describe the power and complexity of interests that were at stake for fascism
once it turned toward Ethiopia.[34] It is true that there were divergences between words and facts as well as between forces and means, or even between
a decisive choice like the aggression toward Ethiopia and the absence of an
exact analysis of its possible influence on Italy's position in the international
scene, but this does not undermine the complexity and modernity of the
forces displayed by fascist colonial imperialism in the first half of the 1930s.

As far as the time of the aggression is concerned, it is clear that it tran-
scended the colonial African theater. It is enough to recall that, in addition
to the Japanese example in Manchuria, the years between 1931 and 1934
were counterpointed by the rise of Nazism and by the unfolding of the decisive rivalry of German revisionism and expansionism with the Italian.[35]
The fascist decision to invade Ethiopia can only be read in relation to Nazi
dynamism, in addition to being seen as an autonomous project matured
within the forces of the regime.

It has been argued that, in order to mark the transformation of the objective and means chosen by the regime, from 1922 to 1932 fascism aimed
mainly at Libya, although from 1932 to 1939 the prevalent objective became Ethiopia.[36] The formula should not make one forget that colonizing
Ethiopia had always been an objective of the fascist regime and that the regime wanted to pursue this objective in spite of both its difficulty and of every
diplomatic counterindication.[37] In any case, the decision to display aggression toward Ethiopia was not made only in late 1935; the occupation of the
African country was not an almost casual accident of reluctant imperialists.[38]

It may be convenient to recall at this point that in 1931 Raffaele Guariglia wrote a report from the Ministry of Foreign Affairs that explained how
Ethiopia remained the sole available site for fascist intervention in Africa.
Guariglia was fully aware that his report would animate interests already existing in Mussolini, in the colonies, and elsewhere.[39] Most indicative of all in
this vein are De Bono's plans of 1932, from the colonies, for a definitive
military action against the empire of the Negus. No later than December of
the same year, Mussolini expressed his appreciation for those plans to De
Bono, began to indicate certain distant dates, and suggested the position
of supreme command of the expedition to the same *quadrumvir*. Although
De Bono's plans received strong criticism from the high ranks of the armed
forces that were informed of these designs, they remained the political
point of departure, despite being later reformulated by Badoglio and by the
Ministry of War. Unsurprisingly, the military's concerns were linked to fears
about the control of the entire expedition and to the Duce's retention of all
the military ministries. A meeting of the leaders in February 1934 estab-

lished more defined times and modalities for the invasion, even though they were not yet irreversible: the spring-to-summer European crisis certainly worried the leaders of fascism. However, the appointment of the first military enjoys in April demonstrated that a choice had been made. After that, the Stato Maggiore and the Ministry of War tried to rearticulate their position in relation to the colonies and foresaw, in their counterplans, a more extensive expedition than that predicted by De Bono, both by virtue of their more realistic and professional analysis of the risks and in order to reassert military supremacy over the rival colonial administration. From May to November of 1934, the combat readiness and the armament of the Italian troops in Eritrea was doubled. It was not yet the massive envoy of men accumulated by 1935–36, but it already represented a clear signal to everybody, from the Ethiopians to international public opinion, that something was being prepared.

In the meantime, the mechanism that would lead to the border incident of Ual-ual on December 5, 1934, had started to function. It was through this incident that the regime justified its aggression toward Ethiopia in 1935, at which time no war declaration was made. The Italian-Ethiopian colonial borders, especially between Somalia and Ethiopia, in fact had never been fixed, and the Italians had always hindered and systematically violated the few agreements that had been reached, even at the time of the accord of 1928. Rome had always refused to accept the more than reasonable, peaceful proposals of Addis Ababa for the resolution of the dispute, and the instructions sent directly from the colonies to the governors and from the governors to the frontier positions were implicitly aggressive.[40]

Less than a month after Ual-ual, on December 30, 1934, Mussolini wrote a personal memorandum: "The time is against us. . . . It is necessary to solve the [Ethiopian] problem as soon as possible. . . . The objective can only be the destruction of the Abyssinian armed forces and the total conquest of Ethiopia. The Empire cannot be made otherwise."[41] The memorandum revealed then that the character of the enterprise had changed from that of a colonial expedition to a full-scale national, fascist war. Surprised, De Bono himself wrote in his diary, "Mussolini would send all his army, all the air force and all the navy."[42] The operations would begin on October 3, 1935, and in May 1936 the army corps, situated between Eritrea and Somalia, reached Addis Ababa. This corps numbered about 330,000 Italian soldiers, 87,000 *ascari* (indigenous soldiers), and 100,000 militarized Italian workers and was equipped with 10,000 machine guns, 1,100 cannons, 250 tanks, 14,000 vehicles, and 350 planes.[43] A good part of the gas weapons that had been prepared for some time had already been released on the Ethiopians. Assuming such dimensions, the Italian aggression toward Ethiopia "was the first war enterprise on a large scale of a European power after the end of the Great War."[44] The colonial politics of the regime had gone that far.

On the internal front, at the beginning of the conflict, the regime had begun to see the results of the complex and at that point decade-long effort of colonial propaganda. It cannot be doubted that this had an impact. In spite of this, Renzo De Felice documented that, at least until October 1935, police sources indicated that the public was not at all convinced, cases of failure to report for military service and clandestine expatriation to escape the war in the Horn of Africa were frequent, and fears were rife among the police of antifascist sabotage. Meanwhile, the communists, for their part, were making significant efforts in anticolonial propaganda through their clandestine press.[45]

In order to conclude my discussion of the role of the regime's colonial politics in the first fifteen years and to define some points of the historiographic debate regarding the older origins, the localization, and the immediate causes of the aggression toward Ethiopia, it is appropriate to go back to the general structural picture and to the points made above about the internal dynamic of the regime's colonial politics. Obviously in 1932, as was true later in 1934–35, Mussolini could choose his colonial politics; his choice, however, was not influenced only by personal opinion, even though the regime was becoming increasingly totalitarian.[46] In addition to his own opinion, il Duce had to take into account the same forces that the regime had been building up gradually. These forces included the military and the diplomatic sector, as well as colonial and expansionistic circles within other sectors of the state. More generally, il Duce had to reckon with the large world of interests linked to the Italian-African interchange, including all those economic groups that after 1929 counted, not mistakenly, on the recovery of profits that a significant military enterprise would entail. Finally, il Duce had to placate the regime's propagandists, who had been preaching the imperial idea for quite some time, and the Italian public, who had been bombarded by rampant colonialist propaganda. All these forces pushed Mussolini toward Africa, toward a politics of open subversion and war.

Interpretations based on the notion that Mussolini considered a great war an opportunity to leave an inheritance for future generations are, therefore, unfounded. Also unfounded is the opinion that Mussolini could have founded an African empire anywhere in the Mediterranean, the Arabian peninsula, or the Horn of Africa.[47] In fact, the fascist colonial expansion after 1929–31 entailed by itself significant risks of destabilization; the prospect of the war was not avoided by the regime but only subordinated to the hope that the liberal European powers would prefer peace. Haile Selassie had initiated a process of centralization and modernization in Ethiopia; therefore, the possibilities for success of peripheral Italian politics had been decreasing for some time, while it was reasonably unthinkable that the Negusa Negast could accept an Italian protectorate or the dismemberment of the Ethiopian country.

On the other hand, in spite of the risks implicit in a similar politics of destabilization and of a war in such a vast and harsh territory, the Ethiopia of the Negus represented much the weakest adversary of fascism. Mussolini's regime had long been engaged in diplomatic preparations for this confrontation. In addition, conflict with Ethiopia did not involve challenging another Western power, as would have been the case in the Mediterranean or the Middle East, not to mention, moreover, that Ethiopia was the only country capable of eliciting residues of old and recent colonial propaganda among the Italians. All this does not mean that, after military preparations had been underway for some time, Mussolini did not have to take into account the movements within the European diplomatic world and, in particular, French support and English reactions.[48] On the contrary, it warns against any overestimation of potential strategies—like that of the dismemberment of the Ethiopian empire linked to the Hoare-Laval plan— that were part of the international diplomatic games or of games internal to the regime, rather than real possibilities.

Once the war machine had been turned on, it was not easy for the regime to decrease its speed or reverse its direction. Nor did Mussolini want this. Once Italy had prepared for war and initiated it, "the alternative to accepting a peace of compromise would have meant to send back to Italy thousands of soldiers and their equipment. A move so costly and senseless would have made Italy the joke of the entire world and would have inflicted a humiliation greater than that which the fascist regime could tolerate."[49]

A great number of the elements that constituted the colonial politics of fascism therefore converged in the final decision to attack Ethiopia: revisionism, racist contempt, and consistency of the mobilized interests. It has been argued that the foreign politics of the fascist regime had aspects of both stabilization and destabilization in the international order. On the colonial front, the destabilizing elements were absolutely superior to the others.[50]

NOTES

The pages that follow will appear, in a modified version, in a more extended historical review in Enzo Collotti, ed., *La politica di potenza del fascismo* (Firenze: La nuova Italia, 2000), a volume of the series *Storia d'Italia nel secolo ventesimo,* sponsored by the National Institute for the History of the Liberation in Italy. My thanks to the editor of the Italian volume and to INSMLI and its president, Giorgio Rochat, who authorized the prior publication of several parts of my contribution. In this chapter I do not propose to offer a complete bibliography, even if I intend to discuss the fundamental themes of fascism's colonial politics in its twelve years of life, until now neglected in comparison with the anniversary of the Ethiopian war.

1. Giorgio Rochat, "Colonialismo," in *Il mondo contemporaneo: Storia d'Italia* (Firenze: La nuova Italia, 1978).

2. Renzo De Felice, *Mussolini il duce,* vol. 1, *Gli anni del consenso 1929–1936,* (Torino: Einaudi, 1974).

3. Nicola Labanca, *In marcia verso Adua* (Torino: Einaudi, 1993).

4. Angelo Del Boca, *Le conseguenze per l'Italia del mancato dibattito sul colonialismo* (Studi piacentini, 1989), n. 5.

5. Vincenzo Pellegrini and Anna Bertinelli, *Per la storia dell'amministrazione coloniale italiana* (Milano: Giuffrè–Isap, 1994).

6. Patrizia Ferrara, "Recenti acquisizioni dell'Archivio centrale dello Stato in materia di fonti per la storia dell'Africa italiana: Ufficio studi e propaganda MAI, in Fonti e problemi della politica coloniale italiana." Atti del convegno (Taormina-Messina, 23–29 ottobre 1989), Roma, Ministero per i beni culturali e ambientali, Ufficio centrale per i beni archivistici, 1996.

7. Luigi Goglia, *Politica coloniale,* in *Bibliografia orientativa del fascismo,* director Renzo De Felice (Roma: Bonacci, 1991).

8. Angelo Del Boca, *Gli italiani in Africa Orientale* (Roma-Bari: Laterza, 1976–84) and *Gli italiani in Libia* (Roma-Bari: Laterza, 1986–88); Raffaele Ciasca, *Storia coloniale dell'Italia contemporanea: Da Assab all'impero* (Milano: Hoepli, 1938); G. Rochat, *Il colonialismo italiano: Documenti* (Torino: Loescher, 1973); Jean-Louis Miege, *L'imperialismo coloniale italiano dal 1870 ai giorni nostri* (Milano: Rizzoli, 1976).

9. See Carlo Sforza, *L'Italia dal 1914 al 1944 quale io la vidi* (Roma: Mondadori, 1944 [consulted edition 1945]); Mario Donosti (pseud. Mario Luciolli), *Mussolini e l'Europa: La politica estera fascista* (Roma: Leonardo, 1945); Ennio di Nolfo, *Mussolini e la politica estera italiana (1919–1933)* (Padova: Cedam, 1960). Still seminal today is Giampiero Carocci, *La politica estera dell'Italia fascista (1925–1928)* (Bari: Laterza, 1969). But also see Enzo Santarelli, "Guerra d'Etiopia, imperialismo e terzo mondo," *Il movimento di liberazione in Italia* 97 (1969).

10. G. Rochat, "La repressione della resistenza araba in Cirenaica nel 1930–31," *Il movimento di liberazione in Italia* 110 (1973); Piero Pieri and G. Rochat, *Pietro Badoglio* (Torino: UTET, 1974); G. Rochat, *Militari e politici nella preparazione della campagna d'Etiopia: Studio e documenti 1932–1936* (Milano: Angeli, 1971); and G. Rochat, *Italo Balbo* (Torino: UTET, 1986).

11. R. De Felice, *Mussolini il duce,* vol. 1, *Gli anni del consenso 1929–1936;* R. De Felice, *Il fascismo e l'Oriente: Arabi, ebrei e indiani nella politica di Mussolini* (Bologna: Il Mulino, 1988).

12. See in general the observations of Romain Rainero and Giorgio Rochat in "Studi storico-coloniali," in *Gli studi africanistici in Italia dagli anni '60 ad oggi: Atti del convegno* (Roma: Istituto italo-africano, 1986).

13. L. Goglia, *Colonialismo e fotografia: Il caso italiano* (Messina: Sicania, 1989); Goglia, "Storia militare coloniale," in *Guida alla storia militare italiana,* ed. Piero Del Negro (Napoli: Edizioni scientifiche italiane, 1997); Claudio Segrè, *Gli italiani in Libia: Dall'età giolittiana a Gheddafi* (Milano: Feltrinelli, 1978); Alberto Sbacchi, *Il colonialismo italiano in Etiopia 1936–1940* (Milano: Mursia, 1980); Mario Isnenghi, *Intellettuali militanti e intellettuali funzionari: Appunti sulla cultura fascista* (Torino: Einaudi, 1979); Adolfo Mignemi, ed., *Immagine coordinata per un impero: Etiopia 1935–1936* (Torino: Forma, 1984); N. Labanca, *L'Africa in vetrina: Storie di musei e di esposizioni coloniali in Italia* (Treviso: Pagus, 1992).

14. Cf. N. Labanca, "Italiani d'Africa," in *Adua: Le ragioni di una sconfitta*, ed. A. Del Boca (Roma-Bari: Laterza, 1997).

15. Elena Aga Rossi, "La politica estera e l'Impero," in *Storia d'Italia*, vol. 4, *Guerre e fascismo 1914–1943*, ed. Giovanni Sabbatucci and Vittorio Vidotto (Roma-Bari: Laterza, 1997). But also see G. Carocci, "Appunti sull'imperialismo fascista negli anni '20," *Studi storici* 1 (1967); Enzo Collotti, "Fascismo: La politica estera," in *Storia d'Italia*, vol. 1, *Il mondo contemporaneo*, ed. Fabio Levi, Umberto Levra, and Nicola Tranfaglia (Firenze: La nuova Italia, 1978); Enzo Santarelli, "L'espansionismo imperialistico del 1920–1940," in *Storia della società italiana*, vol. 22, *La dittatura fascista*, ed. Giovanni Cherubini (Milano: Teti, 1983); Marco Palla, "Imperialismo e politica estera fascista," in *Storiografia e fascismo: Con appendice bibliografica*, ed. G. Quazza, E. Collotti, M. Legnani, et al. (Milano: Angeli, 1985); MacGregor Knox, "Il fascismo e la politica estera italiana," in *La politica estera italiana 1860–1985*, ed. Richard J. B. Bosworth and Sergio Romano (Bologna: Il Mulino, 1991). More generally, see also the anthology of documents by L. Goglia and Fabio Grassi, *Il colonialismo italiano da Adua all'impero* (Roma-Bari: Laterza, 1981).

16. M. Isnenghi, "Il sogno africano," in *Le guerre coloniali del fascismo*, ed. A. Del Boca (Roma-Bari: Laterza, 1991).

17. Paul Kennedy, *Ascesa e declino delle grandi potenze* (Milano: Garzanti, 1989).

18. Lenin, *L'imperialismo* (1917) (Roma: Editori Riuniti, 1971).

19. R. De Felice, *Mussolini il duce*, vol. 1, *Gli anni del consenso 1929–1936*.

20. N. Labanca, *Storia dell'Italia coloniale* (Milano: Fenice 2000, 1994).

21. Carlo Giglio, *Colonizzazione e decolonizzazione* (Cremona: Mangiarotti, 1964); Giampaolo Calchi Novati, *Decolonizzazione e Terzo Mondo* (Roma-Bari: Laterza, 1979); Anna Maria Gentili, "Decolonizzazione e neo-colonialismo nel XX secolo," in *La storia*, ed. Nicola Tranfaglia (Torino: UTET, 1986).

22. Walter Markov, *Sommario di storia coloniale* (Roma: Editori Riuniti, 1975).

23. Pietro Grifone, *Il capitale finanziario in Italia* (Torino: Einaudi, 1971); Felice Guarneri, *Battaglie economiche fra le due grandi guerre* (Milano: Garzanti, 1953) (in which one can also find Luciano Zani, *Fascismo, autarchia, commercio estero: Felice Guarneri un tecnocrate al servizio dello "Stato nuovo"* [Bologna: Il Mulino, 1988]); A. O. Hirschman, *Potenza nazionale e commercio estero* (Bologna: Il Mulino, 1987); Giuseppe Maione, "I costi delle imprese coloniali," in *Le guerre coloniali del fascismo*, ed. A. Del Boca (Roma-Bari: Laterza, 1991); A. Pedone, "La politica del commercio estero," in *Lo sviluppo economico in Italia*, vol. 2, *Gli aspetti generali*, ed. G. Fuà (Milano: Istat, Sommario di statistiche storiche 1861–1955, 1978). One can read a different series in Emilio Canevari, *La guerra italiana: Retroscena della disfatta* (Roma: Tosi, 1950). For the following period, see G. Maione, *L'imperialismo straccione: Classi sociali e finanza di guerra dall'impresa etiopica al conflitto mondiale (1935–1953)* (Bologna: Il Mulino, 1979).

24. Corrado Zoli, *Espansione coloniale italiana (1922–1937)* (Roma: L'arnia, 1949).

25. Even if not wholly objective, the figures concerning exchanges between the metropolis and colonies, as well as between the Italian peninsula and Africa more specifically, identify and measure the extent of interest of relevant sectors of the national economic sphere in the overseas question, depicting the cycles of this market

and allowing us to insert the issue in a broader international context. Since most available studies have a diplomatic-political-military orientation, preparatory studies are lacking in this area, and it will only be possible to make some preliminary observations as a result. See, for reconstructions of the economic history of Italy during this period, Giuseppe Tattara, "La persistenza dello squilibrio dei conti con l'estero dell'Italia negli anni Trenta," in *Ricerche per la storia della Banca d'Italia*, vol. 3, *Finanza internazionale, vincolo esterno e cambi 1919–1939* (Roma-Bari: Laterza 1993); Mariangela Paradisi, "Il commercio estero e la struttura industriale," in *L'economia italiana nel periodo fascista*, ed. Pierluigi Ciocca and Gianni Toniolo (Bologna: Il Mulino, 1976).

26. Gian Carlo Falco, "La bilancia dei pagamenti italiani tra la prima guerra mondiale e il 1931," in *Ricerche per la storia della Banca d'Italia*, vol. 6, *La bilancia dei pagamenti italiani 1914–1931* (Roma-Bari: Laterza 1995).

27. Giuseppe Guarino and G. Toniolo, eds., *La Banca d'Italia e il sistema bancario 1919–1936* (Roma-Bari: Laterza, 1993).

28. It seems necessary to register this discontinuity from within a history of Italian colonialism, even if it is evident that we are dealing with percentages very different from those of the older colonial powers. As we have seen, the colonial holdings of such powers are quantitatively far more significant than those of Italy.

29. Ettore Sori, *L'emigrazione italiana dall'Unità alla seconda guerra mondiale* (Bologna: Il Mulino, 1978).

30. N. Labanca, *Italiani d'Africa*.

31. Juliette Bessis, *La Libia contemporanea* (Soveria Mannelli: Rubbettino, 1991).

32. Annunziata Nobile, "Gli studi demografici sulle colonie italiane: Fonti e problemi," in *Fonti archivistiche e ricerca demografica: Atti del convegno internazionale* (Trieste, 23–26 aprile 1990), Roma, Ministero per i beni culturali e ambientali, Ufficio centrale per i beni archivistici, 1996; Nobile, "La colonizzazione demografica della Libia: Progetti e realizzazioni," *Bollettino di demografia storica* 6, no. 1 (1990); Nobile, "Politica emigratoria e vicende dell'emigrazione durante il fascismo," *Il ponte* 30, nos. 11–12 (1974); Carl Ipsen, *Demografia totalitaria: Il problema della popolazioni nell'Italia fascista* (Bologna: Il Mulino, 1997).

33. Ronald Robinson, "British Imperialism: The Colonial Office and the Settler in East-Central Africa, 1919–63," in *Italia e Inghilterra nell'età dell'imperialismo*, ed. Enrico Serra and Christopher Seton Watson (Milano: Angeli, 1990).

34. G. Carocci, *La politica estera dell'Italia fascista*.

35. E. Collotti, *Fascismo, fascismi* (Firenze: Sansoni, 1989).

36. Giorgio Candeloro, *Storia dell'Italia moderna*, vol. 9, *Il fascismo e le sue guerre 1922–1939* (Milano: Feltrinelli, 1981).

37. For the complex diplomatic ties with Great Britain and France in relation to the hostilities toward Ethiopia, see Renato Mori, *Mussolini e la conquista dell'Etiopia* (Firenze: Le Monnier, 1978); among the most recent studies of Paola Brundu Olla, *L'equilibrio difficile: Gran Bretagna, Italia e Francia nel Mediterraneo, 1930–37* (Milano: Giuffrè, 1980); Giovanni Buccianti, *Verso gli accordi Mussolini-Laval 1931–34* (Milano: Giuffrè, 1984); Francesco Lefebvre D'Ovidio, *L'intesa italo-francese del 1935: Nella politica estera di Mussolini* (Roma: Tip. Aurelia, 1984); Francesco Perfetti, "Alle origini degli accordi Laval Mussolini: Alcuni contatti italo-francesi del 1932 in materia coloniale," *Storia contemporanea* 8, no. 4 (1977); R. Quartararo, "L'Italia e lo

Yemen: Uno studio sulla politica di espansione italiana nel Mar Rosso (1923–1937)," *Storia contemporanea* 10, no. 4–5 (1979); and, with major attention to colonial questions, R. Rainero, *La rivendicazione fascista sulla Tunisia* (Milano: Marzorati, 1978), and E. Serra, "La questione italo-etiopica alla conferenza di Stresa," *Affari esteri* 34 (1977); Enrico Serra, "Dalle trattative sul confine meridionale della Libia al baratto sull'Etiopia," *Nuova antologia* 3 (1980). Remaining in the perspective, this time military, of Africa orientale italiana are the studies of Fortunato Minniti, "Oltre Adua: Lo sviluppo e la scelta della strategia operativa per la guerra contro l'Etiopia," *Quaderno* (1993); and Minniti, "'Il nemico vero': Gli obiettivi dei piani di operazione contro la Gran Bretagna nel contesto etiopico (maggio 1935–maggio 1936)," *Storia contemporanea* 26, no. 4 (1995).

38. R. De Felice, *Mussolini il duce,* vol. 1, *Gli anni del consenso.*

39. Gianfranco Bianchi, *Rivelazioni sul conflitto italo-etiopico* (Milano: Ceis, 1967); G. Rochat, *Militari e politici nella preparazione della campagna d'Etiopia: Studio e documenti 1932–1936* (Milano: Angeli, 1971); R. De Felice, *Mussolini il duce,* vol. 1, *Gli anni del consenso.*

40. Salvatore Minardi, *Alle origini dell'incidente di Ual Ual* (Caltanissetta-Roma: Sciascia, 1990).

41. Op. cit. in G. Rochat, *Militari e politici nella preparazione della campagna d'Etiopia: Studio e documenti 1932–1936.*

42. Franco Fucci, *Emilio De Bono il maresciallo fucilato* (Milano: Mursia, 1989), 109, 111.

43. G. Rochat and Giulio Massobrio, *Breve storia dell'esercito italiano dal 1861 al 1943* (Torino: Einaudi, 1978).

44. Ennio Di Nolfo, *Storia delle relazioni internazionali 1918–1992* (Roma-Bari: Laterza, 1994), p. 192; but see also G. W. Baer, *La guerra italo-etiopica e la crisi dell'equilibrio europeo* (Bari: Laterza, 1970), and Baer, *Test Case: Italy, Ethiopia, and the League of Nations* (Stanford, Calif.: Hoover Institution Press, 1976).

45. Simona Colarizi, *L'opinione degli italiani sotto il regime, 1929–1943* (Roma-Bari: Laterza, 1991), as well as R. De Felice, *Mussolini il duce,* vol. 1, *Gli anni del consenso 1929–1936,* p. 617.

46. R. De Felice, *Mussolini il duce,* vol. 1, *Gli anni del consenso 1929–1936.*

47. Ibid.; R. Quartararo, *Roma tra Londra e Berlino: La politica estera fascista dal 1930 al 1940.*

48. Renzo De Felice, *Mussolini il duce,* vol. 1, *Gli anni del consenso 1929–1936.*

49. Esmonde M. Robertson, *Mussolini fondatore dell'impero* (Roma-Bari: Laterza, 1977).

50. G. Candeloro, *Storia dell'Italia moderna,* vol. 9, *Il fascismo e le sue guerre 1922–1939.*

WORKS CITED

Bessis, Juliette. *La Libia contemporanea.* Soveria Mannelli: Rubettino, 1991.

Bianchi, Gianfranco. *Rivelazioni sul conflitto Italo-Etiopico.* Milano: Ceis, 1967.

Calchi Novati, Giampaolo. *Decolonizzazione e Terzo Mondo.* Roma-Bari: Laterza, 1979.

Candeloro, Giorgio. *Storia dell'Italia moderna.* Vol. 9, *Il fascismo e le sue guerre, 1922–1939.* Milan: Feltrinelli, 1981.

Carocci, Giampiero. *La politica estera dell'Italia fascista (1925–1928)*. Bari: Laterza, 1969.

Ciasca, Raffaele. *Storia coloniale dell'Italia contemporanea: Da Assab all'impero.* Milano: Hoeply, 1938.

Colarizi, Simona. *L'opinione degli italiani sotto il regime, 1929–1943.* Roma-Bari: Laterza, 1991.

Collotti, E. *Fascimo, fascismi.* Firenze: Sansoni, 1989.

De Felice, Renzo. *Mussolini il duce.* Vol. 1, *Gli anni del consenso, 1929–1936.* Torino: Einaudi, 1974.

Del Boca, Angelo. *Gli italiani in Africa orientale.* Roma-Bari: Laterza, 1969.

———. *Gli italiani in Libia: Dal fascismo a Gheddafi.* Roma-Bari: Laterza, 1988.

Del Negro, Piero. *Guida alla storia militare italiana.* Napoli: Edizioni scientifiche italiane, 1997.

Di Nolfo, Ennio. *Mussolini e la politica estera italiana (1919–1933).* Padova: Cedam, 1960.

Donosti, Mario. *Mussolini e la politica estera fascista.* Roma: Leonardo, 1945.

Esmonde, M. Robertson. *Mussolini fondatore dell'impero.* Roma-Bari: Laterza, 1977.

Falco, Gian Carlo. "La bilancia dei pagamenti italiani tra la prima guerra mondiale e il 1931." In *Ricerche per la storia della Banca d'italia,* vol. 6. Roma-Bari: Laterza, 1995.

Ferrara, Patrizia. "Recenti acquisizioni dell'Archivio centrale dello Stato in materia di fonti per la storia dell'Africa italiana: Ufficio studi e propaganda MAI." Paper presented at Fonti e problemi della politica coloniale italiana (Taormina-Messina, 23–29 ottobre 1989, Roma), Ministero per i beni culturali e ambientali, Ufficio centrale per i beni archivistici, 1996.

Fucci, Franco. *Emilio De Bono il maresciallo fucilato.* Milano: Mursia, 1989.

Gentili, Anna Maria. "Decolonizzazione e neo-colonialimso nel XX secolo." In *La storia,* ed. Nicola Tranfaglia. Turin: UTET, 1986.

Giglio, Carlo. *Colonizzazione e decolonizzazione.* Cremona: Mangiarotti, 1964.

Goglia, Luigi. *Colonialismo e fotografia: Il caso italiano.* Messina: Sicania, 1989.

———. "Politica coloniale." In *Bibliografia orientativa del fascismo.* Roma: Bonacci, 1991.

———. "Storia militare coloniale." In *Guida alla storia militara italiana,* ed. Piero del Negro. Napoli: Edizioni scientifiche italiane, 1997.

Grifone, Pietro. *Il capitale finanziario in Italia.* Torino: Einaudi, 1971.

Guarino, Giuseppe, and G. Toniolo, eds. *La Banca d'Italia e il sistema bancario 1919–1936.* Roma-Bari: Laterza, 1993.

Guarneri, Felice. *Battaglie economiche fra le due grandi guerre.* Milano: Garzanti, 1953.

Isnenghi, Mario. *Intellettuali militanti e intellettuali funzionari: Appunti sulla cultura fascista.* Torino: Einaudi, 1979.

Kennedy, Paul. *Ascesa e declino delle grandi potenze.* Milano: Garanti, 1989.

Labanca, Nicola. *L'Africa in vetrina: Storie di musei e id esposizioni coloniali in Italia.* Treviso: Pagus, 1992.

———. *In marcia verso Adua.* Torino: Einaudi, 1993.

———. *Storia dell'Italia coloniale.* Milano: Fenice 2000, 1994.

———. "Italiani d'Africa." In *Adua: Le ragioni di una sconfitta,* ed. A. Del Boca. Roma-Bari: Laterza, 1997.

Lenin, V. I. *L'imperialismo.* Roma: Editori Riuniti, 1971.

Markov, Walter. *Sommario di storia coloniale.* Roma: Editori Riuniti, 1975.

Miege, Jean-Louis. *L'imperialismo coloniale italiano dal 1870 ai giorni nostri.* Milano: Rizzoli, 1976.

Mignemi, Adolfo. *Immagine coordinata per un impero: Etiopia 1935–1936.* Torino: Forma, 1984.

Minardi, Salvatore. *Alle origini dell'incidente di Ual Ual.* Caltanissetta and Roma: Sciascia, 1990.

Mori, Renato. *Mussolini e la conquista dell'Etiopia.* Firenze: Le Monnier, 1978.

Nobile, Annunziata. "Gli studi demografici sulle colonie italiane: Fonti e problemi." *Fonti archivistiche e ricerca demografica: Atti del convegno internazionale* (Trieste, 23–26 aprile 1990, Roma), Ministero per i beni culturali e ambientali, Ufficio centrale per i beni archivistici.

Pellegrini, Vincenzo, and Anna Bertinelli. *Per la storia dell'amministrazione coloniale italiana.* Milano: Giuffre-Isap, 1994.

Piero, Pieri, and Giorgio Rochat. *Pietro Badoglio.* Torino: UTET, 1974.

Quartararo, Rosaria. *Roma tra Londra e Berlino: La politica estera fascista dal 1930 al 1940.*

Rainero, Romain, and Giorgio Rochat. "Studi Storico-Coloniali." In *Gli studi africanistici in Italia dagli anni '60 ad oggi.* Atti del convegno, Roma, Istituto italo-africano, 1986.

Robinson, Ronald. "British Imperialism: the Colonial Office and the Settler in East-Central Africa, 1919–63." In *Italia e Inghilterra nell'età dell'imperialismo,* ed. Enrico Serra and Christopher Seton Watson. Milano: Angeli, 1990.

Rochat, Giorgio. *Militari e politici nella preparazione della campagna d'Etiopia: Studio e documenti 1932–1936.* Milano: Angeli, 1971.

———. "La repressione della resistenza araba in Cirenaica nel 1930–31." *Il movimento di liberazione in Italia* 110 (1973).

———. *Italo Balbo.* Torino: UTET, 1986.

Santarelli, Enzo. "Guerra d'Etiopia, imperialismo e terzo mondo." *Il movimento di liberazione in Italia* 97 (1969).

Sbacchi, Alberto. *Il colonialismo italiano in Etiopia, 1936–1940.* Milano: Mursia, 1980.

Segre, Claudio. *Gli italiani in Libia: Dall'eta giolittiana a Gheddafi.* Milano: Feltrinelli, 1978.

Sforza, Carlo. *Italia dal 1914 al 1944 quale io la vidi.* Roma: Mondadori, 1948.

Sori, Ettore. *L'emigrazione italiana dall'Unita alla seconda guerra mondiale.* Bologna: Il Mulino, 1978.

Zoli, Corrado. *Espansione coloniale italiana (1922–1937).* Roma: L'arnia, 1949.

Italian Anthropology and the Africans

The Early Colonial Period

Barbara Sòrgoni

Italian colonialism in the Horn of Africa officially began in 1890 when Eritrea—the first Italian colony—was founded, and lasted until 1941 when, during the Second World War, Italy lost its recently formed empire of so-called Italian East Africa. The colonial expansion had actually started two decades earlier with the acquisition of a small portion of the Red Sea coast, and by the date of the first colonial foundation Italians had conquered a territory of about 110,000 square kilometers, with a local population of about 250,000 inhabitants. The population was ethnically diverse and was roughly divided up into three different groups: the Coptic Christians of the highlands (agricultural Tigrinyans who represented the largest ethnic group of the territory); the "aristocratic" groups (various pastoral or semipastoral Muslim groups inhabiting mostly the northern part of the colonial area, and perceived as having a strongly elitist social structure); and finally the "democratic" ones (mostly Muslim groups of the southwest, agriculturalists perceived as exhibiting an egalitarian social structure and thus described as the most primitive tribes).[1]

This rough description of the peoples of the area was shared amongst the colonial officers and travelers to the colony: it was formulated out of brief encounters and first impressions and endured throughout the colonial period. It was not the product of classification work or any in-depth study by Italian anthropologists. Indeed, in those years, academic anthropology in Italy was still based on the biological anthropology of the nineteenth century, which has been described by Stocking (1988) as a paradigm based on "bones, bodies and behavior." Anthropology of that era was basically physical anthropology: bones and bodies from faraway places were assembled in Italy and then studied as a means of classifying human races and finding the appropriate place for each group in the evolutionary chain of human beings. Italy's two existing anthropological academic traditions,[2] despite some differences, shared a basic assumption: namely, that through the study of the body it was possible to infer facts about the mind, it then being possible to derive from the psychological features of the various races their level of civilization. In addition, the anthropologists did not travel themselves but rather studied skulls, skeletons, and sometimes handicrafts that were collected by travelers, explorers, or military or colonial administrators and were assembled in the newly founded museums. This particular division of labor, whereby anthropologically unskilled people collected and sent to Italy any type of relevant ethnological material and the scholars then classified and sorted it, continued until the late fascist period. The only intervention from anthropologists was the writing of guides aimed at teaching the travelers how to collect and catalogue the material, and instructing them as to what type of material was anthropologically relevant or needed.

Since anthropology was concerned mostly with bones and behavior and was an armchair discipline, Lanternari (1974) has argued that no social anthropology existed in Italy until the end of the Second World War and that, as a consequence, the study of the relationship between anthropology and colonialism is not relevant in the Italian case. Although the first assertion is true to some extent, the second is more problematic. For example, other scholars have identified a need to explore the roots of the discipline by looking at the colonial period in particular (Angioni 1973; Dore 1980; Solinas 1988a), and an article written by Grottanelli in 1977 was criticized precisely because it failed to place the history of Italian anthropology into its political and colonial context. More recently, other scholars have assessed the strong link between the development of Italian anthropology and the fascist regime (Puccini and Squillacciotti 1980; Leone 1985). Still lacking, however, was an exploration of how colonialism informed and was itself affected by the discipline in the early period.

In this chapter I will focus mostly on the years preceding the advent of the fascist regime, the period between 1890 and 1922. In the following section I will argue that, despite being an armchair discipline in which bones were the main focus, Italian professional anthropology was also much concerned with the classification of the new colonial subjects in Africa from the very beginning of the Italian colonial experience. I will show how a major representative of the discipline in the country, Giuseppe Sergi, spent almost his entire life describing and classifying the people of the Horn of Africa, propounding as he did so a theory of their origin with a strong political dimension that was later perceived as a threat to the fascist regime's new paradigm of Italian superiority to the Africans.

In the next section I will focus on what I call "accidental ethnographers." My goal here is to assess how a large number of travelers, military officers, and colonial civil servants became ethnographers out of curiosity or to serve the colonial administration, thus producing a relevant corpus of ethnographic material. This material has not been thoroughly studied, probably as a result of the discipline's concentration on the "big men" of anthropology and the process of erasing from the history of the discipline those who did not belong to the academic environment (Pels and Salemink 1994). The output of these accidental ethnographers, however, was both richly detailed and politically relevant since its explicit aim was to allow the "better" policing of the new subjects. I give some examples of how these studies were carried out, their ethnological content, and their political import.

ACADEMIC ANTHROPOLOGY AND THE CLASSIFICATIONS OF AFRICANS

In Italy "few among the credited anthropologists . . . were willing to offer their competence to study the newly conquered territories" (Solinas 1988b: 6). Despite the undoubted scarcity of colonial studies in anthropology, and the meager interest in the colonial adventure displayed in general by Italian society, the political relevance of the discipline for the colonial power was widely recognized. Those in power were clearly conscious of the need to have access to the best possible information on the newly colonized territories and peoples.

At the same time, academics of the early period were clearly aware of the political importance of the anthropological discipline, whose role it was to be a guide toward the "better" governance of the colonized. According to the psychiatrist and anthropologist Enrico Morselli (1898: 15), "had we better known the ethnology of the Abyssinians, we would not have faced so naively the disaster of Adwa."[3] In the opinion of another anthropologist of the time, Lamberto Loria (1912: 76–78), "the study of local laws and customs is necessary" in the first place "to organize colonial armies," and secondly "to administer justice." In his view, ethnographic knowledge was the main tool for a "firm" colonial policy, so much so that if in the past "our governors" had known the ethnography of their subjects, they would have surely shown "a stricter rule . . . less generosity."

In those years Raffaele Corso—who was then teaching at the Institute of Anthropology of the University of Rome and who was to be particularly active during the fascist regime—highlighted that in many countries anthropology developed hand in hand with the rise of colonialism. It was the "world expansion" characterizing the modern era that gave "ethnography its place among the other social sciences, and pointed to its specific role, that of attaining a systematic and deep knowledge of those people the civilized states intend to govern and lead along the path of civilization." In his view, the "true results of the discipline are the ones obtained in its political, social, and colonial application" (Corso 1916: 181–86).

Despite acknowledging the relevance of the discipline for the colonial process, professional anthropologists rarely became involved in the discussion of colonial issues. In the three main anthropological periodicals of the time—*Archivio per l'Antropologia e la Etnologia,* founded in 1871 by Paolo Mantegazza; *Archivio di Psichiatria,* founded in 1880 by Cesare Lombroso; and *Rivista di Antropologia,* founded by Giuseppe Sergi in 1893—it is possible to find dissertations about different human groups throughout the world without any specific focus on the Italian colonies, which are markedly underrepresented. Some anthropologists, however, were aware of this gap and called for a more accurate analysis of the new subjects.

Lanternari (1974) has also argued that it was the limited extent of the Italian colonial territories and the "ideological narrowness and cultural blindness" of the fascist regime that hindered the development of anthropology as a discipline for a long time. But what was the academic and institutional situation before fascism? Toward the end of the nineteenth century and at the beginning of the twentieth the boundaries between geography, ethnology, physical anthropology, and psychology were shifting and permeable, and the distinctions between what was considered biological and hereditary and what fell in the realm of culture were ill defined. The two main schools of anthropology in the country, despite some theoretical and methodological differences, shared the same belief: that it was the task of anthropology to reach a full understanding of human nature in its biological, psychological, and social aspects, thus treating the human being as a unique whole. From a methodological point of view, it was possible to infer social or psychological characteristics from biological or linguistic ones, and vice versa, since all characteristics were interconnected. In addition, the two schools also shared an interest in "a historical and often speculative approach, that was primarily concerned with reconstructing the past of mankind" (Stauder 1993: 410).[4] It is against this background and with these tools that some scholars like Aldobrandino Mochi, Vincenzo Giuffrida Ruggeri, Giuseppe Sergi, and Carlo Conti Rossini tried to place the newly colonized people of the Horn of Africa in a rigid classification of human races.

One of the first anthropologists to write about the populations of the Italian colonies of the Horn of Africa was Aldobrandino Mochi. His specific interest was in reconstructing their history and origins in order to classify them. Mochi proposed a reconstruction of the various waves of immigration to the area of different groups at different times—black peoples from "dark Africa," Semitic groups from Asia in a more recent period—that mixed with the preexisting indigenous population. He called the indigenous people Hamitic and described them as follows: "despite some mixing with negroes, [the indigenous population] was almost exclusively Hamitic, *therefore* being able to reach a high level of civilization." Indeed, they were the progenitors of the Egyptians. "Actual Ethiopians," Mochi concluded, "do not belong to a pure race but, taking a middle way between an exaggerated Semitism proposed by some authors, and a pure Hamitism expressed by others, we should consider them as a mixed race . . . nowadays become stable" (1900: 91).

Vincenzo Giuffrida Ruggeri, then professor of anthropology at the University of Naples, held a different view. Though agreeing that there had been waves of migration to the area from both central Africa and Asia, he believed that the indigenous populations were black. Both the lighter complexions seen in the area and the higher level of civilization—compared to the "real black" people—were due, in his opinion, to more recent Semitic migrations from Arabia (Giuffrida Ruggeri 1915). What Giuffrida Ruggeri was opposing was not only the Anglo-Saxon theory of a Caucasian (that is, Aryan) origin for both Egyptians and Hamites, but more importantly the theory proposed in those years by Giuseppe Sergi, which was becoming known internationally. As early as 1897 Sergi had proposed that Mediterraneans and Hamites had the same origin, the first being a subset of the second and both being indigenous to the Horn of Africa.

Sergi's theory, later known as the Hamitic hypothesis, interested scholars at least until the late 1960s. The problems mentioned above confronted by the Italian anthropologists—that of the origin of the Egyptians; the lighter skin color and higher civilization of Ethiopians; Semitism, Hamitism, and Aryanism—can be fully understood only in relation to the Hamitic hypothesis. It is therefore important to have a closer look at this theory and to try to understand the political stances behind it.

The Hamitic hypothesis acquired the meaning it retained until the 1960s only in the eighteenth century, when it could be summarized as follows: "Partout où l'on trouve des sociétés developpées, la régle est: 'cherchez les chamites'" (Saint-Clair 1959: 215). In contrast, from the Middle Ages to the eighteenth century, the term Hamites—derived from the Bible—identified the "black race," following the tradition according to which Noah had cursed his son Ham and decreed for his offspring a destiny of slavery. This interpretation of Genesis thus associated the black race with inferiority and slavery, justifying the latter with the former. It was only with Napoleon's invasion of Egypt and the subsequent archaeological excavations that this interpretation was shaken. The discovery of a civilization that appeared sophisticated enough to compete with that of the Greeks and Romans left a question mark over the origin of the Egyptians: how was it possible that an African group could create such an advanced civilization?

As Young (1995) has shown, the climate became particularly heated in the United States, where most scholars of the nineteenth century tended to ascribe the origin of the Egyptians to the Aryan race, therefore separating them from the Africans and preserving, for the latter, the fate of slavery.[5] This called for a reinterpretation of Genesis itself. In 1800 most scholars argued that Noah had cursed not Ham but rather his son Canaan, and thus it was the offspring of the latter that were the origin of the black race. Ham's own offspring showed instead a light complexion and were therefore to be considered the progenitors of the Egyptians. This new interpretation had two advantages. First, it did not question the link between blackness and slavery, but only found a new origin for the Africans in the cursed Canaan; and second, it could easily explain the perceived higher level of civilization of the Egyptians and all the Hamites inhabiting the Horn of Africa by attributing to them finer somatic traits and a biblical Semitic descent. In this way Egyptians and Hamites, and a lighter complexion and a higher degree of civilization, were each synonymous with one another. What remained to be traced was their actual racial origin.

Seen in this light, the search for the history of these people undertaken by the Italian anthropologists reveals its political dimension. Indeed, any solution to the problem that placed the origin of the Hamites (and thus of the Egyptians) beyond Africa had a precise political use. As Zachernuk (1994: 438) has pointed out, the analogical thought behind it contended that, just as the Africans had needed the Hamites in the past to progress, so they now needed Europeans for the same purpose. Colonialism in Africa thus found its justification. Matters were, however, more nuanced for the Italian colonists, precisely because the portion of Africa they were controlling was not the "inferior" black Africa but rather the place inhabited by the "superior" Hamites. In fact, not a few among the more educated colonizers were proud that Italy had conquered precisely that part of the continent with the most "noble" origin. Later, such a perception was to become a contentious problem with the advent of the fascist regime and the violent policy of racism and strict segregation it established. The belief in the higher civilization of the colonial subjects was then perceived as a threat to the new racist laws and the presence of the colonial administration. As a consequence, this belief had to be wiped out.

It is against this background that we can fully appreciate the originality of Sergi's theory. Being a polygenist, Sergi believed that human beings belonged to two different genera, *Homo asiaticus* and *Homo afer,* the latter comprising three different species. One of these, the *Homo eurafricus,* included, in his view, the Mediterranean, the African and the Nordic peoples. In 1901 Sergi published in English his final thoughts about the relationship between Egyptians, Africans, Mediterraneans, and Aryans, that is to say about all the politically relevant questions raised by anthropology and archaeology at the time. In the text, which he considered "conclusive" of his thought, he claimed that all the primitive populations of Europe originated in Africa; the three varieties—African, Mediterranean, and Aryan—belong to the same species; it is a mistake to believe that the Nordic populations are Aryan because they belong to the Eurafrican species; the Roman and Greek civilizations were not Aryan and the Aryans themselves were nothing but savages when they invaded Europe from Asia (Sergi 1901: 41).

It is clear that such a hypothesis could not easily be used by those in power to sustain the conquest and colonization of Africa. In addition, Sergi himself was perfectly aware of the fact that his criticism of the Aryan theory and his proposal to abandon it would meet strong opposition, since the Aryan theory laid the foundations for the superiority of the Europeans. Sergi's theory of the origin of the Europeans in the Horn of Africa found no followers, while minor aspects—such as the definition of the Hamites as brown in color—did. Indeed Seligman, in his study of the people of Sudan, adopted Sergi's classification using the "brown race" as synonymous with the Hamitic race, but he contended that, precisely because of the higher civilization displayed, they could only be Caucasian. "The incoming Hamites were pastoral 'Europeans'—arriving wave after wave—better armed as well as quicker witted than the dark agricultural Negroes" (Seligman 1930: 96).[6] What was new in Sergi's hypothesis, and difficult to accept, was the absence of the belief that any sign of civilization found in Africa originated elsewhere. Although Africans were widely believed to be unable to create any "progress," for Sergi it was precisely Africa that was the cradle of all the "superior" civilizations, a hypothesis that even in his time both Giuffrida Ruggeri and Seligman found difficult to accept and that, in the fascist period, would be banned.[7]

The last scholar to write about the Ethiopians in the same period was Carlo Conti Rossini. A historian with a juridical background, he taught the history and languages of Ethiopia at the University of Rome. Introducing his own work, Conti Rossini was aware of the fact that he was the only scholar of Ethiopians who actually visited the people he wrote about. From 1899 to 1903 he had served in the civil administration of the Eritrean colony, and his studies drew essentially—as he proudly announced—"from my own observation, from materials I have collected, from my personal research" (Conti Rossini 1913: 62). In contrast to the anthropologists described above, Conti Rossini used various sources in addition to the analysis of bones, including the language, the translation of written documents, and the oral history and traditions. He was interested in the actual history of the Eritreans, rather than in the biological classification of human groups, and in his text the analysis of bones inhabited a marginal position within a complex methodology that utilized linguistics, oral history, and ethnology. These different tools allowed him to conclude, in line with Sergi, that the

Hamites of Ethiopia were indigenous and not from elsewhere, and to discard the Aryan theory through the use of multiple sources.

The classifications proposed by these four anthropologists betrayed different aims. For Sergi and Giuffrida Ruggeri the biological classification was a valid outcome of the research in itself, for they were both mainly concerned with the problem of tracing the origin of the indigenous population of the Horn of Africa in order to place them in the evolutionary chain of human beings. The methodology they adopted was the bones and bodies approach, regarded as the most conclusive in distinguishing between different human races. In contrast, Conti Rossini treated this analysis as a marginal tool and showed innovative and eclectic skills. His main interest was not so much the study of the biology of human groups for a comparative purpose, but rather in the reconstruction of the individual history of a certain group as the first step in a wider research project. In 1916 Conti Rossini published a comprehensive and detailed description of the customary laws of various ethnic groups of Eritrea. In the light of this, his former historical research can be seen as a preliminary study that served as the background for his new ethnological research. Finally, Aldobrandino Mochi shared with Sergi and Giuffrida Ruggeri the same belief in the importance of bones, but he was more in line with the school of his teacher, Mantegazza, and believed in inferring from the bones and other physical traits the culture and the psychology of the people studied. In his approach, biology, culture, and psychology all reflected one another, meaning that one could be deduced from another.

His first concern, therefore, was to draw, from the bones, the somatic features of the "Ethiopian type": "Very tall; brown or chocolate skin color with some reddish shade; long head; high but narrow forehead; black and not long hair, not curly like that of the Arabs but also not frizzy like that of the Negroes; little beard; black eyes; long face; big protruding lips . . . beautiful chest of a conic shape, *just like the statues of ancient Egypt*" (Mochi 1900: 92, emphasis added).

Because of these somatic characteristics, it was possible—in Mochi's opinion—to classify the Ethiopians also in the "psycho-sociological" sense and place them among the "superior barbarians." In addition, a quick look at some handicrafts stored at the Florentine Museum allowed for their moral classification. Indeed, the use of amulets was proof that, despite some education obtained by the superior classes, and some sort of religious belief that "cannot but be superficial, the Ethiopian has in his psychology a primitive ground" that any subsequent progress was unable to wipe out (ibid.: 64–65). The procedure by which the somatic classification allowed for a moral or cultural one was not only characteristic of Italian anthropology, and it points to the existence of a climate in which culture and race were contiguous fields, often overlapping—a process Stocking described thus: "In the diffusely evolutionary milieu of later nineteenth-century European colonial expansion, the traditional developmental sequence of savagery, barbarism and civilisation . . . took on a systematic biological significance."[8]

The outlook was shared by both scholars and laypeople. A good example of how a work for the mass audience could be tailored to blur the distinction between biology and culture is an article from Father Mauro da Leonessa. The article drew substantially from that of Mochi quoted above, and it was the author's intention to produce a "simple and readily accessible" review at the popular level. After enumerating the somatic characteristics in Mochi's fashion, da Leonessa added brief sentences to qualify the psychological and moral characteristics of the Eritrean groups. These were presented as if they derived directly from the biological traits. The Nara were said to be "beautiful in the body" but "prone to vengeance and cowardly"; the Bilen, who were "very beautiful," were also "cowardly, wretched, and traitors"; the Habab were "quarrelsome, arrogant, ignorant, cowardly, and greedy"; and finally the Tigrinyans, despite being "the most civilized," showed "serious deficiencies" (da Leonessa 1927: 120–28).

In concluding this section, it is important to summarize the salient features emerging from this detour into Italian professional anthropology of the early colonial period. In the first place, it emerges how cultural and biological traits were interwoven and how the concept of race and the classificatory efforts retained social and moral judgments and evaluations. In the years when physical anthropology prevailed and social anthropology was still to be born, what was measured and placed in a hierarchical order were not only the physical traits but also the different cultures. Second, despite the fact that most academics did not travel in person to the colonies, this did not prevent them from writing extensively about issues that had a strong colonial and political relevance. In this sense, Italian academic anthropology was very well integrated in the international disciplinary and political debate of its time. Finally, as Young (1995) has pointed out, at the center of the political and scientific debate of the period's various colonial powers was the problem of interracial sexuality: desire and repression of desire. Giuffrida Ruggeri's solution to the problem of the Hamites' origin was in line with the idea of the separation of colonizers and colonized proposed by the colonial power. In the political discourse of the time, different racial origin was held to mean that "mixing" desire was not possible and gave rise to the prohibition of interracial sexual relationships. By concluding that Europeans and Africans were the same species, Sergi's theory pointed rather to an absence of spontaneous separation, to a desire for contact and the fertility of cross-race sexuality. This is why, in the late fascist period, regime anthropologists such as Guido Landra and Lidio Cipriani banned Sergi's theory, using different strategies to manipulate his analysis (Sòrgoni 2002).

ACCIDENTAL ETHNOGRAPHERS

In the previous section I mentioned that some anthropologists lamented the lack of in-depth information and ethnographic descriptions about the colonial subjects. And I stressed that, in their studies, scholars used ethnographic accounts or material objects collected by others. Travelers' accounts, explorers' diaries, and colonial officers' reports constituted a literary corpus that, despite not being academic in nature, provided the means to enrich speculative dissertations about the "Ethiopian type" with first-hand ethnographic data. This type of colonial literature consisted of a variety of texts exhibiting different styles and aims, but all the texts shared the feature of stemming from a direct encounter with the people they referred to. As Solinas (1988b: 5) has pointed out, the result was a type of anthropology we could define as "practical" rather than "applied," less structured and more informal but expressing a vivid picture of the Africans under the European gaze.

Different types of nationals used their colonial experience to present themselves as local experts. In his diary, for instance, Colonel Giovanni Pittaluga (1935: 150) noted that "our officers in Africa, attracted by the novelty and greatness of what they can observe, give a new direction to their spirit. . . . Zoology, botany, ethnology, local languages, law, biography, history, geography, archaeology." The diary also reveals that the colonel himself, as soon as he arrived in the area of Kassala, went directly to meet the local population to "visit their huts, examine the people, the handicrafts, to question their customs." The reason for this ethnographic interest is also stated: we learn that his task was to force the nomadic hunter groups into sedentary agriculture, something that turned out to be particularly painful since their chief had already been begging him to let them go "every day" for months. Others who were not directly involved in the political administration of the colony found in ethnography an entertaining diversion. This was the case for Rosalia Pianavia Vivaldi, who joined her husband in Eritrea in 1893 and lived there for three years. One of the very few Italian women to write about her colonial experience, she said, "in order to know and study directly the intimate life of this people, escorted by some officers and one interpreter, I often wandered around the village, the market, observing, comparing, visiting their dwellings" (Pianavia Vivaldi 1901: 45).

The fact that they were accidental ethnographers—or, as they were called at the time, the "science's labor force" (Società di Studi Geografici 1907: 15)—did not necessarily mean that their ethnographic work was superficial. Some of their texts were considered among the first examples of accurate ethnographic monographs, and in some cases they represented an early attempt at fieldwork.[9] In most cases we also know how these scripts circulated among academic anthropologists and the wider public: to go home, for a traveler, often meant to be invited to present one's first impressions or one's text at public conferences attended by both the general public and scholars. The latter would then use the data collected in the field "as a comparative device to support their speculations on human beings" (Puccini 1988b: 27). In Corso's opinion (1916: 180), ethnography was constantly fed by diaries, guides, and travel books, while for Loria (1912: 75), "it is our colonial officers who study the ethnography of the colony." Finally, there were also cases in which anthropological studies were explicitly commissioned from colonial officers by scholars in Italy. The military doctor Ercole Raimone was requested to measure the differing muscular resistance under effort of whites and blacks, in order both to better regulate labor division and to furnish data to the physiologist Angelo Mosso in Italy for his latest research, published in 1891 (Raimone 1906: 19).

Ethnographic information was so widespread that Conti Rossini (1916: 11) felt the need to warn the reader:

> There is basically no travel book that does not contain some chapters about the institutions and customs of the people visited, either when the traveler writes about his own impressions, sometimes carefully collected and evaluated . . . or when he is content with presenting as his own findings information taken from someone else, thus contributing to the spread, from book to book, of erroneous data.

One of the few scholars in Italy who has analyzed colonial travel literature with an eye on the representation of the indigenous people is Francesco Surdich. In his works, he usefully points out that local women were mostly represented by Italian travelers as loose in their sexual morals and therefore readily "available." At the same time, travel literature also stressed the many and tiring duties allocated to women according to the local division of labor and contrasted them with the laziness and unwillingness to work displayed by the men (Surdich 1979 and 1991). The author rightly stresses that the stereotype of local men being generally lazy also served to justify the exploitation of both land and low-cost manpower by the colonizers, just as the stereotype of local women having loose morals justified widespread concubinage and the prostitution imposed by the citizens on the subjects.[10]

Although this representation of the local population is to be found in much colonial literature, I think one should also recognize and stress the complexity and ambiguity inscribed in some of these texts, or, as Bhabha (1985: 154) has defined it, their hybrid nature. In other words, in this literature there is not a single representative mode for the subjects, but rather a plurality of often contrasting images juxtaposed in the same text. This emerges particularly clearly when one shifts from travel literature to the reports and diaries of colonial officers who lived for some years side by side with the group they wrote about. A fruitful example of the latter type of writing is that of Alberto Pollera, a colonial officer who served the colonial administration from his early twenties until his death, in 1939. His case can better show the process behind the ethnographic writing, and demonstrate how personal thoughts and current stereotypes met in the same text.

Having served in the colonial army from 1894 (when he was twenty-one years old), Alberto Pollera entered the colonial civil administration in 1905. Two years previously he had been appointed first resident of the Gash and Setit district, in the southwestern part of Eritrea. Pollera was to hold this post until 1909, when he was appointed resident in the Seraye region, a position he held for about 10 years. He subsequently held other appointments in both Eritrea and Ethiopia until his death in 1939. Living his whole adult life in the colony, he had relationships with two Eritrean women with whom he had six children; he legitimized all his children, provided for their education in Italy, and married his second partner in protest when the fascist racial laws prohibited interracial unions. In some ways, he was paradigmatic of a particular type of colonial civil servant, the so-called "old colonial officers": well-educated men[11] who spent their entire lives in the colony, learned the local language, formed families, and often wrote about their experiences. Indeed, he wrote extensively about all the different groups he lived with while serving in the administration. It is interesting to note, for example, that in 1922—when in Italy political and social awareness of the woman's condition had yet to spread—he wrote an ethnographic monograph on Ethiopian women.

His first book, *I Baria e i Cunama* (the colonial names for Nara and Baza), published in 1913, was based on his six-year experience in the Gash and Setit area and makes manifest the process through which he turned into an ethnographer or, as it was written after his death, "one of the most prominent Italian Africanists."[12] Indeed, it was thanks to a voluminous ethnographic paper he sent in 1902 to the first civil governor of the colony, Ferdinando Martini, based on a first survey of the recently conquered and still unknown Gash and Setit area, that he was soon thereafter appointed resident of the area, without having to undergo the long service in the colonial offices that was generally expected before appointment to any administrative position.

The 1902 "Notes" is a voluminous manuscript that is mostly about the Baza and marks a change in Pollera's ethnographic style and interest. Earlier in the same year he had submitted to the government a shorter version of his survey of the Baza in which he extensively described how the area could be dominated economically by the Italians—which commercial routes had to be followed or made secure, what changes had to be made for economic purposes. In contrast, the "Notes" showed little interest in issues directly connected to economic exploitation, concentrating rather on the description of social structures and the everyday lives of those visited.

Between the "Notes" of 1902 and the final book of 1913, Pollera prepared an ethnographic questionnaire that he compiled himself.[13] In preparing his own questionnaire he drew inspiration from the "Instructions for the Study of the Eritrean Colony" (Società di Studi Geografici 1907) prepared by those Italian anthropologists who took part in the first colonial conference held in Asmara in 1905, which Pollera also attended.

The monograph *I Baria e i Cunama* echoed the "Notes" in its structure. Both started with a description of the origin and history of the two groups, thus reflecting the typology set out by professional anthropologists analyzed in the section above. They both identified religious beliefs and practices as the core issue and included lengthy descriptions of the social structure of the groups, the role of the elderly, the rituals that marked the important phases of life, and even the content of songs and poems.

What marks the difference between the "Notes" and the book is Pollera's own prolonged field experience. Not only did many questions addressed in the Notes finally find an answer in the book, but more importantly Pollera tried in his monograph to explain what, in the "Notes," were presented merely as awkward or primitive customs. The best indication of Pollera's progress toward a better comprehension is given by his assessment of the local language. In the "Notes," the description of what he perceived to be a "very simple" linguistic structure led him to express a moral judgment: the language reflected a primitive and limited mind, a childish psychology that was unable to evolve. The book attempted a different explanation, shifting from biology to history. In 1913, after more than six years living amongst the Baza, Pollera retracted his previous judgments.

The story of the Baza had been a catalogue of tragic events: both Baza and Nara were repeatedly attacked by neighboring groups who destroyed their villages, killing most of a population that was unable to mount any defense (they were "peaceful peasants," Pollera explained) and enslaving women and children. This wretched story explained how their perceived "primitiveness," far from being a biological condition, was rather a historical outcome. Even the supposedly barbarian custom of men ritually killing members of enemy groups before getting married is now viewed in a different light. Although Pollera had previously called for the adoption of harsh penalties to punish this practice,[14] in the book he described it as a useful device, the "miracle of resistance of a small race" that would have otherwise disappeared long ago (Pollera 1913: 160). Any custom, he reminded the reader, "however barbarian it may seem, is always rooted in its historical context" (ibid.: 159). His goal in writing and publishing a monograph was to help the Italians replace "imagined dreams of a fantastic environment" with knowledge and understanding; because to deeply "comprehend allows also to partially justify barbarianism" (ibid.: 2, 78). The primitivism and inferiority of the colonized are never questioned in his texts; what changes is the way that Pollera looks at them, shifting from a negative judgment to a sort of proto-relativistic comprehension of otherness.

As Pels and Salemink (1994: 13) have argued, "proto-relativism" meant that the fully developed notion "existed in an embryonic, often implicit form." The authors contend that nonacademic colonial ethnography was relevant "for the development of both colonial society and academic anthropology." Mary Louise Pratt (1985) has also explored how colonial ethnography—or the "manner and customs genres"—preceding professional anthropology was continuous with the latter. Indeed, Pollera's writings, his proto-relativistic mode, and his ethnographic holism—concentrating on a specific institution with the assumption that it stands for the whole society—long precede professional anthropological fieldwork, which in Italy was extensively developed only after the Second World War. In the 1907 "Instructions for the Study of the Eritrean Colony"—the first Italian equivalent to the British 1874 *Notes and Queries*—the authors suggested that travelers and colonial officers collect only information that was agreed upon by many informants and that could be directly verified by the researcher himself. Puccini (1998: 150) has argued that this was the first time professional anthropologists recommended such a methodological device. Yet five years before, in the 1902 "Notes," Pollera revealed the fieldwork method he had adopted during his first survey: he had applied exactly the same method, and he had expressed it using the same words.

I mentioned above how colonial ethnographies are often complex texts in which common sense, current stereotypes, and research findings merge. In 1922 Pollera published a monograph on "the Ethiopian woman." The text is extremely interesting if we read it set against the author's private life. Writing about the colonial context, Pollera argued that marriage with a local woman "rightly repels anyone [i.e., the white man] given the big gap between the two civilizations" (Pollera 1922: 82). Yet not only did he marry his second Eritrean partner, with whom he had lived almost his entire colonial life, just before he died, but we also know from his will that he would have married her much earlier, "if only it were not so difficult." The difficulty he referred to was the royal decree issued in 1909 that forced a colonial officer into retirement if he wished to marry a colonial subject.[15] When his book was published, Pollera had six children with his Eritrean partner, and retirement would have made it extremely difficult to provide them the standard of living he wished for them. In publishing a text for the wider public, Pollera chose to adhere to the racial policy adopted by the colonial power and to agree with the political and commonsense argument of white prestige and racial separation. But his private behavior and his unpublished manuscripts reveal a different and more complex personality. And *I Baria e i Cunama,* like other monographs he wrote, juxtaposes stereotypical assumptions with confutation of the widely shared belief that a big gap existed between the two cultures.

Reading the ethnographic writings of a colonial officer is useful for several reasons. On the one hand, it reminds us that outside the academy a whole body of literature exists that contains relevant ethnographic information. This literature is valuable because in many cases it is the only source of information we have about Eritrean groups at the time of the Italian conquest and during the colonial regime. Or, more correctly, it is one of the few sources exhibiting how the Italians perceived the Africans at the outset of the colonial period. Despite the fact that the importance of this literature is largely acknowledged, it has been little studied. These writings are also extremely interesting because they help reconstruct the *"préterrain"* (Pels and Salemink 1994: 14) from which social anthropology was to grow, a theme that has been almost completely neglected in the Italian disciplinary debate. Furthermore, this type of literature reminds us how closely colonial power and the first, improvised ethnographic material were related and that, no matter what induced an officer to write about the people he was in contact with (whether the need to produce a formal government report or the desire to replace exotic dreams with knowledge), the colonial power knew how to use the information to its own advantage. More precisely, this literature highlights the complex relationship between administrative and ethnographic texts, and how administrative officers / ethnographers contributed to the creation of ethnic groups in the colonial context (Amselle 1990). In addition, the early ethnographic literature points to the existence of individuals—later known as "old colonial officers"—who were driven by (or developed) a kind of curiosity and some degree of respect for "difference." The picture presented in their ethnographic scripts could be quite detailed, and the nature of the texts themselves quite complex.

Finally, it is possible to highlight and start to reconstruct the processes through which professional anthropology both informed and was informed by this accidental ethnography. Just as anthropologists at home used materials and information collected by travelers or officers in faraway places, so the latter knew and used the academic anthropological trends, tools, and interpretations to organize their texts and pose questions around their object of fieldwork. Both anthropologists and travelers and officers shared an interest in the classification of races and the origin of the human groups;

both merged—although to different extents—biology with social traits; both never doubted the existence of an evolutionary scale that placed primitives, savages, and civilized people at different levels.

NOTES

This paper draws from a section of my Ph.D. research (Sòrgoni 1998), and from my recent research based on the private archive of a colonial officer, Alberto Pollera, presently held by his heirs (Sòrgoni 2001). It has been translated and published by permission of Liguori Editore.

1. The "aristocratic" groups were the Habab, Marya, Mensa, Bilen, and Afar, the "democratic" ones Baza, Nara, and Saho. For the demographic figures for colonial Eritrea see Labanca and Barrera, this volume.

2. The two anthropological academic traditions were expressed by the Florentine school, initiated by Paolo Mantegazza, who in 1869 held the first university professorship in anthropology; and by the Roman school, instituted in 1893 by Giuseppe Sergi, a former student of Mantegazza. For a discussion of the differences between the two schools see Taylor 1987 and 1988.

3. The 1896 battle of Adwa between Italians and Abyssinians was the biggest defeat a European army suffered in the whole colonial history of Africa. About four thousand Italian and two thousand colonial soldiers died or were captured.

4. This quotation, which refers to early British anthropology, well describes a trend that lasted in Italian anthropology for a much longer period.

5. For the whitening process of the Egyptians see also Bernal 1987.

6. As Sanders has noted (1969: 521), this sentence was identical in the 1966 edition.

7. Sergi was not totally out of step with his time. Indeed, in his classification he never questioned the supposed difference between the "superior" Hamites and the "inferior" southern Africans.

8. Stocking further argues that, even in 1900, both scholars and lay observers still looked at "the differences between savages and civilized men, or between contemporary races, in explicitly or implicitly Lamarkian terms of the inheritance of acquired characteristics—thereby systematically blurring the distinction between cultural behavior and racial heredity, and providing an implicit theoretical justification for the prevailing loose usage of the term 'race'" (Stocking 1988: 8).

9. See, for instance, Perini 1905 and Pollera 1913.

10. For an analysis of Italian travel literature in the early colonial period see also Lombardi-Diop, this volume.

11. Pollera himself was of upper-class origin and could speak and read English and French. His private library shows he was informed about many issues discussed internationally within the colonial debate.

12. *La Nazione,* Aug. 8, 1939: 4.

13. The first survey ("Considerazioni generali sull'importanza della regione dei Cunama," 1902), the "Notes" ("Appunti," 1902), and the questionnaire are contained in Pollera's private collection, Ostia.

14. A. Pollera, Residenza del Gasc e Setit, "Oggetto: Taglie e multe consuetudinarie," June 21, 1903, contained in his private collection, Ostia.

15. See A. Pollera, "Testamento," in his private collection, Ostia; and Regio Decreto, Sept. 19, 1909, n. 839.

WORKS CITED

Amselle, J. L. 1990. *Logiques métisses: Anthropologie de l'identité en Afrique et ailleurs.* Paris: Éditions Payot.

Angioni, G. 1973. "Primitivismo, eurocentrismo, antropologia." In *Tre saggi sull'antropologia dell'età coloniale,* ed. G. Angioni, 9–50. Palermo: Flaccovio.

Bernal, M. 1987. *Black Athena: The Afroasiatic Roots of Classical Civilization.* London: Free Association Books.

Bhabha, H. K. 1985. "Signs Taken for Wonders: Questions of Ambivalence and Authority under a Tree Outside Delhi, May 1817." *Critical Inquiry* 12.1: 144–65.

Conti Rossini, C. 1913. "Schizzo etnico e storico delle popolazioni eritree." In *L'Eritrea economica,* 61–90. Novara-Roma: Biblioteca Geografica dell'Istituto Geografico de Agostini.

———. 1916. *Principi di diritto consuetudinario dell'Eritrea.* Roma: Tipografia dell'Unione Editrice.

Corso, R. 1916. "L'etnografia scienza politica e coloniale." *Rivista Coloniale* 3–4: 178–89.

Da Leonessa, (Padre) M. 1927. "Gruppi etnici della colonia Eritrea." *L'Antischiavismo* 40, no. 5: 120–28.

Dore, G. 1980. "Antropologia e colonialismo italiano: Rassegna di studi di questo dopoguerra." *La Ricerca Folklorica* 1: 129–32.

Giuffrida Ruggeri, V. 1915. "Nuovi studi sull'antropologia dell'Africa orientale." *Archivio per l'Antropologia e l'Etnologia* 45: 123–79.

Grottanelli, V. 1977. "Ethnology and/or cultural anthropology in Italy." *Current Anthropology* 18.4: 493–614.

Lanternari, V. 1974. "Le nuove scienze umane in Italia: Genesi e sviluppi." In *Antropologia e imperialismo e altri saggi,* ed. V. Lanternari, 321–48. Torino: Einaudi.

Leone, A. R. 1985. "La Chiesa, i cattolici e le scienze dell'uomo: 1860–1960." In *L'antropologia italiana, un secolo di storia,* ed. P. Clemente et al., 51–96. Roma-Bari: Laterza, 1985.

Loria, L. 1912. "L'etnografia strumento di politica interna e coloniale." *Lares* 1: 73–79.

Mochi, A. 1900. "Gli oggetti etnografici delle popolazioni etiopiche." *Archivio per l'Antropologia e l'Etnologia* 30: 87–173.

Morselli, E. 1898. "Prefazione." In G. Mondaini, *La questione dei Negri nella storia e nella società Nord-Americana,* ix–xxvi. Torino: F.lli Bocca.

Pels, P., and O. Salemink. 1994. "Introduction: Five Theses on Ethnography as Colonial Practice." *History and Anthropology* 8: 1–34.

Perini, R. 1905. *Di qua dal Marèb (Marèb-Mellàsc').* Firenze: Tipografia Cooperativa.

Pianavia Vivaldi, R. 1901. *Tre anni in Eritrea.* Milano: L. F. Cogliati.

Pittaluga, R. 1935. *Rievocazioni Africane: Con Diario inedito della Campagna Eritrea del Generale Giovanni Pittaluga.* Brescia: G. Vannini.

Pollera, A. 1913. *I Baria e i Cunama.* Roma: Reale Società Geografica.

————. 1922. *La donna in Etiopia.* Roma: Monografie e Rapporti Coloniali, Ministero delle Colonie.

Pratt, M. L. 1985. "Scratches on the Face of the Country, or: What Mr. Burrow Saw in the Land of the Bushmen." *Critical Inquiry* 12: 119–43.

Puccini, S. 1988. "Elio Modigliani: Esplorare, osservare, raccogliere nell'esperienza di un etnografo dell'Ottocento." *La Ricerca Folklorica* 18: 25–40.

————. 1998. *Il corpo, la mente e le passioni.* Roma: CISU.

Puccini, S., and M. Squillacciotti. 1980. "Per una prima ricostruzione critico-bibliografica degli studi demo-etno-antropologici italiani nel periodo tra le due guerre." In *Studi antropologici italiani e rapporti di classe,* 67–93. Milano: Problemi del Socialismo.

Raimone, E. 1906. *Etnofisiologia eritrea.* Napoli: G. Civelli.

Saint-Clair, D. 1959. "Détruire le mythe chamitique, devoir des hommes cultivés." In *Deuxième Congrès des Ecrivains et Artistes Noirs,* 215–30. Rome, Mar. 26–Apr. 1, 1959. Vol. 1, *Presence Africaine,* 1959.

Sanders, E. R. 1969. "The Hamitic Hypothesis: Its Origin and Functions in Time Perspective." *Journal of African History,* 10.4: 521–32.

Seligman, C. G. 1930. *Races of Africa.* London: Oxford University Press.

Sergi, G. 1897. *Africa: Antropologia della stirpe camitica.* Torino: F.lli Bocca.

————. 1901. *The Mediterranean Race: A Study of the Origin of the European People.* London: Walter Scott.

Società di Studi Geografici e Coloniali, Società di Antropologia, Etnologia e Psicologia Comparata. 1907. *Istruzioni per lo studio della colonia Eritrea.* Firenze: Tipografia Galileiana.

Solinas, P. G. 1988a. "Coscienza coloniale e affari indigeni: L'Africa italiana da Ferdinando Martini a Giacomo de Martino." *La Ricerca Folklorica* 18: 41–47.

————. 1988b. "Introduzione." *La Ricerca Folklorica* 18: 5–7.

Sòrgoni, B. 1998. *Parole e Corpi: Antropologia, discorso giuridico e politiche sessuali interrazziali nella colonia Eritrea (1890–1941).* Napoli: Liguori.

————. 2001. *Etnografia e colonialismo. L'Eritrea e l'Etiopia di Alberto Pollera 1873–1939.* Torino: Einaudi.

————. 2002. "Racist Discourses and Practices in the Italian Empire under Fascism." In *The Politics of Recognizing Difference: Multiculturalism Italian-Style,* ed. R. Grillo and J. Pratt, 41–57. Aldershot, Eng.: Ashgate.

Stauder, J. 1993. "The 'relevance' of anthropology to colonialism and imperialism." *'Racial' Economy of Science: Toward a Democratic Future,* ed. S. Harding, 408–27. Bloomington: Indiana University Press.

Stocking, G. W. 1988. "Bones, bodies, behavior." In *Bones, Bodies, Behavior: Essays on Biological Anthropology,* ed. G. W. Stocking, 3–17. Madison: University of Wisconsin Press.

Surdich, F. 1979. "La donna nell'Africa orientale nelle relazioni degli esploratori italiani 1870–1915." *Miscellanea di storia delle esplorazioni* 4: 191–220.

————. 1991. "L'impatto dell'esplorazione dell'Africa sull'Italia di fine Ottocento." *Materiali di lavoro* 2–3: 5–33.

Taylor, P. M. 1987. "Paolo Mantegazza (1831–1910): Reassessing the Florentine School of Anthropology in Pre-Fascist Italy (up to 1925)." *Antropologia Contemporanea* 10.1: 1–16.

————. 1988. "Anthropology and the 'Racial Doctrine' in Italy before 1940." *Antropologia Contemporanea* 11.1: 45–58.

Young, R. 1995. *Colonial Desire: Hybridity in Theory, Culture and Race.* London and New York: Routledge.

Zachernuk, P. S. 1994. "Of Origins and Colonial Order: Southern Nigerian Historians and the 'Hamitic Hypothesis.'" *Journal of African History* 35: 427–55.

The Construction of Racial Hierarchies in Colonial Eritrea

The Liberal and Early Fascist Period (1897–1934)

Giulia Barrera

Maria is an Italo-Eritrean, the child of an Italian father and an Eritrean mother, born in Asmara in 1917.[1] I was asking her about the relations among Italians, Eritreans, and Italo-Eritreans when she replied, "Only during fascism was there a vicious [*feroce*] racism. The Italian is not racist otherwise. This division was a heritage of fascism. Before 1935 Italians had a human and a friendly attitude. To be sure, they did not bring our mothers to restaurants or to the cinema. The division was there, but it was *natural,* it was not imposed" (emphasis mine).[2]

The way Maria characterizes the relations between colonizers and colonized before 1935 is remarkable in many respects. On the one hand, she suggests that Italians had a friendly attitude toward the colonized, but on the other hand she reveals that colonial society was deeply divided along racial lines. Long before the racial laws of the late 1930s, Maria reveals, "human" Italians found it "natural" to discriminate against the Eritreans. This paper intends to unravel this apparent contradiction.

One should notice that when Maria says "during fascism" she refers to the period after 1935. This periodization is commonly shared by many Eritreans and Italo-Eritreans. They often use the expression "when fascism came" to refer to the upheaval caused by the invasion of Ethiopia, and in particular to the racial policy after 1935.[3] The Fascist Party had already been a strong presence in the colony since the 1920s, and governors of indisputable fascist credentials had ruled the colony.[4] But before 1935, the new regime apparently had relatively little impact on the relations between the colonizers and colonized. In this paper I am using Maria's periodization, and I am discussing only the period before the invasion of Ethiopia (1935). I also leave out of the picture the conquest years (1885–96) because they were deeply different from the following period.[5]

The nature of the relations between Italians and their colonial subjects remains a disputed yet underresearched issue. Studies on this issue mostly concentrate on state policies and on colonial discourse at the time of Italy's first African war and of the invasion of Ethiopia.[6] In particular, the focus on fascist racial policy has had the unintended consequence of leaving an aura of ambiguity around the nature of the relations between ordinary Italians and Africans.[7] The prevailing perception remains that the government— and in particular fascist authorities—were solely responsible for any discrimination or violence against the Africans that might have occurred under Italian colonialism. Ordinary Italians, by contrast, are supposed to have been immune to racist attitudes and inclined to have friendly relations with the colonized.[8]

My understanding of the interaction between the colonial state, Italian settlers, and colonial subjects is very different. As in any other colony, in Eritrea the relations between the colonizers and the colonized were by no means idyllic. Everyday life was dotted with acts of abuse by the colonizers against the colonized, and racial discrimination was one of the founding pillars of the colonial edifice.

It is true, however, that in the period under examination Eritrea experienced a lesser degree of racial segregation compared to the years after 1935, and to a certain extent also compared to other African colonies. Physical and social proximity between colonizers and colonized—interracial sexual relations included—calls for very cautious examination. As Ann Stoler has pointed out, "miscegenation signaled neither the presence nor absence of racial discrimination."[9] Stoler's point applies as well to other types of interracial relations, which cannot per se be taken as evidence of lack of racial discrimination. In this chapter I will not explore the nature of interracial sexual relations in Eritrea (I do so elsewhere),[10] but I will provide different examples that point out how the intermingling of the colonizers with the colonized could coexist with racial arrogance and abuse, and with an overall structure of racial discrimination.

Still, the unusual level of intermixing, in contrast both to post-1935 Eritrea and to other colonies, is worth attention, because it signals that the relations between colonizers and colonized in Eritrea assumed particular characteristics in the period from 1897 to 1934. The construction and preservation of colonial hierarchies could take different forms in different contexts. Strict racial segregation was but one of the tools that colonizers could use.

Discussions of Italian "national character" are of little help in understanding why pre-1935 colonial Eritrea allowed such a degree of intermixing. If national character were the key factor that shaped settlers' attitudes, then what would explain why the forty-five thousand Italians who settled in Algeria during the nineteenth century did not behave much differently from other European settlers?[11] We should rather look at which historical factors produced such an outcome.[12]

The first part of this chapter intends to account for what Maria describes as the "friendly attitude" of Italians by looking at the political economy of Italian colonial domination, at the demographic profile of the Italian community, and at how the experience of Adwa influenced Italian settlers' attitudes toward the Eritreans. The second part discusses the strategies followed by the colonial state in order to enforce racial hierarchies (that is, what Maria describes as the "natural" division between Italians and Eritreans).

THANKS TO ADWA, ERITREA WAS THE SAFEST COLONY

The first steps of Italian colonialism in Eritrea were in many ways similar to those of other colonial powers. A private company opened the way, and then the state stepped in. The colonizers used local chiefs against one another. And they benefited from the ecological catastrophes of the late nineteenth century. Also similar to the usual pattern were the killings, the burning of African villages, the fear of African rebellion, and the brutal repression.[13]

The first years of Italian rule in Eritrea were also characterized by an aggressive land expropriation policy. In the early 1890s, the colonial government expropriated more than 50 percent of the cultivated land in the Eritrean highlands with the intention of promoting the settlement of landless Italian peasants. Land confiscation met Eritrean resistance. In 1894, local chief Bahta Hagos led an anticolonial rebellion. The Italians crushed the revolt and continued to advance inland into Ethiopian territory, but in 1896 they were stopped at Adwa by the Ethiopian army led by Emperor Menelik II, who inflicted on the Italians the most devastating defeat suffered by a European power on African soil. Italy lost four thousand Italian and two thousand colonial soldiers. Adwa was a unique event in African colonial history and established unique conditions for the development of the Italian colony.

Adwa forced the Italians to drastically redefine their ambitions in the Horn of Africa. The defeat had a dramatic impact on Italian public opinion. Both in the streets and in the Parliament, colonial opponents demanded a complete end to colonial adventures (Rainero 1971). The government, however, opted for keeping the colony, but at the lowest possible cost, both politically and economically. It appointed a civilian, Ferdinando Martini (1897–1907), as governor of Eritrea and gave him a clear mandate: keep the colony and limit colonial expenses. The Italian government could no longer bear the financial cost of keeping a large contingent of Italian troops in Africa, and it could not bear the political cost of another military defeat.

For the Italians, thus, it became crucial to avoid an Eritrean rebellion and a war against Ethiopia. The two dangers were intimately connected, since an Eritrean revolt was likely to prompt an Ethiopian attack.

The prevention of Eritrean rebellions required, first and foremost, repudiation of large-scale land-alienation programs. As historian Tekeste Negash has pointed out, "The main lesson learnt from the Bahta uprising was that any colonial policy of land alienation would arouse such political unrest that would bring forth support from Ethiopia" (Tekeste 1987: 126). After Adwa, therefore, the government silently dropped the expropriation decrees issued in the early 1890s and returned the land to Eritrean villagers.[14] Martini and his successors carried out new land alienation, but on a limited scale. The region where conflicts over land were likely to arise (and where, in fact, Bahta Hagos's rebellion took place) was the plateau, which was densely populated by local agriculturists and enjoyed a climate palatable to Italian settlers. In the highlands, the concessions to Italians amounted to about 2 percent of the cultivated land.[15] More extended areas were declared state land *(terre demaniali)*, especially in the lowlands.[16] More than 90 percent of land alienated to Italians in the highlands was concentrated in Hamasien (the region of Asmara), and especially in the fertile area of the eastern escarpment.[17] This limited policy of alienation caused much distress to Eritrean peasants in some specific areas, and we have news of some instances of Eritrean resistance.[18] But, on the whole, land alienation was limited, and equally limited were confrontations between the colonizers and the colonized over land.

The colonial government did not pursue a large-scale land alienation policy because it progressively came to realize that "European agriculture in the highlands, besides being politically hazardous, was also not profitable."[19] Therefore, after 1910 the colonial government virtually stopped land alienation in the highlands.[20] Italians rather pinned their hopes for Eritrean economic development on capitalist agriculture in the lowlands; on the exploitation of Eritrean natural resources (ivory palm, gum arabic, livestock, etc.); and on the development of Eritrean transit trade (Tekeste 1987: 39).

But most of all, the Italian government found it profitable to exploit Eritrea as a source of colonial soldiers (Tekeste 1987). By using Eritreans, and not Italians, as cannon fodder, the Italian government was able to continue pursuing an expansionist colonial policy in Somalia and Libya without running the risk of the political backlash that the death of Italian soldiers could have caused (Scardigli 1996: 51). Especially from the conquest of Libya (1911–12) on, Eritrea constantly provided a large contingent of soldiers (known as *ascari*) to the Italian colonial army.[21] Other colonial powers also used African soldiers for their African conquests. The Eritrean case, however, stands out because the colonial army absorbed a particularly high

percentage of the local labor force. The *ascari,* in fact, largely outnumbered Eritreans who worked for the Italians as agricultural or industrial
wageworkers.[22]

The limit on land alienation and the use of Eritreans as colonial soldiers
had important consequences for the relations between Italians and Eritreans. In the first place, both contributed to reducing pressure on land. And
land was the most important source of conflict between Europeans and
Africans in colonial Africa. Furthermore, the income of the *ascari,* as well
as of seasonal wageworkers, helped shield peasants from starvation when
crop failures or locust invasions occurred. Prolonged peace and the development of veterinary services allowed for the considerable growth of livestock. Overall, this was a period of food security for Eritrean peasants.[23] All
these factors contributed to the easing of tensions between colonizers and
colonized.

Another obvious consequence of the limit on land alienation was that
only a small percentage of Italian settlers lived off the land. In 1913, sixty-
two Italian concessionaires shared a total of 6,500 hectares in the highlands
(Tekeste 1986: 45). At the time, the Italian community numbered 2,410. In
other words, the community as a whole was small, and concessionaires were
only a minor fraction of it.[24] The size of the Italian community slowly
increased over time, reaching 4,188 in 1931 (Ciampi 1995). Concessions,
however, did not correspondingly increase, also because there was little interested in investing Italian capital in Eritrea.[25] The image of white settlers in
Africa is often associated with plantation owners. Such an image, however,
would be misleading in the Eritrean case. Among the Italians in Eritrea there
were many more workmen, craftsmen, and masons than landowners.[26]

If one looks at sheer numbers, the Italian community in Eritrea until
1935 can be likened to those of West African colonies, which had equally
small numbers of settlers. But if one looks at the social composition, namely
at the large percentage of poor whites, then one should rather liken the
Italian community in Eritrea to the white communities of settler colonies of
North or Southern Africa. The Italian community's peculiar features influenced the type of interaction that Italians had with Eritreans.

Racial and class hierarchies did not always overlap. This was a source of
concern for the colonial government, and a source of tension for Italians
who competed with Africans for similar jobs. However, the Italian community was too small to allow for the existence of businesses that served whites
only. Mixing with Eritreans was an economic necessity for Italian working-
class settlers, craftsmen, and small traders, and even for some members of
the upper class. For example, Italian lawyers, who were prominent among
the colonial elite, worked frequently for Eritreans, at least during Martini's
times.

As a consequence, Eritrea saw a degree of intermingling between colonizers and colonized during the era prior to racial laws that surprised West-ern visitors. In September of 1935, a reporter for *National Geographic* tour-ing Eritrea noticed, to his amazement, how an Italian shopkeeper could serve African customers: "I was astonished. In no other *black* colony, in my experience, have I seen white shopkeepers, unembarrassed, selling wares for a few cents to native customers. Such a thing would be unthinkable in India, for instance" (Lechenperg 1935: 287).[27] I should emphasize that workers, craftsmen, and small traders, who comprised more than 50 per-cent of the Italian civilian population, gave their special imprint to the settler community. However, the Italian community also included a large contingent of military personnel, as well as a significant number of public employees and a few entrepreneurs. There was not just one "Italian behav-ior" in the colony. The trend that I am describing coexisted with others.

In addition to the colony's political economy, the Italian community's de-mographic profile also influenced Italians' interaction with Eritreans. In 1905, almost 80 percent of the European men older than sixteen were un-married, and quite a few of the married ones did not have their wife with them. White women were few and mostly married. There were more than 1,300 single European men, while single European women numbered only 73 (De Angelis 1921).[28] This unbalanced ratio impelled a number of Ital-ian men to consort with Eritrean women. Since the very beginning of Ital-ian rule in Eritrea, colonial authorities had set up state-controlled brothels. Long-term residents, however, tended to leave prostitutes to soldiers and preferred more stable sexual partners for themselves. Concubinage with lo-cal women was widely practiced by Italians of all walks of life, especially dur-ing the first decades of Italian colonization. The colonial government did not approve of interracial concubinage, but it did not have the political strength to promote the migration to the colony of Italian women. As a re-sult, it could do little to prevent Italian men from taking African concu-bines. By and large, the government could only wait until the ratio of Ital-ian women to men gradually became more balanced.[29]

Finally, one should consider a subtler feature of the Italian community that influenced its interaction with the colonized. Compared to other set-tler communities (I am thinking, for instance, of the French in Algeria, or the British in Eastern and Southern Africa, or the Germans in Southwest Africa) Italians seem to have had significantly less fear of the Africans. The frequent outbreaks of the so-called "black peril" (a paroxysm of anxiety about black men raping white women) that haunted white settlers in South-ern and Eastern Africa did not have an equivalent in Eritrea. I should em-phasize that I am talking about perceptions, not about the actual threat that Africans posed. As much scholarship has pointed out, the "black peril" hys-teria was not caused by actual increases in rapes (Van Onselen 1982: 45–53; Kennedy 1987: 128–47). Neither was German settlers' fear that their Hereros servants would poison them caused by actual incidences of poisoning (O'Donnell 1999). Such paroxysms of fear had little to do with what Africans actually did, and much to do with the white communities' internal dynamics.

Among Italian settlers, fear of the Eritreans occasionally surfaced.[30] But it did not reach the level of collective hysteria, not even when, in some rare occurrences, Eritrean men harassed Italian women.[31] Paradoxically, one of the elements that contributed to Italian feelings of greater self-confidence about their position in the colony seems to have been the historic defeat that Italians suffered at Adwa.

The births of many colonies were tainted by bloodshed. This was especially true for settler colonies, where vast land expropriation took place. In colonies like Algeria, Kenya, and Rhodesia the colonizers successfully crushed African resistance by ruthless repression. The experience of such violent confrontations with Africans remained deeply entrenched in the settlers' memory and amounted to founding events for the settler communities. It was a memory that settlers passed on to newcomers and to new generations, and that shaped settlers' culture. As Dane Kennedy has pointed out, in such colonies, "white settlers saw themselves as aliens in a darkly hostile land." And they reacted by erecting an invisible wall to isolate themselves from the colonized (Kennedy 1987: 128).[32]

Eritrea's birth as a colony was also baptized in blood. But the founding event that remained deeply entrenched in Italian memory, unlike that of other colonies, was a war with an external enemy, not an internal rebellion. It was a war in which only the military participated, and which did not cause victims among Italian civilians. Italian settlers did not fight at Adwa, nor did they directly participate in the repression of the Africans, as British settlers did. The memory of Adwa suggested that danger was more likely to come from outside than from inside the colony. And an external enemy, although dangerous, is less unsettling than an internal one.

As already mentioned, the colonial government considered an Eritrean rebellion or an Ethiopian attack a serious danger for the colony, and therefore operated in order to prevent them. When occasionally Eritrean peasants' malcontent surfaced, it caused serious concerns in governmental circles. Italian governmental concerns, however, were different from the fear that settlers experienced elsewhere; they did not affect settlers' collective attitudes. During the period that I am considering, in fact, it seems that Italians perceived Eritrea as a safe place.[33]

The relatively low level of conflicts over land, which I have already discussed, was a major factor that encouraged Italians to feel safe. The large Eritrean participation in the colonial army also contributed to Italian perception of Eritrea as a safe place. Italians came to have complete trust in their Eritrean soldiers. The "faithful *ascaro*" became a topos in Italian colonial literature. Also colonial authorities did not spare praise for them. For example, in 1926 Federzoni, the minister of colonies, stated that the Eritrean battalions were "the most solid, effective, and safe pillar of our military might in all our African colonies."[34] Italians, then, perceived many Eritreans not as a threat but as a potential bulwark against external enemies.

Confidence increased Italian willingness to intermix with the Africans. Intermingling between colonizers and colonized, however, did not necessarily imply a respectful or friendly relationship. Meaningful in this regard is the story of Oscar Agresti, by any standard a rogue. He went to Eritrea in 1889, at the age of twenty-seven; he initially worked as a gardener and then as a mason. He lived for several years with a local woman, by whom he had six children. Before the government decided to expel him from the colony in 1912, Agresti had accumulated a record of wrongdoing, mostly against Eritreans. Eritrean notables had entrusted him with the construction of different buildings, but he did not complete the jobs "and seriously damaged all those who had made use of his work."[35] He had contracted debts with a number of Eritreans; had abandoned his partner and their children in misery; had swindled an Italian company and several Eritreans, and so on. Some Eritreans had filed complaints against him, but to no avail. The Carabinieri described him as "a violent man, ready to fight, who for frivolous reasons resorted to violence against the natives. And to make his lifestyle even more unbecoming, he behaved in all—from food to clothing—like a native of the lowest kind."

It is interesting to note how the Carabinieri stigmatized Agresti's behavior both because he bullied Eritreans and because he had adopted their lifestyle. In the Carabinieri's eyes, by both behaviors he had proven himself "unworthy of the good name of Italy."[36] Oscar was by no means the typical Italian settler. His case, however, is significant because it effectively illustrates how intermingling with the colonized and abusing them could go hand in hand.

We do not know what Oscar thought of the Eritreans he abused. Whether he considered Eritreans equal to any other human being, biologically inferior, or backward but susceptible to civilization is beside the point. More relevant to our discussion is that—in all likelihood—one of the reasons he found Eritrea attractive was that he thought that in the colony he could get away with his wrongdoing more easily than in Italy. And it is equally likely that, once in Eritrea, he treasured and exploited a political system that granted him, as an Italian, a privileged position with respect to the Eritreans. This attitude was by no means unusual among white settlers. Debate over Italian colonial racism has tended to focus on the definition of "racism" and failed to answer what—in my opinion—is a more compelling question: in which ways and by which means, before the racial legislation of the late 1930s, did Italian colonizers build and maintain colonial hierarchies, that is, a social order that granted Italians supremacy over the Africans. The following section provides a first answer to this question.

RACIAL POLICIES

In 1897, when the colonial government was establishing the foundations for the new course of Italian rule in Eritrea, in a report a colonial judge effectively summarized the principles that, in his opinion, had to inform colonial legislation and governmental action in Eritrea.

a) On every occasion, strengthen and underline European superiority over the natives;
b) Protect the natives against the very easy and very frequent vexations and abuses committed by the unruly Europeans who live in the colonies;
c) Secure governmental prestige and authority over both the natives and the Europeans with an iron fist, more firmly than is necessary in Europe.[37]

If one looks at Italian colonial policy in the period between Adwa and the invasion of Ethiopia, one can see that indeed from Martini's times on, colonial governments moved precisely according to such guidelines. There were certain variations from governor to governor, with some (e.g., De Camillis, 1919–20) emphasizing the protection of the "natives" and others (e.g., Zoli, 1928–30) stressing "European superiority."[38] But the governmental course of action remained fundamentally consistent. We can thus follow such guidelines in order to analyze Italian racial policy in the post-Adwa period.

"Strengthen and underline European superiority"

A first obstacle to the achievement of the goal of strengthening European superiority was based on the settlers' class. Colonial authorities were not at all pleased by the presence of a large contingent of proletarians among Italian colonists. Governor Salvago Raggi (1907–15) effectively explained the nature of the colonial government's concerns in a long report to the ministry.

> Since the Italian must be respected by the native, it is necessary that European migration be limited. It should comprise only craftsmen, people who can supervise the work of the native workers, or people who have some capital. . . . We thus tried to discourage the mass of proletarians and people who do not have any skills from migration to Eritrea, because they would be in a social condition lower than that of the natives. There are already Italians of this sort in the colony. There are cases of Italians who have been living for months begging from the natives; needless to say we must eliminate such elements. All the more so considering that the Italian worker here is in such a condition only because here he has a much higher standard of living than in Italy. He almost

always maintains a servant and a concubine. He certainly spends less than he would in Italy for them, but he spends all that he earns. And when he becomes unemployed, he ends up begging, or being supported by his concubine.[39]

The Italian colonial government, thus, consistently discouraged the migration to the colony of unqualified and unemployed proletarians.[40] As a result, before 1935 migration to Eritrea was very limited. The colony dramatically failed in its proclaimed goal—to provide an outlet for Italian migration—but succeeded in limiting the disgrace of having destitute Italians side by side with Eritreans. Italian workers in Eritrea numbered in the hundreds. They made up an important component of the Italian community only because the community as a whole was small. But if one considers that in the period 1880–1930 more than nine million Italians migrated to non-European countries, one can see to what extent Italian migration flows bypassed Eritrea (Duggan 1994: 20).[41]

In many respects, Italian governors used tools similar to those used by other colonial rulers in order to enhance Italian prestige, mark racial hierarchies, and legitimize colonial rule. For example, Martini's fondness for public ceremonies and pomp was not only the result of his personal vanity (Del Boca 1976: vol. 1, 758, 836; Salvago Raggi 1968: 458–59), or of his desire to enhance his authority vis-à-vis the military and the metropolitan government (Labanca 1991: 31). To a good extent, in fact, his style of rule paralleled the efforts of British and French colonial rulers to use "invented traditions" in order to legitimize colonial rule (Ranger 1983).

Another tool typically used in the colonies to mark racial hierarchies was urban segregation. Racial zoning in Asmara was first introduced in 1908 by Governor Salvago Raggi, who issued a city plan that divided the town into three residential areas. The first two zones were for Europeans and for Africans, respectively, while the third one was mixed.[42] Though not as strict as in the period after 1935, urban segregation did work to consolidate the idea of racial separation as "natural" (as Maria says).

The domain in which Italian racial policy departed most dramatically from that of the British and the French was education.[43] Martini's educational philosophy was simple: no schooling for Africans. Showing indisputable acumen, Martini maintained that educated subjects were more difficult to dominate than untutored ones. In Eritrea, there were enough working-class Italians to fill lower-level positions in the public administration. So, unlike other colonial powers, Italy did not really need to train Africans to fill such positions. Martini could clearly see the political hazard of having educated Africans in a colony where more than 10 percent of the Europeans were illiterate.[44] In order to strengthen "European superiority over the natives," Martini believed it was necessary to deny them access to education.[45]

The subsequent governor, Salvago Raggi, partially departed from Martini's policy. He opened three schools for male children of chiefs and other notables. Such schools had a strong vocational character and imparted elementary education equivalent to the Italian third grade (Tekeste 1987: 80). Eritreans were strongly dissatisfied with the vocational character of such schools and demanded access to higher education.[46] In the late 1920s, the government extended the school program to a fourth year, and in the early 1930s it allowed a handful of Eritrean students to have another two years of education. Otherwise, the Italian government remained adamant in denying Eritreans access to higher education.[47] In colonial Eritrea, educational restrictions remained one of the pillars of the color bar.

The assimilation of the colonized was not part of Italian colonial rhetoric, let alone colonial practice. Rather, Italians progressively rigidified the criteria for racial exclusion. For example, in the early years, for judiciary purposes Italians considered Indians and Middle Easterners "assimilated to Europeans" (that is, Egyptians Italians were under the jurisdiction of the same judge). But from 1908 on, the Italian government started to consider these same Indians and Middle Easterners as "assimilated to the colonial subject."[48] In order to underline European superiority over the Africans, the gap between the colonizers and the colonized needed to be wide and clear.

The colonial army also strictly followed the principle of always enhancing "European superiority over the natives." Italians were ready to praise the military—or, more precisely, the warlike—virtues of Eritrean soldiers. However, they allowed Eritreans only promotion up to the rank of NCO (Scardigli 1996: 198). Eritreans, of course, resented such limitation.[49] Throughout the colonial period there were recurrent discussions about the possible introduction of some sort of officers ranks for Eritreans.[50] But since in the colony there were always also Italian rank and file, in Italian eyes the political hazardous of having Eritrean officers always outnumbered the advantages.[51]

The principle that Eritreans must always be subordinated to Europeans posed a thorny problem when it came to using Eritreans as policemen, or in any circumstance in which the Eritrean military dealt with white civilians. In such circumstances, two different principles were in conflict: the principle of European superiority over Africans, and the principle of military authority over civilians.

Since the times of Governor Baratieri (that is, before Adwa), Italians had agreed not to let Eritreans arrest Europeans, testify against them, or act as *pubblici ufficiali* (officers vested with a public interest function). Baratieri justified this course of action on the grounds of Eritreans' alleged "lower moral standards" *(sentimento morale inferiore),* "inclination to intrigue," and "religious fanaticism."[52] The praxis started by Baratieri later became law.[53]

The shortcomings of such a norm became apparent in 1915, when an *ascaro,* who was serving as a sentinel in front of the Italian national bank, the

Banca d'Italia, in Asmara drove away an Austrian citizen. The Austrian reacted by biting the sentinel. The Italians arrested the Austrian, but then they
realized that they could not charge him with resistance and violence against
a *pubblico ufficiale,* which under Italian law is a special crime.[54] This case in-
cited a lively discussion between the colonial troops command, the colonial
government, and the government in Rome. The military proposed to amend
the law, introducing an exception for African sentinels. For the military, in
this circumstance, the need of enhancing military authority prevailed over
racial concerns.[55] But after lengthy discussions, an ad hoc committee[56] for-
bade the introduction of any exception to the rule.

Without seeing the irony in talking about "European prestige" when Europeans went around biting Africans, the committee explained that the
need to enhance "color prestige and racial superiority vis-à-vis the natives"
remained unchanged. To be sure, the more unbecoming the behavior of
Europeans, the more decrees were needed in order to enhance "white prestige." The committee gave a long list of reasons for its decisions: Eritreans
were too ignorant to become *pubblici ufficiali;* they were morally unfit for
such a delicate task; it was politically risky to grant them such status because
of their "foolish nationalist ambitions"; and so on. Most interestingly, the
committee argued that it was "highly dangerous to modify even slightly a law
so important for a sound colonial life, because to a first exception, a second
always follows, and then a third one, and so on."[57] The principle that a European must always be superior to an African allowed for no exceptions.
Otherwise, a chain reaction would ensue, undermining the foundation of
the colonial edifice.[58]

"Protect natives against European abuses"

In Eritrea, as in other Western colonies, ruling by sheer force had proved
too costly both in terms of taxpayers' money and in terms of soldiers' lives.
After the conquest stage, when the use of force generally prevailed, the colonial state needed to attain internal legitimization by means other than
machine guns. This required that the state prove that it was not a mere
agent of settlers' interests.[59] Thus, in all the colonies, in different degrees
and in different ways, the colonial state provided some protection to the
colonized against white settlers' rapacity. Furthermore, some individual idealistic officials, who sincerely believed in the "white man's burden," tried to
advance African interests.

In Eritrea as elsewhere, settlers by and large wanted more land and a co-
ercive system that forced Eritreans to work for them for a low salary. The colonial government, however, had learned the hard way that it could not afford to expropriate large amounts of land in the highlands. Furthermore,
as already mentioned, during the governorships of Martini (1898–1907)

and Salvago Raggi (1908–15), colonial authorities realized that letting Eritrean peasants farm the highlands was not only politically expedient, but also economically convenient. After Adwa, then, compared to other colonies, the colonial state in Eritrea had both a greater need to build a legitimacy not based on the use of force and less economic interest in yielding to the settlers' claims.

To be sure, the colonial state was committed to the promotion of the colony's valorization (that is, exploitation for the colonizers' benefit). This translated into substantial help to Italian entrepreneurs, such as concessions for the exploitation of natural resources, the construction of the railroad (entirely financed by Italian taxpayers), a favorable import/export tax system, and so on (Tekeste 1987: 43–44; Yemane 1988: 153–63, 187–200). In Eritrea, then, the colonial state was certainly willing to serve the interests of Italian capital. It was not willing, however, to grant individual Italians a free hand in exploiting and abusing Eritreans in a way that fueled Eritrean malcontent without providing any economic benefit for the colony as a whole. Martini, thus, exposed the wrongdoing of the concessionaires:

> Some [of the concessionaires] let their concessions to the natives for an extravagant rent. Some took advantage of the water sources in their concessions or in their vicinities. Their contract provided for the free access of the natives to the water. Instead, they imposed tolls and rights of way. Others extorted money from the natives every time they had to pass near their concessions. Finally, others invented a usury-type of sharecropping, which accorded all the benefits to the one who had received the land from the government for free, and placed all the burden on the native tiller.[60]

The "European abuses" that the colonial government was willing to curb for the most part did not concern the economic relations between colonizers and colonized, but rather behaviors that the government considered detrimental to Italian "prestige." In particular, Martini set for himself the task of disciplining the military. During the years of military rule (1885–97), military officers had enjoyed unbounded authority. Many abuses had ensued, at the expense of both Italian taxpayers and Eritrean subjects. Martini's mandate was to cut expenses, and he did not forgive the military—which he described as consisting of "either idiots or criminals"—for their squandering of public money. But Martini was even more outraged by the military lifestyle, which damaged Italian prestige. White prestige, and in particular state prestige, was one of the pillars of Martini's colonial building. Shabby officers who squandered their money in gambling or dedicated their best energies to running after Eritrean women were at odds with Martini's colonial project. He thus kept the military to a higher standard, and he repatriated the most unruly officers.[61]

A similar rationale was behind the repression of petty violence and

abuses perpetrated by Italian civilians. In May 1899, an enraged Martini
noted in his diary that Asmara's *commissario* had asked him what he had to
do with two reports against a certain engineer named Capucci, for assault
and battery against "natives"; the reports had been on the *commissario's* desk
for some time. Martini wrote, "For God's sake! Act. Since Capucci is white,
Italian, and an engineer, should we allow him to whip and beat the natives?
We cannot prevent him from skinning them by usury; but beating them, no
[we cannot allow]."[62]

As in the case of military men, the most important tool that the colonial government used to discipline Italian civilians whose behavior could
undermine the colonial edifice was expulsion. From Martini's times on, in
fact, there was a small but constant flow of Italian civilians expelled from the
colony.

A good example of the kind of behavior that the colonial state repressed
is provided by Giovanni Bianco's case. In the colony from 1902, Bianco had
initially worked as a domestic servant for an Italian officer. At the time of
his expulsion, he was irregularly working as a mason for Eritreans. He mo-
lested local women, was a habitual alcohol abuser, and borrowed money
from villagers without returning it. Villagers thus "laughed at him, pitied
him, and hated him," and they frequently complained about him to the Italian *commissario.*[63]

This case, like that of Oscar Agresti, involved a lower-class Italian. One
could infer that abusive behavior was a characteristic of only the lowest stra-
tum of Italian settlers. But this was not the case. Much evidence, in fact, suggests that even middle-class settlers considered abusing the colonized a normal aspect of colonial life. Martini's remarks about Capucci are telling in
this regard. Also quite revealing is a comment by a certain A. Signorini,[64]
chief engineer of the railroad. Signorini was reporting about the battery
that another railway engineer, Corti, had inflicted on an Eritrean employee.
The two lived in the same railway facilities, and Corti was trying to force the
Eritrean to move out in order to get his room. "Mr. Corti," the chief engineer reported, "told me about this event as if it was *the most normal thing*"
(emphasis mine).[65] What is significant about this incident is not the fact of
the abuse, but that the abuser considered it "normal." (To be sure, it is significant as well that Signorini did not consider it "normal" at all. Different
Italians had different ideas about how to behave with the colonized.) Colonial Eritrea was not King Leopold's Congo. Violence against the colonized
was limited. Nevertheless, mistreatment of the colonized was a component
of everyday life, as in any other colony. This is a truism, but it is worth
remarking to counter the persisting myth of the benign nature of Italian
colonialism.

The analysis of criminal records confirms both the relatively modest
character of colonial violence and its racial connotations. The level of crim-

inality in general was very low, and violent crimes, in particular, were rare.[66] The low criminality rate is an indication of the relatively low degree of racial conflict in the post-Adwa period, which I have already mentioned.

Crimes that involved interaction between Italians and Eritrean were usu-ally one of two types: thefts by Eritreans from Italians (but occasionally the other way around), and assault and battery by Italians against Eritreans. Vio-lent crimes by Eritreans against Italians were almost nonexistent.[67] In 1907, for example, the only case reported was that of an Eritrean who slapped an Italian boy. Thefts committed by Eritreans were a consequence of pov-erty. Eritreans got arrested for stealing food (a bag of flour, a basket of fruit, etc.), clothes, or similar items with greater use value than exchange value. Crimes committed by Italians against Eritreans, by contrast, were the conse-quence of racial arrogance.

In 1920 the regent governor De Camillis issued a circular letter in which he "deplored the behavior of some Europeans residing in the colony against the natives," and called Italian officials to take severe measures to stop mis-treatment. In recent times, the circular stated, there had been repeated "disgusting incidents" that had "damaged European prestige and caused scandal among the local population."[68] In a report to the ministry, the re-gent governor recited a meticulous catalogue of the incidents that had oc-curred in the previous few months and that had provoked his initiative. "Girolamo R. injured a native. Carlo E. and Silvestro B. battered a na-tive and slandered another one. Ottavio L. battered a worker . . ." The re-port went on and on, listing more than two dozen cases of battery against Eritreans—often committed, according to De Camillis, "for frivolous rea-sons"—and a few major crimes. An Italian had raped an underage virgin girl, and other Italians had killed two Eritreans. In one such case an Italian, Dante B., had killed a boatman by striking him with an oar because the boatman "did not want to carry him beyond the destination they had previ-ously agreed upon."[69] In cases such as these, as in Corti's case, one can see how racial arrogance played an important part. It was not simply violence such as that present in any other society, but it was *colonial* violence.

The repressive action carried out by colonial authorities against such vio-lence also had a special rationale that set it apart from the usual govern-mental function of ensuring public order. While in the metropole, ruling elites could conceive of their actions as the honoring of a social contract; in the colony, they imagined their role as that of civilizers who take paternal care of savages. Unruly settlers who perpetrated blatant abuses against the colonized contradicted an ideological pillar of the colonial edifice, that is, the supposed superiority of the whites over the blacks. Quite meaningfully, when colonial rulers talked about curbing white abuses, they phrased it in terms of "preservation of white prestige."[70] Curbing abuses by whites and stressing European superiority over the Africans were thus two sides of the same coin. They were also insidiously at odds, since exposing white abuses proved how questionable the notion itself of "white prestige" was.

At an ideological level, colonial rulers were able to reconcile the systematic subordination of the colonized vis-à-vis the colonizers, and the repression of colonizers' abuses, by stressing the special responsibilities of the civilized. In order to honor the "white man's burden," colonizers needed to maintain standards of behavior that would prove their preeminence and thus the legitimacy of colonial domination.

We have only a hazy picture of how colonial rulers were able to reconcile the systematic subordination of the colonized and the repression of colonizers' abuses at the level of daily administration. Most colonial court archives have apparently been lost, other colonial series are badly incomplete, and—even more importantly—many sources still need to be explored. We do not know, for instance, what happened to the Italians listed in De Camillis's report, and what kind of action colonial officials took after his circular letter. It seems that colonial authorities often pressured Eritreans in order to make them withdraw their lawsuits against Italians.[71] In this way, the authorities avoided the disgrace of having a white person in a courtroom witness box as a defendant, with a black person as a plaintiff.

Two 1923 reports by Governor Giovanni Cerrina Feroni provide us with some disturbing clues about how colonial judges handled the cases that ended up in court. The case concerns an Italian who was found guilty of attempted murder of an Eritrean but was set free. It is worth following this lengthy story in some detail, because it is quite revealing of many aspects of colonial life.

Italian settler Aristide Zelinotti was jealous of Abdalla Agos, a servant of high colonial official Riccardi. Zelinotti suspected Abdalla of having a relationship with the Eritrean woman with whom he lived. Zelinotti, therefore, assaulted and battered Abdalla before having Abdalla arrested, adding insult to injury. However, thanks to the intercession of Riccardi (Abdalla's master), Abdalla was released. For the record, Riccardi made it clear that "he really had no partiality for natives," and that he had just administered twenty-five lashes to another of his servants who was guilty of negligence. Following his release, Riccardi kept Abdalla secluded at home. But once he brought Abdalla with him on a trip. Zelinotti, knowing about the trip, ambushed Abdalla and fired four shots at him, crippling him for life.[72]

The Asmara criminal court (Corte di Assise), however, ruled that Zelinotti was not punishable because he was insane. The court also specified that Zelinotti was affected by a very special type of insanity that manifested itself only in the colony. The judge thus recommended Zelinotti's expulsion from the colony. The governor readily expelled him, not least because, he explained, the court decision had shocked "the natives." Eritreans, in fact, were "unable to precisely appraise Zelinotti's mental condition." According to Governor Cerrina Feroni, they mistakenly believed that Zelinotti had been discharged only because he was Italian. A few days earlier, the governor further explained, the same court had condemned an Eritrean guilty of assault and battery against an Italian soldier to thirteen years of prison.[73]

In 1907, Martini wrote that Eritreans maintained that in controversies between them and whites, the whites always prevailed. Of course, Martini claimed that this was not the case (1913: 137). It does not require much imagination, however, to understand what generated such belief.

"Secure governmental prestige and authority against both the natives and the Europeans"

Colonial governors agreed that an exceptional situation in the colony required exceptional powers in governmental hands vis-à-vis both the colonized, Italian settlers, and the central government in Rome.[74] Although autocratic rule of the colonized was intrinsic to the colonial relation, a less obvious fact was that governors ruled their own citizens "with an iron fist." Competition for preeminence among colonial governments, white settlers, and metropolitan governments was by no means unusual. What characterized the Eritrean case was the unusual weakness of white settlers vis-à-vis the colonial government. The colonial government was thus able to impose on the settlers its model of "legitimate" exploitation of the colony.

As we have already seen, before the Italo-Ethiopian war the Italian community was numerically small. It was also economically weak. A good percentage of the Italians were on the state payroll, either as military personnel or as public employees. Only a few concessionaires had been able to invest some capital in the colony, but their economic success depended to a good extent on favorable import-export tariffs and on massive state investment in infrastructure. Fiscally, the colony was never self-sufficient; rather, it was heavily subsidized by the metropole. Even if in the 1920s some settlers fantasized about establishing a "settler republic,"[75] Italian settlers were not in a position to aspire to self-rule. And they were by no means able to lobby in the metropolitan Parliament, or to pressure the colonial government as much as the British or French settlers did.

Confronting such a weak settler community were governors with a strong sense of their role who were convinced that they possessed a better understanding than both the settlers and the central government in Rome. Italy had an administrative tradition of bureaucratic centralism. The colonial administration, however, progressively shifted toward the British model of the crown colony, which allowed for the significant autonomy of colonial governments. The historian Nicola Labanca (1991: 31) has indicated the high degree of autonomy enjoyed by the Eritrean government vis-à-vis the metropolitan state. Within the colony, however, in accordance with Italian bureaucratic tradition, the government established a centralized and hierarchical model of administration.

At the same time, colonial rulers seemed to consider the checks and balances that regulated state authority in Italy as an unnecessary burden in the colony. The outcome was a colonial state that provided its own citizens with few guarantees. For example, departing from metropolitan norms, the colonial judiciary law dictated that ordinary judges did not have competence over the controversies between the colonial administration and Italian citizens. In such controversies, the judge was the governor himself, who therefore was at the same time judge and judged.[76]

Another element that concentrated power in the hands of colonial rulers was the indeterminacy of the norms that regulated colonial life. Italian rulers agreed that metropolitan legislation could not simply be exported to the colony, and that modifications in order to accommodate local needs were needed. Under Martini's tenure, thus, the government appointed an ad hoc committee that elaborated special codes for the colony. The codes were duly approved, but they were never formally enforced. Salvago Raggi, in fact, recurred to a captious procedural devise in order to postpone *sine die* the enforcement of the new codes. The succeeding governors followed Salvago Raggi's steps, and the Eritrean codes were never formally enforced. Nevertheless, colonial judges and officials tended to follow them in their rulings. This situation of legal haziness left great discretionary power to colonial officials. And this was precisely what the colonial government wanted.[77]

During the long elaboration of the Eritrean codes, both the colonial government and the jurists had come to the conclusion that it was better to leave the articulation of a corpus of colonial laws to the gradual work of court decisions. This line of action, modeled after the British system, was an important departure from the Italian judicial tradition. If one considers that governor and *commissari* were vested with wide judiciary powers, one can appreciate the concentration of power in the colonial government's hands.

Last but not least, one should consider that unlike what generally happened in settler colonies, Italian settlers did not enjoy any form of political representation.[78] In 1900, Governor Martini could hardly temper his rage when he learned that in Massawa some settlers were meeting in order to demand that Italians in the colony be allowed to participate in political elections.[79] This demand was utterly unsuccessful and settlers remained disenfranchised.

An argument used to justify the denial of political representation to settlers was that it contributed to the protection of the colonized against settlers' exploitation. In 1891, the Committee of Inquiry on the Colony of Eritrea articulated its firm opposition to any form of political representation for the Italians in Eritrea by arguing that electoral bodies in the colonies "become almost always a formidable instrument of exploitation and oppression" of the colonized in the hands of the settlers.[80] Of course, this was not the only reason behind the committee's support for authoritarian rule in the colony, but there was a kernel of truth in it. In colonial Africa, strong settler communities were able to push for rules that allowed for harsh exploitation of the colonized. In Eritrea the authoritarian conduct of the colonial state vis-à-vis its own citizens helped to temper the degree of exploitation of the colonized by bridling the settlers. The analysis of the most important public confrontation between the governor and the settlers that occurred in colonial Eritrea will help clarify my point.

In 1911, more than eighty settlers staged a protest against Governor Salvago Raggi, accusing him of favoring the Eritreans over the Italians. The protest had a significant echo in Italy, not only in the press, but also in the Parliament, where an MP voiced the settlers' complaints.[81] The occasion for the protest was the expropriation of 40 hectares of land from four Italian concessionaires. In order to do some public works, the government had expropriated 120 hectares from some Eritrean villagers and had partially compensated them with 40 hectares taken from Italian settlers. The settlers had received monetary compensation in return. The colonists claimed that the government planned to progressively despoil the Italians of "their" land in order to give it to the Eritreans.

Salvago Raggi argued that the real causes for the protest lay elsewhere. Several colonists had personal grievances against the government because the government had not yielded to their illegitimate claims. In every colony, the governor argued, "there are persons inclined to live by exploiting the native and the government, instead of working."[82] One of the settlers who supported the governor reported:

> One of the colonists who signed [the petition against the governor] one day talking to me expressed his surprise because the government had not enslaved the native population. Another concessionaire, who complained about labor shortages, was astonished because the government did not force the native to work in whites' concessions. "It is pointless," he argued, "that they grant us land, if they leave the natives free to work their own land, while we are lacking a labor force. Why did we sacrifice so many lives and so much money if the Italian has to come here to work? If one wants to work, one goes to America." (Goglia and Grassi 1981: 135–36).

There were, however, also other reasons behind the protest against the governor. According to Salvago Raggi, the most active organizers of the protest had been the Italian lawyers residing in the colony. They were enraged by a governor's decree that prevented lawyers from participating in the controversies between Eritreans decided by Italian *residenti* and *commis-*

sari (that is, land conflicts and other civil cases). According to the governor, Italian lawyers used to cynically exploit Eritreans, extracting from them extravagant fees. Lawyers had also allegedly encouraged Eritrean litigation out of personal interest. Some Italians agreed with the governor in his critique of the lawyers.

Others, however, held a totally different opinion and accused the governor of administrative despotism. According to the colony's state attorney, Ernesto Conte, Eritreans were now abandoned to the colonial officers' whims. In a long memoir addressed to the ministry, Conte also stigmatized the reform of the Eritrean judiciary carried out by Salvago Raggi. In order to simplify the system and cut expenses, the reform had abolished the local court of appeal, diminished the number of Italian judges, and granted wide judiciary power to the *commissari*. In Conte's opinion, the reform had unduly concentrated power in colonial officials' hands, fostering their bossy attitudes. "It seems that all the branches of the pubic administration have been pervaded by a true libido for arrogance and abuse," Conte argued.

One of the new laws promoted by Salvago Raggi provided for the transfer to Italy of all the trials against colonial officials.[83] This norm, according to Conte, amounted to a further act of administrative arrogance. The state attorney thundered:

> In order to justify this norm, they will certainly say that one has to avoid a scandal in front of the natives. They will talk also about the need of preserving governmental prestige. But "prestige" at this point has become a banner to cover up too many contraband goods.[84]

Salvago Raggi had urged the central government to issue such a law during a dramatic case, which had deeply impressed both Italians and Eritreans.[85] In 1908, Italian *residente* Rinaldo Bruna was arrested and charged with raping a six-year-old Italian girl. Immediately tried in Eritrea, Bruna was convicted. But in 1912, the Court of Appeal of Rome reversed the verdict and acquitted him. Bruna's lawyers successfully argued that Bruna had been a victim of false accusations by some settlers who were acting out of personal grudges. In particular, the main witness against Bruna had been a certain Luigi Ernesto Beltramo, who had held a grudge against Bruna because the *residente* had refused to grant him some contracts for supplies to the colonial administration.[86]

This dreary story is quite revealing about the quality of the relations between the colonial administration and Italian settlers, or at least a significant percentage of them. To be sure, the Bruna case was exceptional for the quality of cross-accusations between the resident and the settlers. And it seems that under the governorship of Salvago Raggi the relations between colonial administration and settlers were particularly strained. One should remember that in 1909, Salvago Raggi issued the land law that severely lim-

ited the granting of concessions in the highlands. The clash between the colonial government and the settlers thus erupted at a crucial moment in Eritrean colonial history. It was a clash about who—the government or the settlers—had the authority to define what should be considered "legitimate"
exploitation of the colony and its population, and what should be considered "abuse." And it was a clash that the settlers lost. The echoes of their
protest progressively faded, and the governor was able to continue pursuing his policy.

In the conclusion to her book *Eritrea colonia,* Irma Taddia calls for studies
on Italian colonialism that focus on the making of the colonial society and
question the supposed "uniqueness" of Italian colonialism (1986: 353).
This chapter is a contribution to this project.

It has suggested, in fact, that the relations among the settlers, the state,
and the colonized in Eritrea had significant parallels to those of other colonies. The popular myth that ordinary Italians in the colonies had nothing but friendly relations with the Africans has proved to be without foundation. As in other colonies, there were settlers who went by the rules set by
the colonial government, and others who interpreted the colonial relation
as a license to abuse the colonized. Just as in other colonies, the colonial
government worked to prevent the rapacity and violence of some settlers
from endangering the colonial edifice by igniting African rebellion. At the
same time, the colonial state worked to make sure that the colonized were
systematically subordinated to the colonizers.

The unique aspect of Eritrean colonialism seems to have been the weakness of the colonial state vis-à-vis the Africans on the one hand, and the
weakness of the settler community vis-à-vis the colonial state on the other.
Italian weakness in Eritrea had its roots in both Italy (in the deficiency of
Italian capital) and Africa (in the devastating defeat at Adwa). Because
of Adwa, Italians in Eritrea were far less successful than their counterparts
in other colonies in seizing Africans' land. As a consequence, the political
economy of Italian colonial domination assumed particular characteristics,
which eased tensions between colonizers and colonized. Paradoxically, because of the experience of Adwa, Italian settlers seem also to have had less
of a siege mentality compared to other settlers. Adwa put an end, as well, to
any project of large-scale Italian migration to Eritrea. In short, it was not because of a thriving Italian civil society but because of a weak one that Eritrea
before 1935 saw a relatively low level of racial conflict.

Because of the weakness of the colonial state vis-à-vis the Africans and
the weakness of the settler community, the state had both a great need to
and relative ease in enforcing a paternalistic mode of relationship with the
colonized. By carefully balancing the legal and social subordination of the

Eritreans with the curbing of Italians' unbecoming abuses, the state was able to shape the relations between colonizers and colonized in a way that could be perceived—as Maria said—as "naturally" unequal. What could appear in Maria's words as a contradiction—that is, the coexistence of friendly attitudes and racial discrimination—was actually the operational mode of colonial paternalism.

NOTES

This chapter is a revised version of the first chapter of my Ph.D. dissertation (2002). I am grateful to the Center for International and Comparative Studies of Northwestern University and to the American Association of University Women for their financial support. I would also like to thank Dario Gaggio, Jonathon Glassman, Nicola Labanca, Micaela di Leonardo, Barbara Sòrgoni, and the participants in my dissertation seminar (Amal Fadlalla, Jenna Johnson-Kuhn, and Elise Levine) and the CICS interdisciplinary workshop for their valuable comments on earlier versions of this chapter.

1. *Italo-Eritrei* (which I translate as "Italo-Eritreans") is the Italian term that persons of mixed Italian and Eritrean descent use to describe themselves. They perceive the terms *"meticcio"* and—even worse—*"mulatto,"* both of which translate as "mixed-race," as derogatory.

2. Interview with author, Rome, Nov. 7, 1997.

3. Many people I interviewed in Eritrea in 1998 adopted such a periodization. See also Taddia (1996).

4. In 1930 the Eritrean Federation of the Fascist Party had 350 members, the Dopolavoro Fascista (Fascist Leisure Organization) 570 members, and the Opera Balilla (Fascist Children's Organization) 600 members. At the time, Italians in Eritrea numbered 4,188; the percentage of party members in the colony was thus even higher than in Italy. Governo dell'Eritrea, Segreteria del governatore, *Notiziario politico Eritrea-Etiopia,* no. 3 (Mar. 1930), p. 2. Archivio storico diplomatico del Ministero affari esteri (hereafter ASDMAE), *Archivio storico del Ministero Africa italiana* (hereafter *ASMAI*), 35/1, f. 3.

5. The periodization that I am adopting is congruous with my specific object of study. If one looks at colonial policies from the metropolitan point of view, as Labanca does in this volume, the periodization should be different, as he points out.

6. The bibliography is too extensive to be listed here. For a good overview of the recent literature on Italian colonialism, the reader is referred to Labanca (1996). An essential bibliography on fascist racial policy in the colonies would include Pankhurst (1969), Bernardini (1977), Goglia (1988), Mignemi (1986), Centro Furio Iesi (1994), and Labanca (1999). A most relevant study embracing the entire colonial period that analyzes colonial discourse and governmental policies regarding interracial sexual relations is that by Sòrgoni (1998). On colonial concubinage see also Campassi (1987), Barrera (1996), Gabrielli (1996 and 1997), and Iyob (2000).

7. There are some relevant exceptions to this trend. Some scholars have done pioneer studies on working-class settlers and soldiers, mostly—once again—at the

time of the first African war or of the conquest of Ethiopia. See, for example, Dore (1983), Labanca (1990), Guerrini (1990), Le Houérou (1994), and Taddia (1988).

8. For a recent discussion on "the myth of Italian humanity," the English-speaking reader is referred to Doumanis (1997: 163–65), Fuller (2000), and Del Boca and Pickering-Iazzi in this volume.

9. Stoler (1991: 86). Sòrgoni (1998: 255–56) has confirmed Stoler's analysis in reference to the Eritrean case.

10. I address such issue in depth in my dissertation (Barrera 2002).

11. Commissione d'inchiesta sulla colonia Eritrea (1891: 9).

12. Jonathan Steinberg (1990) has made a similar point in his study on the reasons why, during World War II, in the countries under Italian military occupation several Italian officers and officials saved Jews. Other scholars had explained Italian officers' behavior with Italian national character. Steinberg convincingly points out how such generic explanations do not explain, for example, why Italians on the one hand saved Jews in Croatia in 1942, and on the other hand sent them to extermination camps in 1944, under the Repubblica Sociale Italiana.

13. The Italian penetration of Eritrea started in 1869, when the Rubattino Shipping Company acquired the port of Assab. In 1882 the Italian government took over Assab; in 1885 it occupied Massawa and started heading inland. On January 1, 1890, the Italian government formally established the colony, naming it Eritrea. On the history of Italy's first African war (1885–96) see Battaglia (1958), Del Boca (1976), Labanca (1993), and Scardigli (1996).

14. Between 1893 and 1907 the government had declared 207,639 hectares in the highlands "state land" *(terre demaniali)*. But the *Ordinamento della Colonia Eritrea*, the law of May 24, 1903, no. 205, provided for the revocation of all of the expropriation decrees not published in the official collection of colonial governmental decrees *(Raccolta degli atti dell' autorità pubblica anteriori alla promulgazione della legge 24 maggio 1903, n. 205, in vigore nella Colonia Eritrea, approvata con R.D. 30 dicembre 1909, n. 845)*. Since the official collection did not include the expropriation decrees issued before 1903, such decrees were automatically revoked. Only the decrees issued after 1903 remained valid. Agnesa [contribution to the debate] in *Atti del secondo congresso degli italiani all'estero (11–20 giugno 1911)*, vol. 2, pp. 482–85. Bartolommei-Gioli and Checchi (1913: 387), Valenti (1913: 39).

15. According to historian Irma Taddia, in 1910 in the highlands there were 301,434 hectares of cultivated land and 347,504 hectares of "cultivable" land (probably for the most part land that Eritrean peasants were allowing to lay fallow). Concessions to Italians amounted to 6,819 hectares (Taddia 1986: 235–36). According to British official Gerald Kennedy Trevaskis (1960: 53), in the highlands the cultivable land available to Eritreans amounted to only 178,000 hectares. Different scholars have accepted such figures (see, for example, Markakis [1989] and Pateman [1990]). However, I consider more reliable Taddia's data, since she has done in-depth research on this topic. Yemane (1988) gives data that is similar to Taddia's (1986: 145). For a recent compelling discussion on the issue, see Tronvoll (1998: 196–202).

16. In 1913, state land in the highlands amounted to 29,553 hectares; two-thirds of the state land was in Shimezana. It is difficult to get a precise picture of how much

land was seized from the Eritreans in the highlands. One should think that the concessions to Italians (6,819 hectares) were a fraction of state land (29,553); but, apparently, to a good extent they were not. At the time, in fact, Italians for the most part held concessions on land whose expropriation decree had been revoked. The legal status of such land was thus very confused. To know how much land was seized from the Eritreans in the highlands, then, it seems that one should actually add, at least in part, the two figures (state land and alienated land). One should also consider, however, that state land was often let out for cultivation to Eritrean peasants. Finally, one should consider that state land included rivers, roads, and other areas for public use (Bartolommei-Gioli and Checchi 1913: 387, n. 3; Nadel 1946: 19).

17. In 1910, land alienated to Italian settlers in Hamasien amounted to 6,241 hectares (Bartolommei-Gioli and Checchi 1913: 384, n. 2). In 1907, concessions in the Medrì Baharì amounted to 5,339 hectares (Martini 1913, also published in Goglia and Grassi 1981: 124).

18. For example, in 1908 the population of Hamasien refused to enroll in the colonial reserve battalions. It was the first time that disobedience to governmental orders of this sort occurred. The Italian resident Paolo Teodorani blamed it first and foremost on land alienation and argued that the only solution was to return the land to Eritrean peasants. "The highland can be exploited only by the natives," he concluded. Teodorani to Salvago Raggi, *Le condizioni politico-amministrative dello Hamasien sul finire del 1908,* Asmara, Nov. 7, 1908, ASDMAE, *Archivio Eritrea* (from now on *AE*), b. 510, f. "Hamasien." For other instances of Eritrean peasants' protest see Tekeste (1986: 45).

19. "L'agricoltura in Eritrea dal 1882 ad oggi: La colonizzazione," *L'Agricoltura coloniale* 26 (1932), nos. 9–10: 418. Since the turn of the century, fear of Eritrean rebellion in case of large-scale land alienation is constantly evoked in Italian writings about the valorization of the colony. See, for example, the panel on "Del regime fondiario nelle nostre colonie" in *Atti del secondo congresso degli italiani all'estero (11–20 giugno 1911),* vol. 2, pp. 481–87, Stanga (1913: 53–54), Bartolommei-Gioli and Checchi (1913), Dainelli (1929), and Gabelli (1936).

20. The 1909 land law (R.D. Jan. 31, 1909, no. 378, *Ordinamento fondiario per la colonia Eritrea*) recognized Eritreans' property rights over land in the highlands to a significant extent, but Eritrean ownership of land still allowed for the granting of concessions to Europeans in such regions. The land law of Feb. 7, 1926, no. 269, excluded altogether the granting of new concessions in the highlands. In 1907, land alienated to Italians amounted to 6,483 hectares; it increased to 6,819 hectares in 1910. It progressively decreased in the following years, reaching 5,905 in 1930, and 4,479 in 1939 (Taddia 1986: 235–36).

21. In the period 1912–28, the number of *ascari* ranged from about six thousand to about nine thousand and constituted from 5.5 percent to 8.1 percent of Eritrea's productive male labor force (Tekeste 1987: 51–54).

22. As yet we have data about Eritrean wageworkers only from the 1930s on. In the previous decades their number was certainly smaller (Taddia 1986: 252; Killion 1985: 112–16, 275–85).

23. In 1928, per capita animal herds were apparently the highest in the century. Italian investments were insufficient to produce large-scale proletarianization, and Eritreans generally received extremely low salaries, insufficient to support a family.

Nevertheless, wage work became a valuable complement to agricultural activity (Niaz Murtaza 1998: 58–62, 113–17).

24. In 1913, the Italian population of working age totaled 1,420, more than one-third of which were military men (475). Concessionaires comprised only about 4 percent of the active population. Even if one considers only the civil active population, the percentage of the concessionaires remained limited (6.5 percent). Furthermore, for most of the concessionaires, agriculture was not their main source of income, but rather a supplement to their income as public employees, professionals, traders, and other. "Censimento 1913"; De Angelis (1921), Valenti (1913: 60, n. 1).

25. The exception to this trend was the large farm at Tessenei, in the lowlands, which was, however, owned by a state company (Taddia 1986: 320–29).

26. In 1913, among the Italian civilian population of working age, about 25 percent were workers (mostly masons), and another 25 percent were craftsmen. Of the latter, more than 25 percent were carpenters, and another quarter were mechanics. The rest of the craftsmen were cobblers, tailors, blacksmiths, barbers, stonecutters, goldsmiths, typographers, and so on. The rest of the total Italian population was comprised of traders (10 percent), private employees (6 percent), and professionals (2 percent). One hundred sixty-four Italian civilians (17 percent) were employed by the public administration. The missionaries comprised 5 percent of the Italian population, while Italians who worked full time in agriculture were less than 5 percent. The so-called nonactive population included 13 rentiers and pensioners, 354 homemakers, and 147 students. *Censimento 1913*.

27. Lechenperg was probably overstating his point; white shopkeepers who served African customers were not unique to Eritrea. Still, his reaction remains significant.

28. I am taking the demographic data from De Angelis (1921), who is apparently more precise than Martini (1913).

29. The government prohibited military and colonial officers from cohabiting with local women but otherwise did not prevent them from keeping African mistresses (Sòrgoni 1998; Barrera 2002).

30. One of the few expressions of fear by Italian settlers that I found is a petition by worker Giovanni Festa to the king. Festa complained that—in his opinion—the colonial government offered more job opportunities to Africans than to Italians, and raised the specter of an Eritrean uprising. Whether Festa's expression of fear was sincere or instrumental, it is meaningful that it came from a poor white, who was in direct economic competition with Eritrean workers. Festa to Re d'Italia, Asmara, June 11, 1905, ASDMAE, *ASMAI*, 35, b. F2, f. "Festa Giovanni."

31. In 1917, for instance, an Eritrean was condemned for insult and battery against an Italian woman. The incident does not seem to have caused any special reaction in the Italian community. Commissariato Reg.le dello Hamasien, *Relazione annuale per il 1917*, p. 9, ASDMAE, *AE*, b. 828, f. "Relazioni Commissariati," sf. "Hamasien." In 1922, a civil servant, Riccardo Facchini, "repeatedly hit with a stick and kicked Salem Menahim, because the latter had made indecent proposals to his wife." Once again, no special reactions among the Italian general public were reported. CCRR, *Relazioni giornaliere dei reati ed avvenimenti, degli arresti eseguiti dall'Arma e delle consegne e costituzioni all'Arma stessa*, Asmara, June 13, 1922, no. 321/6, ibid., b. 906.

32. Kennedy has thoroughly discussed in his book how fear of the Africans shaped settlers' culture in Kenya and Rhodesia. On fear among white settlers in Algeria, see Nora (1961: 170–74).

33. For instance, an Italian who toured the colony in 1913 commented, "I do not think that any Italian region is safer than Eritrea" (Stanga 1913: 89; see also 38, 90, and 91).

34. Federzoni to Mussolini, Nov. 24, 1926, Archivio centrale dello Stato (hereafter ACS), *Segreteria Particolare del Duce—Carteggio Riservato,* b. 23, f. 224 "SE Federzoni Luigi (colonie, affari generali)."

35. Cagnassi (Commissario Akele Guzai) to Governo Asmara, Adi Caieh, July 12, 1912, no. 301, ASDMAE, *AE,* b. 9, f. "Agresti Oscar."

36. Compagnia dei Carabinieri reali to Direzione affari civili, Asmara, May 3, 1912, no. 257/2, ASDMAE, *AE,* b. 9, f. "Agresti Oscar."

37. G. Mucci, draft report on the 1897 activities of the Keren court *(Tribunale di arbitrato),* ASDMAE, *AE,* b. 189, f. "Commissariato regionale di Cheren."

38. On Zoli's aggressive racial policy, see Zoli to Min. Colonie, June 30, 1930, no. 272, ASDMAE, *ASMAI,* 35/5, f. 18.

39. Salvago Raggi to Min. degli esteri, Asmara, June 8, 1911, ASDMAE, *ASMAI,* 11/8, f. 73. Salvago Raggi's report has also been published, with some modifications, in Ministero affari esteri, Servizio storico e documentazione, Ufficio studi (1977: 91–92). See also, for instance, economist Paoli, who argued that Italian workers in the colony damaged Italian prestige (Paoli 1908: 95–97). Similar concerns were widespread in other colonies as well. See, for example, Vellut (1982: 97–98) and Stoler (1989: 150–51).

40. Before Adwa, the state and a Catholic organization sponsored the settlement of some landless peasants in Eritrea, but such schemes miserably failed (Rainero 1960). On the measures taken by the colonial state to limit proletarian migration to the colony in the pre-Adwa years, see Labanca (1993: 155–57). For the Martini years, see the *Decreto governatoriale* (hereafter DG), Feb. 22, 1898, no. 17, *Norme atte a regolare l'emigrazione di persone in colonia* (republished in Rainero 1971: 356–57); DG Oct. 2, 1902; and DG Sept. 30, 1904, no. 310.

41. The thesis of the "demographic" nature of Italian colonialism has been very popular among both scholars and the Italian general public. For a convincing refutation of this thesis, see Labanca 1996.

42. DG Dec. 19, 1908, no. 814, "Zone del piano edilizio di Asmara." On racial segregation in Asmara, see Onnis (1956–57).

43. On Italian educational policy in Eritrea, see Tekeste (1987: 66–91) and Araia (1986).

44. In 1905, 11.6 percent of the Europeans older than twenty and 19.3 percent of those between seven and twenty years old were illiterate (Martini 1913: 47).

45. Martini was not the only one to have such ideas about African education. For example, prominent colonial official Alessandro Allori shared Martini's scorn for Catholic schools, and he suggested that it was probably better not to educate Eritreans at all "in order not to estrange them." Allori, *Relazione (ed allegati alla stessa) del commissario regionale di Asmara,* May 20, 1899, ASDMAE, *AE,* b. 1.028, f. "Commissariato Hamasien."

46. According to the apostolic vicar Camillo Carrara, Eritreans were "really craving for learning" *(una vera smania d'imparare).* Carrara, *Rapporto generale,* Asmara, Sept. 25, 1913, Archivio Generale dei Cappuccini (Roma), H/42/II. See also the letter of grievances addressed by a group of Eritreans residing in Addis Ababa, "Gli umili eritrei" (the humble Eritreans) to Mussolini, Mar. 20, 1927, ASDMAE, *ASMAI,* 35/4, f. 14. Oral interviews also confirm that Eritreans deeply resented being denied access to education. See also Taddia 1996.

47. The only Eritreans who were able to attain higher education were those who attended the Lutheran missionary school and those who attended the Catholic seminary.

48. The *Ordinamento giudiziario per l'Eritrea* (Eritrean judiciary law), R.D. Feb. 9, 1902, no. 51, art. 1, considered "assimilated to the European . . . Egyptians, Syrians, Americans, Australians, and in general anyone who belongs to a European stock or to a stock that has a civilization similar to the European." However, the 1908 judiciary law (R.D. July 2, 1908, no. 325) classified as "assimilated to the colonial subject," "the foreigner who belongs to a population that does not have the same degree of civilization as the European" (art. 2). A later gubernatorial decree (DG Oct. 8, 1908, no. 787) made it clear that "Arabs, Egyptians and Indians" had to be considered "assimilated to subjects." We know that a group of Jews from Aden and Yemen protested against such a norm. See *Promemoria* (no date, but May 1911) by "Gli israeliti dimoranti in Asmara," ASDMAE, *ASMAI,* 11/11, f. 130. For a contemporary Italian critique of such a norm, see Conte, memoir, Asmara, May 1911, ASDMAE, *ASMAI,* 11/8, f. 80. For a juridical study on citizenship and subject status under Italian colonialism, see Capuzzo (1995).

49. See, for example, Direzione Generale Affari Politici to Ufficio Militare, Nov. 6, 1933, no. 485, which reports a censored letter from an *ascaro* who had deserted and fled to Ethiopia, and who commented that although in Ethiopia an Abyssinian could become an officer, in Eritrea he could not. ASDMAE, *ASMAI,* 35/5, f. 18.

50. Governor Riccardo Astuto to Min. Colonie, Jan. 13, 1931, no. 194, ASDMAE, *ASMAI,* 35/5, f. 18. Moreno (director general of the Direzione generale affari politici, Ministero Africa italiana), *Promemoria per il sottosegretario di Stato,* Rome, June 3, 1939, ASDMAE, *ASMAI, Direzione generale affari politici,* b. 91, f. 288. Moreno to Ufficio militare, Rome, Sept. 21, 1940, no. 316640, ASDMAE, *ASMAI, Gab.,* b. 68, f. "Nominativi vari."

51. Actually, during the early days of Italian colonialism, Eritreans could reach a rank *(jubasci)* equivalent that of an Italian lieutenant. But Baratieri reformed the organization of colonial troops and reduced the *jubasci* to the rank of a NCO (Scardigli 1996: 81, 112–13).

52. Baratieri to Min. Esteri, Dec. 3, 1892, no. 13/237, ASDMAE, *AE* b. 52, f. "Questioni indigene: Ufficiali reduci dall'Equatoria." Also ASDMAE, *ASMAI,* 11/9, f. 101.

53. The Eritrean judiciary regulation (*Regolamento giudiziario per l'Eritrea,* DG July 11, 1908, no. 756) stated that "the native policeman, when dealing with Europeans, has never the status of a *pubblico ufficiale,* and cannot arrest a European" (art. 231). According to the 1902 judiciary law (R.D. Feb. 9, 1902, no. 51, art. 38), Eritreans could testify against Europeans only in special cases. The 1908 judiciary regu-

lation (DG July 11, 1908, no. 756, art. 65) gave wider decision-making power to judges on this point. On the Eritrean codes' provisions on this matter, see Sagù (1986: 594).

54. Comandante Regio Corpo Truppe Coloniali to Min. Guerra, Apr. 29, 1915, ASDMAE, *ASMAI,* 11/11, f. 136.

55. There were also other reasons: If African sentinels were not granted the status of *pubblici ufficiali,* then the army had to use only white sentinels, which in fact ultimately happened. Min. Guerra to Colonie, July 12, 1916, no. 11515, and Agnesa to De Martino, Nov. 17, 1916, ASDMAE, *ASMAI,* 11/11, f. 136.

56. The committee was composed of Director of Civil Affairs Alessandro Allori, Judge Adalgiso Ravizza, *Procuratore del re* (Public Prosecutor) Michele Libonati, and the state attorney Ugo Bozzini. Cerrina Feroni to Min. Colonie, Apr. 19, 1916, no. 3112/415, ASDMAE, *ASMAI,* 11/11, f. 136.

57. Cerrina Feroni to Min. Colonie, Apr. 19, 1916, no. 3112/415, ASDMAE, *ASMAI,* 11/11, f. 136.

58. In 1920, Eritrea's *procuratore del re* (public prosecutor) raised once again the issue of the status of Eritrean *ascari* and *zaptiè,* who were used to perform police services. The *procuratore* exposed the fact that some Europeans insulted and harassed Eritrean servicemen for no reason. Since the Eritreans were not *pubblici ufficiali,* he could not prosecute the offenders without the victim needing to report the offense (*"procedere d'ufficio"*). In order to "protect the principle of authority," the *procuratore* suggested the issuing of a decree that, without granting the status of *pubblici ufficiali* to Eritreans, made it possible to prosecute Europeans who harassed Eritreans engaged in public services without requiring an official complaint. To my knowledge, the *procuratore*'s initiative had no effect. Procuratore del re to Reggente di governo, May 6, 1920, no. 332, ASDMAE, *AE,* b. 877, f. 20, "Reati commessi in danno di militari indigeni addetti a pubblici servizi: Proposta del procuratore del re."

59. For a discussion of the relations between white settlers and the colonial state in the British empire, see the seminal studies by Berman and Lonsdale (1992) and by Berman (1990); see also Robinson (1990) and, for the Algerian case, Prochaska (1990).

60. Martini (1913: 167–68), also published in Goglia-Grassi (1981: 125–26). Martini in his diary also described other types of Italian abuses, such as those perpetrated by Italian contractors who promised a certain pay to Eritrean workers and then refused to pay it, or those committed by some colonists "whose special industry is to swindle the natives (Mazè, Bentivoglio, Berinetti, etc.) or to fleece them with usury (Capucci, etc.)" (Martini 1946: vol. 2, pp. 537, 554).

61. Del Boca (1976: vol. 1, p. 752). On the military's mischief, see also Martini (1946: vol. 1, pp. 37, 89, 126, 130, 178, 181, 257; vol. 2, p. 539). On Martini's rocky relations with the military, see Aquarone (1989: 161–254). After Martini's cleaning up, things seem to have improved markedly. In later periods, we have only occasional news of military abuses against Eritreans (both civilian and military). Comando RCTC, *Relazione III trimestre 1929,* ACS, *Ministero dell'Africa Italiana, Archivio Segreto,* b. 1, f. 2/2.

62. Martini (1946: vol. 1, pp. 21–22). Eritrea at the time was divided into ad-

ministrative districts called *commissariati* and *residenze,* headed respectively by *commissari* and *residenti.*

63. On Bianco's expulsion see Andreini *(Comandante Compagnia Carabinieri Reali)* to Governo colonia, Nov. 4, 1906, no. 2945, ASDMAE, *AE,* b. 477, f. "1906, IX, PS, 27 Esercizi pubblici, 28 Sfratti dalla colonia, 29 Meretricio." In the colonial archives there are several files regarding the expulsions of Italians from the colony; see for instance ASDMAE, *AE,* b. 680 (for expulsions in 1917); b. 951 (for expulsions in 1924); ACS, *Ministero dell'Interno, Direzione Generale Pubblica Sicurezza, Divisione Polizia Giudiziaria,* 1913–15, b. 6, f. 10900.3 "Colonia Eritrea, Benadir, Somalia." In the 1930s, news regarding Italians expelled from Eritrea was reported in the *Notiziario politico Eritrea-Etiopia;* see ASDMAI, *ASMAI,* 35/2, f. 6 and 35/2, f. 31. The expulsion of "demimondaines and rogues" *(donnine galanti e fior di mascalzoni)* from the colony in Martini's times is also mentioned by Paoli (1908: 98–99).

64. I am not sure I have correctly interpreted his signature.

65. Ingegnere capo A. Signorini (Ufficio speciale per le costruzioni ferroviarie), to Governo colonia, Oct. 13, 1914, ACS, *Ministero dell'Africa italiana, Governo dell'Eritrea* (hereafter *MAI, GE*), b. 1250, f. 3931 "Corti Vincenzo."

66. My analysis of criminality in Eritrea is based on the following sources. For 1902–5: Andreini, *Copia di relazione sulla pubblica sicurezza—anni 1902, 1903, 1904, 1905—della Compagnia Carabinieri Reali diretta al Governo della Colonia,* Jan 25, 1906, no. 296/3; ASDMAE, *AE,* b. 41; Falcone (1913: 3). For 1907, 1920, and 1922: Carabinieri's daily reports (Compagnia Carabinieri Reali di Asmara, *Relazione giornaliera dei reati ed avvenimenti, degli arresti eseguiti dall'Arma e delle consegne e costituzioni all'Arma stessa*) in ASDMAE, *AE,* b. 495, f. "IX PS 23 Rapportini"; b. 877, f. "Reati e contravvenzioni (Dir. AA.Civili, pratica 20/1920)"; b. 906, file without title. For 1924–25 and 1927: incomplete collection of extended reports on different crimes in ASDMAE, *AE,* b. 951, files without title; b. 979, files without title.

67. In addition to the sources that I have already mentioned, see also a 1927 telegram by Governor Gasparini, who stated that "in the past five years there hasn't been the slightest incident against Italians." Gasparini to Federzoni, Dec. 20, 1927, no. 17363, ASDMAE, *ASMAI,* 35/4, f. 13, sf. "Incidente di Cheren: Ferimento Brigadiere carabinieri reali."

68. De Camillis *(Reggente del Governo),* Circular letter May 7, 1920, in "Disposizioni di servizio e variazioni nel personale dipendente," supplement to *Bullettino ufficiale della Colonia Eritrea,* no. 8–9, Apr. 30–May 15, 1920.

69. De Camillis to Min. Colonie, Sept. 24, 1920, no. 8565, ASDMAE, *ASMAI,* 35/4, f. 13, sf. "Circa offese e violenze di taluni europei verso indigeni." We do not know whether settlers' violence against Eritreans was unusually high in 1919–20. However, we do know that De Camillis was possibly the most enlightened ruler that colonial Eritrea had. One can suspect, then, that in 1920 it was the governmental reaction that was unusually energetic rather than the colonists' behavior that was unusually aggressive.

70. On the notion of "white prestige" in a colonial situation see Kennedy (1987: 153–54).

71. Browsing colonial police files, I have found several clues that support such a hypothesis. See, for example, the reports regarding Ignazio Giacalone, Michele Lac-

cetti, and Sebastiano Rizza, in ASDMAE, *AE,* b. 979; and a telegram draft, no author (Corsi?), to Commissario Saganeiti, Asmara, Nov. 25, 1904, regarding the assault by Ferdinando Dastola against Amlesù, ACS, *MAI, GE,* b. 1315, f. 5308 "Dastola Ferdinando."

72. Cerrina Feroni to Min. Colonie, Mar. 1, 1923, no. 1859, and May 29, 1923, no. 4547, ASDMAE, *ASMAI,* 35/4, f. 13, sf. "Ricorso Zelinotti Aristide contro Abdalla Agos servo del Comm. Riccardi."

73. Cerrina Feroni to Min. Colonie, May 29, 1923, no. 4547, ASDMAE, *ASMAI,* 35/4, f. 13, sf. "Ricorso Zelinotti Aristide contro Abdalla Agos servo del Comm. Riccardi." To the governor's honor, I should say that he did not seem pleased by the court decision.

74. On Martini's efforts to gain autonomy from the burdensome bureaucratic control of the metropole, see Aquarone (1989: 161–254).

75. Taddia (1988: 53). See also Goglia's review of Taddia's book (Goglia 1991).

76. Here I am oversimplifying a very complex matter. In Italy as well not all of the controversies between the public administration and individuals were decided by ordinary judges. Laws regarding administrative justice in the colony changed several times from 1894 on. Only in the 1930s did administrative justice in the colony start to provide individuals (citizens and subjects) with guarantees similar—but still inferior—to the ones enjoyed by Italians at home. See Capuzzo (1996).

77. Salvago Raggi was very open in this regard in his memoirs (1968: 464). On the tormented vicissitudes of the Eritrean codes, see Sagù (1986).

78. Ironically, Italians in Eritrea could participate in a consultative—but not elective—body in Massawa when the colony was under an authoritarian governor like General Baratieri (1892–96). Under his more enlightened successor, Governor Martini, this council was abolished because of the conflicts between the committee and the governor. See Dir. Gen. Africa orientale, Ufficio II Affari civili, *Sull' istituzione dei municipi in Eritrea ed in Somalia,* no date, but early 1930s, ASDMAE, *ASMAI,* 180/17/49.

79. Martini 1946: vol. 2, p. 103, Mar. 25, 1900.

80. Commissione d'inchiesta sulla colonia Eritrea (1891: 96). Future governor Martini was one of the committee's members.

81. On the settlers' protest against Salvago Raggi, there is a rich documentation in ASDMAE, *ASMAI,* 11/7, file 71, and 11/8, files 73–87. See also Atti parlamentari, *Camera dei deputati,* Legislatura XXIII, I sessione, *Discussioni,* II tornata, 3 luglio 1911, pp. 16702–15.

82. Salvago Raggi to Min. affari esteri, May 25, 1911, no. 6806; see also Salvago Raggi to di San Giuliano, July 30, 1911, respectively in ASDMAE, *ASMAI,* 11/7, file 71, and 11/8, file 76. The governor was not the only one to have such an opinion of the settlers. In 1908, the *commissario* of Hamasien Teodorani described the settlers as "rude, mean, greedy, unfair, and ignorant" *(rozzi, gretti, avidi, ingiusti e ignoranti).* Teodorani to Salvago Raggi, *Le condizioni politico-amministrative.* See also Ostini, Valenti, and Stanga (1913: 54) and Garaviglia to Ascani, Agordat, June 12, 1911, ASDMAE, *ASMAI,* 11/8, f. 84.

83. R.D. Jan. 5, 1911, no. 18.

84. Ernesto Conte, memoir, Asmara, May 1911, pp. 8 and 49, ASDMAE, *ASMAI,* 11/8, f. 80.

85. Salvago Raggi to Min. affari esteri, June 22, 1908, ASDMAE, *ASMAI,* 12/12, f. 105.

86. Apparently, a major source of conflict between Bruna and the settlers had been the city plan for Adi Cahie (the capital of Acchelè Guzai). Italian settlers had set up a Comitato di agitazione permanente contro il cavalier Bruna (Committee of permanent opposition against Cavalier Bruna). See Gregoraci to Agnesa, Nov. 26, 1912, ASDMAE, *ASMAI,* 12/12, f. 105. On the Bruna case, see also Salvago Raggi to di San Giuliano, July 30, 1911, pp. 24–26, ASDMAE, *ASMAI,* 11/8, f. 76; and Atti parlamentari, *Camera dei deputati,* Legislatura XXIII, I sessione, *Discussioni,* II tornata, 3 luglio 1911, p. 16707 (Riccio).

WORKS CITED

Aquarone, Alberto. 1989. *Dopo Adua: politica e amministrazione coloniale,* ed. Ludovica de Courten. Roma: Ufficio centrale per i beni archivistici.

Araia, Tseggai. 1986. "Historical Analysis of Infrastructural Development in Italian Eritrea: 1885–1941." *Journal of Eritrean Studies* 1, no. 1 (1986): 19–33 and 1, no. 2 (1987): 10–26.

Astuto, Riccardo. 1940. "Gerarchia di razza o reciprocità egualitaria penale?" *Il Diritto razzista* 2, nos. 5–6: 170–90.

Atti del secondo congresso degli italiani all'estero (11–20 giugno 1911), vol. 2. Roma: Istituto coloniale italiano, [1911?].

Barrera, Giulia. 1996. "Dangerous Liaisons: Colonial Concubinage in Eritrea (1890–1941)." PAS Working Papers 1, Northwestern University, Program of African Studies, Evanston, Ill.

———. 2002. "Colonial Affairs: Italian Men, Eritrean Women, and the Construction of Racial Hierarchies in Colonial Eritrea (1885–1941)." Ph.D. diss., Northwestern University, Department of History.

Bartolommei-Gioli, Gino, and Michele Checchi. 1913. "La colonizzazione dell'Eritrea." In *L'Eritrea economica: Prima serie di conferenze tenute in Firenze sotto gli auspici della Società di studi geografici e coloniali, da Ferdinando Martini, Olindo Martinelli, Carlo Conti-Rossini, Attilio Mori [et al.],* 375–418. Novara-Roma: Istituto geografico De Agostini.

Battaglia, Roberto. 1958. *La prima guerra d'Africa.* Torino: Einaudi.

Berman, Bruce. 1990. *Control and Crisis in Colonial Kenya: The Dialectic of Domination.* London: James Currey; Nairobi: Heinemann Kenya; Athens: Ohio University Press.

Berman, Bruce, and John Lonsdale. 1992. "Crises of Accumulation, Coercion and the Colonial State." In Berman and Lonsdale, *Unhappy Valley: Conflict in Kenya and Africa,* 101–26. London: James Currey; Nairobi: Heinemann Kenya; Athens: Ohio University Press.

Bernardini, Gene. 1977. "The Origins and Development of Racial Anti-Semitism in Fascist Italy." *Journal of Modern History* 49: 431–53.

Campassi, Gabriella. 1987. "Il madamato in Africa Orientale: Relazioni tra italiani e indigene come forma di aggressione coloniale." Studi di storia delle esplorazioni, no. 21, in *Miscellanea di storia delle esplorazioni* 12: 219–60.

Capuzzo, Ester. 1995. "Sudditanza e cittadinanza nell'esperienza coloniale italiana nell'età liberale." *Clio* 31: 65–95.

———. 1996. "Sulla giustizia amministrativa nelle colonie italiane." *Clio* 32: 233–50.

Castellano, Vittorio. 1948a. "Considerazioni su alcuni fenomeni demografici della popolazione italiana dell'Eritrea dal 1882 al 1923." *Rivista italiana di demografia e statistica* 3: 386–417.

———. 1948b. "La popolazione italiana dell'Eritrea dal 1924 al 1940." *Rivista italiana di demografia e statistica* 2, no. 4: 530–40.

"Censimento 1913: Popolazione italiana ed assimilata." *Bullettino Ufficiale* 15, no. 23 (Dec. 1923).

Centro Furio Jesi, ed. 1994. *La menzogna della razza: documenti e immagini del razzismo e dell'antisemitismo fascista.* Bologna: Grafis.

Ciampi, Gabriele. 1995. "La popolazione dell'Eritrea." *Bollettino della Società geografica italiana,* series 11, vol. 12: 487–524.

Commissione d'inchiesta sulla colonia Eritrea. 1891. *Relazione generale della R. Commissione d'inchiesta sulla colonia Eritrea.* Roma: Tip. delle Mantellate.

Dainelli, Giotto. 1929. "The Italian Colonies." *Geographical Review* 29: 404–19.

De Angelis, Francesco. 1921. "Il Censimento del 1913 della popolazione italiana ed assimilata nella Colonia Eritrea." *L'Africa Italiana: Bollettino della Società Africana d'Italia* 40: 65–73.

Del Boca, Angelo. 1976–1984. *Gli italiani in Africa orientale.* 4 vols. Roma-Bari: Laterza.

Dore, Giovanni. 1983. "Guerra d'Etiopia e ideologia coloniale nella testimonianza orale di reduci sardi." *Movimento operaio e socialista:* 475–87.

Doumanis, Nicholas. 1997. *Myth and Memory in the Mediterranean: Remembering Fascism's Empire.* Houndmills and London: MacMillan; New York: St. Martin's Press.

Duggan, Christopher. 1994. *A Concise History of Italy.* Cambridge: Cambridge University Press.

Falcone, Ranieri. 1913. "L'amministrazione della giustizia nella colonia Eritrea: Resoconto letto nel dì 23 gennaio 1905 dal procuratore del re cav. Ranieri Falcone all'assemblea generale del Tribunale d'appello sedente in Asmara." In Ferdinando Martini, *Relazione sulla Colonia Eritrea del R. Commissario civile deputato Ferdinando Martini, per gli esercizi 1902–907, presentata dal ministro delle colonie (Bertolini) nella seduta del 14 giugno 1913,* 309–24. Atti parlamentari, Legislatura XXIII, Sessione 1909–13, Camera dei Deputati, Roma.

Fredrickson, George M. 1981. *White Supremacy: A Comparative Study in American and South African History.* New York and Oxford: Oxford University Press.

Fuller, Mia. 2000. "Blame, Innocence, and Agency in the Historiography of Italian Colonialism." Paper delivered at the 114th Meeting of the American Historical Association, Chicago, Ill., January 2000.

Gabelli, Ottone. 1936. "Le vicende della colonizzazione italiana in Eritrea e in Somalia." In *L'Affrica orientale italiana e il conflitto italo-etiopico,* 113–26. Studi e documenti raccolti e ordinati da Tomaso Sillani. Roma: La rassegna italiana.

Gabrielli, Gianluca. 1996. "La persecuzione delle 'unioni miste' (1937–1940) nei testi delle sentenze pubblicate e nel dibattito giuridico." *Studi piacentini* 20: 83–140.

————. 1997. "Un aspetto della politica razzista nell'impero: il 'problema dei me-ticci.'" *Passato e presente* 15, no. 41: 77–105.

Goglia, Luigi. 1988. "Note sul razzismo coloniale fascista." *Storia contemporanea* 19: 1223–66.

————. 1991. Review of Irma Taddia, *La memoria dell'impero: Autobiografie d'Africa orientale.* In *Africa* 46: 146–48.

Goglia, Luigi, and Fabio Grassi. 1981. *Il colonialismo italiano da Adua all'impero.* Roma-Bari: Laterza.

Guerrini, Irene. 1990. "Esotismo, conquista coloniale ed introspezione personale nel diario di un marinaio di leva." *Materiali di lavoro* 8, nos. 1–2: 117–23.

Iyob, Ruth. 2000. "Madamismo and Beyond: The Construction of Eritrean Women." *Nineteenth-Century Contexts* 22: 217–38.

Jordan Gebre-Medhin. 1989. *Peasants and Nationalism in Eritrea: A Critic of Ethiopian Studies.* Lawrenceville, N.J.: Red Sea Press.

Kennedy, Dane. 1987. *Islands of White: Settler Society and Culture in Kenya and Southern Rhodesia, 1890–1939.* Durham, N.C.: Duke University Press.

Killion, Thomas C. 1985. "Workers, Capital and the State in the Ethiopian Region, 1919–1974." Ph.D. diss., Stanford University.

Labanca, Nicola. 1990. "Coscritti in colonia: Appunti in tema di percezione dell'Africa e scrittura popolare." *Materiali di lavoro* 8, nos. 1–2: 93–115.

————. 1991. "Ferdinando Martini in Eritrea, 1897–1907: Per il riesame di un mito del colonialismo italiano." *Farestoria* 10, no. 17: 26–42.

————. 1993. *In marcia verso Adua: Esercito, politica e società alle origini dell'imperialismo coloniale italiano.* Torino: Einaudi.

————. 1996. "L'imperialismo coloniale dell'ultima delle grandi potenze: Una rassegna di studi e problemi." *Africa e Mediterraneo* 2: 4–17.

————. 1997. "Italiani d'Africa." In *Adua: le ragioni di una sconfitta,* ed. A. Del Boca, 193–230. Roma-Bari: Laterza.

Le Houérou, Fabienne. 1994. *L'épopée des soldats de Mussolini en Abyssinie, 1936–1938. Les "ensublés." Préface de Pierre Milza.* Paris: L'Harmattan.

Lechenperg, Harold P. 1935. "With the Italians in Eritrea." *National Geographic Magazine* 68, no. 3 (Sept.): 265–96.

Markakis, John. 1989. *National and Class Conflict in the Horn of Africa.* Cambridge: Cambridge University Press.

Martini, Ferdinando. 1913. *Relazione sulla Colonia Eritrea del R. Commissario civile deputato Ferdinando Martini, per gli esercizi 1902–907, presentata dal ministro delle colonie (Bertolini) nella seduta del 14 giugno 1913.* Atti parlamentari, Legislatura XXIII, Sessione 1909–13, Camera dei Deputati, Roma.

————. 1946. *Diario eritreo.* Firenze: n.p.

Mauro da Leonessa. 1937. "I diritti degli italo-eritrei." *Rivista giuridica del Medio ed Estremo Oriente e giustizia coloniale* 2: 35–40.

Mignemi, Adolfo, ed. 1984. *Immagine coordinata per un impero: Etiopia, 1935–1936.* Torino: Forma.

Ministero affari esteri, Servizio storico e documentazione, Ufficio studi. 1977. *Giuseppe Salvago Raggi.* Roma.

Murtaza, Niaz. 1998. *The Pillage of Sustainability in Eritrea, 1600s-1900s: Rural Com-*

munities and the Creeping Shadows of Hegemony. Westport, Conn., and London: Greenwood Press.

Nadel, Siegfried F. 1946. "Land tenure on the Eritrean Plateau." *Africa* 26: 1–22, 99–109.

Nora, Pierre. 1961. *Les Français d'Algerie.* Paris: Julliard.

O'Donnell, Krista. 1999. "Poisonous Women: Sexual Danger, Illicit Violence, and Domestic Work in German Southern Africa, 1904–1915." *Journal of Women's History* 11, no. 3: 31–54.

Onnis, Eleonora. 1956–57. "La città di Asmara." Thesis, Università degli studi di Padova, Facoltà di Magistero.

Ostini, Giuseppe. 1907. "Gli italiani all'Eritrea e gli inglesi in Egitto." *Rivista coloniale* 2, no. 4: 340–47.

Pankhurst, Richard. 1969. "Fascist Racial Policies in Ethiopia, 1922–1941." *Ethiopia Observer* 12, no. 4: 270–85.

Paoli, Renato. 1908. *Nella colonia Eritrea. Studi e viaggi. Con in fine il discorso di Ferdinando Martini tenuto alla Camera dei Deputati il 15 febbraio 1908. Illustrato da 18 fototipie.* Milano: Fratelli Treves.

Pateman, Roy. 1990. *Eritrea: Even the Stones are Burning. New and Revised Edition.* Lawrenceville, N.J., and Asmara: Red Sea Press.

Prochaska, David. 1990. *Making Algeria French: Colonialism in Bône.* Cambridge: Cambridge University Press; Paris: Editions de la Maisons des Sciences de l'Homme.

Rainero, Romain. 1960. *I primi tentativi di colonizzazione agraria e di popolamento in Eritrea, 1890–1895.* Milano: Marzorati.

———. 1971. *L'anticolonialismo italiano da Assab ad Adua (1869–1896).* Milano: Edizioni di Comunità.

Ranger, Terence O. 1983. "The Invention of Tradition in Africa." In Eric Hobsbawm and Terence O. Ranger, *The Invention of Tradition.* Cambridge: Cambridge University Press.

Robinson, Ronald. "British Imperialism: The Colonial Office and the Settler in East-Central Africa, 1919–63." In *Italia e Inghilterra nell'età dell'imperialismo,* ed. E. Serra and C. Seton-Watson, 195–212. Milano: Angeli, 1990.

Sagù, Maria Letizia. 1986. "Sui tentativi di codificazione della colonia Eritrea." *Clio* 22: 567–616.

Salvago Raggi, Giuseppe. 1968. "Memorie dell'Ambasciatore Giuseppe Salvago Raggi." In Glauco Licata, *Notabili della terza Italia,* 211–592. Roma: Edizioni Cinque Lune.

Sbacchi, Alberto. *Ethiopia under Mussolini: Fascism and the Colonial Experience.* London: Zed, 1985.

Scardigli, Marco. 1996. *Il braccio indigeno: Ascari, irregolari e bande nella conquista dell'Eritrea, 1885–1911.* Milano: Angeli.

Sòrgoni, Barbara. 1998. *Parole e corpi: Antropologia, discorso giuridico e politiche sessuali interrazziali nella colonia Eritrea (1890–1941).* Napoli: Liguori.

Stanga, Idelfonso. 1913. *Una gita in Eritrea.* Milano: Cogliati.

Steinberg, Jonathan. 1990. *All or Nothing: The Axis and the Holocaust.* London and New York: Routledge.

Stoler, Ann L. 1991. "Carnal Knowledge and Imperial Power: Gender, Race, and Morality in Colonial Asia." In *Gender at the Crossroads of Knowledge: Feminist Anthro-*

pology in the Postmodern Era, ed. Micaela di Leonardo, 51–101. Berkeley: University of California Press.

Stoler, Ann Laura. 1989. "Rethinking Colonial Categories: European Communities and the Boundaries of Rule." *Comparative Studies in Society and History* 31: 134–61.

Taddia, Irma. 1986. *L'Eritrea colonia (1890–1952): Paesaggi, strutture, uomini del colonialismo.* Milano: Angeli.

———. 1988. *La memoria dell'impero: Autobiografie d'Africa orientale.* Manduria: Lacaita.

———. 1996. *Autobiografie africane: Il colonialismo nelle memorie orali.* Milano: Angeli.

Tekeste Negash. 1986. *No Medicine for the Bite of a White Snake: Notes on Nationalism and Resistance in Eritrea, 1890–1940.* Uppsala: Uppsala University Press.

———. 1987. *Italian Colonialism in Eritrea, 1882–1941: Policies, Praxis and Impact,* Uppsala: Uppsala University.

Trevaskis, G. Kennedy N. 1960. *Eritrea: A Colony in Transition: 1941–52.* London: Oxford University Press.

Tronvoll, Kjetil. 1998. *Mai Weini: A Highland Village in Eritrea. A Study of the People, Their Livelihood, and Land Tenure during Times of Turbulence.* Lawrenceville, N.J.: Red Sea Press.

Valenti, Ghino. 1913. "Introduzione: Le cause politiche ed economiche dello stato attuale." In Angelo Omodeo, Vittorio Peglion, and Ghino Valenti, *La colonia Eritrea: Condizioni e problemi,* vol. 1, 9–77. Roma: Società italiana per il progresso delle scienze.

Van Onselen, Charles. 1982. "The Witches of Suburbia." In Van Onselen, *Studies in the Social and Economic History of the Witwatersrand, 1886–1914,* vol. 2: *New Nineveh,* 1–73. Johannesburg: Ravan Press.

Vellut, Jean-Luc. "Matériau pour une image du Blanc dans la société coloniale du Congo Belge." In *Stéréotypes nationaux et préjuges raciaux aux XIXe et XXe siècles: Sources et méthodes por une approche historique,* ed. Jean Pirotte, 91–116. Louvain-la-Neuve: Collège Erasme, Bureau de Recaueil; Louven: Editions Nauwelaerts, 1982.

Yemane Mesghenna. 1988. *Italian Colonialism: A Case Study of Eritrea, 1869–1934: Motive, Praxis and Result.* Lund, Sweden: [University of Lund].

PART II

Colonial Literature

From Exploration to a Domestic Empire

Gifts, Sex, and Guns

Nineteenth-Century Italian Explorers in Africa

Cristina Lombardi-Diop

The exchange of commodities evolves originally not within primitive communities, but on their margins, on their borders, the few points where they come into contact with other communities. This is where barter begins and moves thence into the interior of the community, exerting a disintegrating influence upon it.
KARL MARX, *A Contribution to the Critique of Political Economy*, 1859

GIFTS AND COMMODITIES: CARLO PIAGGIA AMONG THE AZANDE

In 1857, while Karl Marx was meditating on the development of the commodity form within precapitalist societies, the Italian explorer Carlo Piaggia reached Khartoum for the first time to join an expedition along the White Nile. Khartoum was at the time an important commercial center, a place of exchange and the point of departure for all the expeditions headed to equatorial Africa. Many of the commercial expeditions along the Nile utilized captured slaves as a form of payment for hired soldiers or in exchange for ivory. Piaggia signed a contract with the French merchant Alfonse de Malzach and experienced—unwillingly and with utmost disgust, according to his biographers[1]—the daily brutality of the slave trade. During this expedition he collected indigenous artifacts and weapons that he donated to the Museo di Storia Naturale (Museum of Natural History) of Florence.

In 1860 Piaggia was again in Khartoum. Here he met with Giovanni Miani and Orazio Antinori[2]—two Italian explorers traveling in the Nile area—and joined the latter in an expedition to the Bahr-el-Ghazal region. In 1863 Piaggia was again traveling in the Sudan, this time with the Copt merchant Ghattas and his escort of armed soldiers. Due to the violence involved in the kidnapping and deportation of slaves, traveling along the Nile had quickly become a very dangerous enterprise. Following an exchange of shots between Ghattas's soldiers and the Bongo tribe, Piaggia made a radical decision. He got rid of his escort and established himself for almost two years among the Azande tribes, the first and only European to do so at that time. This experience is recorded in a series of notes published for the first time in their unedited version only in 1978, under the title *Nella terra dei Niam-Niam (1863–1865)*[3] (In the land of the Niam-Niam), which is the focus of the following section. During his stay with the Azande, Piaggia acquired the status of chief and relative political power. He visited various tribal chiefs while functioning as diplomatic mediator not only between his hosts, the Zande chief Tombo and his brother, but also between the Azande and the Arab slave traders. His isolation from both the Europeans and the Arabs, however, would cost him a great deal of trouble. The Arabs in particular saw Piaggia's presence among the Azande as a hindrance to their trade in the area. They thus tried more than once to compromise his good relations with his hosts. In the end, troops hired by the Ghattas company found him, surprised that he was still alive, and brought him back to Khartoum. Piaggia returned to Italy in 1865 where he tried in vain to publish his travel notes.

Piaggia's career as explorer is indeed a remarkable example of a particular nineteenth-century diasporic phenomenon that saw thousands of Italians depart for Africa in search of opportunities—a phenomenon that remains to be studied.[4] Son of a Tuscan miller, Piaggia migrated to Tunisia in the 1840s in search of employment and found a job as gardener in Egypt, where many Italian migrants settled before Italy's unification. After learning all sort of trades and skills, including embalming, bookbindery, upholstery, and weapon construction and repair, Piaggia decided to dedicate his time to hunting rare animals for shipment to Europe's zoological museums (Battaglia 1958: 16–28). In Egypt Piaggia also learned French and Arabic, while saving money to devote himself to explorations. As an "experiential narrative," Carlo Piaggia's travel memoir shares significant similarities with the writings of the British explorer Mungo Park, published at the end of the eighteenth century. According to Mary Louise Pratt, Mungo Park's *Travels in the Interior of Africa* (1799) offers a good example of how, in a colonial context, sentimental writing allowed a particular form of cultural relativism. This resulted in reciprocity of vision and perspective, one that called into question some of the common positions of imperial ideology (Pratt 1992). The adventures and writings of Carlo Piaggia, who spent most of his life exploring and hunting rare animals in the region of the High Nile, present remarkable similarities with Mungo Park's antiheroic stance. Like Mungo Park, Piaggia is a lonely figure of the colonial pioneer, isolated from the scientific and political community of his time. Like his British counterpart, Piaggia made his way into the interior of Africa alone, gradually alienating himself—both physically and culturally—from the slave traders, merchants, and official explorers with whom he had set off from Khartoum. Like Park, Piaggia negotiated his Europeanness in exchange for indigenous goods, food, shelter, and language lessons.

Piaggia's travel writings constitute a remarkable example of cultural relativism and reciprocity of perspective in Italian colonial literature. How can we explain this phenomenon without necessarily attributing this uniqueness solely to the author's intention? In other words, what can be said about this remarkable text that is not only limited to Piaggia's biography? Italian colonial historians have attributed the absence of evolutionary perspective and cultural racism in Piaggia's text to his peasant origins and lack of proper academic education. I argue, rather, that Piaggia's specific mode of exchange with African tribal cultures allowed him reciprocity of vision because it was embedded in precapitalist models of economic interaction absent in late modern colonial encounters. Piaggia and the Zande chief Tombo engaged in a system of gift exchange that did not partake of the symbolic rules produced in monetary and market economies. In order to explain how the traveler's material practices produced a specific symbolic and ideological system of meaning, I will diverge briefly from the text. I will thus inscribe my discussion within a theoretical framework that supports the shift in my argument from textual to material considerations.

Jean-Joseph Goux has argued for the legitimacy of the extension of Marx's notion of the general equivalent from the field of political economy to other domains where values are no longer economic, such as semiotics, linguistics, and psychoanalysis. In particular, he interprets the emergence of the father as the privileged subject, the phallus as a centralized object of drive, and language as a phonic signifier as a consequence of the institutionalization of the monovalent measure of commodity exchange. Monetarocentrism, Goux argues, carries along phallocentrism, logocentrism, and patricentrism. Goux traces the philosophical aspect of these particular forms of symbolizing back to the genealogy of Western metaphysics and idealism (Goux 1990).

Absent from Goux's discussion, but central to my concerns, is the question of ethnocentrism. Alongside phallocentrism, logocentrism, and patricentrism, one could argue that the logic of the general equivalent, in which "a constant value [is] to be postulated in spite of difference and an ideality [is] to be maintained throughout changes in materiality" (Goux 1990: 5), also produced Eurocentrism. In Eurocentrism, a particular geopolitical, ethnic, cultural, and racial constituency is raised to the value of universal equivalent, thus becoming a unique measure of the values of all other geopolitical localities, ethnicities, races, and cultures. Evolutionary racism posits the superiority of the white race and the exclusion of others at a moment when a particular mode of signifying is needed in order to support and justify capitalist colonial expansion. If we accept the correspondence of the mode of economic exchange with the mode of signifying exchange, we can also posit a reversal of the terms of such correspondence. Evolutionary racism is not yet present in a system of exchange, such as the one Piaggia encountered among the Azande, where there is no general equivalent. But what kind of system of exchange was established between the Italian foreigner and the Azande people?

In his famous ethnographic study of the Azande tribes, Evans-Pritchard explains that a sense of equal reciprocity structured Azande societies at the time Piaggia resided among them. "*Ru ae,* the giving of things [to a prince], ought to be balanced by *fu ae,* the giving of things [to his subjects]" (Evans-Pritchard 1971: 215). Piaggia's first encounter with Tombo is marked by gift exchange: "tutti si accamparono in quel punto aspettando che la gente della tribù ci portassero farina e galline e patate in cambi di verotterie. Di fatto al buon mattino del 15 detto arrivava da ogni parte selvaggi carichi di robba da cibarsi; questo intiero giorno si occupò in baratti" ("everybody camped on that spot while waiting for the tribesmen to bring flour, hens, and potatoes in exchange for trinkets. In fact, in the early morning of the fifteenth, savages arrived from everywhere loaded with food. That entire day was spent in bartering").[5] On another occasion, Piaggia offers copper rings while the chief Tombo offers back ivory and women. "Questa sorta di saluto è il più grande che si possa fare fra questi popoli, ed anche serve alla fedele amicizia, e che non danno a tutti, ma solo ai più grandi tra i loro capi, anche in segno di pace, in caso di guerra tra loro" ("This type of welcome is the greatest that can be offered among these peoples, and also encourages faithful friendship, but they don't give to everyone, only to the greatest among their chiefs, also as a sign of peace, in case of war among them") (TNN 104). The exchange obviously serves to establish social relations between tribal authorities and their foreign guest, soon accepted within the tribe as chief. This position entails prestige and social status but also responsibilities, bonding respect, and reciprocal dependence. Moreover, Piaggia's elevation to the status of chief serves to domesticate, incorporate, and thus neutralize, his foreignness within the Azande societal order.

As Marcel Mauss and other anthropologists have argued, the bond produced in a system of gift exchange is not wholly of an economic nature but has social, legal, and moral significance.[6] In gift exchange, "goods are not only economic commodities but vehicles and instruments for realities of another order: influence, power, sympathy, status, and emotion" (Levi-Strauss 1996: 19). Although in commodity exchange, the result is tangible and profit is direct—inherent in the objects exchanged—in gift exchange the reward is often expressed in terms of prestige, power, and privilege of position within the community in which the exchange takes place.[7] Gift exchange thus produces excess that must be accounted for socially: it creates social bonds and interdependency.[8] The immediate dialogue that takes place in this type of exchange produces tropes that embody equality of a material and cultural nature.

As Karl Marx had understood, however, the entanglement of indigenous economies with European capitalist trade and colonial occupation gradually changed the nature of gift exchange in indigenous societies,[9] producing mixed forms of exchange. Mungo Park, writing from Africa in 1799, eloquently describes how the shift from gift to monetary forms of exchange occurred: "In their early intercourse with Europeans, the article that attracted most notice was iron. Its utility, in forming the instruments of war and husbandry, made it preferable to all others; and iron soon became the measure by which the value of all other commodities was ascertained" (Park 1971: 27). This passage anticipates and strangely recalls Marx's history of the evolution of the monetary form.

According to Evans-Pritchard, the rule of reciprocity between the Zande prince and his subjects followed a specific pattern: subjects paid metal spears in fines and fees and these were returned to them as gifts or in labor performed within and outside the household by the prince's wives. Although Evans-Pritchard does not mention it, the payment of fees in the form of spears reveals that the Azande economic exchange system is not exclusively a form of barter, but approximates monetary exchange in that spears are used both as a standard measure and a real instrument of exchange. Spears, in Mauss's terms, become "concept money." In this respect, the Azande's economy confirms Marx's idea that primitive economies are never pure gift economies, but show signs of the "disintegrating influence" of commodity exchange. Among the Fijians, for instance, barter was critically modified after the 1813 arrival of Captain David Porter of the U.S. Navy. As Nicholas Thomas argues, "after Porter almost anything could be exchanged for muskets and gunpowder" (Thomas 1991: 100). Guns and ammunition thus became a form of general measure that determined the value of indigenous goods. Not by chance weaponry was, at least at the beginning, an exclusive possession of the Europeans. Similarly, as I discuss in the next section, the nature of gift exchange changed after the Italians introduced guns in their material interactions with the Ethiopians. Guns, as inalienable gifts associated with colonial power, became a form of universal equivalent in the colonial context.

Significantly, Piaggia holds tightly to the only gun he possesses. While the slave merchants of the Sudanese town of Ghattas bring cattle with them to exchange for ivory and slaves, Piaggia offers copper rings and glass beads in exchange for flour and hens. Instead of ivory or slaves, Piaggia collects birds and indigenous artifacts to be shipped to museums in Italy. He is an early "accidental ethnographer" who provided firsthand, experiential, and non-academic information about the things and people he encountered. If, as Crystal Bartolovich argues, the act of collecting indigenous things promotes a "supplementary logic" (Bartolovich 1998: 230) that has important general implications for capital, Piaggia does not participate in the colonial economy of capitalist trade. In the absence of an economy based on a general equivalent (whether guns, cattle, or money), Piaggia's encounter with the Azande does not partake of the logic of monetary capitalism and therefore of evolutionary racism, necessary corollary to capitalist colonial expansion.

The particular mechanism of exchange, between barter and gift exchange, established between the Italian traveler and his host also sheds some light on Tombo's insistence on Piaggia's acceptance of a woman. As chief, Piaggia had to return his dues to his subjects in the form of labor performed by his women and, more specifically, in the form of cooked meals. Food, which the Azande tribes often denied to ivory merchants as a way to jeopardize their survival miles away from Khartoum, is accorded to Piaggia by virtue of his unique status as foreign chief, but also because, according to the rule of reciprocity, it can be returned to the community in the form of cooked dishes prepared by Piaggia's women.

During his visits to other chiefs, the ritual of gift exchange repeats itself: "Il secondo giorno venne da me il capo detto Ingioma e li feci alcuni regali come è l'uso, e che pretendono questi capi" ("On the second day, the chief called Ingioma came to see me and I offered him a few gifts according to custom, and as requested by these chiefs") (TNN 31). In the course of this encounter with Ingioma, Piaggia asks him for tobacco and food, while refusing a gift of ivory from Tombo. As this incident reveals, the Italian traveler had immediately understood that the rules of reciprocity comprised a chain of reciprocal gifts and countergifts which, as Malinowski remarks, "in the long run balance, benefiting both sides equally" (Malinowski 1996: 15). He in fact refuses ivory from Tombo in order to avoid association with the rest of the Arab slave merchants—whom the Azande repeatedly ostracized—but nevertheless accepts the gift of a woman. "A questa sorta di regalo non potevo rinunziare, poichè volevo passare qualche anno tra loro" ("Since I wanted to spend a few years among them, I could not renounce such a gift") (TNN 104). If Piaggia needs a woman for sexual consumption, he also needs one in order to stabilize his presence among the Azande, so as to be able to reciprocate by using women as active producers of material value.

Piaggia thus accepts the gift of women—not only one, but a few—in what I interpret as his awareness of the reciprocity rule. The Italian traveler, however, cannot but infuse this act of exchange with some of the assumptions he carries with him from his own culture. On first being offered a woman, he writes: "Io pensai subito al potere che acquista un marito sopra d'una moglie in paesi liberi e di potersene disfare a suo bell'agio, ero contento assai del grato regalo, ma chiesi alla giovine se fosse restata contenta di restare con me e mi rispose con spirito franco un bel no" ("I immediately thought of the power a husband acquires over his wife in free countries, to be able to get rid of her as he wishes; I was happy about the gift, but I asked the girl if she was happy to be with me and she replied very frankly with a sound no") (TNN 39). In another remarkable episode, Piaggia spanks a woman for stealing meat. This episode enrages Tombo, who comes with spears as a sign that he seeks revenge. The Zande chief makes clear that "le sue donne non dovevano essere minacciate di bastone da bianco, e che lui poteva minacciare il bianco con la sua lancia" ("A white man could not threaten his women with a big stick, but that he could threaten the white man with his spear") (TNN 48). Reciprocity clearly works both ways. Moreover, as Tombo makes clear, Piaggia can only accept a limited number of women because he does not have enough subjects with whom to reciprocate: "in suo paese era lui il grande e . . . che io non dovevo avere molte donne, perche' non avevo uomini da fare il capo" ("He was the greatest in his country and . . . I could not have too many women, because I did not have enough subjects to be a chief" (TNN 111). As Tombo knows, too many women without enough subjects would mean a surplus of labor production that would not be absorbed by the reciprocity system, thus creating an imbalance in social relations.

Among the women Piaggia accepts as gifts is Mambia, daughter of the chief Inido. Mambia is the first of a long series of African women in colonial literature who serves to counterpoint an ideal of Italian femininity, and whose description sets the parameter for future writers:

> "Questa giovine non dimostrava più che quattordici o quindici anni; la sua altezza non meno di una donna delle più grandi d'Europa; le sue fattezze non potevano essere così regolari per quanto più potesse desiderarle il modello della beltà. Il suo colore della pelle era di un rosso scuro, liscia e gentile; pelle come d'una figura in cera. La sua vita stretta sui fianchi come se avesse vestito fasce fino da piccola. I suoi lunghi capelli accordellati, cadendo fino alle spalle. I suoi fitti e minuti denti bianchi e appuntati come sogliono sin da piccoli, davano il più leggiadro aspetto alle rosse e regolari labbra. Non altro copriva le vaghe fattezze, che un qualche anello di ferro posto alla clavicola dei piedi e ai polsi delle braccia. (TNN 51)

> [This girl looked not more than fourteen or fifteen, her height no less than that of the tallest woman in Europe. Her features could not be more regular than what could be desired by the model of beauty. The color of her skin was a dark red, smooth and gentle. She had the skin of a wax figure. Her waist was as thin at the hips, as if she had worn bands since childhood. Her long braided hair fell to her shoulders. Her thick and small white teeth, sharp since childhood, gave the most exquisite appearance to her red and even lips. Nothing covered her pleasant features but a few iron rings on her feet, ankles, and wrists.]

This ideal must be signified through images of constriction and submission, such as the imagined "bands" surrounding Mambia's waist and the real "iron ring"—reminiscent of imprisonment and slavery—around her ankles and wrists. Curiously, although Piaggia places himself outside the society of slave traders, slavery returns through the back door in his text through his representations of Azande women. Imagined in a role that denies them agency and independence, women are thus better "understood" in terms culturally familiar to the Italian traveler and his society of origins.

The above description is nevertheless challenged in Piaggia's text by social interactions in which the role of Azande women appears far more complicated and difficult to grasp. Even if Piaggia never fails to explain that women are offered to him "a titolo di saluto" ("as a welcome"), numerous details in the narrative reveal that Piaggia is actually expected to return something to their fathers in the form of "payment." This particular request contradicts the rule of reciprocity as described by Evans-Pritchard, because it establishes a form of individualized reward that transcends communal exchange and marks the passage, according to Levi-Strauss, from restricted to generalized exchange: "it is a process whereby the woman provided as a counterpart is replaced by a symbolical equivalent." [10]

A key episode, whose narration Piaggia revises twice, serves to elucidate this point. In one version, Piaggia offers Mambia a cotton skirt, we are told, as a gift. In a revised version of the same episode, it is Mambia herself—on behalf of her father—who asks for a gift "come segno che io l'avessi comprata, e come in pari tempo essa apparteneva all'uomo bianco" ("as a sign that I bought her, and at the same time that she belonged to the white man") (TNN 110). The detail of the skirt, which takes considerable space in the narrative, reveals Piaggia's symptomatic confusion vis à vis women's status as elements of exchange within Azande society and his desire to be kept outside monetary transactions. "Io gli [Mumbia's father] diedi 2 grossi anelli di rame in segno di saluto e non per la sua figlia che era sparita con la veste." ("I gave him [Mumbia's father] two large copper rings as a welcome and not for his daughter who had disappeared with the skirt") (TNN 146). The exchange of a skirt for Mambia transforms what Piaggia interprets as a symbolic exchange ("a titolo di saluto") into a real market transaction that follows less the logic of barter than the logic of trade. But unlike Mungo Park, whose language reflects his knowledge of and familiarity with the workings of capitalist trading, Piaggia is not able, or is unwilling, to interpret Mambia's father's request in terms of economic transaction, and he considers it an act of reciprocal exchange.

Yet Piaggia repeatedly revises the seemingly trivial episode of the skirt. His need to repeat and change this event reveals the traveler's uneasiness about this matter. By establishing the terms of the cohabitation between the white man and the Zande woman, this episode provides clues, and simultaneously conceals them, about the real nature of their relationship. On other occasions when the exchange of women takes place, Piaggia feels the need to emphasize repeatedly the voluntary nature, on the part of the women, of the cohabitation. Mambia, Piaggia tells us, leaves her father's house without his consent. The Italian traveler, we are told, asks Mambia's father for permission to marry her, but he refuses. Moreover, Mambia decides to live in her own hut, "già che non voleva restare in compagnia di uomini, per conservare la sua nubiltà" ("because, in order to keep her marriageable status, she did not want to be in the company of men") (TNN 57). What is then Mambia's status vis-à-vis the foreigner? And how is sexual exchange, manifestly omitted from the narrative, inscribed within this relationship?

In his otherwise astute reading, the historian Roberto Battaglia—who relies exclusively on Pellegrinetti's 1941 embellished edition of Piaggia's text—refers to Mambia as "la troppo innamorata fanciulla" ("the too enamored young girl") and transforms their relationship into an "idillio nascente" ("blooming romance") (Battaglia 1958: 22). This reading inscribes the narrative within the tradition of British sentimental literature. As Mary Louise Pratt shows, sentimental narratives fused captivity and romance in order to convey antislavery sentiments in favor of the abolitionist cause. Because Battaglia reads Piaggia's text as an antislavery text, he also inscribes romance within it. I find that, despite Piaggia's refusal to be involved with the slave merchants, the abolitionist tradition is completely absent from Piaggia's original text. Romance and antislavery rhetoric are more the result of Battaglia's good will and Pellegrinetti's manipulations than of Piaggia's writing.

In his revision of Piaggia's work, Pellegrinetti infused the narrative with the stylistic and ideological devices that fascist colonial literature had established at the time he was writing. The inscription of romance within Piaggia's narrative not only sells, in Pellegrinetti's view, but also yields a temporal and ideological displacement that is particularly productive in Italian colonial fiction in the late 1930s. The manipulation of the text by its editor in fact effects a "modernization" that reinscribes it within fascist colonial expansionist ideology. This functions according to the logic of belatedness that produces *mal d'Africa,* a form of disrupted sentimentality that extends romance to colonial relationships where there is none, and in so doing manages to sublimate the coercion and violence involved in colonial interactions. In Italian colonial production, *mal d'Africa* projects male sexual dominance over Africa and its women, who become easy prey of their fascination. As enamoured concubine, Mambia is thus no longer a partner within a reciprocal exchange between equal members, but becomes a subordinate within a transactional exchange whose logic leaves the white man complete power of negotiation. Moreover, Piaggia's own reading of the role of women in exchange—based on his own cultural background—and the particular mixed nature of the Azande economic system create an ambiguity in the text that facilitates Pellegrinetti's manipulation.

There is, however, an aspect of Piaggia's text that underscores the discourse of capital modernity and resists its co-optation. Piaggia states that the primary objective of his stay among the Azande is to dispel the myth concerning their alleged reputation as cannibals. But rather than through eloquent explanations, Piaggia prefers to leave the theme of anthropophagy conspicuously aside from this text, except for one particular episode. This appears at the very end of the narrative, in the context of a final "ethnographic" report on the behaviors and customs of the *Niam-Niam.* Here, Piaggia first declares that he has seen half-eaten corpses. He then narrates how, on one occasion, Tombo offered him a piece of meat, which he found "dolce e assai buono" ("sweet and very good") (TNN 136). It is only after eating it that he suspects it might have been human flesh. In the report, Piaggia thus uses a twofold strategy. On the one hand, he satisfies his readers' curiosity about the spicy topic of the alleged cannibalistic tendencies of his hosts; on the other, he simultaneously frustrates their expectations. He employs but at the same time violates the eye-witnessing rules that produce reliability in ethnographic reports.

As Peter Hulme states, the eyewitness is "somebody whose evidence can be accepted because they saw what happened without them being involved in what happened" (Hulme 1998: 22). Even if unaware, Piaggia participates in cannibalism, breaks the taboo, and thus renounces his authority as ethnographic eyewitness. By breaking the ultimate taboo of anthropophagy, Piaggia not only underscores European cultural superiority—which sets in cannibalism the parameter for the separation of African savageness and European civility—but also puts himself in a participatory position that undermines the objectivity of his testimony. In so doing, he also violates the cultural separation that the discourse of civility established between modern economy and preindustrial values, Europeans and savages.[11] We, Piaggia says, are the cannibals. This final statement sheds light onto the nature of gender relations in this text. European men's cannibalistic tendencies constitute in fact the basis of Piaggia's inability to understand the place of women within the Azande's social system of reciprocal economy.

As some critics have noticed, the fragmented, unedited nature of Piaggia's travel notes gives his writings an immediacy and reciprocity of perspective missing in other diaries of the period. Although Piaggia had sought the collaboration of best-seller writer Edmondo De Amicis in order to publish a revised edition of his travel notes,[12] this was never completed.[13] Despite De Amicis's opinion that "una certa ingenua rozzezza di forma accresca efficacia a questo genere di scritti"[14] ("a certain naive roughness in style enhances this kind of writings"), stylistic embellishments and fictional additions had made other exploration narratives attractive to a wider public and had contributed to the establishment of the genre. Their lack explains Piaggia's failed attempt at editorial fame in his lifetime. In their disorganized, unedited format, Piaggia's notes represent an unfinished product of the colonial encounter, that is, simple "raw material" out of which a marketable commodity might have been manufactured. But since they were left unstructured and fragmented, Piaggia's writings never managed to participate in the monetary and ideological exchange between travelers, colonial policymakers, the public, and the publishing industry. By remaining outside the monetary economy of what was then an emerging branch of the publishing industry in Italy, Piaggia's writings once again avoided embracing the fetishistic logic of commodity capitalism and the racist ideology it inevitably produced in other travel narratives. I will now turn my attention to these other forms of colonial writings.

GUNS AND LIBERAL IDEOLOGY: GIOVANNI MIANI AND GUSTAVO BIANCHI IN ETHIOPIA

Carlo Piaggia's travel notes constitute an exception to the corpus of Italian exploration writings. As governmental and private funding increasingly required detailed accounts of the state of the potential colonies and of their population for future colonial occupation, a pseudoscientific rationalism became the prevailing mode of travel writing. The present section focuses on two travel narratives written a few years after Piaggia's. Unlike Piaggia's, these texts articulate an evolutionary and racist ideological perspective that marks the inception of Italy's colonial liberal economy. In this economy guns, rather than gifts, become the privileged object of exchange, while native women increasingly disappear as economic actors, leaving the space of action to homosocial relations among Western men.

Giovanni Miani's diary notes are a case in point.[15] These record the Italian explorer's 1859–60 expedition in southern Sudan. Unlike Piaggia's, Miani's description of the different tribes inhabiting the Bahar-el-Ghazal region, including the *Gniam-gniam*,[16] is based on hearsay rather than firsthand experience. Miani—unlike Piaggia—belongs to the northern classes, is highly educated, and was a member of the prestigious Société Géographique of Paris.[17] Although his objectives were ostensibly scientific, Miani obtained Napoleon the Third's support in the form of weapons and ammunitions, and French merchants' backing in the form of funds and diplomatic connections.

It comes as no surprise that Miani's ethnographic notes privilege a detached scientific tone that differs enormously from Piaggia's. Miani's descriptive style contrasts with Piaggia's experiential narrative, where subjectivity and sensorial experience prevail. A typical entry reads:

Quattro giorni distante da Condokoro sopra i monti si trova la tribù dei *Berri*. Essi parlano la lingua dei Sceluki, e si trovano sei giorni distanti dal Sobat. I berri seppelliscono i loro morti, sono agricoltori, lavorano molto bene il ferro con due pietre, vivono di caccia e di latte. Essi come al Sobat portano barba e capelli. (DC 208)

[A four-day distance from Condokoro in the mountains are the *Berri* tribes. They speak the Sceluki language and are a six-day distance from Sobat. The Berri tribes bury their dead, are farmers, work the iron very well with two stones, live on hunting and milk. Like people at Sobat, they grow a beard and long hair.]

Although Piaggia discouraged the Azande from trading ivory with Arab merchants, Miani's perspective is inevitably vitiated by his close connection with the merchants' troops. Although the explorer harshly condemns slavery, he nevertheless profits from the gains obtained by the merchants' troops and adopts their punishing methods (baton and gun) against the Sudanese tribes. On one particular occasion, three of his wethers are stolen. Miani threatens: "che mi sieno portati altrimenti sarei andato a prenderli, che avevo molti regalli sulla bocca del fucile e dei miei revolver" ("that they better return them to me, otherwise I would go to get them, that I had lots of gifts in the muzzle of my rifle and guns") (DC 211). Unlike Piaggia's, Miani's exploration project heavily relies on commodities and guns, rather than social bonding, for its success. Miani makes a list of gifts, which includes trinkets and infantile trifles for the indigenous chiefs. In Miani's notes, gift exchange is a ritual by which the European asserts his military power, sense of national superiority, and right of possession: "Ho regalato al sultano una bandiera tricolore che sarà una prova che fu primo un italiano a penetrare sin qui" ("I have given the Sultan an Italian flag that will prove how I have been the first Italian to penetrate this far").[18] According to Miani's expansionist mentality, gifts are no longer trading goods considered for their use value. Rather, their exchange produces ideological meaning, as they signify European imperial presence and conquests.

Gustavo Bianchi, a former soldier employed as bookkeeper in an Italian firm, left Milan in 1879 as a member of the first Italian expedition in the Shawa regions of Abyssinia.[19] The expedition was organized by the Società di Esplorazione Commerciale in Africa, with major funding provided by Italy's main industrial groups, such as Carlo Erba and Pirelli,[20] and the magazine *Esploratore*. The results of the expedition, together with an account of Bianchi's adventures in Africa, were published in 1884 under the title *Alla terra dei Galla* (In the Land of the Galla). Although the main objective of the exploration was to find in the Horn of Africa a potential market outlet for Italy's emergent industrialism, Bianchi's perspective opens the way to a vision of Ethiopia as an ideal stage for Italy's ideological preparation for colonial expansion. If Miani's expansionist mentality remains confined within the practice of mercantile economy, Bianchi's encounter with the Ethiopians convinces him that trade is only a limited aspect of Italy's future in Africa. In his approach, which he defines as more "practical" and less "senti-mental," what really matters is not the limited, material value that trade can yield, but a long-term plan of production, which would allow financial and ideological investments in both commodities and desire.

According to Bianchi, a full-fledged program of colonial settlement and occupation must help create a need for European commodities. Bianchi admits that the natives "si mostrano avidi di possedere armi, oggetti, gingilli e strumenti appartenenti agli Europei" ("show greed for weapons, objects, trifles, and instruments belonging to the Europeans"), but do not appreci-ate their value. "Essi non possono desiderare le cose di cui odono parlare dal momento che non sanno comprenderne la necessità" ("They cannot desire the things they hear about since they do not understand their nec-essity") (TDG 10). The knowledge of this "necessity" must be derived not only from the appreciation of the use value of commodities, but from their recognized "utility" in a system of value judgement that transcends use. In an eloquent appeal to the wealthy members of the Società di Esplorazione, Bianchi clarifies this: "Questi popoli, dunque, non avranno bisogno di voi se non quando avrete loro insegnato i vostri bisogni. Insegnate loro a vestirsi, insegnate loro con l'esempio a fabbricar case, a coltivare i terreni, e così im-pareranno a desiderare, e ricorerranno a voi" ("These people, then, will not need you until you teach them your needs. Teach them how to dress, teach them by your example how to build houses, to farm the land, and thus they will learn how to desire, and they will come to you") (TDG 477).

Bianchi's perspective is thus no longer that of a trader whose immediate interests focus on the exchange of commodities, but rather of a long-term political planner whose interests coincide with the interests of the nation-state. In the 1870s, Italy was still in the process of developing those in-dustrial and banking structures that would enable the state to finance an imperialist economic policy. Bianchi nevertheless already envisions a devel-oped colonial economy and the emergence of a mass of African workers and consumers who would assimilate through labor and consumption. Bianchi also foresees the formation of a pool of alienable labor as the pri-mary condition for capitalist development in Africa, as well as the circula-tion of the values of a liberal capitalist economy: utility, wealth, property. The market economy Bianchi envisions in Ethiopia is based on class and racial separations and inequalities, that is, on the opposition of a rich Euro-pean elite to poor African working masses.

What Bianchi then outlines in his diaries is not only a policy of agrarian development in Africa, but also a massive national colonial operation by which Italy's industrial capitalism will develop and prosper. Like Luigi Ein-audi's "healthy imperialism,"[21] Bianchi's program also envisions a free trade economy, colonial self-government, indirect rule, and the formation of set-tlement colonies. This plan of development would allow the grafting of

Western liberal values onto the African soil, "the cult of work and respect for goods, utility, propriety." These, according to Bianchi, must be the key elements of Italy's *mission civilisatrice*, together with guns and land expropriation, the only possible civilizing factors in Africa. But why does Bianchi's vision differ so radically from Piaggia's, and what kind of changes have occurred from one text to the other?

Once again, a brief consideration of the material conditions in which the writing of Bianchi's texts took place will yield some interesting responses. Unlike Piaggia, who managed to assimilate in Azande society because he understood and accepted the reciprocity rule, Bianchi is constantly annoyed by gift requests. Significantly, it is Bianchi's lack of understanding of the social responsibilities that go along with the reciprocity rule that will compromise his relationship with the Ethiopians, as well as the relations of the Italians who followed after him. While traveling through Ethiopia, Bianchi considers gift demands as a telling example of the natives' greedy nature. Moreover, as Bianchi explains, the negus Menelik, future emperor of Ethiopia, imposes on Europeans who travel in his territories heavy tributes in the form of Western goods—medicine, instruments, utensils, weapons, ammunitions. During his stay in the negus's residence, Bianchi is constantly asked for "gingilli, stoffe, camicie da regalare" ("trifles, fabrics, shirts to offer as gifts") (TDG 168). On one occasion, he unwillingly gives up three cotton shirts in exchange for an ox, two rams, *engera,* and *tegg.*[22] On another occasion, he refuses to offer gifts to a local resident because of his low social rank. "Io facevo le cose per bene; i doni li presentavo alla residenza dei capi, per mezzo del capo dei miei servi e del mio dragomanno" ("I did things the right way. I offered my gifts in the chiefs' residence and by means of my servants' chief or my dragoman") (TDG 325). For Bianchi, gift offering is a ritual that can only take place in the presence of chiefs and kings as a measure and visual materialization of their respective powers.

Unlike Piaggia's, Bianchi's main objective is not simply social interaction. His goal is to convince the negus Menelik to agree to a new expedition that would open Italy's direct commercial relations through the Shawa regions, an expedition that Bianchi will eventually undertake in 1884 but that will cost him his life. In 1884, Bianchi was thus again in Africa with another expedition, whose official objective was to bring promised gifts to the emperor Johannes. In reality, the explorers' intention was to champion ambitious commercial and colonial plans. This time, "victim of [his own] zeal,"[23] Bianchi will never return to Italy. After having refused the advice of both his Italian colleagues and the emperor Johannes, and in a state of exalted excitement, he decided to take a dangerous and unknown route towards the Red Sea through the Danakil desert areas, inhabited by populations traditionally hostile to the Europeans. A few days before being killed, Bianchi wrote to his superiors in Italy: "Non siamo una spedizione, siamo tre uomini

liberi, che vogliono andare, correre, camminare, star fermi a lor talento. . . .
I miei impegni, il compito mio verso il Governo, sono finiti"[24] ("We are not
an expedition, we are three free men who want to go, run, walk, and stay as
they please. . . . My duties toward the government are over"). He thus sev-
ers forever his links with the Italian government and with the rest of the
world.

At the close of his travel narrative, weapons are the only possible currency the Italian explorer has left in order to establish any form of dialogue
with the Ethiopians. Significantly, weapons were to become again a major
point of contention between the negus Menelik and the Italians in the following years. In 1887, in the wake of the Italian defeat at Dogali, a treaty was
signed in which the Italians promised Menelik 5,000 Remington rifles in
exchange for his neutrality in the impending conflict with the emperor
Johannes. This agreement was incorporated in the 1889 Wechale Treaty
which—by binding Menelik, now emperor, to make all his foreign contacts
through the agency of Italy—marked the height of Italian colonial ambition and the beginning of the hostilities that led to the Italian defeat at
Adwa.[25] Broken promises, misplaced gifts, and ambiguous agreements characterized the inception of Italy's colonial politics in Africa.

In the extreme circumstances of Bianchi's last days, African men acquire
an increasing importance as the explorer gradually cuts his ties with the fatherland and needs their help to survive in the Danakal desert. Bianchi em-
ploys a great number of them to perform all sort of services, from transportation to translation, and their opinion is offered especially on matters
regarding diplomatic and economic transactions and local geography, customs, and language. The exploration of the African wilderness, which becomes possible in the absence of women, is thus the dominion exclusively
of men. The male bond sealed by the experience of the African frontier
glorifies self-sufficiency, autarchy, and homosociality. Although in Piaggia's
narrative women participate as actors in social relations, the invisibility of
women as social and sexual actors in Bianchi's text is also the result of the
passage from a system of reciprocity to relations based on monetary transactions. In the sociosymbolic regime of the general equivalent, as Goux reminds us, women are placed within a logic of difference based on the "phallic standard" in a position of marginality: "The phallus transcends its status
as a part object in the same way that gold transcends its commodity status. . . . The phallus is erected as general equivalent for objects of drive"
(Goux 1990: 21–22).

Although Piaggia describes how he is constantly made object of women's
sexual desire, sexual desire in Bianchi is exclusively male. The glorification
of homosociality on the African frontier entails an acceptance of men's centrality in sexual relations. In Bianchi's vision, colonialism would then not
only transform Africans into mass consumers, but it would also "teach them

how to desire," that is, how to accept European male sexual dominance over Africa and its women. Rooted within Bianchi's ambitious colonial project is thus the shift from a particular need, which differentiates between men and women, to a general logic of desire in which the phallus "possesses all pleasures in potentiality."[26] Significantly, this is the legacy fascist colonial literature will receive from its predecessors.

Gustavo Bianchi's rejection of women from the colonial scene and the exaltation of free individuality against the constraints of the nation-state in his last diaries set a paradigm for Gabriele D'Annunzio's construction of a colonial hero in his 1907 drama *Più che l'amore* (More than love). In a parallel but opposite move, romance with native women and loyalty to the nation-state in fascist colonial literature will later mark the passage from the Dannunzian hero's subjective experience to mass consumption of colonial culture and the formation of a fascist male subjectivity. In fascist colonial literature, the combination of heroism and eroticism will sanction the rise of the fascist state while consolidating mass consumption of colonial texts. If Piaggia's unfinished notes opened the genre of Italian colonial writings in the name of a genuine material and symbolic form of reciprocity, in later years state colonial expansion will offer the Italian readership a blank vision of Africans as subjected people lacking the dignity of political autonomy, cultural expression, and societal forms of organization. And although Piaggia's unedited notes, full of grammatical mistakes and unfinished sentences, did not sell on the colonial literary market, fascist colonial writers will learn how to embellish their works with exotic scenarios in order to make colonial violence a marketable exotic commodity. Yet, during fascism, the combination of the political with the exotic had to be orchestrated in ways to prevent the latter from overshadowing the former. Africa could offer romance and sexual fulfillment only in exchange for patriotism and heroism. In the exchange, all forms of equality were inevitably lost.

NOTES

1. See Roberto Battaglia, *La prima guerra d'Africa* (Torino: Einaudi, 1958) and Ezio Bassani, "Introduction," in Carlo Piaggia, *Nella Terra dei Niam-Niam (1863–1865)*, ed. Ezio Bassani (Lucca: Maria Pacini Fazzi, 1978). All translations of this and following texts are my own.

2. Giovanni Miani, author of *Le spedizioni alle origini del Nilo* (Venezia: Longo, 1865) and *Diari e Carteggi: 1858–1872*, ed. Gabriele Rossi (Milano: Longanesi, 1973), died in the High Nile region in 1872. Born in Rovigo in 1810, Miani migrated to Venice, where he completed his academic training in arts and letters and fought for the defense of Venice in 1849. Roberto Battaglia describes him as "the first Risorgimento patriot who chose Africa as his land of exile" (Battaglia 1958: 29). Perugian Marchese Orazio Antinori, hunter and trader in Africa and head of the 1876 expedition of the Società Geografica Italiana through the Shawa regions, put

together what Carlo Piaggia told him of his travels in Zandeland. Antinori is the author of *Viaggio tra i Bogos* (1887), ed. Manlio Bonati (San Sisto [Perugia]: Effe, Fabrizio Fabbri Editore, 2000).

3. Niam-Niam is the term that was in use among the Arabs and the European merchants at the time Piaggia was writing to designate not only the Azande but all the tribes that inhabited the equatorial regions of Sudan. These tribes were thought to practice anthropophagy. Azande is the current term used to designate a rich variety of different ethnic groups, focus of E. E. Evans-Pritchard's ethnographic study *The Azande: History and Political Institutions* (Oxford: Clarendon Press, 1971). For further details see Bassani (1978) and Evans-Pritchard (1971).

4. Italian migration to Mediterranean Africa was a steady phenomenon all through the second half of the nineteenth century and beginning of the twentieth century. According to the 1871 census, there were 23,645 Italians in the whole of Africa, distributed for the most part in Egypt (10,679), Algeria (6,482), and Tunisia (5,889). The total number increased in the following years, and reached 188,702 in 1927. Despite Italy's colonial occupation of Eritrea, Ethiopia, Libya, and Somalia from 1890 to 1940, Italians largely preferred the Maghreb, and particularly Tunisia, to the Italian colonies. According to the 1927 census, the number of Italians in Tunisia reached 97,000. In the same year, only 196 Italian civilians lived in Ethiopia. This data contradicts the image of the "fiumana" (flow) of people leaving Italy to reach the colonies, a persistent topos of Italian colonial propaganda. See Nicola Labanca (1997: 193–229).

5. Piaggia, *Alla terra dei Niam-Niam,* 27. Hereafter referred to as TNN.

6. See Marcel Mauss, *Essai sur le Don* [1923], translated as *The Gift: The Form and Reason for Exchange in Archaic Societies* (London: Routledge, 1990).

7. See Bronislaw Malinowski, "The Principle of Give and Take," in *The Gift: An Interdisciplinary Perspective,* 15–17.

8. See Nicholas Thomas, *Entangled Objects: Exchange, Material Culture, and Colonialism in the Pacific* (Cambridge, Mass: Harvard University Press, 1991).

9. This argument constitutes the main objection to Marcel Mauss's view of tribal societies as exclusively communal or 'gift' societies. For a discussion see Thomas, *Entangled Objects: Exchange, Material Culture, and Colonialism in the Pacific,* and C. A. Gregory, *Gifts and Commodities* (London: Academic Press, 1982).

10. Claude Levi-Strauss, 1949, cited in C. A. Gregory, *Gifts and Commodities* (London: Academic Press, 1982), 22.

11. For a discussion see Hulme, *Cannibalism and the Colonial World.*

12. For their exchange of letters see Bassani, "Introduction," in Piaggia, *Nella terra dei Niam-Niam.*

13. In 1941, Alfonso Pellegrinetti published an edited and revised version, in narrative form and standard Italian, of Carlo Piaggia's manuscripts and correspondence. See G. Alfonso Pellegrinetti, *Le memorie di Carlo Piaggia* (Vallecchi, 1941). For further details see Bassani, "Introduction," in Carlo Piaggia, *Nella terra dei Niam-Niam.*

14. Cited in Bassani, "Introduction," in Piaggia, *Nella terra dei Niam-Niam,* 151.

15. Giovanni Miani, *Diari e Carteggi: 1858–1872,* Gabriele Rossi-Osmida, ed. (Milano: Longanesi, 1973). Hereafter referred to as DC.

16. This is the spelling Miani uses to refer to the *Niam-niam* or Azande.

17. Gabriele Rossi-Osmida, "Introduzione," in Giovanni Miani, *Diari e Carteggi: 1858–1872,* 39. For further information refer to footnote 4.

18. Cited in Battaglia, *La prima guerra d'Africa,* 36.

19. As the hinterland of Assab, Italy's first coastal acquisition, Shawa represented a logical line for the extension of the Italians' interests in the area. The first geographical mission to Shawa was the 1876 exploration headed by Marquis Orazio Antinori. The mission, like Bianchi's, "was a good example of the interconnection between geographical exploration and colonial expansion which had been a characteristic feature of colonialism in Africa." Bahru Zewde, *A History of Modern Ethiopia: 1855–1974* (London: James Currey, 1991), 74.

20. For a discussion of the expedition see Angelo Del Boca, *Gli italiani in Africa orientale,* vol. 1, *Dall'Unità alla marcia su Roma* (Milan: Mondadori, 1992), 85–98, and Anne Hugon, *The Exploration of Africa: From Cairo to the Cape* (New York: Abrams, 1993).

21. For a discussion of "democratic imperialism" see Aldo A. Mola, ed. *L'imperialismo italiano: La politica estera dall'Unità al fascismo* (Roma: Editori Riuniti, 1980) and Luigi Goglia and Fabio Grassi, *Il colonialismo italiano da Adua all'impero* (Roma: Editori Riuniti, 1981), 21–22.

22. *Engera* is a flat, sour fermented pancake that is used in Ethiopian and Eritrean cooking to serve stews made with spices, meats, and pulses such as lentils, beans, and split peas. *Teff* is the cereal most commonly used to make *engera*. *Tegg* (also spelled *tej* in Amharic) is an alcoholic drink also known as Ethiopian honey wine, made from raw honey with its comb and cooked with hops.

23. Pietro Antonelli, "Lettera del 25 gennaio 1884," cited in Del Boca, *Dall'Unità alla marcia su Roma,* 157.

24. Gustavo Bianchi, *L'ultima spedizione affricana di Gustavo Bianchi: Diari, relazioni, lettere e documenti editi and inediti,* vol. 1, Carlo Zaghi, ed. (Milano: Alpes, 1930), 300–301.

25. Zewde, *A History of Modern Ethiopia: 1855–1974,* 75. As both Del Boca and Zedwe explain, the Treaty of Wechale is an example of how hollow diplomatic agreements were destined to be. Article XVII, which in the Amharic version had made optional Menelik's use of Italy's services, in the Italian version ineluctably bound Menelik to Italy, thus reducing Ethiopia to the status of an Italian protectorate. For further details see Zewde and Del Boca.

26. Karl Marx, *Capital,* cited in Goux, 117.

WORKS CITED

Antinori, Orazio. 2000. *Viaggio tra i Bogos* (1887), ed. Manlio Bonati. San Sisto (Perugia): Effe, Fabrizio Fabbri Editore.

Bartolovich, Crystal. 1998. "Consumerism, or the Cultural Logic of Late Cannibalism." *Cannibalism and the Colonial World,* ed. Francis Baker, Peter Hulme, and Margaret Iversen. Cambridge: Cambridge University Press.

Bassani, Ezio. 1978. "Introduction." In Carlo Piaggia, *Nella Terra dei Niam-Niam (1863–1865),* ed. Ezio Bassani. Lucca: Maria Pacini Fazzi.

Battaglia, Roberto. 1958. *La prima guerra d'Africa.* Torino: Einaudi.

Bianchi, Gustavo. 1930. *L'ultima spedizione affricana di Gustavo Bianchi: Diari, relazioni, lettere e documenti editi and inediti,* ed. Carlo Zaghi. 2 vols., vol. 1. Milano: Alpes.

Del Boca, Angelo. 1992. *Gli italiani in Africa orientale.* 4 vols., vol. 1: *Dall'Unità alla marcia su Roma.* Roma: Mondadori.

Evans-Pritchard, E. E. 1971. *The Azande: History and Political Institutions.* Oxford: Clarendon Press.

Goglia, Luigi, and Fabio Grassi. 1981. *Il colonialismo italiano da Adua all'impero.* Roma: Editori Riuniti.

Goux, Jean-Joseph. 1990. *Symbolic Economies: After Marx and Freud.* Translated by Jennifer Curtiss Cage. Ithaca, NY: Cornell University Press.

Gregory, C. A. 1982. *Gifts and Commodities* London: Academic Press.

Hugon, Anne. 1993. *The Exploration of Africa: From Cairo to the Cape.* New York: Abrams.

Hulme, Peter. 1998. "The Cannibal Scene." In *Cannibalism and the Colonial World,* ed. Francis Baker, Peter Hulme, and Margaret Iversen. Cambridge: Cambridge University Press.

Labanca, Nicola. 1997. "Italiani d'Africa." In *Adua: Le ragioni di una sconfitta,* ed. Angelo Del Boca, Bari: Laterza.

Lévi-Strauss, Claude. 1996. "The Principle of Reciprocity." In *The Gift: An Interdisciplinary Perspective,* ed. Aafke E. Komter. Amsterdam: Amsterdam University Press.

Malinowski, Bronislaw. 1996. "The Principle of Give and Take." In *The Gift: An Interdisciplinary Perspective,* ed. Aafke E. Komter. Amsterdam: Amsterdam University Press.

Marx, Karl. 1976. *Capital: A Critique of Political Economy.* 2 vols., vol. 1. Translated by Ernest Mandel. New York: Penguin Books.

———. 1971. *A Contribution to the Critique of Political Economy* (1859). Trans. S. W. Ryazanskaya; edited and with an introduction by Maurice Dobb. London: Lawrence and Wishart.

Mauss, Marcel. 1990. *Essai sur le Don* [1923]. Translated as *The Gift: The Form and Reason for Exchange in Archaic Societies.* London: Routledge.

Miani, Giovanni. 1973. *Diari e Carteggi: 1858–1872,* ed. Gabriele Rossi-Osmida. Milano: Longanesi.

———. 1865. *Le spedizioni alle origini del Nilo.* Venezia: Longo.

Mola, Aldo A., ed. 1980. *L'imperialismo italiano: La politica estera dall'Unità al fascismo.* Roma: Editori Riuniti.

Park, Mungo. 1971. *Travels in the Interior Districts of Africa* [1799]. New York: Arno Press.

Pellegrinetti, G. Alfonso. 1941. *Le memorie di Carlo Piaggia.* Firenze: Vallecchi.

Piaggia, Carlo. 1978. *Nella terra dei Niam-Niam (1863–1865),* ed. Ezio Bassani. Lucca: Maria Pacini Fazzi.

Pratt, Mary Louise. 1992. *Imperial Eyes: Travel Writing and Transculturation.* New York: Routledge.

Rossi-Osmida, Gabriele. 1973. "Introduzione," in Giovanni Miani, *Diari e Carteggi: 1858–1872,* ed. Gabriele Rossi-Osmida. Milano: Longanesi.

Thomas, Nicholas. 1991. *Entangled Objects: Exchange, Material Culture, and Colonialism in the Pacific.* Cambridge, Mass.: Harvard University Press.

Zewde, Bahru. 1991. *A History of Modern Ethiopia: 1855–1974.* London: James Currey.

Incorporating the Exotic

From Futurist Excess to Postmodern Impasse

Cinzia Sartini-Blum

The debate on colonial literature is one of many initiatives orchestrated by fascist state agencies to promote a new art for the new times. In keeping with the self-definition of fascism as a cultural-political revolution, fascist art was viewed as a means of shaping the collective's mind and body into the mold of the revolution's values. As shown in recent studies, the debates generated by such initiatives reveal a varied scenario that complicates our understanding of cultural life under the regime.[1] Most importantly, there emerges a disjunction between aesthetic/spiritual and political/pragmatic concerns. A frequent (albeit largely unacknowledged) cause of contradiction and controversy, this disjunction can be traced to a fundamental paradox of fascism: the project of building a powerful, industrial mass society with old values salvaged from the impact of modernity's "plagues," namely capitalist materialism and Marxist collectivism. For the many intellectuals attracted by the fascist appeal to values such as heroism and virility, the regime's bureaucratic machine was bound to summon up the specter of the standardized, depersonalized mass society they sought to exorcise.

The quandary facing the fascist intellectual becomes most apparent when projected onto a distant object of individual and collective desire, namely the African territories. The regime sought to incorporate these territories, depicted by orientalist literature as exotic retreats for heroic individuality, and turn them into a regimented extension of the fatherland, a testing ground for the newly molded fascist subject. This vantage point allows us to view the fascist paradox in relation to the paradoxical project of exoticist literature: the doomed attempt to salvage the romantic figure of the individual by displacing it to a land beyond the reach of modernity. As Chris Bongie argues, this project arose in response to "the absorption of the individual into the abstract unity of the modern European State": it was, at least in part, motivated by a desire to escape the ills of mass society and to achieve self-realization in exotic territories where "the archaic model of subjectivity [the autonomous, sovereign individual] still persisted as a political system."[2] But literary fantasies of heroic individuality would only survive as long as exoticist writers could avoid facing the realities of colonialism and their own inescapable involvement in the very system they sought to transcend. Similar desires and ambiguities underwrite the fascist rhetoric of heroic virility, which fostered fantasies of (vicarious) identification with the sovereign individual (paradigmatically embodied by Benito Mussolini) when, in fact, the bureaucratic apparatus of the totalitarian state was pragmatically geared to produce a strictly regimented fascist mass.

Such a pragmatic bias clearly informs the "referendum" on colonial literature launched in March 1931 by *L'Azione Coloniale,* a publication devoted to "the diffusion and popularization of the major problems and aspects of [Italian] colonial expansionism."[3] The writers and intellectuals who participated in the poll expressed a variety of opinions on the questions of the existence, adequacy, desirable characteristics, and future prospects of a "healthy and effective colonial literature."[4] Overall, the inquiry pointed to a state of lack or inadequacy. The answers gave a more or less negative assessment of the situation, depending mainly on whether literary or propagandistic value was taken as criterion. Some—a minority—lamented a shortage of true works of art and expressed skepticism about the usefulness of any promotional initiatives. To produce such works, as Margherita Sarfatti noted, one needed not build a colonial empire but rather resort to the power of the creative imagination.[5] Most respondents, however, taking their cue from the questionnaire and focusing on the political function of colonial literature ("to form a colonial consciousness"), criticized the predominant tendency to indulge in "local color" and advocated the production of more informative, pedagogical texts.

As the founder and leader of the futurist avant-garde—the first to break traditional barriers between art and life—Filippo Tommaso Marinetti is, not surprisingly, among the most optimistic and proactive respondents. Speaking in vague terms on the valuable achievements and proven credentials of almost all Italian authors of "colonial books," he summarily offers some predictable input: Italian colonial literature must become more and more "futurist"—i.e., rich in technical/practical elements and free from sentimental/romantic trappings—in order to be "more representative, more virile, more worthy of [the Italian] race launched by Fascism toward an ever-greater colonial empire."[6] In keeping with futurism's vociferous commitment to the nationalist cause, this formula posits an unproblematic relationship between political and aesthetic goals. But as we shall see, Marinetti's own writing turns out to be caught in the paradoxical dynamics of the exoticist project. The futurist leader may seem an obvious paragon for colonial writers: the son of an Italian lawyer who made his fortune in Egypt, he covered the Italian campaign in Libya as a reporter, participated as an officer in the Ethiopian war, and throughout his career wrote several books staged in Africa. Yet his works were not generally cited as models of colonial literature. Marinetti himself, despite his notorious lack of modesty and penchant for self-promotion, quotes Mitrano Sani's works as "excellent from the perspective of colonial propaganda" in his response to the inquiry promoted by *L'Azione Coloniale.* But in a 1939 essay that spells out his programmatic vision of Africa as matter to be assimilated and transfigured by the futurist imagination, he lists himself among the few original writers inspired by Africa, including some Italian authors but also prestigious foreign names such as Victor Hugo, Gérard de Nerval, Charles Baudelaire, Gustave Flaubert, and André Gide.[7] Thus, insofar as he discriminates between literature valuable for colonial propaganda and (his own) inspired art, Marinetti leaves room for a discrepancy between aesthetic and political concerns.

Since futurism is generally identified with virulent cultural and political nationalism, this might seem to be a moot point, easily dismissed with an obvious conclusion: the futurist exploitation of Africa as a new domain for creative expansion is simply the aesthetic equivalent of the imperialist conquest of new territories for the augmentation of Italy's economic and political strength. Ultimately such a conclusion is a fair assessment of the political implications of Marinetti's stance. But it fails to account for the complexities in his work, which are noteworthy in themselves and, moreover, provide a unique angle on exoticist desire. The most conspicuous aspect of Marinetti's "incorporation" of Africa is, of course, his celebration of Italian colonialism in the works inspired by the Libyan and Ethiopian campaigns: *La battaglia di Tripoli* (The battle of Tripoli; 1912) and *Il Poema africano della Divisione "28 Ottobre"* (The African poem of the "October 28" Division; 1937), where the poet-turned-colonizer transfigures war into a source of aesthetic pleasure providing artistic justification for imperialist violence. Another more complex dimension—especially apparent in *Mafarka il Futurista* (Mafarka the futurist; 1910) and *Il tamburo di fuoco* (The drum of fire; 1922)—is what can be termed "futurist primitivism": in particular, the staging of an exotic hero in a primitive setting. This scenario suggests a desire for self-exoticism (a desire to be an "Other"), which can be related to the Nietzschean call for a new barbarism and to the European avant-garde's rejection of liberal-bourgeois culture.[8] A third, even more problematic aspect is most clearly apparent in *Il fascino dell'Egitto* (Egyptian fascination; 1933): inspired by Marinetti's 1930 visit to his native land, this collection of fragments in poetic prose dramatizes the inner conflict between a futurist will to progress and a decadent regret for the past, as Marinetti puts it, "the tragic struggle that took place in my veins between that lamenting past and the magnificent future that strangled it."[9] All three aspects can be viewed as instances of exoticism in its aggressive, escapist, and nostalgic manifestations. Writing well into the age of New Imperialism, but early from the standpoint of Italy's colonial ambitions, Marinetti offers a seemingly contradictory recapitulation of the three modes. His exoticist nostalgia, in particular, appears to run against the general understanding of futurist ideology as centered on *modernolatria,* the unequivocal cult of the modern.

Upon closer examination, Marinetti's literary exploitation of Africa—like his writing in general—forces the reader to forgo the security of prefabricated judgments, in particular the dismissive view of the second phase of futurism, roughly coinciding with its connection with fascism, as a tired recycling of the stock materials of the futurist warehouse, which often merely served a propagandistic function and lacked the aesthetic and ideological interest of earlier works. Taking issue with this view, I will focus on a 1929 play entitled *Luci veloci* (Swift lights), perhaps the most problematic of Marinetti's "African" works. This little-known text exhibits an ambivalent attitude toward colonization, but also proposes a remedy for the ethical dilemma of the artist facing an "Africa chewed and devoured by the Europeans."[10] In light of this analysis, I will then theorize an overarching principle that informs Marinetti's "incorporation" of the exotic into fictions of individual and collective regeneration. In its excessive futurist enactment, such a principle foregrounds a persisting logic in the Western approach to the Other. My goal is twofold: to reach a better understanding of scarcely studied dimensions of Marinetti's work and participate in current efforts to explore the heterogeneous discursive manifestations of the desire for the exotic.

EPHEMERAL IMMORTALITY: THE FUTURIST POET'S PARADOXICAL MISSION

Luci veloci takes place in a fictitious Egyptian town that Marinetti imagines soon transformed into an oil-trade hub and a hotbed for the conflict between British imperialism and African nationalism.[11] The scene represents a room in a boarding house. The protagonist is a world-famous poet bearing obvious resemblance to the author: he is a fifty-year-old World War I veteran dubbed "Musoduro" (Tough face) for his defiant countenance displayed against the Austrian enemies. (Marinetti, who often boasted of his participation in the Great War, was fifty-three in 1929.) But this figure of the poet is a far cry from the exuberant persona of Marinetti's earlier writings. Afflicted by health problems and confined to his room, he no longer takes an active part in life. He lives with his thirty-year-old wife and a daughter, also thirty, from a previous marriage. Given that the futurist program prescribed the rejection of Woman as a prerequisite for heroic self-affirmation, Musoduro's affective ties can be considered symptomatic of a passive, or weakened condition. One can also argue that the two female figures stand for conflicting aspects of the protagonist's personality: the materialistic and the idealistic. Musoduro is growing distant from his sexy, fickle wife, and relies instead on the unwavering devotion and the "pure" love of his daughter, Perlina, who turns down attractive offers of marriage and devotes her life to her father's mission.[12] The bond between Perlina and Musoduro, which has central thematic relevance in the play, will not be weakened by the discovery that they are not father and daughter. As we shall see, by casting an ambiguous light on the nature of their relationship, this revelation leads the protagonists to deal with some general ethical issues that also invest another central, and equally ambiguous question: the nature of the poet's mission in Egypt, and his position in the conflict between British imperialism and African nationalism.

Musoduro expresses sympathy for Sir John Roll, the British officer, who is a heavy drinker "but gets things done," and suspicion toward Mahmud, the Arab petty politician ("politicante") whom he describes as "mellifluous, fawning, ambiguous" (282). Stereotypically depicted as a womanizer and a liar, Mahmud will be accused by the Arabs of selling their plan for insurrection to the English. His faults, however, appear to be the product of the corrupting impact of Western greed. He drinks, in fact, like everybody else, to kill nostalgia "among the machines and oil of this Africa chewed and devoured by the Europeans" (297). Musoduro echoes these sentiments as he declares himself tired of Bassabulà, calling it "a vortex of frenzied Europeanisms, a brawl of middlemen competing for Africa's last remnants of virginity" (284). He desires to leave this chaotic brawl and regenerate himself by assimilating the invisible forces that fill the "intoxicating" desert, upon which he projects a paradoxical mood of "virile and optimistic despair" (283). (The attribute "intoxicating" suggests that this may be a sublimated version of the alcoholic's escape, the ordinary means of intoxication for both colonizer and colonized.) But Musoduro's room seems to hold him captive with its mysterious magnetic force and crushing weight: "How can we get out or rather, how can we break free from this room? I carry this room on my back like a knapsack. It has become my skin! I would have to tear my own skin in order to get out . . . Yet if I leave, it will catch me, it will catch me again!" (308). Symbolizing the modern power structure that forces individuals into preordained roles, the boarding house has a similar effect on the British officer and the Arab schemer: "This room," remarks Musoduro, "defeats everything and everyone. It doesn't let go of its prey, or else it creates new ones similar to the first" (323). The common predicament dramatizes the global, homogenizing system of an increasingly bureaucratic, impersonal society, which both produces and thwarts dreams of heroic individuality, such as Musoduro's desire to find freedom in the majestic solitude of the desert. The protagonist's dilemma, in other words, is symptomatic of the inescapable ambivalence of exoticist desire: an unavoidable complicity with the historical process of colonialism and an impossible desire for the exotic as a reservoir of heroic individuality.

Indeed, although Musoduro seems to deplore Europe's greedy stranglehold on Africa, the political implications of his attitude are ambiguous at best. His anticolonial stance is weakened by the fact that it coincides with a patriotically strong gesture against Italy's colonial competitors. His desire to cut off the suffocating "tangle of European tentacles" reveals an explicit nationalist bias: "It is necessary to cut off the non-Italian tentacles. Will I succeed?" The possibility that the protagonist's anticolonial sentiments may be part of a dubious political project is dramatized by the doubts surrounding his mission in Egypt. Alleging that Musoduro is an agent of the Italian government, on a mission to stir up the Arab rebellion against the British (299), Mahmud remarks that the world-famous poet must hate the job he is forced to do, just as he himself hates his own schemes. It is interesting to note that on the occasion of his 1926 trip to Buenos Aires, about three years before writing *Luci veloci,* Marinetti had been clamorously attacked by local antifascist militants who regarded him as a political envoy of the fascist regime.[13] Perlina spiritedly defends her father, portraying him as an "utterly pure patriot" consumed by his passion for art (299). And Musoduro himself defines his mission in idealistic terms: he claims to be "a sort of spy of the invisible and of the afterworld" (285). Having cut short his political career "to quickly reach the peak of [his] artistic thought and the most splendid imagination," he aims to build "a luminous lyrical architecture with the pieces of life that destiny hurls at [him]" (305). He is also pursuing a study on historical truth and on the deformation of facts through the collective imagination (280), a project through which he intends to debunk the pretended objectivity of realist aesthetics and defend his own poetic practice, which has been accused of excessively transfiguring reality (295).

One must recall that similar accusations were often directed at Marinetti, who was regarded with some mistrust by fascist authorities. The following example is especially relevant as it relates to colonialist propaganda: in February 1941, Marinetti was invited to deliver a conference on the Italian colonies and, contrary to his earlier practice, requested payment because of his deteriorating economic situation. In agreeing to pay, Ronchi of the Istituto fascista per l'Africa italiana (Fascist Institute for Italian Africa) imposed the condition that Marinetti's speech should be "not artistic but celebratory," thus manifesting a common misgiving about the obscurity and counterproductivity of futurist art for the purposes of fascist propaganda.[14] It is also worth noting that Musoduro's antirealist stance is consistent with Marinetti's aesthetic program, and anticipates his August 1937 declaration against Hitler's prejudice in favor of "an art that is realist, analytical, static, and photographic."[15] In the play this kind of art is embodied by a filmmaker ("filmista di guerra") who turns out to be part of a mysterious "Ditta Roll" (Roll

Company), an allusion to possible ties between his work and British interests, since Roll is the British officer's name. Significantly, during a preemptive strike by the British, his camera is not pointed at the fighting, but rather at the shadow of Mahmud's revolver projected against a wall by means of a "lanterna cieca" (309). What is being recorded, in other words, is the shadow of a shadowy character projected by means of a "dark lamp."

In the seclusion of his study, Musoduro himself has an indirect take on the swift lights of life, which he only views filtered through a door or framed by a window. These "luci veloci" are signs of dynamism and progress, the inexorable laws of life that futurism had confidently set out to embrace and master. In the play, however, the artist is atypically disconcerted by and removed from the bewildering forces of progress: "England the colonizer and Africa the petty politician have become imponderable. But the lights persist. And they are swift. They are hurrying. Where?" (287). Later, from his desk, the "privileged writer" takes pride in his ability to render lyrically the beauty of the swift lights, which explode in the sky as the British bomb Bassabulà in order to foil the nationalist insurrection. Musoduro describes his artistic effort as an attempt to transfigure the raw material of "an imperious life's burning impressions" (containing "the calories and breaths of carnal desire and cruelty, the wrangling sparks of the mind's frenzied batteries") into the ideal work of eternal and ephemeral fire: "an art of light that is intense and swift, broad and synthetic, alive to the point of giving the sense of immortality but winged fleeting already vanished" (281). The paradoxical goal of ephemeral immortality points to the founding paradox of the futurist project: the (impossible) desire to revitalize hollowed-out ideals such as the absolute, the infinite, and the immortal through assimilation of the ephemeral, chaotic, and aggressive materiality that drives progress.

Perlina makes the ambiguity of Musoduro's mission evident as she delivers to him the plans for the Arab insurrection, which she found in a folder left unattended by Mahmud. While it remains unclear whether Musoduro's aims are artistic or political (he insists, in fact, that he is spying on things extraneous to Arab interests), his justification for taking Mahmud's papers only confirms his ambiguous position: "In reality we are two friends who defend themselves any way they can against the sinister, aggressive confusion of life! A father and a daughter who strive to extract from life a juice, yes, a juice transformable into Italian greatness and beautiful art." In response to his daughter's objection that this "juice" may be oil and not an ideal artistic distillation, he replies: "and yet it can be proven that this colonial war's ideals are light and speed, our saints!" (302).

Later, upon discovering that she is not Musoduro's daughter, Perlina questions the ethical implications of their love and of reprehensible actions such as stealing and killing. Musoduro responds by advocating a voluntarist ethic that arises from, and offers an anchor against, the unsettling premise of epistemological instability: "Each atmosphere imposes its moral, absolves or condemns neutral life, coloring it with virtue or sin, nobility or baseness" (317). Hence even killing may be a duty: for the soldier at war, for instance. This "atmospherically variable" perspective allows the poet to stand precariously above the ambiguities played out in the drama: condemnation of the colonial greed of countries like England can be reconciled with a desire to strengthen Italy's weak hold on the African continent. Patriotic faith (just as love for Perlina), being raised to the status of absolute value by sheer will, is thus reclaimed from the play's mire of unresolvable ambivalence and provides a firm point of reference "against the sinister, aggressive confusion of life": a differential space whereupon the futurist poet's will to action can be grounded and rescued from his decadent sensibility, his sense of foundering in the overwhelming dissolution brought about by the global advance of modernity. The voluntarist ethics advocated by Musoduro will be fully enacted in the later *Poema africano della Divisione "28 Ottobre,"* which celebrates Italy's conquest of Ethiopia. In the new context or "atmosphere" of a "heroic" Italian war, Marinetti (who joined the ranks as an officer at age fifty-nine) displays the inevitably colonialist nature of his incorporation of Africa, and yet can avoid the mire of materialist greed thanks to the "absolute" value of patriotism. But considering his patriotic enterprise against the background of *Luci veloci,* one realizes that such a vital "juice," distilled by dint of willpower and imagination, is actually as volatile and variable as any atmosphere. The exchanges between Musoduro and Perlina also point to a relationship between the voluntarist and antirealist aesthetics defended in the play and enacted in the poem on the Ethiopian war: they both rely on a surfeit of will and imagination to recover some residual value from the chaos of reality. Failing to confront the tangle of aggressive forces, such a surfeit sublimates it.

At the end, in order to flee from the international police, Musoduro and Perlina disguise themselves as Arab beggars and seek refuge in the desert, invoking its "absolute gift": presumably a sublimated form of existence, sustained by the "water of [Musoduro's] poems" (324). But the fickle wife, Floflò, seduced by the trappings of civilization and by a charming Arab officer, follows reluctantly the beggar-poet's call and promises the officer that she will soon return to give him a full account. Leaving the uncertainties at work in the play unresolved, this conclusion reproposes a central topos of exoticism: the majestic, inviolate desert is the ultimate retreat offered by nature to the frustrated heroic subject, an absolute elsewhere irreducible to the homogenizing forces of society. This is no exotic Eden, but rather a symbol for the harsh truths/laws of the existential condition against which the hero's mettle can be tested, and a metonymy for his unquenchable "thirst"—his unrestrained desire/ambition.[16] Musoduro's survival strategies—the disguise hiding his Western identity and the poetic "distillation" that is supposed to sustain him—suggest that the poet's exotic retreat is nothing but the fruit of his imagination. Ultimately, such an evasion poses no challenge to the system of power relations established by colonial domination. In fact, ambivalence and discontinuities in the discursive manifestations of Orientalism, rather than subverting its power system, may help it to maintain its cultural hegemony by catering to changing conditions in the relation between the West and its Elsewhere.[17] The shifting role of the exotic in Marinetti's texts offers evidence in support of this argument. The recurrent trope of incorporation, in particular, provides a vehicle to explore a consistent strategy that underlies the various manifestations of futurist exoticism.

INCORPORATING THE EXOTIC

Musoduro's disguise at the end of the play recalls the figure of the poet in *Destruction* (1904) and *La Ville charnelle* (The carnal city; 1908), the late-symbolist poems that predate Marinetti's shift from decadent pessimism to the artificial optimism of futurist modernolatria. The prefuturist poetic subject is a "beggar of love" hungering for the Ideal and repelled by reality's abjection, the limited and limiting material(istic) world that is his lot. Driven by his insatiable hunger, the decadent "I" risks drowning in the chasm created by the modern collapse of value systems. Although allowing for the poet's escape from the reality he abhors, the irrational forces unleashed by this collapse produce, in fact, a destructive surfeit of affect, a boundary-dissolving eruption of drives that is recurrently associated with the primitive, the exotic, and the feminine. Self-destruction is averted through the empowering solution anticipated in the final section of *La Ville charnelle* and dramatized in Marinetti's first futurist works, in particular "Fondazione e Manifesto del Futurismo" (Founding and manifesto of futurism; 1909), "Uccidiamo il Chiaro di Luna" (Let's murder the moonshine; 1909), and *Mafarka il Futurista.* The futurist strategy involves both drawing on vital, libidinal forces and channeling these forces into a geometric, mechanical "armor": the machine viewed as paradigmatic vehicle for progress. The result is the multiplied, metallized man: the embodiment of a new mode of being whose essential features are, in Marinetti's words, "hygienic oblivion, hope, desire, harnessed force, speed, light, willpower, order, discipline, and method" (TIF 98–99). Significantly, the birth of the futurist superman is staged in a primitive, exotic locale, or in a setting that somehow evokes the "flavor" of such a locale. In the founding manifesto, for instance, the poet breaks free from his decadent past and is reborn to face the challenges of the future by drinking the "fortifying sludge" of a maternal factory drain, which reminds him of "the blessed black breast" of his Sudanese wet nurse (TIF 9). The event is a primal fantasy with a technological twist: the mater-

nal "factory drain" is a hybrid image in which regressive, feminine, and exotic elements (the maternal womb and the breast of the black wet nurse of
Marinetti's childhood in Egypt) are linked with and contained by a modern
emblem (the drainage ditch filled with fortifying industrial waste), thus signifying regeneration. By assimilating the unpalatable sludge of the industrial age as "exotic" milk, the futurist poet transforms it into prime nourishment for his inspiration.[18]

Like the feminine, with which it is often associated, the exotic is laden
with ambivalent connotations in Marinetti's writings. In *Mafarka il Futurista,*
Africa is the mythical stage in which a heroic, sovereign individual—un-
hindered by the fetters of modern democracy—can effect an "ingenious"
fusion of savagery and progress: the regeneration of himself through a mechanical, superhuman son. But it is also a locus of abjection—insatiable
desire, feminine weakness, festering decay, and mortal disease—which the
African king confronts outside and inside himself, and which he must repress in order to achieve his futurist goal. Thus, with a fateful kiss, Mafarka
exhales his vital force into the all-powerful son he has engineered—the
machine-man Gazourmah—and, becoming the ballast that the newborn
hero must drop in order to rise up from the earth, is finally jettisoned to a
watery death. As already noted, the eruption of irrational drives unleashed
by the decay of Western values and associated with the exotic is both a crucible and a threat for the new futurist man: it expands and also dissolves the
boundaries of the self, hence the need to transfuse these drives into a new
value system, modeled after the metallic, mechanical power of the machine.
This transfusion serves an additional strategic purpose: by incorporating
the "spirit" of the machine into an exotic, sovereign version of himself, and,
conversely, by imbuing the machine with a human essence, the futurist man
can exorcise the alienating effects of the technological world. (Anxieties
about this new world are the unavowed underpinnings of futurism's artificial optimism.) [19] Marinetti, in other words, constructs an exotic-modernist
fiction that envisions the historically impossible. Opting for a mythical
rather than a historical setting, and thus occluding the realities of colonialism and mass society, he creates a scenario in which the futurist superuomo
can incorporate both the unfettered sovereignty/vitality of an exotic individual and the empowering forces of progress.

But in the African play *Il tamburo di fuoco,* Kabango—a later embodiment
of the exotic sovereign individual—succumbs to the world he is seeking to
redeem. Like Mafarka, Kabango is a product of Marinetti's tendency to self-
exoticize, a cross of exotic prowess and Western ambition. Both leaders are
figures of the futurist artist: Mafarka, for instance, having relinquished
political power to pursue a creative mission, announces his new "religion
of manifested Will and daily Heroism" in a "futurist speech" (TIF 255–66);
and Kabango characterizes himself as an antisentimental poet, chastising

Lanzirica—the "effeminate," lustful, and cowardly dreamer—for being a "devoted subject of queen Disease" rather than a poet (28, 60–61).[20] Mafarka, however, is a despotic Arab king at war with other African tribes and driven by a solipsistic vision: having overcome the "black hordes" of his enemies, he sacrifices his kingdom, his subjects, and his own flawed self to an ambition of omnipotence and immortality. Kabango, by contrast, is an "enlightened" version of the exotic sovereign. A mixture of different races (Arab, Berber, and black) and cultures (he has studied Western science in Timbuktu, a city synonymous with exotic remoteness), he aims not to re-create himself into a superhuman being, but rather to create a better Africa for all Africans. This is to be accomplished by incorporating Western science and primitive culture into the Sinrun: "the Mystery, fetish of fetishes" (48), a formula for progress that does not dispel mystery, magic, and heroic individuality. The differences between the two leaders signal a shift in perspective, from a purely mythical, ahistorical space to one vaguely placed at the crossroads of the primitive world and encroaching Western influences. But even this slight concession to the historical context of colonization comes with a steep price for the heroic individual. At the end of the play, Kabango is killed by his own people whose primitive nature—stereotypically depicted as stagnating in a vegetative and animal state—has already been corrupted by the dishonest ways of the White world. And the vision inscribed in the Sinrun, Kabango's legacy, is only provisionally rescued by Bagamoio, a faithful officer entrusted with the mission of delivering it to the leader's brother.

Arguably, Kabango's failed effort to redeem his people can be read as a reflection of Marinetti's frustrated commitment to political action in the aftermath of World War I. *Il tamburo di fuoco* was first performed in 1922 and published in 1923, after the delusions of 1919–20 and at a time of crisis for the futurist movement.[21] I refer, in particular, to the defeat of the Fasci Italiani di Combattimento or Italian Battle Fasces (a coalition of futurists, Fascists, and war veterans) in the 1919 elections, and to the severance of the futurist alliance with Mussolini's Fasci in 1920, when Marinetti resigned his post in the party executive, accusing it of monarchism and clericalism. The process of reconciliation with fascism took place in the mid-1920s and coincided with Marinetti's avowed confinement of futurism's ambitions to the artistic sphere. In *Futurismo e Fascismo* (Futurism and fascism; 1924), the work that sealed Marinetti's rapprochement to Mussolini, the futurist leader programmatically (and diplomatically) declared: "Futurism is an artistic and ideological movement. It intervenes in political battles only when the Nation faces the gravest danger" (TIF 494).

This strategic separation of the political and artistic domains provides an illuminating context for the ambiguities that we have earlier identified in Musoduro's mission and in Marinetti's attitude toward colonial literature.

It also offers a background for yet another figure of the futurist, self-exoticizing poet: the belated traveler-writer of *Il fascino dell'Egitto*. In many respects this collection of travel impressions evokes the predominant mode of late Orientalism that futurism rejected and that the proponents of colonial literature criticized for its tendency toward descriptivism and melancholia: to use Ali Behdad's definition, "the fragmentary reflections of an ambivalent traveler who finds the place of his or her displacement and the locus of his or her discontent in the Orient."[22] In nineteenth-century orientalist traveler-writers, the condition of belatedness—the dilemma "of finding alternative horizons to explore, discover, and conquer" at a time when "Western tourism and colonialism had already turned the exotic into the familiar"[23]—produced a melancholy discourse of nostalgia. Bongie compares this "attempt at figuring as real what has become patently unreal" to a fetishist's strategy of recognition and disavowal.[24] Just as the fetishist disavows a painful experience of absence through surrogate objects, so the belated traveler, either consciously or unconsciously, tries to transform the signs of the Other's absence into tokens of a presence, the semblance of a residual ground for the exoticist project. Characterized by discursive ambivalence and ideological uncertainties, this belated Orientalism is inscribed within both the economies of colonial power and the exoticist desire for the disappearing Other. Its protagonist is "the hedonistic traveler," a "consumer of sights," and a "passive observer of the already seen."[25]

Marinetti's fragmentary recollections constitute a complex and revealing instance of this split discursive practice. In *Il fascino dell'Egitto,* the frustrated desire for the "authentic" Orient is interrelated with the impossible wish of returning to the enchanted place and time of youth. Various layers of nostalgia intertwine as the futurist poet re-experiences the disappointment of his longing for the exotic, the "fall" from exotic grace. The sight of Alexandria's Ancient Harbor, for instance, evokes a romantic vision of "invisible sumptuous galleys," bringing the poet back to his youthful delusions:

> This was my mother's favorite evening walk. A sixteen-year-old, I accompanied her trying to harmonize my dreamy steps with hers, determined and hurried. She seemed to pursue some painful regret; I was magnetized by the blazing sunset, which again and again scenically rehearsed, as a master of war and heroism, all the possible battles of clouds, purple cavalries, musketries of rays, collapsing golden castles, etc. (TIF 1078)

But maternal regrets and collapsing golden castles usher in an abject scenario of death and decay, and the daydream of heroic battles is overcome by the invasive foulness of a slaughterhouse:

> We were assaulted by the piercing stench of the large slaughterhouse, a purple mass of hovels besieged by piles of bloody hides, heaps of garbage and furious lowing. My nostrils remember the horrible breath of omnipresent Death

in that sinister landscape of smells, among the shadows of ghostly cattle which scared the feet of Arab passersby in skirts and black slippers along the shimmering water. (TIF 1078–79)

Returning to the present, Marinetti remarks that a large embankment, shored up with concrete blocks, has replaced the slaughterhouse and allows "smooth access" to ancient Roman ruins. However, this watershed of progress can not hold back the surge of his decadent sensibility, and, once more, "the turbid sunset changes into the large slaughterhouse of the past, a fuming mass of reddish entrails collapsed over a banana plantation with leaves of emerald and pearls that burn to ashes" (TIF 1079). Progress is occasionally presented in a positive light, as when King Fuad praises the "Italian colony" for its "intelligence[,] industriousness[,] and speed," resuscitating in Marinetti's "visionary heart" the "iron life" of his enterprising father, and arousing the proud vision of the fatherland as a dynamic ship launched to conquer the future ("all electrified by the orders of the Leader and by the inexhaustible fervor of the crews" [TIF 1957–58]). But the futurist will projected in this vision is caught in a devastating battle with a resurgent decadent sensibility, which had been repressed, but not suppressed. Under the weight of British domination, the inexorable advance of progress has crushed both the ancient Egypt of exotic, heroic rulers, and the Egypt of the writer's personal memories, the product of a youthful imagination shaped by orientalist literature and art. These memories "break" in the poet's hands like fragile old toys as he surveys the new reality that has taken over the emotion-charged sites of his youth (TIF 1058). And the anamnestic experience evokes recurrent images of dismemberment and mutilation.[26]

Torn by the clash between orientalist nostalgia and futurist modernolatria, Marinetti colors his descriptions of the Egyptian landscape with a mixture of precious and abject hues, and likewise depicts his encounters with the sociopolitical effects of modernization in an ambivalent light. The splendid desert, which preserves the ruins of ancient glory, is set against the feminine-connoted Nile valley, a hyperorganic and sensual scenario of a battle between life and death (TIF 1074–75). And the glorious memories of erstwhile sovereigns are contrasted with the image of the present leader, King Fuad: in the feminine softness of his countenance and demeanor Marinetti views the embodiment of an enfeebled Egypt, which responds to Europe's aggressive greed with seductive moves. King Fuad's mustache is highlighted as the only remaining trace of Egypt's heroic past: "His curvy mouth smiles under the hook-shaped mustache that still recalls the sultans on horseback under the double arch of scimitar and moon" (TIF 1055). Similarly, the monumental vestiges of ancient Egypt appear to represent mere surrogates or fetishes of a lost grandeur. Upon closer examination, however, one realizes that Marinetti goes beyond the melancholic wiles of orientalist fetishism and, with typical futurist excess, deploys his trademark rhetorical strategy of incorporation. An abundance of alimentary images points to both a continuity and a shift in his approach to the exotic Other. Whether embodied in an architectural marvel or in a feminine specimen of oriental beauty, the mythical exotic is recurrently debased and reduced to the mere object of (Western) appetite.

In the episode tellingly entitled "Una piramide tutta da mangiare" (A pyramid good enough to eat), the traveler-writer's "hunger" is stimulated by the famous pyramid of Ghiseh: "It has nothing nostalgic," he comments, "Nothing eternal. It doesn't teach. It doesn't rule. Rather, it makes you immediately want to eat it at the table or even better in this desert sumptuously set for a feast" (TIF 1077–78). Driving away from the pyramid, Marinetti knowingly evokes and debunks the fetishistic mode of orientalist discourse as he momentarily (re)assumes the position of a romantic observer, enjoying a recomposed image of the whole monument against the picturesque background of a stereotypical sunset: "The pyramid of Ghiseh appeared to me all built of crystallized pistachios. I ate more of it, anticipating what would happen upon returning to Cairo, when, as I quickly turned back, I saw it recompose itself into the old romantic visions. It was already floating in the reddish liquid gold of a sunset à la Victor Hugo" (TIF 1077). The preemptive move of "eating" the pyramid like candy in anticipation of falling under its ancient spell—if only for the duration of a fleeting glance—underscores the distance between Marinetti's futurist approach (modeled after the consumerist dynamics of progress) and the "old romantic visions" (inspired by the orientalist literature that influenced his literary beginnings). At the same time, this episode helps us recognize a connection between the futurist and the romantic observer. As the final scene of the episode reveals, Marinetti's "oral fixation" on the sensual landscape is a symptom of frustrated idealism, that is to say, a product of his romantic roots. Underlying his regressive desire is the fear that even the debased vestiges of the exotic may be taken away: "Lest it would be stolen from me, I ate the moon, convinced that appetite is always right: such was the charm of this exalting contest of Arab deserts" (TIF 1978). In keeping with his overarching strategy, Marinetti assimilates the ruthless rule of progress according to which "appetite" (for things, power, pleasure, knowledge, and so on) can override all concerns, and thus transforms fin-de-siècle melancholia into futurist "hunger" for life. In so doing, he takes the belated traveler's "scopophilic" tendency to revealing extremes.[27] The rhetorical transfiguration of even the most sacred monuments of ancient Egypt into mouthwatering tidbits exposes the unconscious of orientalist discourse: an affinity between the all-consuming voracity that drives Western expansionism and the belated traveler's unrestrained desire to dispose of the Other in order to sustain his own debilitated self.

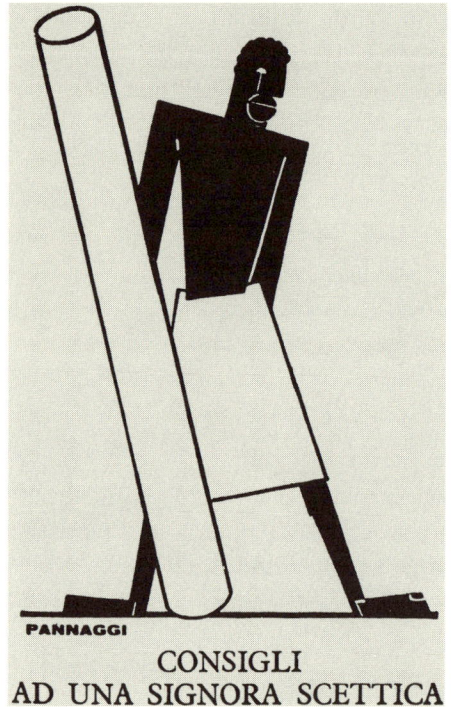

PANNAGGI

CONSIGLI
AD UNA SIGNORA SCETTICA

Figure 2. Illustration of "Consigli a una signora scettica," in F. T. Marinetti's *Scatole d'amore in conserva.* Reprinted by permission of the University of Iowa Libraries (Iowa City).

Such a connection between exoticist desire and the dynamics of progress is most blatantly and crudely displayed in "Il negro" (The black man): a grotesque tale of Western cannibalism and futurist eroticism, which was first published in *Gli amori futuristi* (Futurist loves; 1922) and was later reprinted, with the title "Consigli a una signora scettica" (Advice to a skeptical lady), in *Scatole d'amore in conserva* (Canned love; 1927) and *Novelle con le labbra tinte* (Stories with painted lips; 1930). This short story is one of a number of futurist texts in the genre of social-erotic literature, which acquired great popularity after World War I. As declared in Marinetti's preface to *Novelle con le labbra tinte,* the purpose of futurist storytelling was to prepare the reader for the challenge of the modern "simultaneous" world by offering a new kind of "nourishing" entertainment in the form of variable "Programs for Life":

> The old forms of the novel and the short story are ruined and unsuitable for entertaining, nourishing and energizing the spirit.
>
> All forms of novel and short story regret what once was. From Homer to D'Annunzio all literature can be reduced to this rhythm of dejected tale: Once upon a time . . .

> We want instead a literature that tells the reader: don't give a damn about
> what once was! What once was is always wrong! Choose, find, decide, make
> and master what will be![28]

Generally addressed to a male audience, these futurist programs of simultaneous living often present woman as a key ingredient in the tonic treatment for the endangered masculinity of modern man.[29] In the story under
consideration, however, Marinetti offers advice to a jaded femme fatale, the
kind of feminine figure that typically embodies male anxieties regarding identity and power. A beautiful, rich, idle widow and an amoral "man-
eater," this lady can no longer experience excitement because she has
already "drunk the most original men of Europe like egg yolks" (173). Marinetti admits that even he, with his renowned skills as an imaginative lover,
will not be up to the challenge. His recommendation is therefore "to cross
the ocean in search of exotic males and truly exciting nights of love" (173).
The erotic adventure he prescribes and depicts in full color takes place in
Kuroo, an imaginary little town in Florida where the black man appears to
have lost most of his cultural "Otherness," but not (yet) his body's exotic appeal: by taming the "massive exuberance" of his race, assimilation into the
Western world has in fact refined and enhanced his physical beauty (174).
The lady—herself exotically sensual in her fragrant body, torrid breath, and
in the "soft, black ennui" of "eyes floating in the golden adventure of her
hair" (174–75)—will immediately attract the prized catch of her erotic expedition: Kam-Rim, the extremely handsome and intelligent son of a rich
landowner. Kam-Rim, in turn, will inevitably seduce her with his superior
ability as a lover: "being most intelligent, he can surpass all the earth's races,
besides his own, as a lover at once passionate and courteous. He will also be
able to whisper in your ear, between kisses, the most sweet, joyous, and unruly black songs" (175).

In his good looks and seductive power, Kam-Rim may recall Mafarka: the
foremost futurist incarnation of the exotic, sovereign subject. Like Mafarka,
Kam-Rim also displays the futurist tendency to reverse an excess of sensual-
ity into violence (on the second night, he attempts to kill his lover with a
razor blade, accusing her of betrayal). But as the story makes abundantly
clear, he is only a degraded incarnation of the exotic hero: transplanted
from his native land into a new society where colonization has followed its
extreme course, he is reduced to an exotic body that can be consumed to
appease Western desires and anxieties. His sexual prowess and the synco-
pated rhythm of his voice are the sole residue of the "indomitable" vital
force of his "vanquished race" (175–76), and his sovereignty is limited to
his ability to seduce a bored Western lady. Even this residual power is short-
lived. According to the unwritten law of the land ("the black men, hated
and closely watched by the white in Florida, always pay for their very rare

sexual encounters with white women," 174), Kam-Rim must pay the ultimate price for making love to a white woman. An angry mob (recalling the
feminine-connoted masses of Marinetti's prefuturist works, embodiment of
the homogenizing social forces that destroy heroic individuality) lynches
him and hangs him from the pole of an electric street-lamp (an obvious
icon of progress), as a satisfied "white moon" (the paramount target of
futurist antisentimentalism and antipasséism) pours its vindictive light over
the entire scene. Both Western progress and Western passéism, in other
words, conspire to kill the exotic, sovereign subject. But even dead, Kam-
Rim casts a threatening, phallic shadow over the white crowd: "He seems to
be charged by the ferocious electric currents of the arc lamp which cheerfully showers him with explosive milk. Kam-Rim is naked. Naked. Athletic
power. His chest is monstrously swollen with menace. Suddenly the hanged
man's member rises over the crowd, projecting the enormous shadow of a
bold cigar on the white pavement" (180). This last display of power is met
by the mob's gunfire, which riddles the corpse, tearing it to shreds. In a final
"Supplementary Advice," the author enjoins the lady, who narrowly escaped
the attack of her suspicious lover, to follow the crowd and "satiate" herself
with the barbaric spectacle of the lynching (182). Marinetti pushes his fantasy even further and, envisioning the retail-sale of Kam-Rim's flesh by a
street vendor, prescribes the ultimate cure for the jaded Westerner:

> without bargaining or arguing, at any price, buy the two best pieces of your
> handsome black seducer! It will be easy for you because you are an expert on
> the matter of male anatomy. Don't make the mistake of cooking them. They
> must be eaten raw. The following winter you will be able to return to the
> Hotel Excelsior in Rome carrying in your blood something that no man or
> woman has! That exasperated force of enraged black man will finally give you
> the moral, erotic sentimental balance for which certainly you would beg in
> vain through a thousand stupid flirtations or dreadful, weary loves. (183)

In the end, the complex role of the lady as an intermediary for male exoticism becomes apparent—a role which may account for the exotic features
she shares with Kam-Rim. The two protagonists flesh out Marinetti's desire
to re-incorporate the power lost by the European man. On the one hand,
the exotically virile Kam-Rim, embodying the principle of futurist primitivism, is a suitable match for the man-eater who has consumed the best
champions of European manhood. On the other hand, the femme-fatale
becomes a pretext for racist reprisal, and an instrument of the impersonal
crowd that destroys even the last remains of exotic individuality. Ultimately
however, thanks to Marinetti's "cure," the castrating crowd is exorcised and
exotic individuality is reborn in the lady herself. By displacing the act of incorporation onto a woman, Marinetti also dispels the homoerotic implications with which the tale would otherwise be fraught. Through these twists

and turns, his cannibalistic fantasy displays both the drive toward self-expansion through incorporation that informs the Western approach to the Other, and the drive's phobic undercurrents: fears about the homogenizing effects of progress (e.g., the destruction of exotic difference), but also fears of the Other, namely, anxieties about the perceived advances of women and non-white peoples.

THE END OF THE JOURNEY AND BEYOND

One may be tempted to dismiss Marinetti's tale of Western cannibalism as either a provocative gesture aimed at "bourgeois" tastes and conventions, or simply the grotesque product of a sick imagination. The most disturbing aspects of Marinetti's writing, such as his misogynist outbursts and violent erotic fantasies, are frequently dismissed in this fashion. What I have been arguing, by contrast, is that Marinetti's recipe for self-healing graphically exposes the Western strategy of assimilation/annihilation of the Other, a strategy that governs both discursive, imaginative gestures of appropriation (such as colonialist stereotyping or the exoticist fantasy of an alternative space) and actual practices of economic and sexual exploitation.[30] I will now take this argument even further, as far as our postcolonial, postmodern present. Having become unpalatable to self-proclaimed civilized societies that ostensibly embrace the principles of democracy and tolerance, the blunt tactics—both discursive/cultural and economic/political—of colonialism have progressively given place to subtler, "weaker" forms of assimilation. Overt imperialist rule has been replaced by the impersonal, all-encompassing market rule of "the New World Order," according to which the so-called Third World is differentially inserted into the international division of labor and thus incorporated into the ever-expanding global economy dominated by multinationals. Concomitantly, Western academia has incorporated the (post)colonial world into its sphere of interests, thus creating a fresh reservoir of research material to sustain scholarly endeavors in today's competitive job market. In drawing this parallel I do not mean, of course, to suggest that scholars are agents or accomplices of international capitalism and its neocolonial strategies, but rather to underscore the principles of productivity and competitiveness that govern both the business world and academia, often at the expense of other values and concerns. I hasten to add that the field of postcolonial studies has greatly contributed to the struggle for cultural decolonization by revising ethnocentric historical accounts, overhauling the literary canon, and undermining the authority of Western epistemologies and regimes of representation. Postcolonial theory, in particular, advances a reading practice that can act "as a safeguard against the dangers of 'repetition-in-rupture'" by deconstructing traditional dichotomies and ideological imperatives such as the "organicist" conception of the nation, the essentialist "myths of origin," and the figure of the sovereign subject—white, middle-class, and male—celebrated by imperialist discourse or nostalgically/ambivalently evoked by exoticist fantasies.[31] This very reading practice, however, alerts us to the possibility that deconstructive projects may also unwittingly reproduce the West's assimilative approach to the Other. The most poignant objection raised against postcolonial theory is precisely that in its tendency to overvalue the semiotic domain, it discounts material forms of colonial oppression and resistance to colonial power alike.[32] And indeed some prominent exponents of the theoretical approach have demonstrated awareness of the risks involved in applying a poststructuralist framework to the postcolonial arena: Gayatri Spivak, for instance, warns against the exclusive or "exorbitant" advancement of theory to the exclusion of the domains of social practice; and Homi Bhabha acknowledges that in some cases, "while decentering the claims of Western knowledge by the invocation of its Others," contemporary Western theory may end up foreclosing "on those Others, usually by in some way essentializing them."[33]

One step to avoid falling back into the essentializing, assimilative rut of exoticist discourse might be to recognize the genealogical link between the protagonists of exoticism and postmoderinism. Though by negation rather than by affirmation—the one being the disillusioned reverse of the other— contemporary theoretical projects remain anchored in the (now pulverized) notion of sovereign (united, authentic, authoritative) subjectivity. The landscape that these projects evoke is the wasteland produced by the collapse of logocentric thought with all its false idols. Nothing seems to lie beyond the ruins of the humanist tradition (or, to use other abused commonplaces, beyond "the end of history," which seems also to mark "the end of the journey" toward identity and self-representation) except an all-encompassing "lack," a bleak desert where any positive vision on the part of the stranded traveler is bound to appear as a mirage of the ever-thirsty imagination. I use the desert as a figure for today's intellectual aporias in order to draw a connection between the decentered, disseminated subject of postmodern theory and the long lineage of protagonists in exoticist discourse: most notably, the heroic explorer embodying the ethnocentric arrogance of Western thought; the conqueror/colonizer, following in the footsteps of the explorer and enacting the aggressive exploitative drives that the latter's knowledge authorizes; the belated, exoticist traveler, searching for an elusive fantasy of authenticity, and thus playing out the modern subject's division between a desire for progress through self-expansion/control and nostalgia for the myth of uncorrupted origins; and at "the end of the journey," poised on the brink of total ideological bankruptcy, the deconstructed protagonist of "weak" thought, for whom the exotic Other remains a (haunting) memory of a mirage in a never-never land, the memory of what never was.[34]

But this need not be the end of the line for the Western "traveler" in search of identity and self-representation. The journey, I believe, appears to be over only for those who opt to remain trapped within the crumbled walls of failed ideological systems. I will therefore conclude this chapter by shifting attention onto a different kind of scholarly and poetic project, one that seeks to depart from the nostalgic, melancholic, and nihilistic impasse of the "end-of-the-journey" mentality. I refer to Biancamaria Frabotta's sustained effort to revise the metaphor-concept of the journey from a woman's perspective. Driving such effort is a need to trace new, viable parameters for self-representation and identity without envisioning a definitive route toward a programmatically defined destination/resolution, i.e., without recourse to prefabricated ideologies. The project is premised on the belief that a woman cannot recognize herself in the images of the traveler consecrated by Western culture, and thus should not remain attached to the value system they embody. A less explicitly articulated premise is the recognition of an affinity between the feminine and the non-Western Other, two paradigmatic objects of the Western male subject's desires/anxieties. As suggested in the following passage, for these previously silenced subjects the crisis of the West's "universals" marks not the end of the journey but the possibility of new beginnings:

> In the minds of weaker subjects, civilization is still a goal to be reached, not a conquest to be preserved. The journey we must undertake is not the exploratory mission immediately ratified by the conquistadors; or the philosophical adventure that oscillated, through centuries of glorious history, between two opposite dreams: the return to the origins of civilization and the less and less likely escape toward an exotic Elsewhere. Today nothing is more unstable than the concept of center and margin and their mutual relationships; therefore, the crisis of the humanistic tradition of the journey is a given, not a melancholic projection of the travelers' mood. Driven by imposing migratory currents, human masses move toward the center of power and wealth and the fortunate inhabitants of the surrounded citadel react with the scarce elegance that is typical of a siege.
>
> And yet we are one step from the end of the millennium. Is it possible that we can not imagine anything other than this obtuse instinct of self-preservation?[35]

Frabotta elaborates the trope of *viandanza* (wayfaring) as a possible way of imagining something different from the Westerner's "obtuse instinct of self-preservation," an expression by which she indicates not just a political reaction but also, and perhaps primarily, a cultural one. She defines her metaphor-concept as "a continuous return to a new departure," a journey conducted not in the name of "authenticity that refers back to the close circle of the autós [self], of repossession and of belonging" but in a spirit of "humbleness" and in the "precariousness of fleeting hospitality."[36] Frabotta's arguments allow us to perceive both the limitations and the value of projects such as the one she pursues. While the non-Western immigrant and the Western intellectual may, on some level, share a similar position vis-à-vis the now-decentered subject of phallogocentric and ethnocentric discourse, their experiences remain separated by irreducibly different realities and concerns. As one of the fortunate inhabitants of the citadel of privilege, Frabotta (an established poet and scholar) is of course not involved in the sort of uprooting that continues to be a forced choice for many "weaker subjects" around the world. Thus their struggles cannot be subsumed within (and will not be directly aided by) the kind of journey she undertakes. Yet such a journey constitutes a valid attempt to move beyond the hopeless or defensive stasis in which the intellectual establishment has remained entrenched after the failure of totalizing ideologies. As already noted, this move beyond the postmodern impasse is not a return to the teleological path of some definitive resolution/destination. The defining attitude of the "wayfarer"—a willingness to accept the precarious conditions and rewards of the existential journey, which also involves humbly accepting (and returning) the "hospitality" of other people and things—marks the distance between Frabotta's poetic persona and the other figures of the writer we have encountered in this essay. This is true, in particular, of the belated traveler of the fin-de-siècle (both modernist and postmodernist), who occupies "the scene of decadence rather than attempting to overcome it,"[37] and the futurist conqueror of modernity, with his aestheticizing surrogate, the desert-bound poet who ends up surviving solely on his artistic distillation because he can neither achieve nor relinquish his impossible dream of totalizing pursuits. Encouraging an attitude that is positive but not incautiously euphoric (euphoria, as Frabotta warns and Marinetti's "optimistic despair" shows, is the flip side of dejection), the "wayfaring" poet thus invites the reader to be hospitable to precarious, partial pursuits that are sustained by vital encounters.

NOTES

1. See, in particular, Jeffrey T. Schnapp and Barbara Spackman, eds., *Fascism and Culture,* special issue of *Stanford Italian Review* 8, nos. 1–2 (1990); and Jeffrey T. Schnapp, *Staging Fascism: 18 BL and the Theater of Masses for Masses* (Stanford, Calif.: Stanford University Press, 1996).

2. Chris Bongie, *Exotic Memories: Literature, Colonialism, and the Fin de Siècle* (Stanford, Calif.: Stanford University Press, 1991), 38.

3. All translations are mine. For a survey of this inquiry see Giovanna Tomasello, *La letteratura coloniale italiana dalle avanguardie al fascismo* (Palermo: Sellerio, 1984),

13–24. A number of useful documents, including the questionnaire and the responses originally published in *L'Azione Coloniale,* are reproduced in Tomasello's book.

4. Tomasello, *La letteratura coloniale italiana dalle avanguardie al fascismo,* 120.

5. Ibid., 124–25.

6. Ibid., 120.

7. See F. T. Marinetti, "L'Africa generatrice e ispiratrice di poesia e di arti" (Africa as a source and inspiration of poetry and the arts), originally published with the proceedings of the Eighth Convention of the Fondazione Alessandro Volta (*Africa* [Rome, 1939], 198–201), and reprinted in Tomasello, *La letteratura coloniale italiana dalle avanguardie al fascismo,* 131–33.

8. On avant-garde primitivism, see John J. White, *Literary Futurism: Aspects of the First Avant-Garde* (Oxford: Clarendon Press, 1990), 289–358. White outlines programmatic differences between the "retrospective, archaizing, 'sentimental'" neo-primitivism predominant among the historical avant-gardes (cubists, vorticists, and Russian futurists) and the brand of primitivism embraced by the Italian futurists: "a modernist primitivism, one which is not backward-looking to the same degree (if at all), but seeks to create a new sensibility appropriate to its own culture, especially those elements of the modern world which point towards the future" (316). In White's view, an even more crucial distinguishing characteristic of futurist primitivism is that this ideologically progressive stance and its equally progressive aesthetic manifestations are contaminated by morally objectionable, reactionary tendencies: savage vitalism, barbarous aggressiveness, violent iconoclasm, and regressive anti-intellectualism.

As my discussion of Marinetti's writings makes apparent, I take issue with such a sharp distinction between progressive/aesthetically valuable and regressive/morally objectionable aspects of futurist primitivism.

9. F. T. Marinetti, *Il fascino dell'Egitto* (Milano: Mondadori, 1933); reprinted in *Teoria e invenzione futurista* (hereafter TIF), ed. Luciano De Maria (1968; Milano: Arnoldo Mondadori Editore, 1983), 1056. Subsequent page references to TIF will be given parenthetically within the text.

10. F. T. Marinetti, *Luci veloci: Dramma futurista in sei sintesi,* in *Teatro,* ed. Giovanni Calendoli (Roma: Vito Bianco Editore, 1960), vol. 3, 297. Subsequent page references to the play will be given parenthetically within the text.

11. The stage directions read: "Ten years from now in Bassabulà, an Egyptian coastal village turned into a major oil port" (277). There is no record of Bassabulà either in old or contemporary maps.

12. Musoduro makes Perlina's role explicit as he tells her, "you are me, more transparent and more serene" (283). She gives voice to his ideals and portrays an idealistic version of him. As the object of Mahmud's desire, Perlina also stands for the attraction that Italian culture exerts on the Arab world—a perspective that reverses the exoticist position and is consistent with the goals of fascist propaganda.

13. Benedetta Cappa, Marinetti's wife, reports the incident in a letter to her brother, Alberto Cappa. See Gianni Eugenio Viola, *L'utopia futurista: Contributo alla storia delle avanguardie* (Ravenna: Longo, 1994), 101.

14. See Viola, *L'utopia futurista: Contributo alla storia delle avanguardie,* 142. For another significant episode, see Lucio Villari, "Inediti di F. T. Marinetti: una poesia

di guerra e una lettera," in *Nuovi argomenti* 22, nos. 33–34 (1973), 7–11. Villari documents the uneasy relationship between the futurist leader and the minister of Popular Culture, Alessandro Pavolini, highlighting a gap between Marinetti's efforts at offering poetic "support" to Mussolini's war and the response of both the fascist leadership and the public at large.

15. Viola, *L'utopia futurista: Contributo alla storia delle avanguardie,* 130.

16. This interpretation is confirmed by the role that the desert recurrently plays in Marinetti's writing. See, for instance, *Il tamburo di fuoco,* in *Teatro,* ed. Giovanni Calendoli (Roma: Vito Bianco Editore, 1960), vol. 3, 29–31 and 42. Subsequent page references will be given parenthetically within the text.

17. This is the central argument in Ali Behdad's *Belated Travelers: Orientalism in the Age of Colonial Dissolution* (Durham and London: Duke University Press, 1994).

18. Throughout Marinetti's writing, the assimilative strategy of metaphorically incorporating a hostile or alien object/environment is the precondition for artistic creation. See Cinzia Sartini-Blum, *The Other Modernism: F. T. Marinetti's Futurist Fiction of Power* (Berkeley: University of California Press, 1996), 52, 134, 152, and passim. In this work, relying on Paul Ricoeur's *Freud and Philosophy: An Essay on Interpretation,* trans. Denis Savage (New Haven, Conn.: Yale University Press, 1970), 315–16, I have given a psychoanalytical reading of Marinetti's trope of incorporation as indicative of a semantics of desire restricted to the perspective of the "pleasure-ego," an archaic stage in the psychic constitution of the self, antecedent or regressive with respect to the consciousness of the "reality-ego," the ability to recognize and accept the limitations imposed upon the subject's desire by reality (or by another subject's desire). Philosophically, such a stance is a regressive one, marked by inability or unwillingness to accept the limitations of life and avoid the resurgence of narcissistic illusions. This very stance is at the core of the futurist tendency to primitivism, violent antagonism, and juvenile rebelliousness (Blum, *The Other Modernism: F. T. Marinetti's Futurist Fiction of Power,* 14 and 93–99).

19. See Blum, *The Other Modernism: F. T. Marinetti's Futurist Fiction of Power,* 48–54, 157, and passim.

20. Lanzirica embodies the "sickly" drift of passéist poetry that Marinetti elsewhere identifies with Gabriele D'Annunzio. Lanzirica's lyrical address to Kabango (51)—an enticement to leave the virile desert for the forest's soothing, sensual lures—echoes "La pioggia nel pineto," one of D'Annunzio's most famous poems.

21. See Enrico Crispolti, *Storia e critica del Futurismo* (Bari: Laterza, 1986), 219–24; Emilio Gentile, "Il futurismo e la politica: Dal nazionalismo modernista al fascismo (1909–20)," in *Futurismo, cultura e politica,* ed. Renzo De Felice (Torino: Edizioni della Fondazione Giovannni Agnelli, 1988), 105–59; Niccolò Zapponi, "Futurismo e fascismo," in *Futurismo, cultura e politica,* ed. De Felice, 161–76; and Claudia Salaris, *Artecrazia* (Firenze: La Nuova Italia, 1992), 7–63.

22. Behdad, *Belated Travelers: Orientalism in the Age of Colonial Dissolution,* 54–55.

23. Ibid., 92.

24. Bongie, *Exotic Memories: Literature, Colonialism, and the Fin de Siècle,* 76

25. Behdad, *Belated Travelers: Orientalism in the Age of Colonial Dissolution,* 63–64.

26. Blum, *The Other Modernism: F. T. Marinetti's Futurist Fiction of Power,* 138–40.

27. Behdad defines the belated traveler as a "*voracious* observer" (58; emphasis

in original) who indulges in scopophilic desire: "The tendency to have a wide angle of vision is symptomatic of the modern orientalist's fragmentation. Since he can no longer achieve a sense of epistemological totality, he indulges in a scopophilic desire that situates him in a panoptic position from which he can have a panoramic view" (58).

28. F. T. Marinetti, *Novelle con le labbra tinte* (Milano: Mondadori, 1930), xvi. Quotes from the story refer to this edition; page numbers will be given parenthetically within the text.

29. For an in-depth analysis of the trope of incorporation in futurist erotica, see Blum, "The Heart with Watertight Compartments and the Travel-Size Woman: Futurist Strategies in Love and War," in *The Other Modernism: F. T. Marinetti's Futurist Fiction of Power*, in particular the section "Cooking with Women," pp. 89–99.

30. Two essays included in this collection are especially relevant to my discussion of the Western strategy of incorporation. In "Colonial Autism: Whitened Heroes, Auditory Rhetorics and National Identity in Interwar Italian Cinema," Bertellini calls attention to the appropriatory strategy by which movie characters like Maciste change nationality and color while retaining their primitive strength. Lombardi-Diop's "Gift, Sex, and Guns: Italian Explorers in Africa, 1860–1910" underscores the contrast between the Europeans' "cannibalistic" system of economic/sexual exploitation in Africa and an indigenous system of reciprocal economy that also entails reciprocity of perspective and the acceptance of social responsibility.

31. See Bart Moore-Gilbert, *Postcolonial Theory: Contexts, Practices, Politics* (London and New York: Verso, 1997), 162–63. Moore-Gilbert offers a balanced survey of the debate on postcolonial theory.

32. Moore-Gilbert, *Postcolonial Theory: Contexts, Practices, Politics,* 162.

33. Ibid., 161–66.

34. One can find an example of this stance in Bongie's *Exotic Memories,* an excellent study of exoticist literature, which illustrates the genealogical connection between turn-of-the-century exoticism and postmodern thought. While offering a cogent analysis of the contradictions at the heart of the exoticist project, Bongie advances an elegiac, recollective attitude toward the subject of exoticist discourse, the "posthumous" sovereign individual, an attitude by which he consciously places himself in the same position as the allegorizing, commemorating "writer among the ruins" that takes center stage in his book. As Bongie argues, echoing Walter Benjamin's *The Origins of German Tragic Drama* (1928), this writer adopts a commemorative rhetoric and an allegorical mode to approach "the alterity of the past from the perspective of a present that ruins and masks (or fictionalizes) what has come before it. With a melancholy gaze the allegorist 'revives the empty world in the form of a mask, and derives an enigmatic satisfaction in contemplating it'; an equivocal figure, he situates himself *both* between the past and the present *and* entirely to one side, the fallen side, of this opposition. Through his work, we envision the path that lies before us but that we cannot take, or can take only in a dream" (181–82; emphasis in original). From this vantage point, the melodramatic fictions—or "posthumous (re)creations"—of self-mastery by writers like D'Annunzio appear "supremely ethical" strategies for coping with the "unending decline" of our world (185–86). However, I would argue, the hardly "ethical" implications of the will to mastery that

such fictions "commemorate"—but also announce and celebrate, given modernism's position vis-à-vis fascism—are notably obfuscated by this focus on the posthumous individual.

35. Biancamaria Frabotta, "La viandanza femminile e la poesia," *Horizonte* 1 (1996): 76–77.

36. Ibid., 79. For a discussion of the difficulties and dangers involved in sublating the postcolonial within other political and critical projects, see Moore-Gilbert, *Postcolonial Theory: Contexts, Practices, Politics,* 199–203.

37. Bongie, *Exotic Memories: Literature, Colonialism, and the Fin de Siècle,* 186.

Alexandria Revisited

Colonialism and the Egyptian Works of Enrico Pea and Giuseppe Ungaretti

Lucia Re

In his essay "The Empire at Work: Verdi's *Aida*," Edward Said judges Verdi's opera to be essentially complicit in the violence of European imperialism. When Verdi wrote *Aida* (1870–71), Egypt was still officially part of the Ottoman Empire; the opera was commissioned by Khedive Ismail for the Cairo Opera House in 1870, the year after the opening celebrations for the Suez canal (which included the opera house's inauguration with a performance of Verdi's *Rigoletto*). Khedive Ismail—descendant of the dynasty of viceroys that started with Muhammad Ali in the early nineteenth century and that laid the foundation of the modern state of Egypt—was then attempting to establish Egypt's independence from the Ottoman Empire. Some of the music from *Aida* was later incorporated into the Egyptian national anthem. Yet Verdi had no feelings at all for modern Egypt, Said claims; modern Egypt was a place that Verdi could not relate to in any way other than through the colonizing optic of the European conqueror, "premised upon the subordination and victimization of the native" (Said 131). Said bases much of his analysis on Verdi's connection with Auguste Mariette, the French Egyptologist and archaeologist (deeply implicated in the Napoleonic "imperial genealogy") on whose knowledge of ancient Egypt Verdi relied for *Aida*. Verdi even asked Mariette to design the sets and write the scenario for the libretto. Even Verdi's desire to control every aspect of the production in Cairo is, in Said's eyes, a form of imperial domination, and he derides Verdi's "comic effort" to have the famous Egyptian ceremonial trumpet built in Italy on the basis of studies of ancient music by French musicologist François-Joseph Fétis.

In Said's allegorical reading, *Aida*'s story is itself the dramatization of a colonial plot. In the opera, the Egyptian army defeats an Ethiopian force, but the young Egyptian hero (Radames) is judged to be a traitor and sentenced to death. According to Said, a French colonial perspective underlies this plot, for the opera evokes the dangers for France of the Egyptian policy of force in Ethiopia, which was pursued by Khedive Ismail as a way to assert Egypt's independence from Istanbul. In the struggle over Egypt between 1840 and 1882 (the year of British occupation), the British encouraged Ismail's moves in East Africa in order to block French and Italian ambitions in Somalia and Ethiopia.

Although it is undeniable that *Aida* in many ways is an orientalizing fantasy, Said's argument ignores several facts. The plot of *Aida* does not necessarily embody a French-colonial or imperial perspective; indeed, it can be read (and has been read) as anticolonial, anti-imperialist, and nonracist.[1] As grand and magniloquent and (as Said rather snobbishly points out) rather vulgar the "sound" and the operatic trappings of "empire" are in *Aida* (ancient Egyptian empire, that is), the opera is, nonetheless, a tragedy; it points to the bloody costs of imperialist power struggles between nations. If anything, the plot seems to embrace Khedive Ismail's perspective and point to the desirability of Ethiopia joining Egypt.[2] The story of the Ethiopian princess's tragic love affair with the Egyptian Radames is reminiscent of the tale of the star-crossed lovers of *Romeo and Juliet,* and it similarly indicts the kind of political hatred and fanatical prejudice that prevents the lovers' union in Shakespeare's tragedy. If one considers that Italy for centuries had been a battleground for French, Spanish, and Austrian imperialism, that 1870 was the year of Italy's final unification that—with the declaration of Rome as capital—sanctioned its independence, and that Verdi and his music were among the most revered and popular symbols of the Risorgimento, *Aida* may appear to hold an altogether different meaning. Many Italian patriots sought refuge in Egypt during the Risorgimento. In 1819, five hundred Italian political exiles resided in Egypt and were in contact with Mohammed Ali (Ilbert 103; Briani 22). Political emigration from the Italian peninsula into Egypt continued throughout the Risorgimento. Several Italians participated in Mohammed Ali's abolitionist expedition in the Sudan in 1838, and in the Egyptian independence struggle against the Ottoman Empire in the 1840s.[3] Khedive Ismail is likely to have seen in Verdi's music a political symbol of the spirit of national independence rather than a means to enslave Egypt economically, culturally, and politically to Europe.

Under Ismail's reign, the Egyptian cotton boom (caused by the American Civil War) linked Egypt's economy inextricably to Europe, sharpening the dichotomy between big landowners and impoverished fellahin, and ultimately leading to the erosion of the peasant family and traditional culture. Yet, as Michael Reimer shows in his study of Alexandria in the nineteenth century, the idea that the khedives single-handedly led Egypt into a submissive form of dependency is false, for the process of Egypt's incorporation into the wider European and Mediterranean economy was already well under way in the eighteenth century. Nonetheless, the khedives were responsible for tilting the balance toward Europe. Arabization in Egypt and the notion (officially sanctioned by an 1870 khedival decree) that native Egyptians should rule their country along with the non-native political elite developed only in the nineteenth century, paradoxically at the very same time that Europeanization was under way and Levantines were being extensively employed in administration. The "Egypt for Egyptians" movement led to the Arab riots of 1882, and was crushed by British military force and subsequent occupation. (Asked to participate in the repression of the Arab riots, Italy, then under the presidency of Agostino Depretis, declined to be involved.) Indigenous aspirations to self-rule were thwarted by the installation of a thoroughly colonial regime subservient to British and other European interests. When Verdi wrote *Aida* in 1870, then, Arabization was still a relatively novel concept. That Verdi, as Said claims, had no personal connection to modern Egypt and Egyptians may be true. As for his "feelings," they are more difficult to gauge, although any interest in the question of Arabization on Verdi's part would have been anachronistic.

One might avoid Said's generalizations and the risks involved in lumping Verdi with the French under the vague category of "European imperialism" by considering the specific realities of Italy and the Italians' relationship with Egypt around 1870. A movement of nationalist imperialism began to develop in Italy only around the 1890s; the first nationalist journal was *Il Regno,* which began publication in 1903. Prior to the 1890s, colonialism and imperialism were widely perceived as glaringly contradictory with respect to the spirit of the Risorgimento (Isnenghi 53–54). Furthermore, the vast majority of Italians in Egypt around 1870 were impoverished emigrants. In 1868, for example, Giuseppe Ungaretti's father, Antonio—a peasant from the countryside near Lucca—emigrated to northern Egypt with thousands of others (most of whom were native Egyptians from the southern regions of the upper Nile) to work on the digging of the Suez canal. He became gravely ill with elephantiasis from digging in the mud of the Red Sea, and he died of gangrene only two years after Giuseppe's birth in Alexandria. Along with the descendants of Italian political exiles, poor emigrants (mostly from Sicily and the Veneto, initially) formed the core of the Italian community that established itself in Alexandria in the nineteenth century. Although native Egyptians outnumbered foreigners in most categories of labor, in the 1870s Egypt saw the growing presence of Mediterranean immigrant groups, above all Italians and Greeks, many of them joining the ranks of manual laborers and the urban poor (Reimer 168). About 10,000 Italians resided in Egypt by 1870 according to Briani, a number that grew to about 19,000 by 1882 and 35,000 by 1907.

Newspapers in Italian (*L'Avvenire d'Egitto, L'Eco d'Egitto, La Trombetta*) had started to appear earlier, in the 1860s, at the time of the cotton boom, when thousands of people embarked every year from the Italian peninsula to seek work in Egypt. As early as the 1830s, a more affluent professional Italian population—mainly businessmen, bankers, architects, and engineers—had also begun to establish itself in Egypt. This group contributed to the modernization of Egypt and to the construction of railroads and roads (a development that Said acknowledges as beneficial, even though it accelerated Egypt's dependence on Europe). These affluent "European colonizers" were the intended audience and the consumers of Verdi's operas, Said points out; yet he forgets that the Italian presence in Egypt was hardly limited to the affluent and that Verdi's operas were hugely appealing to working-class audiences of all nationalities and races. Whatever his personal feelings about Egypt might have been, then, it is clear that Verdi was not as removed from the country as Said indicates, if only because Italians were very much an integral part of modern Egypt, an active presence that was highly diversified and stratified rather than monolithically "imperial." Thus the meaning of the letter, cited by Said, to the critic Filippo Filippi in which Verdi decries the excess of publicity mounted to advertise the opening of *Aida* in Cairo is not to be sought in Verdi's aristocratic faith in the value of "European" pure art, but is explainable rather in terms of the author's desire to see how the opera would pass the unadulterated test of popular opinion in a multicultural context.

Yet what I would like to address in this chapter is not the specific weakness of Said's reading of *Aida* as "imperial artifact," but rather the larger critical and theoretical framework that it implies, and that I consider representative of colonial and postcolonial studies in general. The opening of *Aida* in Cairo may not have been, as we have seen, necessarily a function of "empire," but it was, to be sure, a "colonial" event. I wish to question the equation of "colonial" with "imperialist" that subtends Said's essay, and especially the assumption that the colonial (situation, position, or artifact) is necessarily predicated on violence and informed by an ideology of racist domination (Said 131). Is the "non-native" art that comes out of or is produced in (as in the case of *Aida*) the colony necessarily complicit with imperialist oppression? To answer this question, and to develop the hypothesis of a nonimperialist or even anti-imperialist colonial discourse, I have chosen to focus specifically on Alexandria in the late nineteenth and early twentieth centuries, with an eye to the particular repercussions that Alexandria's colonial culture had on Italian modernism.

Some of Italian modernism's most interesting and seminal figures, including Filippo Tommaso Marinetti, Giuseppe Ungaretti, Enrico Pea, and Fausta Cialente, were born in colonial Alexandria or resided there for a substantial period. This has seemed a simple coincidence thus far, but I will argue otherwise. Marinetti and Ungaretti are well known as founders of, respectively, the futurist avant-garde movement and the new modernist movement in post–World War I Italian poetry. Enrico Pea and Fausta Cialente are less familiar figures, yet they were nonetheless important—if eccentric—exponents of modernism in Italian literature. Pea was one of the very few actual working-class Italian modernists, a man who always struggled to make a living and was almost entirely self-taught yet achieved remarkable originality in his literary work.[4] He went to Alexandria in 1896 when he was still a boy—one of many desperate emigrants from the Versilia region of Tuscany—and lived and worked there until 1914, when he returned to Italy. Pea's wife, whom he met and married in Alexandria, was born there, the daughter of Tuscan emigrants who named her Aida after Verdi's heroine. Fausta Cialente is considered one of the two or three most important Italian women modernists of the period between the two world wars. She lived in Egypt for more than thirty-five years, from 1921 to 1956. Interest in her has undergone something of a renaissance in recent years as feminist scholars have begun to study her work, especially in light of her outspoken antifascism and feminism, although the importance of her early Egyptian works has not been established yet.[5]

What do these four have in common aside from their time in Egypt? As different as these four writers are from one another, they nevertheless share a quality of "separateness" that sets them apart from other Italian modernists. Their distance from the Italian context and their particular colonial position as citizens of Alexandria were crucial factors that shaped their originality. The first three, Marinetti, Ungaretti, and Pea, made a startling new use of literary language. Roughly between 1910 and 1920, Marinetti's "words in freedom," Ungaretti's shockingly laconic verses (often of only one or two words), and Pea's raw iconoclasm exploded the literary conventions of late-nineteenth-century and early-twentieth-century literary discourse in Italy (where Giovanni Pascoli and Gabriele D'Annunzio were the leading figures). The first two helped define the discourse of the avant-garde and of modernism in Italy and in the world. Cialente came to writing later (her first novel dates from 1929), and she was influenced especially by André Gide (whose novels *Voyage au Congo* [1927] and *Le Retour du Tchad* [1928] were decidedly anticolonialist) and Proust, as well as other modernists (Petrignani 84–85; Cialente 208–9). Cialente is unique in that she was the only Italian woman writer of the fascist era who combined a highly refined modernist lyrical prose with politically charged, subtly antifascist themes. She thus breaks the mold of the "consensual," "passive," or "seduced" female subject under fascism that scholars such as Victoria De Grazia and Maria Antonietta Macciocchi, among others, have identified. It is my view that the fundamental, formative experience of the colony that these four shared, and, as we shall see, of the specific kind of colony that

Alexandria was, gave them a degree of mental freedom (which was cultural, intellectual, and political) and a mindset that allowed them to do what they did. In this essay I will focus in particular on the work of Pea and Ungaretti, and on the influence of Alexandria's colonial culture. The spirit of Alexandria, however, equally permeates, though in radically different ways, the work of Marinetti and Cialente.[6]

The Italian colony in Alexandria was far from being a mere extension of Italy abroad; rather, it was part of Alexandria's larger, complex, and multicultural colonial society. Marinetti, Ungaretti, Pea, and Cialente were neither exiles nor expatriates but rather—at least for substantial parts of their lives—actual members of Alexandria's multicultural community. Although all maintained considerable links with Italy, being in Alexandria freed them from the constraints of conventions and traditions that residence in Italy and membership in any of the various literary circles active at the time would have imposed on them. Politically, it allowed them to gain perspectives that were distinct from those of most of their contemporaries in Italy. It also established for these writers a mental space, a frame of reference to which they would return for nourishment again and again, even after leaving Alexandria for good. "Alessandria d'Egitto è pure il mio paese" ("And yet Alexandria is surely my country"), Ungaretti wrote nostalgically to Pea in 1913 in the midst of a heady period in Paris, then the capital of modernism and the avant-garde (Ungaretti, *Lettere a Pea,* 50).[7] And he repeated "Sono d'Alessandria d'Egitto" ("I am from Alexandria") in the autobiographical note appended to his collected poems only about a year before his death (*Vita d'un uomo: Tutte le poesie,* 505). While living in Alexandria, Ungaretti subscribed to the journal *La Voce* and even corresponded briefly with its editors, eventually developing an intellectual passion for the iconoclast Giovanni Papini in particular.

But if one compares Ungaretti to Papini, it is clear that the former did not share in the least the provincialism, misogyny, homophobia, and racism that characterize much of Papini's and, generally speaking, *La Voce*'s production.[8] Even Marinetti, whose privileged bourgeois upbringing in Alexandria isolated him to some extent from aspects of the city's social and political life that deeply affected Ungaretti and Pea, was influenced in crucial ways by the experience of Alexandria's multiethnic and cosmopolitan community. In spite of his notorious and ambivalent strategic allegiance with Mussolini and Italian fascism, Marinetti did not share the regime's reactionary view of women as reproductive machines, and he was an outspoken critic of Nazism and of the Italian racial laws of 1938. Marinetti's passionate patriotism and even his aestheticization of war were—as Giovanna Tomasello has observed in her study of Italian colonial literature—fundamentally extraneous to Mussolini's imperialist ideology. Marinetti's early cosmopolitan formation in Alexandria contributed to his keen awareness of the need for art to address a global audience, not just an Italian-speaking one. Thus, while the members of the so-called Florentine avant-garde were speaking mostly to one another, Marinetti became the first "Italian" intellectual in modern times to conceive of an international rather than a national art movement and to envision a worldwide constituency for futurism. And although the actual launching of futurism was possible only from Paris, futurism's cosmopolitanism is to a large extent comparable to that of Alexandrian culture. It is therefore incorrect to assume, as Claudia Salaris and others do, that for Marinetti Africa represented only the "primitive" and the "instinctive," in contrast to "civilization" and the absolute modernity epitomized by Paris. On the contrary, Alexandria for Marinetti represented a model of modern metropolitan civilization that incorporated elements of both Europe and Africa, effectively decentering both, and thriving on the multiple contrasts between the two. Alexandria was not, as is sometimes assumed, simply a colonial extension of Paris, and Marinetti's (as well as Ungaretti's and Pea's) transfer from Alexandria to Europe was not equivalent to going from the margins to the center. The composite, hybrid, and to a large degree anarchic nature of the city of Alexandria finds its equivalent in the futurist aesthetics of words-in-freedom, assemblage, and a decentered, multiplied visual language. Alexandria, an "ugly," incoherent, yet spellbinding modern city where the past is invisible because monuments (unlike Paris and Rome) have been mercilessly wiped out, provided Marinetti with a first glimpse of the possibilities of "antigrazioso" ("antigraceful" and "antigracious") aesthetics and of a future-oriented temporality emptied of the burdens of history.

ALEXANDRIA

What was Alexandria like, what were its links with Italy, and why was this colonial city a place that was so deeply loved and evoked such strong feelings in the hearts of natives and foreign residents alike, inspiring a range of memorable works? Writers who wrote about colonial Alexandria include the modernist poet Constantin Kavafy (who was born and lived most of his life in Alexandria, writing exclusively in Greek), E. M. Forster and Lawrence Durrell, the Nobel prize winner Naguib Mahfouz (whose 1967 novel about postcolonial Alexandria, *Miramar,* is filled with nostalgia for the colonial city), Edwar al-Kharrat (one of the founders of Egyptian modernism and author of the novels *City of Saffron* and *Girls of Alexandria*), and André Aciman (author of the moving 1994 memoir *Out of Egypt*).[9] Each of these writers positions himself differently vis-à-vis the city, and the spectrum of colonial visions in their works is enormously varied. None, however, comes closer to Said's notion of orientalizing (and imperialist) artifact than Durrell in his *Alexandria Quartet* (1957–60).[10] The first novel in particular, *Jus-*

tine, with its portrait of the central character as an out-of-control, over-sexed, and transgressive "jewess," conforms to the European convention of displaying feminine eroticism and "making Oriental women central to any exotic practice" (Said 121). Ungaretti's and Pea's depictions of Alexandria could not be further removed from Durrell's, with his cast of colonial characters oscillating between self-conscious bohemia and unabashed economic and intellectual privilege. Ungaretti grew up and Pea (who was seven years older than Ungaretti) lived and worked in one of those suburbs of Alexandria where Durrell's Justine or her Oxford-educated, Rolls-Royce-driving husband would occasionally go slumming.[11]

The suburb of Moharam-Bey, as Pea describes it in *Vita in Egitto,* was a poor multiethnic neighborhood with unpaved streets and humble little shops. On the edge of the desert, it was populated by Jewish, Arab, and European laborers. Here one could hear the muezzin's call to prayer from the minaret of the local mosque and see the Jews light their fires every Friday evening when "ridiventati in questo giorno, per fede, nomadi come i padri, preparano in mezzo allo sterrato, fuori dall'uscio di casa, sul focolare di fortuna, come se rifossero nel deserto, la loro magra cena" ("having in this day become nomads once again by faith, like their forefathers, they prepare their meager dinner on the ground in front of their house, on an improvised hearth, as if they were in the desert") (210). After her husband's death, Ungaretti's mother—who was also an immigrant peasant from the Lucchesia ("energica popolana," or "energetic woman of the common people," Pea calls her)—made a living by baking bread. Through her industriousness and economizing she was able to open a bakery in her house ("a shack with a courtyard with chickens and a vegetable garden," as Ungaretti recalls in *Quaderno egiziano*) and give work to Arab laborers. Eventually she saved enough money to send her son to a good school in Alexandria (the École Suisse Jacob, with an ethnically diverse student body that included Arabs and Jews), and later, at the age of twenty-four, to the Sorbonne (where Ungaretti, just like Marinetti a few years earlier, studied law before changing to literature). Ungaretti's schooling and his twenty-four years in Alexandria shaped his antinationalistic, anti-imperialist, and non-racist vision of humanity—a vision that stayed with him and set him quite apart from most of his contemporaries then living in Italy, including the intellectuals and leading modernist writers who then constituted the *La Voce* circle. As Ungaretti himself remarked:

> I miei compagni erano ragazzi che appartenevano a tutte le credenze e alle piú varie nazionalità. E' un'abitudine presa dall'infanzia quella di dare, certo, un'importanza alla propria nazionalità, ma insomma di non ammettere che non potesse essermi fratello chi ne avesse un'altra. . . . Sono fatto in modo che non so che cosa sia la ripugnanza per altre razze o per altri popoli, e ciò forse

dipende anche dall'essere nato a Alessandria d'Egitto, dove affluiva gente, la più diversa per provenienza e origine. (*Vita: Poesie* 504)

[My schoolmates were boys from a wide variety of religious backgrounds and all kinds of different nationalities. For me it was a habit picked up in childhood to value one's nationality, yes, but also to find it inadmissable that if someone was from another nationality he should not be my brother . . . I am made in such a way that I know nothing about repugnance for another race or for other peoples, and this perhaps is also due to my being from Alexandria, where people of the most different origins and provenances were constantly converging.]

Ungaretti's schooling in Alexandria, where he read Nietzsche, Baudelaire, Rimbaud, and Mallarmé, was also unlike any education that he could have received in an Italian school at the time. Ungaretti grew up speaking Italian, French, and street Arabic, which apparently he knew "perfectly" as a young man.[12] A few years earlier Marinetti, whose parents moved to Alexandria in 1873 because Alexandrian colonial society was more tolerant of their living together as an unmarried couple than the Milanese bourgeoisie (Marinetti's mother was already married and Italian law did not allow divorce), had a similar education at the Saint François Xavier Jesuit school, attended by a multiethnic and multicultural student body.

The Alexandria that Ungaretti, Pea, and Marinetti knew was a very special city in several respects, although other commercial port cities such as Odessa, Shanghai, and Saigon (whose specific cultural productions still remain to be studied) had multiracial cosmopolitan communities structurally similar to Alexandria's. At the end of the nineteenth century and the beginning of the twentieth, Alexandria was a crucible of races and nationalities where Arab Egyptians (both Muslims and Christian Copts) and native Africans (mostly from the upper Nile valley and the Sudan) lived next door to Greek, Italian, French, Maltese, German, Russian, and "Levantine" (especially Turkish, Armenian, and Syrian) immigrants, both Christian and Jewish, who came to look for work and business opportunities. A multitude of languages was spoken, including not only Arabic in its profusion of dialects, Italian, French, German, Greek, Armenian, Russian, and Turkish, but also Nubian, Ladino, Provençal, and a Mediterranean pidgin used mostly for business. Although the layout of Alexandria conformed in part to that of a typical colonial city, with separate European and Arab quarters, several middle-lower- and lower-class neighborhoods were mixed. One such neighborhood was the suburb of Cleopatra, described in Cialente's novel *Cortile a Cleopatra*. The attempt, typical of the colonizing process in the nineteenth century, to rationalize, compartmentalize, and regulate the city's structure by building a central square and a series of geometrically ordered boulevards was only partially successful.[13] Not only did Alexandria preserve much of its labyrinthine character in the Arabic quarters, but the city's growth and renovation were often anarchic and chaotic, with frequent compromises, infractions, and mixed or unorthodox usages of buildings and urban space that reflected the leniency of the Commissione dell'Ornato, the urban planning commission (which had retained its original Italian name).[14] This distinctly unordered and undisciplined aspect of Alexandria emerges in Ungaretti's diary of his return journey to Egypt in 1931, initially as a sharp sense of shock. Compared to Paris or Rome (which had just undergone in 1930 a process of radical urban reordering and rationalization in the fascist spirit), Alexandria appeared insanely disorderly to Ungaretti, but the shock almost immediately turned into déjà-vu and to an almost resentful sense of belonging:

> Com'è disordinata questa città! Tutte queste lingue che s'incrociano; queste insegne, italiane, francesi, arabe, greche, armene, delle botteghe; l'architettura; il gusto! Quale Merlin Cocai s'è divertito a inventarla? Non so quale rancore m'invade, d'amarla, questa mia città natale! (*Il deserto* 20)

> [How disorderly this city is! All this crisscrossing of languages; this multitude of shop signs in Italian, French, Arabic, Greek, Armenian; the architecture; the taste! What mad Merlin created it for fun? A strange resentment overtakes me for loving this city of mine, this city of my birth!]

Alexandria's cosmopolitanism was the result of Egypt's incorporation into the world market in the nineteenth century, especially with the cotton boom and the unprecedented expansion of the commercial activities of the port. As the major port linking the fields of Africa to the factories of Europe, Alexandria had not only facilities for docking, loading, and discharging goods, but also a community of merchants and a variety of related services: warehouses, banking, money lending, currency exchange, insurance, postal and telegraph service, food services, construction, and transportation. A substantial part of the immigrant community (which included a large number of indigenous people who had moved to Alexandria from within Egypt as well as other sections of the Ottoman Empire) engaged in these activities. There was a thoroughgoing interdependence among the various communities that coexisted in Alexandria, an interdependence that was often better appreciated by native Egyptians than by their "foreign" counterparts, whose number never exceeded about 10 percent of the population (Reimer 12). Unlike most typical colonial cities, Alexandria did not have a unified administration. A unique administrative structure, developed in the nineteenth century, characterized Alexandria and reflected its cosmopolitanism, contributing to make it a very particular kind of colony. Alongside the khedival administration the city had a complex system of intersecting offices, such as the Intendence Sanitaire (health board) and the Commissione dell'Ornato, many of which were started and continued to be administered by khedival administrators in conjunction with foreign consulates. These and other offices were born from the confluence of interests between the khedival state and the foreign colonies (Reimer 75). At the same time a system of consular privileges and immunities (the system of the so-called "capitulations") developed, which had particularly interesting implications for the administration of justice. In cases of legal disputes or criminal offenses, "foreign" defendants had the right to be judged in their own consulates and according to the laws of their country of origin. This at first may seem an extraordinarily unjust system (and in many ways it was), yet the creative ways in which it was used by natives and non-natives alike in order to elude the law (or some law somewhere) made Alexandria one of the few places where one could escape—among other things—the political and racial persecution of any number of European and Mediterranean countries.

Alexandria became a space of immunity for many. There were mechanisms in place whereby one could place himself under the "protection" of a particular consulate in Alexandria and become a *protégé* or putative citizen of that country, enjoying its legal benefits. Thus, for example, a large number of Levantine Jews became Italian *protégés* or "Italians," even though they might have had only imaginary roots in Italy (especially in Leghorn, where the register of births had burned down at some point in the nineteenth century). This situation was made more complex by the ambiguities of Egyptian citizenship laws. As Robert Ilbert has shown in his fascinating study of Alexandria between 1830 and 1930, the difference between native and non-native, between indigenous and foreigner, and the very meaning of the word "Ottoman" or even the implications of religious affiliation were rather fluid and ambiguous in Alexandria. Given the centuries-old multiethnic and religiously mixed reality of the Egyptian territory, restricting Egyptian citizenship to Muslims or to people who were not originally from the Levant or Turkey was impossible, so that the principle was adopted in 1866 of considering Egyptian or "indigène" any Ottoman subject established in Egypt since 1848. "Arabs" were considered to be the "fellahs" or peasants who lived outside the urban areas and who constituted the vast majority of immigrants into Alexandria, but during the nineteenth century "Arab" began to be used interchangeably with "Egyptian." Also developed were in-between categories such as "extérieur" and "étranger par tradition," the latter referring to descendants of families that had been in Egypt since the eighteenth century.[15] And in Alexandria it was often possible to slide from the category of native to non-native and vice versa (Ilbert 89). One could even find siblings who were citizens of different countries.

Far from becoming—like so many other African cities—a mere colonial bridgehead for the exploitation of an enslaved country, Alexandria, on the contrary, gave birth in the nineteenth century to a particular kind of sociability, an amalgam of peoples and races (Ilbert 102). Colonial Alexandria belied the essentialist myth of race, nation, and cultural tradition that is the basis for the authority of colonial domination and subjection.[16] Thus the word "colony" needs to be redefined in Alexandria's case, for even though a colony, Alexandria was a society without the usual essentialist markers traditionally associated with coloniality. It was this particular kind of colonial society that left its mark on both Pea and Ungaretti. Although published only in 1949, Pea's *Vita in Egitto* draws on Pea's diaries and notes from his time in Egypt before the First World War and incorporates notes and articles written (and in some instances published in periodicals) in the late 1930s and in the 1940s. The book recounts episodes of Pea's and Ungaretti's earlier life and their impressions of Alexandria under the British-controlled regime. Pea refers several times to the British military presence in the city and to the 1882 shelling, still very vivid in the city's collective memory when he went to live in Alexandria.

PEA AND ITALY'S DOUBLE COLONIALISM

Pea went to Alexandria around 1896 and found work first as a house servant and then in a foundry, later becoming a mechanic in a naval shipyard and a railroad worker. He suffered serious injuries in two accidents he had while working as a mechanic, so in order to do something less dangerous he started a small commerce in marble, wood, and wine. His enterprise's warehouse, a shack named "La Baracca Rossa," became, as we shall see, a mythic place for both him and Ungaretti. In *Vita in Egitto* and in the 1931 novel *Il servitore del diavolo,* Pea describes very effectively the social topography of the city, highlighting its division into the affluent section with its gardens and boulevards, populated mostly by the European elite (including the "Austriaco avaro e tiranno" ["The avaricious and tyrannical Austrian"] in whose house he was a servant) and the poor neighborhoods with unpaved muddy streets (*Vita in Egitto* 74–75). However, it is clear from Pea's descriptions that the series of oppositions "European vs. native," "affluent vs. poor," and "exploiter vs. exploited" characteristically used to diagram the conflictual dichotomies of the colonial situation is not valid. In the stratified and mixed reality of his and Ungaretti's neighborhood (Moharam-Bey), poor European laborers shared the predicament of Arab and Jewish laborers. Pea's portrait of Alexandria also belies Durrell's aestheticizing (and certainly more seductive) version of the European luxury and decadence of the "Levantine city." Pea does not idealize Alexandria in any way. Although he acknowledges that his experience of Alexandria's cosmopolitanism was beneficial and distanced him from philistine nationalism ("la convivenza internazionale in questa Babele d'Egitto m'aveva convinto dell'inutilità e del danno delle patrie," "the international living together of this Egyptian Babel had convinced me of the uselessness and harmfulness of homelands"), he is also highly critical of what he sees as the aberrations of colonial hybridity (*Vita in Egitto* 26). For example, he deprecates the tyrannical treatment of women among the Alexandria's Greeks and Copts, who, he observes, in using their wives and daughters as mere objects have adopted and even outdone the worst traits of Muslim behavior (*Vita in Egitto* 52–53). Arab women servants, on the other hand, are subject to an even more implacable exploitation. Amina, an Italian-speaking servant girl who befriended Pea (then also a servant) and told him the story of her life, was raped by her first master, an Italian, and then sent to be a sexual slave as well as a servant in the house of a Greek merchant. The indictment of the mistreatment of women is a recurrent theme in all of Pea's work. One of the most striking pages of *Vita in Egitto* is the description of an evening of belly dancing, attended by both Arabs and Europeans. In contrast to the titillating voyeurism that makes the description of belly dancing or other erotic displays by women a classic topos in European literature about Egypt, Pea presents the spectacle as repulsive, painful, and demeaning to the women as well as the spectators. He finds the excitement of the Arab audience as false as the expectations of the polite European observers, who believe themselves to be watching something "authentic." Pea comments:

> Ma questa non è la vita del paese. Questo non è il popolo nei suoi costumi. Questi indigeni di stasera sono una minoranza d'Egitto, degenerata di *hasciascin*. Il popolo io lo conosco bene: è quello che lavora nei campi da secoli. Che lavora con me al porto, all'officina, dentro la caldaia. Ed è come me, oppresso da un'ingiustizia sociale. (*Vita in Egitto* 116)

> [But this is not the life of the country. This is not the simple people with their way of life. Tonight's natives are a degenerate Egyptian minority of *hasciascin*. The people, I know them well; they are the ones who have been working in the fields for centuries. They are the ones who work with me in the harbor, in the mechanic shop, in the boiler room. They are, like me, oppressed by a social injustice.] [17]

In Pea's view the exoticizing spectacle only hides a reality of sexual and economic exploitation.

While Pea gives us a clearly gender- and class-based vision of the complex and diverse nature of the European presence in Alexandria, he displays at the same time a critical understanding of the colonial framework of Alexandria's cosmopolitanism. This understanding emerges most effectively in a page devoted to the spectacle of Alexandria "emptying out" in the heat of summer as everyone who can afford it leaves the city:

> L'estate spopolava l'Egitto in quei tempi di benessere. I vapori delle Messagerie Marittime che andavano a Marsiglia, toccavano Napoli, facevano concorrenza alla nostra Navigazione Generale per Catania, Napoli, Livorno. E così quella della Nord Llloyd Deutsch per Brindisi, Trieste. Mentre i nostri va-

pori da quella parte toccavano Brindisi e Venezia. C'era dunque da scegliere.
I levantini andavano a Parigi per divertirsi. Quelli col mal di fegato a Vichy o
a Montecatini. I mercanti a Trieste, per la Germania a comprar paccottaglie,
a Genova, per Milano e a Marsiglia per il Belgio o per altrove. E i viaggi quasi
di nozze: gli sposati di fresco rinnovano la luna di miele sbarcando a Venezia.
Tutta gente che poteva spendere . . . soltanto i poveri restavano in Egitto, al
torrido dell'estate, e gli indigeni, e quelli che lavorano la terra e non la pos-
seggono: i fellah, che sono poi i veri artefici del benessere di questa cosmo-
polita popolazione che infesta le due grandi città: Cairo ed Alessandria. Io
naturalmente non potevo partire per i diporti estivi. (*Vita in Egitto* 36)

[Summer emptied Egypt out in those times of affluence. The steamers of the
Messagerie Marittime that went to Marseilles also went by Naples, and competed with our Navigazione Generale for Catania, Naples, and Leghorn. And
so did the Northern Lloyd Deutsch for Brindisi and Trieste. Our steamers on
that side, on the other hand, went to Brindisi and Venezia. There was therefore a vast choice. The Levantines went to Paris to have fun. Those with liver
ailments went to Vichy or to Montecatini. Merchants went to Trieste, and on
to Germany to buy junk, or to Genoa, Milan, and Marseilles to go on to Belgium and beyond. Then there were the honeymoon-type travelers. The recently married renewed their honeymoon traveling to Venice. All were people
who could spend . . . only the poor stayed on in Egypt, in the torrid heat of
summer, along with the natives, and those who work the land but do not own
it: the fellah, who are actually the real makers of the wealth of this cosmopolitan population that infests the two big cities: Cairo and Alexandria. I of
course was not able to leave and take part in the summer fun.]

Whatever wealth and even modest well-being is generated in Alexandria,
Pea thus explains, is fundamentally the product of colonial oppression. Pea
lucidly includes himself among the colonizers (and thus the exploiters)
who "infest" Egypt, yet as an immigrant from a desperately poor region of
Italy he is also the victim of a colonial situation. The passage cited above is
immediately followed by another in which Pea contrasts the luxury steamers in which the vacationing Alexandrians traveled with the miserable ships
on which he himself had journeyed in the opposite direction as an emigrant:

Ma quelli erano stati viaggi di terza classe, sui vecchi battelli dalla ciminiera
bianca e nera. Sotto coverta di quei vapori una parte di stiva era adibita a dor-
mitorio, e consisteva in un intavolato a due ordini posto in giro ai fianchi del
bastimento come se fossero state scansie, una sopra l'altra, e su quelle scansie
tanti materassi gli uni accosto agli altri ed alla rinfusa uomini e donne e bambini sdraiati. (*Vita in Egitto* 37)

[But those had been third-class journeys, on old steamers with black and
white chimneys. Under the deck of those steamers a section of the hold was
turned into a dormitory, with two shelf-like wooden planks one on top of the
other all around the sides of the steamer, and those shelves were lined with

many mattresses one right next to the other, on which men, women, and children lay haphazardly.]

In contrasting the emigrants' ships with the luxury steamers of the great Italian naval merchant companies, Pea evokes the economic and political situation of Italy at the end of the nineteenth and the beginning of the twentieth century. Two-thirds of the working population of Italy was still made up of peasants who, although responsible for more than half of the national product, lived in conditions of abject poverty and disease and were increasingly forced to emigrate. The liberal government, partly in the hopes of raising money for its parties' political interests, staked all on industrialization, especially the merchant naval industry; it was thus progressively tied to international capitalism and hence, fatefully, colonialism. The Rubattino naval company was among the initiators of the first Italian forays into the Red Sea coast and East Africa, where in 1882 Italy established its first officially recognized possession in the Bay of Assab (Eritrea). The birth (from the fusion of Rubattino with several smaller naval industries) of the Navigazione Generale Italiana (mentioned by Pea in one of the above passages) and its development into a colossal trust with a network of interests in construction and banking was the most eloquent display of the alliance of government with international capitalism in liberal Italy (Quazza 10–11).[18]

In the years between 1882 and the First World War, Italy's colonial designs and its supposed rights in East Africa and the Red Sea (however uncertain its strategies and incompetent or botched its actual military campaigns)[19] were increasingly asserted and acknowledged by the other European nations. The violent expropriation of land, and the establishment through the use of deportations, internment camps, torture, and indiscriminate killings[20] of Italy's first colonies in Eritrea (1890) and Somalia (1889–1892), was followed in 1911 by the bloody invasion and annexation of Libya (1912), where Italian troops were stunned by the strenuous resistance of native Arabs and Ottomans alike. (Ironically Mussolini, who at the time was still a socialist, was among the few who opposed the invasion of Libya.)

But Pea's text clearly indicates that Italy was actually in a doubly colonial situation. The "southern question" that plagued Italy, and the uneven development between industrial north and rural "south" (a south that included by extension poor sections of central and northern regions, such as the Lucchesia and parts of Versilia), amounted in effect to a colonial relationship in which the south was often considered the equivalent of "barbaric" Africa. The racist rhetoric that characterized much of the political discourse pertaining to the southern question only confirms its essentially colonial nature.[21]

It was precisely to alleviate the tensions of colonialism within Italy that

Premier Giovanni Giolitti welcomed and encouraged the development of Italian nationalism in the first decade of the twentieth century. Italian nationalism, unlike Risorgimental patriotism, had a decidedly colonialist and imperialist emphasis and perceived the conquest of colonial territories in Africa as a means eventually to make Italy queen of the Mediterranean. The chief Italian theorist of nationalism, Enrico Corradini, passionately advertised the need to shift the violence of class warfare toward a more productive target for the well-being of the entire nation: imperial conquest. Imperial conquest was supposed to create "a place in the sun" for the masses of Italian peasants who would otherwise be forced to emigrate; it would solve the southern question by allowing the expropriation of land not from Italian landowners, but from African peoples judged incapable of properly cultivating the land (Isnenghi 57).

Corradini's nationalism had enormous resonance and was echoed (albeit with different emphases) in the works and public appeals of the most representative intellectuals of the time, including D'Annunzio and Pascoli (the latter authored the famous speech "La grande proletaria s'è mossa"). Corradini's myth of the proletarian nation was meant to defuse the violence of the proletariat *within* the nation, and was thus eagerly embraced by Giolitti's government. Along with this myth, Giolitti embraced the discourse of colonial racism in order to justify the Italian attack on Libyan territory: "The colonial war"—he said in a speech delivered to Parliament in the midst of the invasion—"signifies the civilizing of nations that otherwise would continue to be barbaric" (Quazza 30).

Most Italian intellectuals at the time were thoroughly infected with this rhetoric, some becoming passionate proponents of Italy's "heroic" and civilizing mission. D'Annunzio's bellicose *Canzoni delle gesta d'oltremare,* for example, were published in 1911–12 in the daily newspaper *Il Corriere della Sera.* This nationalist and imperialist rhetoric was later adopted with little variation by Mussolini, who also resurrected and updated the Risorgimental discourse of patriotism in the (largely successful) attempt to gather support for the invasion of Ethiopia and the creation of the Italian empire in East Africa in 1935–36. The Italians, however, met with unforeseen and unyielding resistance during their occupation of Ethiopia. As Angelo Del Boca and other historians have determined, the "empire" was an economic disaster that managed to survive until 1941 only by using constant and devastating violence against the native insurgents.

How far Pea was from the pre-fascist and fascist rhetoric of racism and imperialism may be measured by reading the passage immediately following the description of the immigrant ships in his *Vita in Egitto.* Here Pea tells of a journey back to Italy. He had been called to Italy by the military draft board for a medical check (which found him physically unfit to serve due to his work injuries). During that journey, Pea recalls, he had traveled in the company of two caged horses that were being sent as a gift to the king of Italy from the Italian governor of Eritrea, Ferdinando Martini. During that trip he had occasion to see a silver coin—a coin that was already out of circulation and worthless, he adds ironically—that pictured the king himself, portrayed wearing an imperial crown, But even more critical is the image that follows of the exotic caged fauna—with which Pea and the other third-class passengers had to share the bridge—being carried back to Italy from the Red Sea:

> Il ponte . . . era ingombro di gabbie con dentro bertucce e tartarughe pure quelle provenienti dal Mar Rosso e dalle foreste dell'Eritrea. Le bertucce somigliavano proprio agli uomini, anche nei vizi: durante il viaggio, che fu di otto giorni, le teorie di Darwin, di cui avevo saputo all'università popolare, dettero spago alle mie osservazioni dirette. Passavo le intere giornate davanti alle gabbie di queste bertucce, con le quali parlavo. Soffrivano il mal di mare come me e come me si lamentavano della prigionia. E verso sera come me s'immalinconivano, proprio come me sospiravano allo sparir del sole. Alla fine del viaggio abbondonai le bertucce a malincuore, come se fossero state persone umane a cui mi ero affezionato. (37–38)

> [The deck . . . was loaded with cages containing monkeys and tortoises from the Red Sea and the forests of Eritrea. The monkeys really resembled human beings, even in their vices. During the journey, which lasted eight days, Darwin's theories that I had studied at the university for the people were confirmed by my direct observations. I spent entire days in front of the cages containing the monkeys, with whom I spoke. They were seasick like me, and like me they complained about their captivity. And toward evening like me they became melancholy, just like me they sighed when the sun disappeared. At the end of the journey I was sad to leave the monkeys, as if they were human beings to whom I had become attached.]

In this passage Pea clearly associates himself with exotic animals. Animals and humans are on the same level (as they are on the same deck): they are incidental victims in the colonial and imperialist design that has them cross the Mediterranean together like so much merchandise. The reference to Darwin and thus to the racialist discourse of the late nineteenth and early twentieth centuries—which consistently placed lower-class, poor, and "underdeveloped" humans, as well as "barbaric" people of inferior races, on the same level as animals (monkeys and apes in particular)—also has a specific and polemical significance in this context. The colonial logic that victimizes Africans because they are subhuman is the same that continues to exploit the peasants by forcing them to emigrate. Pea thus reads through the populist demagoguery of Italian colonialism in Africa, which in fact ended up generating no benefits at all for the peasants.

PEA, UNGARETTI, AND MULTIETHNIC ALEXANDRIA

It was through his beloved friend Mohamed Sceab (who was a student with him at the École Jacob, and whose tragic and untimely death Ungaretti never stopped mourning) that Ungaretti met Pea and became involved with the crowd of the Baracca Rossa in Alexandria, where they both received their first political education. The cavernous room upstairs from Pea's business warehouse was the gathering place for an anarchist group and a reference point for any number of political refugees from all over Europe and the Mediterranean, as well as serving as the classroom for the "Università popolare" founded by Pea himself. In 1908, the Baracca Rossa gave shelter to a group of Russian sailors who had defected; later members of the group sabotaged the sailors' deportation by occupying the train tracks. Pea, Ungaretti, and the others were reported to the police but, due to the capitulations system, each "criminal" was tried in his own consulate. The trial was a mere formality, and both Pea and Ungaretti were immediately exonerated (Piccioni 41). Ungaretti's mother often gave shelter to anarchists, refugees, atheists, and any number of runaways in Alexandria; it was through their stories that Ungaretti learned about Italy. Both Pea and Ungaretti wrote for a number of Italian-language periodicals in Alexandria, including the daily *Il Messaggero Egiziano* and the anarchist periodicals *L'Unione della Democrazia* and *Risorgete*. Only their contributions to *Il Messaggero* have been recovered (Rebay, "Ungaretti"). They include Ungaretti's enthusiastic review of *Revolverate* by the anarchic poet and futurist sympathizer Gian Pietro Lucini and the first creative prose Pea ever published, a *fola* (fable) later included in the volume *Fole* (1910), lovingly edited by Ungaretti.[22]

The small and fragmented cosmopolitan literary society that Pea and Ungaretti frequented regularly in Alexandria included Kavafy and Socrate Zervos, who went almost every night to the same café for dinner and conversation,[23] and the writers Jean Léon and Henri Thuile, brothers who were both engineers who worked at the Alexandria harbor (Jean-Léon was a poet, Henri a novelist and critic). The Thuiles' simple, stark wooden house on the edge of the desert and overlooking the sea, called "Le Mex," became a legendary place for both Pea and Ungaretti. They went there by train every week across the desert to talk about Foscolo, Verlaine, Rimbaud, Apollinaire, and Gide. The house contained a library (which had belonged to the Thuiles' father, also an engineer) where Pea and Ungaretti both spent many hours reading.[24] It was there that Ungaretti, while looking from the terrace toward the harbor below, first heard about the legendary monumental port of Alexandria buried in the sea in ancient times: the buried port was to become a central metaphor for Ungaretti and the title of his 1916 collection of poems, *Il porto sepolto*.

A peasant like Pea, almost illiterate until the age of ten, and then mostly self-taught, would probably never have become a writer if he had stayed in Italy. The lack of a dominant literary culture—or of even a dominant language—in Alexandria, and the felicitous encounter with the eighteen-year-old Ungaretti, who corrected his punctuation and encouraged him, made it possible for Pea to begin writing with extraordinary stylistic freedom in a language filled with syntactic and lexical oddities (later admired by both Eugenio Montale and Ezra Pound). In 1912 Pea published a volume of tales written in verse, *Montignoso,* followed in 1914 by the long narrative poem *Spaventacchio.* Both were inspired by the stories, legends, and folktales of his native Versilia as told to him by his grandfather and presumably his mother, rumored to have been a folk poet herself (she had emigrated to Alexandria ahead of her two sons, who later joined her). It was precisely his distance from his place of birth, along with his distance from the Italian literary establishment, that allowed Pea to return in his imagination to his roots in Tuscan popular culture and to reinvent them, as it were, from Alexandria, creating poetry of great strength and originality. By the same token, the multicultural and multiethnic experience of Alexandria came alive in his work only after he crossed the sea again and went back to Italy.

After his return to Tuscany, where he became a founding member of the anarchist group Repubblica d'Apua, Pea published the first play of his *Jewish Trilogy,* a tragedy entitled *Giuda* (1918) that was staged the same year and caused enormous scandal. The play, written in an expressionistic language filled with violent imagery, reversed Christian orthodoxy and was seen as blasphemous because it made a hero of the figure of Judas as the legendary king of the Jews—opposed to Roman imperialism—while accusing Christ of cowardice in inducing his people to submit to oppression. The other two plays of the trilogy, *Prime piogge di ottobre* (1919) and *Rosa di Sion* (1920), also deal with Jewish history and culture, turning this time from the theme of the Roman invasion to that of the diaspora, and the plight of people without a home who must travel among people of other cultures and beliefs.

In highlighting religious and ethnic diversity and conflict, both plays reflect Pea's experience as an immigrant in Alexandria, yet they neither idealize nor romanticize the city. One of the most remarkable features of these two plays is that they focus on figures of Jewish women, sensitively portrayed as both victims and rebels, and on the heightened symbolic value of women's sexuality in a patriarchal culture that fears loss and dissolution. Pea's work, with its interest in women and Jewish culture, appears all the more extraordinary in contrast to the rampant anti-Semitism and misogyny of the Italian intellectual elites at the time. The Florentine avant-garde in particular (Giuseppe Prezzolini, Giovanni Papini, Scipio Slataper, Giovanni Boine, and Piero Jahier) had welcomed the 1912 publication in Italian translation of Otto Weininger's *Sex and Character,* embracing (with the exception of Ardengo Soffici) its demeaning vision of both women and Jews. Although Ungaretti was an admirer of Papini in some respects, his vision of Jewishness was even more enthusiastic than Pea's. In a 1913 letter to Pea written from Paris he exalts and romanticizes what he sees as the restless spirituality, heroic defiance, and prophetic, perennially avant-garde intellectual energy of Jewish thinkers from ancient times to Spinoza, Marx, and Durkheim, placing himself and Pea ideally in that same heroic lineage (Ungaretti, *Lettere a Enrico Pea,* 44–45).

Most readers of Pea and Ungaretti have tended to divide their respective literary careers into an early rebellious phase, and a later, mature phase of "return to order" marked by religious conversion and political conservatism. (A similar pattern is often discerned also in Marinetti's career.) But although it is true that both Ungaretti and Pea in the 1920s experienced a spiritual crisis that led them to recant their youthful atheism (an atheism that did not deny God, according to Ungaretti's paradoxical formulation),[25] their writings indicate that they did not relinquish their openness of mind or the egalitarian, antiracist, antinationalist, and anti-imperialist feelings derived from their experience of colonial Alexandria. Pea's *Il servitore del diavolo,* for example, offers a critical reflection on the delusions of anarchic rebellion and atheism, as well as an especially cogent critique of the irresponsible attitude of Pea's and Ungaretti's fellow anarchists toward women and sexuality. This dense, lyrical, and allegorical book recounts episodes from Pea's early years in Alexandria and looks back on the *Baracca Rossa* experience from the point of view of the author's religious conversion, reflecting on the meaning of the motto "Né Dio né padrone" ("Neither God nor master") inscribed over its door. In hindsight, only the first half of the motto, however, is rejected by the author. Apparently fragmentary, the book tells many stories and autobiographical episodes, but retrospectively they all turn out to be segments of a single sustained meditation on violence, abuse, and oppression. This is the link that ties together the story of Pea's own servitude and his experience of being treated as a black African ("servo di razza negra, per caso con la faccia pallida" [*Servitore* 5]) with the stories of Judas (the servant who is an anarchist but has himself become an oppressor to his fellow servant, the black African Barberino), the anarchist Piero Vasai (maniacally persecuted by the Italian police, he sought refuge in Alexandria), the young Sudanese slave girl, and the young Jewish women who fled Russia because they could remain there only if officially classified as either slaves or prostitutes. The book's attack on European imperialism in Africa is explicit, and Pea decries the fact that "the Europeans brought guns to Africa and made the Africans into their servants" (*Servitore* 12–13). In the last episode, Pea recalls his being mortified by the violence inflicted by an Italian foreman on his Arab co-workers. Written between 1929 and 1931, when Mussolini's regime had fully revealed its foundations in systematic violence, abuse, and oppression, Pea's book is profoundly antifascist and anti-imperialist. In 1929, the regime had already confined rebels in its Cirenaica colony into five concentration camps. And, as the explicitly racist official pamphlet *Dieci anni di fascismo nelle colonie italiane* by Alberto Giaccardi observed, the border between Cirenaica and Egypt had been closed off with barbed wire in 1931 to prevent the guerrilla fighters from seeking shelter in Egyptian territory.[26]

UNGARETTI'S EROTICS OF ROOTLESSNESS

The constant presence of Alexandria in Ungaretti's imaginative world has often been noted, and Ungaretti himself reiterated his identity's inseparability from Alexandria. Although Ungaretti spoke modern Arabic (and probably mostly "street" Arabic), he did not read it, and Arabic's major influence on his poetry seems to have been a phonic one. The rhythm and cadences of Arabic funeral chants in particular were associated for him with the very essence of poetry (*Vita: Poesie* 504). Ungaretti's first published poem, "Il paesaggio di Alessandria d'Egitto," which appeared in *Lacerba* in 1915, was about the landscape of Alexandria. In its provocative refrain, written in a witty and mordant spirit reminiscent of Aldo Palazzeschi's poetry and of *Lacerba*'s style at the time, the poem incorporated a sexual invitation from an Arabic folksong. (A reference to the same song appears in Pea's *Il servitore del diavolo* as part of a song sung by the black servant, Barberino.)[27] Ungaretti transformed his origins in a hybrid cosmopolitan city such as Alexandria (where from his mother's house he could see the Bedouin nomads' encampments in the desert), and his subsequent peregrinations from Italy to Paris and then to Brazil (where he lived with his wife and taught Italian literature for six years, from 1936 to 1942) and back to Italy, into a mythic narrative of perennial nomadism and rootlessness that became one of the richest motifs in his poetry.

Ungaretti's mythology of nomadism and rootlessness, like Dante's mythology of exile, was tremendously productive in poetic terms. Italy always appeared as a kind of promised land in his poetry ("La terra promessa"), a place that could never really be his, remaining forever the "Patria" or, literally, the land of his parents, but never his own. "Je suis étranger en Italie, comme en France, aussi bien qu'ailleurs" ("I am a foreigner in Italy as well as France, as well as everywhere else"), he wrote in 1920 when he was living in Paris (*Vita: Saggi* 39). The 1932 poem "1914–1915" (*Vita: Poesie* 161) evokes Ungaretti's first journey to Italy from Alexandria, and his feeling of estrangement from both Alexandria and Italy, along with his contradictory desire for both places. The erotics of rootlessness in Ungaretti is always in

the shadow of loss and death. The feeling of being "déraciné" could be experienced as sheer tragedy, and Ungaretti was well aware of this syndrome,
to which he attributed the suicide of his friend, the "nomads' son" Mohamed Sceab, in Paris in 1913.[28] The devastating experience of being an
"African in Paris" is the theme of a 1919 prose poem with that title in which,
as Rebay observes, Ungaretti closely identifies with his friend's predicament.
Two letters sent to Soffici from Paris in 1920 indicate how close Ungaretti
came to committing suicide himself.[29]

Ungaretti's sense of eroticism, desire, and sexuality, including homosex-
uality, was profoundly influenced by his experience of Alexandria and the
Arab world, although this aspect of Ungaretti's vision has yet to be convincingly explored. Unlike Italian society, Alexandrian society was tolerant of
a wide spectrum of sexual and erotic behaviors, including homoerotic,
homosexual, and interracial relationships. Although when he was asked by
Pier Paolo Pasolini (in an interview for the 1964 documentary film *Love
Meetings*) whether he had ever had a homosexual relationship Ungaretti
gave an evasive answer, he was clearly sympathetic to Pasolini's plight. With
a candor rather unusual among Italian poets, Ungaretti revealed that his
first amorous passion as an adolescent in Alexandria was for another boy in
his school. His official biographer Leone Piccioni tells us that this passion
was "pure," but perhaps that is beside the point. As the pages on the eroticism of the desert in *Il deserto* (among others) indicate, Ungaretti derived
from his youth in Alexandria a sense of desire and pleasure less bound by
a strictly heterosexual paradigm—and the pursuit of purity—than most
Italian poets. The madness of desire for Ungaretti is linked to the phe-
nomenology of the desert and of the mirage: "Il miraggio . . . e le nostre
pazzie più intime, a che sono dovute se non a una separazione falsificatrice
dell'immagine dall'oggetto?" ("The mirage . . . and our most intimate mad-
nesses, where do they come from if not from a falsifying separation of the
image from the object?") (*Il deserto* 80). The phantasmatic nature of the object of desire for Ungaretti is both an erotic and a poetic necessity, however
tragic it may be.

Another fundamental dimension of Ungaretti's poetry, his sense of temporality, or "sentimento del tempo," was marked by the experience of the
desert and of Alexandria. As Ungaretti observes in the autobiographical
note to his collected poems (and also in a radio interview), Alexandria is in
the desert, where all traces of life and civilization are mercilessly wiped out
and erased, while the city lives only in the present. It has no monuments to
remember its past. It is a city in constant flux, where everything changes and
people come and go all the time: "Muta incessantemente. Il tempo la porta
sempre via, in ogni tempo. E' una città dove il sentimento del tempo, del
tempo distruttore, è presente all'immaginazione prima di tutto e soprat-
tutto" ("It changes continuously. Time always takes it away, in every era. It is

a city where the feeling of time, of time the destroyer, is present to the imagination before and above everything else") (*Vita: Poesie* 497). The fragile, unmonumental, and seemingly eroded language of Ungaretti's early and most influential modernist poetry mirrors Alexandria. Ungaretti links the feeling of the ephemeral associated with the desert with an even more fundamental and ancient sense of provisionality and transitoriness inherent in Arabic nomadism, with which he profoundly identifies (*Il deserto* 88–89).

More than Paris or Rome, then, Alexandria is the emblem of nomadic modernity for Ungaretti, or even a premonition of postmodernity: an ephemeral, polyglot city without memory and without interest in either national traditions or the past. In this desert city (unlike Proust's Paris) even personal memories are mirages. This notion of memories as mirages, and of modernity as quintessentially ephemeral and nomadic, shapes Ungaretti's modernism and intersects (although it does not at all coincide) with Marinetti's futurism in ways that have yet to be explored. (Marinetti, like Ungaretti, had a distinctly unmonumental vision of time and language.)[30] The naked and isolated words of *Il porto sepolto* and *Allegria di naufragi*, seemingly unanchored to a past or a tradition or a recognizable poetic heritage, emerge as so many mirages, barely visible remains—the exposed tips of ruins buried in the glistening sand of the Egyptian desert. The devastating experience of death and destruction in the First World War, during which the poems of *Il porto sepolto* and *Allegria di naufragi* were written, precipitated Ungaretti's awareness of the meaning of Alexandria for him. Images of war and of his Egyptian past are interwoven like so many vanishing shapes, as in "Ricordo d'Affrica": "Il sole rapisce la città / Non si vede più / Neanche le tombe resistono molto" ("The sun ravishes the city / It is no longer visible / Not even tombs last long") (*Vita: Poesie* 11). Even when, with *Sentimento del tempo* and *La terra promessa,* Ungaretti undertook his reconstruction and restoration of a literary tradition to use as a frame of reference for his poetry, he did it from the point of view of the nomad and the outsider.[31]

UNGARETTI AND FASCIST IMPERIALISM

Il deserto: Quaderno egiziano 1931 is a composite, hybrid text, a travelogue and a memoir that includes pages of cultural and political history, anecdotes, reportage, poetic meditation, and lyric fragments and prose poems. This composite nature is in part a result of the book's origin as a series of articles that Ungaretti wrote for the newspaper *Il gazzettino del popolo* on the occasion of his first return "home" since 1912. Yet the book also stands as a journey of self-discovery, one that maps out the itinerary of the poet's reappropriation of his past while charting a path for the future. As pointed out by Mario Petrucciani and Glauco Cambon, who have privileged and studied only the more literary sections of this work, the book is important and fascinating because it comes between *L'Allegria* and *Il sentimento del tempo*, offering invaluable insights into the changes undergone by Ungaretti's poetics and testifying to the importance of Egypt for Ungaretti's poetic vision.[32] However, the book is also illuminating for political reasons, which cannot, as Ungaretti himself makes a point of emphasizing, really be separated from the poetic. Indeed, by mixing and "contaminating" poetry with history and politics, this book belies the myth of the essential "purity" of Ungaretti's modernism, which many critics have deemed superior, indifferent or—at worst—tacitly complicit with fascist imperialism.

The sections that have been dismissed as mere "chronicle" or journalism are in fact essential for any understanding of Ungaretti's position on imperialism and, by extension, fascism. The first part of Ungaretti's book offers a thoughtful overview of Egyptian history and a polemical meditation on the meaning of "empire" since Alexander the Great, as well as a lucid analysis of British colonialism and of the effects of the worldwide recession on Alexandria's economy. Ancient Alexandria, Ungaretti says in the chapter entitled "The Roman Column," must have been a rather pompous-looking place, somewhat reminiscent of a late-nineteenth-century universal exhibition, to judge from the available descriptions. But time in Alexandria does not just weather things: it destroys them, Ungaretti continues, implying how fortunate this really is. Roman imperialism—the model for fascist imperialism— and the fascist obsession with monumental exhibitions, phallic virility, and aggressiveness (which found visual expression in the profusion of columns and other neo-Roman elements typical of fascist architecture in both Italy and Africa) implicitly become objects of irony in Ungaretti's text. In the section of this chapter entitled "Non è rimasto ritto nulla?" ("Has nothing remained erect?"), Ungaretti describes the lonely and derelict column known as Pompey's column (a symbol of both Rome and Christianity, for it was thought to have been erected by Emperor Theodosius to commemorate the victory of Christianity) standing in the midst of a working-class neighborhood in Alexandria as the sole remaining testimony of Rome's power. Decapitated of the imperial statue that it presumably once bore on the top, the column's survival is but an accident of time.[33] In the nineteenth century, Ungaretti observes, the top of the column was used as a picnic site by Italian and French immigrants:

> Sopra il suolo, di ritto non è rimasto che una colonna romana. . . . I pionieri della nuova occidentalizzazione dell'Egitto, mattacchioni del primo Ottocento, Italiani e Francesi andavano sulla colonna . . . tutta circondata di scale di corda, a fare ogni tanto un pranzetto. (36)

> [On the ground, the only thing still standing erect is a Roman column. . . . The pioneers of the new occidentalization of Egypt, Italian, and French fun-lovers of the early nineteenth century every once in a while climbed the column . . . enveloped with rope ladders on all sides, to have a nice little lunch.]

The sight of the ruined column inspires humorous irreverence rather than patriotic pride. In Ungaretti's text the column effectively becomes a symbol of the irony of temporality rather than of the endurance of the idea of imperial Rome.

In contrast to Turkish, European, and even—as the khedives sought to incorporate Ethiopia and the Sudan as stepping stones to an empire— Egyptian imperialism, Ungaretti openly advocates a multicultural and non-antagonistic model of cross-fertilization between Europe and Africa, one that is clearly based on his own idealized memory of Alexandria. He emphasizes what in his view is, historically, the positive value of the reciprocal influence and cross-contamination of Europe and Africa, East and West, Christians and Arabs, yet he decries imperialist oppression. Italians, he claims, historically have not partaken in the predatory struggles over Egypt; he sees the relationship of Italians with Egypt since the nineteenth century as one of mutual enrichment rather than aggression. The embodiment of this ideal for Ungaretti is Carlo Piaggia, who had emigrated from Tuscany to Egypt. There Piaggia became an explorer, and he was often a guest of Ungaretti's mother in Alexandria. Piaggia, about whom Ungaretti remembers hearing endless tales as a boy, had learned Arabic and French and exemplified a rare, nonaggressive form of colonialism that valued cultural reciprocity.

The significance of Ungaretti's public intervention on the question of imperialism can be gauged only by considering what was happening in fascist Italy at the time. In his articles Ungaretti was in fact not simply writing a harmless travelogue, but implicitly taking a stand vis-à-vis Italian foreign policy. Published between July and December 1931, Ungaretti's articles followed by only a few months a series of reports given by the Italian foreign minister Dino Grandi to the Gran Consiglio del Fascismo, in which Italy's pressing need to assert its "rights" in Africa were explicitly and forcefully put forward (De Felice, *Mussolini,* 374–75). The idea of an Italian empire in Africa was then circulating widely, and Mussolini's designs included the conquest of Ethiopia (actually undertaken only in 1935–36, just when Ungaretti readied his decision to leave for Brazil) and eventually the joining of the Ethiopian and Libyan territories under Italian rule through conquest of the Sudan and even Egypt.[34] The racism implicit in fascist imperialism was particularly aberrant in Ungaretti's eyes. *Il deserto* not only reiterates Ungaretti's old admiration for the Jews but provides, by reporting a conversation with an Egyptian childhood friend, an evenhanded assessment of the new Muslim solidarity and of Arab-Egyptian nationalism, and concludes that Egypt was fully entitled to independence, although Ungaretti opposes any form of intolerance, violence, and fanaticism (*Il deserto* 77).

One of the things that Ungaretti cherishes most about Alexandria is precisely that it is an unmonumental city, where all is quickly eroded and consumed by time. Yet his return journey to Alexandria gives him new, palpable, and this time painful evidence of what Alexandria had originally taught him, namely that there is no end to the irony of temporality, for even the cherished Alexandria of his youth has now vanished forever. Rather than the nostalgic, melancholy, and exoticism-filled memories of a typical "belated traveler," however, Ungaretti's observations constitute a vivid critique of what in his eyes are the drawbacks of "modernization" and the negative consequences of European colonialism in Egypt.[35] Although in the Alexandria of his youth (whose disorder and promiscuity were exhilarating) European and African cultures seemed to mix freely, if sometimes antagonistically, with neither demeaned nor dominated by the other, what he now sees at the beginning of the 1930s is the end result of a process of hybridization in which European elements have become dominant and have been superimposed on Arabic and African traits, ironically at the very moment in which Arab-Egyptian nationalism is on the rise. In fact, Ungaretti observes, Arab-Egyptian nationalism itself has become a hybrid discourse that incorporates some of the most objectionable aspects of European culture.

This paradox emerges most clearly for Ungaretti during a performance in Alexandria described in the chapter entitled "Pianto nella notte" ("Cry in the night"). It is a "pochade," or comic farce, performed in Arabic for a popular audience, but its plot and performance style are an imitation of French and Italian models. Ungaretti is stunned when, in the midst of the performance, the audience erupts in cries of "Vive, vive, vive!" which—as is immediately explained to him—stands for "Vive la liberté," an Egyptian nationalist rallying call. He reflects on how ironic this call for freedom—uttered in French—is, as it testifies paradoxically to a profound lack of freedom. The nationalists of the "Egypt for the Egyptians" movement clamor for the freedom to preserve Egyptian traditions, yet all that is considered "Egyptian" now, from manuals for the schools to ways of dressing, to poetry, painting, and theater, bears the traces of colonial penetration. Ungaretti does not nostalgically advocate a return to the purity of an uncontaminated tradition, however, for he knows this to be an impossible utopia. He nevertheless chastises as "naive" the nationalists' enthusiasm about the future of independent Egypt. This new Egypt, in Ungaretti's eyes, reflects the country's grotesque mimicry of Europe and internalizes rather than rejects colonial dependency.[36] Ultimately, of course—Ungaretti reflects—"one is never free," for humans are basically all victims of "incessant transformation," even as they blindly fight one another. The only thing one can hope for is that nations will undertake to shape their future in a spirit of moderation rather than aggression. This observation may ultimately reflect in part Ungaretti's panic as a European confronted with the threat of rising Arab-Egyptian nationalism, but it also voices Ungaretti's feelings about political violence coming out of Italy. The experience of the First World War for Ungaretti, unlike Marinetti, caused him to reject all forms of violence, a fact that makes his subsequent admiration for Mussolini "the revolutionary," and his warm relationship with him in the early postwar years (when he wrote for Mussolini's newspaper *Il popolo d'Italia*), all the more ironic. Ungaretti misread Mussolini completely. As late as 1927 he was still comparing him to Gracchus Babeuf and Karl Marx.[37] In 1923 Ungaretti asked Mussolini to write a prefatory note to the new edition of his volume of poetry, *Il porto sepolto*. Mussolini complied (writing a few rather inane laudatory lines), but Ungaretti subsequently had a change of heart, and Mussolini's preface was not included in any of the later editions (1931, 1936, and 1943).[38]

<h2>FASCISM AND THE DECLINE OF ALEXANDRIA</h2>

The Italian colony in Alexandria was stunned by the fascist racial laws of 1938. In the 1930s, Alexandria's Italian colony still had a substantial Jewish population. Most of these Jews were lower-middle class, but the business and administrative leaders of the community, responsible for maintaining relations with the other segments of Alexandrian society and with government bureaucracy through the capitulations system, were also Jewish. As Anouchka Lazarev has shown, after the First World War the 25,000 Italians of the colony still considered themselves Alexandrians first, and were proud of their long-standing Egyptian heritage. Although a considerable portion of the male population of the colony had fought for Italy in World War I, most had returned to Alexandria. Being Italian was only one element in a fluid system of identities and allegiances, and many were "passport Italians" who neither spoke Italian nor had ever been to Italy. With the advent of fascism, however, which suspected Italians abroad of being unpatriotic, displays of national and fascist allegiance were increasingly demanded of them. Fascism was unable and unwilling to deal with the fluid and indeterminate nature of the Alexandrian community and its ambiguous national and religious identity games. The regime thereby attempted to impose a new kind of order and build a new type of fascist colony that was to be "Roman and imperial" in nature. It succeeded only in dislocating the community, cutting it off from Alexandria and depriving it of the life that nourished it.

The decline of the colony was already under way after the First World War, with Italian (as of 1917) no longer one of the official languages of the mixed tribunals. In these same years, although the entire patchwork system of Alexandria was rapidly dissolving under the pressure of Arabization and Egyptian nationalism, fascism accelerated its collapse. The twenty years of the colony's "forced marriage" (as Lazarev defines it) with fascism amounted to a long balancing act by the Italian community that, although superficially "fascistized," was congenitally averse to all forms of authoritarianism and sectarianism. The Italian consul complained in 1937 that Italians in Alexandria used the *fascio* as just another *associazione di mutuo soccorso* (mutual aid societies) typical of the Alexandrian colonial system: rather than a fascistization of the colony what was taking place was a colonization of the *fascio*. Although the brand-new Scuole del Littorio (with an impressive gymnasium and teachers trained exclusively in Italy to replace Italian natives of Alexandria) were inaugurated with much fanfare in 1933, they failed to attract many students. Most parents preferred to continue sending their children to the French schools, at least until the threat of removal of citizenship forced them to comply with Rome's desires.

The Italian invasion of Ethiopia in 1935 made the Italian colony in Alexandria suddenly suspect in the eyes of Egypt, calling into question the very basis of Alexandria's communal life and effectively destroying the equilibrium on which the Italian colony relied for its existence. The coup de grace, however, was the promulgation of the racial laws. Not only was the Italian community itself suddenly deprived of its elite, which could no longer exercise its functions, but the international Jewish community in Alexandria organized a complete boycott of all Italian hires and commercial activities. Only a year earlier, the 1937 Montreux conference had officially abolished the capitulations system and thus effectively dissolved the anachronistic colonial structure of Alexandria. Alexandrian Italians became simply Italians for the first time, although a few (to the shock of the consular authorities) opted for Egyptian citizenship and even converted to Islam (Lazarev 103). A surprisingly large number of Italians remained in Alexandria well after 1938; many of them were sent to British concentration camps during the war.[39] Others, like Fausta Cialente, joined the international antifascist resistance, which had in Egypt one of its principal centers. The surge of Arab-Egyptian nationalism in the 1950s finally drove out the European and Levantine communities that had made their home in Alexandria in the nineteenth century, but well before then fascism had already succeeded in substantially destroying the spirit of the Italian colony.

NOTES

I would like to thank Arnold Band, Françoise Lionnet, and Luciano Rebay for reading the manuscript of this chapter and offering comments and suggestions.

1. See, for example, Leontyne Price's retelling of *Aida* for children, *"Aida" as Told by Leontyne Price* (San Diego: Voyager Books, 1990). On *Aida*'s orientalism see Robinson. For a critique of Said's notion of orientalism, see especially Porter, "Orientalism and Its Problem."

2. Some evidence in fact points to the khedive possibly authoring the scenario himself or at least contributing to it. See Phillips-Matz, *Verdi: A Biography*, 577.

3. Ersilio Michel provides a meticulous account of the Italian emigration into Egypt and of Italian patriotic demonstrations in Egypt during the Risorgimento in his *Esuli italiani in Egitto (1815–1861)*.

4. The best overall discussion of Pea's work and of his relationship with Alexandria is Arslan, *Enrico Pea*. See also Bellora, *Il mondo di Pea,* which includes fascinating photographs from Ungaretti's and Pea's days in Alexandria.

5. Cialente wrote two novels set in Egypt, *Cortile a Cleopatra* (published in 1936) and *Ballata Levantina* (1961), as well as several short stories, including "Pamela o la bella estate," which appeared in the journal *Occidente* 13 (1935), published in Alexandria. On Cialente's feelings toward Alexandria, see Petrignani, *Le signore della scrittura,* 83–89.

6. The importance of Alexandria for Marinetti and Cialente, to which I can only allude briefly here, will be discussed in a larger work on Alexandria's colonial culture.

7. See also the introductory note to the 1969 edition of *Vita d'un uomo*: "Sono di Alessandria d'Egitto: altri luoghi d'Oriente possono avere *le mille notti e una,* Alessandria ha il deserto, ha la notte, ha il nulla, ha i miraggi, la nudità immaginaria che innamora perdutamente e fa cantare a quel modo senza voce che ho detto" (*Vita: Poesie* 505).

8. For an analysis of *La Voce*'s misogyny, see Nozzoli, "*La Voce* e le donne."

9. On the myth of Alexandria in Kavafy, Forster, and Durrell, see Jane Lagoudis Pinchin's pre-post-colonial studies book, *Alexandria Still,* and Errera, "Le rêve d'Alexandre ou le mythe littéraire."

10. On Durrell's orientalism and homophobia, see Boone, *Libidinal Currents,* 353–88. Durrell was a British citizen born in India, where he spent his first ten years before going back to England for schooling. During and after World War II he served Great Britain in various diplomatic capacities in Athens, Cairo, Rhodes, and Belgrade. In 1944 he was posted as press attaché in Alexandria, but he lived there only briefly.

11. About the "real" Alexandria (as opposed to the one of his orientalizing fantasies), Durrell wrote in a letter to Henry Miller: "No, I don't think you would like it . . . this smashed up broken down shabby Neapolitan town, with its Levantine mounds of houses peeling in the sun." Wickes, ed., *Lawrence Durrell and Henry Miller,* 195.

12. See the testimony of Issa I. Naouri, "Ungaretti nel mondo arabo," 1232.

13. On this aspect of the colonizing process in Egypt, see Mitchell, *Colonizing Egypt*. Mitchell studies mostly Cairo, however, and devotes only a few lines to Alexandria.

14. The task of the Commissione dell'Ornato, beginning in 1834, was the supervision of remodeling and new construction. The chief engineer was Francesco Mancini, who was also responsible for some aspects of the city's urban renewal; he designed the rectangular Place des Consuls and many of the most famous mansions of Alexandria. On the Commissione dell'Ornato and Alexandria's urban planning, see Reimer, *Colonial Bridgehead,* and Ilbert, *Alexandrie 1830–1930*.

15. See, for example, the case of Benedetto and Abramino Tilche in Ilbert, *Alexandrie 1830–1930,* 86.

16. Alexandria was arguably an example of hybridity as defined by Bhabha, "Of Mimicry and Men," although Bhabha has a more optimistic view of the political potential of colonial hybridity than either Pea or Ungaretti did.

17. Pea's critique of exoticism and colonialism is also an important element in his 1945 novel, *Rosalia,* which reconstructs the experiences of three Italian mer-

chants in the small provincial villages of Egypt and among the fellahin and the immigrant workers, whose world is minutely and lovingly described.

18. The need to obtain funding to support political interests and to prevail in the power struggles among political parties was a chief incentive behind the government's rash policy of risky investments and its support of a vast and precarious banking system.

19. In 1887, after Italy's "peaceful" occupation of Massawa, 433 Italian soldiers were killed in Dogali by Abyssinian troops. The year of Pea's probable arrival in Egypt, 1896, was also the year of Italy's traumatic defeat by Menelik II at Adwa.

20. Angelo Del Boca has documented the horrors of the African campaigns in several of his works. For a brief account, see "I crimini," 233–34.

21. A glaring example can be found in a letter to Cavour dated October 27, 1860. Luigi Carlo Farini, who was the chief administrator of the south during the first months of Piedmontese rule, wrote: "But, my friend, what lands are these, Molise and the south! What barbarism! This is not Italy! This is Africa: compared to these peasants the Bedouins are the pinnacle of civilization." *Carteggi di Camillo Cavour*, 3: 208. For a discussion of the image of the Italian south as Africa, see Nelson Moe's study *The View from Vesuvius: Geographies of Cultural Production in Nineteenth-Century Italy*.

22. Ungaretti also convinced Pea to throw into the fire his first poems, the "Sonetti del Harem," thus turning him away forever from the exoticizing, decadent mode of certain "orientalist" poetry that Pea mimicked, as can be gathered from a few surviving texts. See, for example, "Fahima" in Livi, ed., *Ungaretti, Pea e altri*, 144.

23. See Ungaretti, "Cavafy, ultimo alessandrino" (1957), in *Vita: Saggi*, 666–69. Ungaretti calls Kavafy one of the "four or five great poets of the twentieth century."

24. The somewhat Borgesian atmosphere of this library in the desert is suggestively evoked in Henri Thuile's *Littérature et Orient* (1921), a book of meditations on a variety of Arabic, Persian, and European texts, written in the form of letters to a Greek friend during the First World War.

25. See the letter to Pea dated February 10, 1913.

26. Giaccardi's pamphlet is analyzed in detail by Isnenghi.

27. On Ungaretti's poem, which he later chose not to publish, see Rebay, *Origini*. The line "Vieni, bella anatrotta" (Come here, beautiful dear little duck) appears in Pea, *Il servitore del diavolo*, 8. Gabrieli, "Ungaretti e la cultura araba," discusses the Arabic original.

28. The 1916 poem "In memoria" is dedicated to the memory of Sceab.

29. See especially the letter dated April 11, 1920, in Ungaretti, *Lettere a Soffici*. On these letters, see Rebay's comments, *Origini*, 23–24.

30. Ungaretti always professed to dislike Marinetti and futurism, decrying their excessively "phallic" stand, yet he acknowledged futurism's influence, especially on his early work. The relationship between Ungaretti's early style and the futurist poetics of words-in-freedom remains to be fully explored, as does the possible influence of the skeletal, asyntactical, and anarchic lingua franca spoken on Alexandria's streets on the linguistic inventions of both Marinetti and Ungaretti. Only literary sources (especially Mallarmé) have been deemed relevant for Ungaretti, but several elements point to the considerable role of popular culture as well as high culture.

31. On this aspect of Ungaretti's position vis-à-vis the Italian tradition, see Luzi's

insightful observation in his essay "La presenza l'attualità di Giuseppe Ungaretti" in Bo, vol. 2: 310–11.

32. Petrucciani's discussion of Ungaretti's "Egyptian memory" is in *Il condizionale di Didone,* 253–72. See also Cambon.

33. E. M. Forster argues that the imperial statue might have represented Diocletian rather than Theodosius. His comment on the column is also ironic and noteworthy: "An imposing but ungraceful object. Architecture has evolved nothing more absurd than the monumental column; there is no reason that it should ever stop nor much that it should begin, and this specimen is not even well proportioned" (*Alexandria* 161).

34. For Mussolini's imperial design on Egypt, see Del Boca, "I crimini," 248. According to Del Boca, Mussolini was planning to put together an army of a million men in AOI (Italian East Africa), the largest army ever seen in Africa, in order to undertake the conquest of the Sudan, Egypt, and Somalia. In *Il fascismo e l'Oriente* (18–25 and passim), De Felice argues that actual territorial conquest was favored by the Catholic right wing, but that Mussolini envisioned Italy's penetration of Egypt and the surrounding African countries as an economic, political, spiritual, and cultural "amicable" overtaking and expansion that would still allow for national independence. However, De Felice himself grants that the Duce's public declarations and his friendly gestures toward Arab nationalist leaders in the 1930s were purely strategic and meant to put pressure on England and France. What De Felice fails also to note is that Mussolini's model of "natural expansion" and amicable penetration was based on an essentially racist outlook that assumed Arab inferiority on all fronts and the desirability of a beneficial fascist infusion and takeover in all levels of cultural, political, and economic life.

35. According to Ali Behdad, *Belated Travelers,* 15, the "belated Orientalism" of travelers such as Nerval, Flaubert, and Pierre Loti "vacillates between an insatiable search for a counterexperience of the Orient and the melancholic discovery of its impossibility; they are, as a result, discursively diffracted and ideologically split."

36. The description of the "pochade" is followed by that of an even more grotesque masquerade in a variety show to which an Egyptian friend took Ungaretti. In the masquerade young Arab dancers (referred to with the English word "girls") dressed in military khakis and white sailor suits sing a patriotic song and salute, alternating military steps with a provocative dance that is "between belly dancing and the fox-trot" (42). Ungaretti finds this hybrid spectacle of double mimicry (Arab women mimic men mimicking European military gestures) ludicrous as well as uncannily disturbing. The scene both invokes and displaces the orientalist topos of the exotic and seductive female dancer. Ungaretti's critique of colonial mimicry is directly opposed to Homi Bhabha's theory, according to which "the menace of mimicry" consists precisely in its "double vision" that discloses "the ambivalence of colonial discourse [and] disrupts its authority," allowing for native intervention (Bhabha, "Signs Taken for Wonders"). In Ungaretti's eyes, on the other hand, mimicry is but a futile act of false intervention and a symptom of subjection.

37. "Originalità del fascismo" (1927) in *Vita: Saggi,* 153.

38. Even in the 1930s, however, Mussolini still took care not to alienate Ungaretti and vice versa. Although Ungaretti, during return trips to Italy from Brazil, was detained twice (once for attempting to intercede on behalf of Umberto Saba, who

after 1938 was required to shut down his bookshop due to the new racial laws against Jews), he was almost immediately released, once by direct order of Mussolini. Ungaretti returned to Italy in 1942 because as "Italians" he and his wife (although she was French) were considered fascist sympathizers in Brazil and were about to be sent to a concentration camp. Ungaretti received several official acknowledgments for his work as a poet on his return; during the war he was given a chair at the University of Rome; and, like Marinetti, he was elected to the Italian Academy. He underwent a painful series of *epurazione* trials or purges after the Liberation and was suspended from teaching for a time, although he was eventually fully exonerated.

39. A small Italian community actually remained in Alexandria even after the Second World War. Only with Nasser's anti-Western reaction to the Suez expedition by Britain, France, and Israel did the Italians accept *a malincuore* (reluctantly) that their Alexandria was and could be no longer. For a vivid description of this last phase of Alexandria's cosmopolitan phase see Aciman, *Out of Egypt.*

WORKS CITED

Aciman, André. *Out of Egypt: A Memoir.* New York: Riverhead Books, 1994.

Arslan, Antonia. *Enrico Pea.* Florence: La Nuova Italia, 1983.

Behdad, Ali. *Belated Travelers: Orientalism in the Age of Colonial Dissolution.* Durham, N.C.: Duke University Press, 1994.

Bellora, Giovanni, ed. *Il mondo di Pea.* Lucca: Maria Pacini Fazzi editore, 1981.

Bhabha, Homi. "Of Mimicry and Men: The Ambivalences of Colonial Discourse." *October* 28 (1984): 125–33.

———. "Signs Taken for Wonders: Questions of Ambivalence and Authority Under a Tree Outside Delhi, May 1817." *Critical Inquiry* 12 (1985): 144–65.

Bo, Carlo, Mario Petrucciani, Marta Bruscia, M. C. Angelini, E. Cardone, and D. Rossi, eds. *Atti del convegno internazionale su Giuseppe Ungaretti.* 2 vols. Urbino: Edizioni 4 Venti, 1981.

Boone, Joseph Allen. *Libidinal Currents: Sexuality and the Shaping of Modernism.* Chicago: University of Chicago Press, 1998.

Briani, Vittorio. *Italiani in Egitto.* Roma: Istituto Poligrafico e Zecca dello Stato, 1982.

Cambon, Glauco. *La poesia di Ungaretti.* Torino: Einaudi, 1976.

Carteggi di Camillo Cavour, La Liberazione del Mezzogiorno e la Formazione del Regno d'Italia. 5 vols. Bologna: Zanichelli, 1949–54.

Cialente, Fausta. *Le quattro ragazze Wieselberger.* Milano: Mondadori, 1976.

De Felice, Renzo. *Il fascismo e l'oriente: Arabi, ebrei e indiani nella politica di Mussolini.* Bologna: Il Mulino, 1988.

———. *Mussolini il Duce. Gli anni del consenso: 1929–1936.* Torino: Einaudi, 1974.

Del Boca, Angelo. "I crimini del colonialismo fascista." In *Le guerre coloniali del fascismo,* ed. Andrea Del Boca, 232–55. Bari: Laterza, 1991.

Del Boca, Angelo, ed. *Le guerre coloniali del fascismo.* Bari: Laterza, 1991.

Errera, Eglal. "Le reve d'Alexandre ou le mythe littéraire." In *Alexandrie 1860–1960,* ed. Robert Ilbert and Ilios Yannakakis, 154–70. Paris: Editions Autrement, 1992.

Forster, E. M. *Alexandria: A History and a Guide* [1922]. London: Michael Haag, 1982.

Gabrieli, Francesco. "Ungaretti e la cultura araba." In Bo, vol. 1: 655–70.

Ilbert, Robert. *Alexandrie 1830–1930: Histoire d'une communauté citadine.* 2 vols. Cairo: Institut d'Archéologie Orientale, 1996.

Ilbert, Robert, and Ilios Yannakakis, eds. *Alexandrie 1860–1960.* Paris: Editions Autrement, 1992.

Isnenghi, Mario. "Il sogno africano." In *Le guerre coloniali del fascismo,* ed. Andrea Del Boca, 49–72. Bari: Laterza, 1991.

Lazarev, Anouchka. "Italiens, italianité et fascisme." In *Alexandrie 1860–1960,* ed. Robert Ilbert and Ilios Yannakakis, 92–110. Paris: Editions Autrement, 1992.

Livi, François, ed. *Ungaretti, Pea e altri: Lettere agli amici "egiziani."* Roma: Edizioni Scientifiche Italiane, 1988.

Luzi, Alfredo. "La presenza l'attualità di Giuseppe Ungaretti." In Bo, vol. 2: 310–11.

Michel, Ersilio. *Esuli italiani in Egitto (1815–1861).* Pisa: Domus Mazziniana, 1958.

Mitchell, Timothy. *Colonizing Egypt.* 2d ed. Berkeley: University of California Press, 1991.

Naouri, Issa I. "Ungaretti nel mondo arabo." In Bo, vol. 2: 1227–33.

Moe, Nelson. *The View from Vesuvius: Geographies of Cultural Production in Nineteenth-Century Italy.* Berkeley: University of California Press, 2001.

Nozzoli, Anna. *"La Voce e le donne."* In *Les Femmes-écrivains en Italie (1870–1920): Ordres et libertés. Chronique Italiennes* 39/40 (1994), Université de la Sorbonne Nouvelle.

Pea, Enrico. *Il servitore del diavolo: Romanzo.* Milan: Treves, 1931.

———. *Vita in Egitto.* Milano: Mondadori, 1949.

Petrignani, Sandra. *Le signore della scrittura: Interviste.* Milano: La Tartaruga, 1984.

Petrucciani, Mario. *Il condizionale di Didone: Studi su Ungaretti.* Napoli: Edizioni Scientifiche Italiane, 1985.

Phillips-Matz, Mary Jane. *Verdi: A Biography.* Oxford: Oxford University Press, 1993.

Piccioni, Leone. *Vita di Ungaretti.* Roma: Rizzoli, 1979.

Pinchin, Jane Lagoudis. *Alexandria Still: Forster, Durrell, and Kavafy.* Princeton, N.J.: Princeton University Press, 1977.

Porter, Dennis. "Orientalism and Its Problem." In Francis Barker, Peter Hulme, Margaret Iversen, and Diane Loxley, eds., *The Politics of Theory.* Proceedings of the Essex Sociology of Literature Conference, University of Essex, Colchester, 1983, pp. 179–93.

Quazza, Mario. "Continuità e rottura nella politica italiana da Mancini a Mussolini." In *Le guerre coloniali del fascismo,* ed. Andrea Del Boca, 5–30. Bari: Laterza, 1991.

Rebay, Luciano. *Le origini della poesia di Giuseppe Ungaretti.* Roma: Edizioni di storia e letteratura, 1962.

———. "Ungaretti: Gli scritti egiziani 1909–1912." *Forum Italicum* 14, no. 1 (1980): 3–31.

Reimer, Michael J. *Colonial Bridgehead: Government and Society in Alexandria, 1807–1882.* Boulder, Colo.: Westview Press, 1997.

Robinson, Paul. "Is *Aida* an Orientalist Opera?" In *Revisioning Italy,* ed. Beverly Allen and Mary Russo. Minneapolis and London: University of Minnesota Press, 1997.

Said, Edward. *Culture and Imperialism.* New York: Vintage Books, 1994.

Tomasello, Giovanna. *La letteratura coloniale italiana dalle avanguardie al fascismo.* Palermo: Sellerio, 1984.

Ungaretti, Giuseppe. *Il deserto: Quaderno egiziano 1931.* 2d ed. Milano: Mondadori, 1996.

———. *Lettere a Enrico Pea.* Jole Soldateschi, ed. Milano: Libri Scheiwiller, 1983.

———. *Lettere a Soffici 1917–1930.* Paola Montefosci and Leone Piccioni, eds. Firenze: Sansoni, 1981.

———. *Vita d'un uomo: Saggi e interventi.* Mario Diacono and Luciano Rebay, eds. Milano: Mondadori, 1974.

———. *Vita d'un uomo: Tutte le poesie.* Leone Piccioni, ed. Milano: Mondadori, 1969.

Wickes, George, ed. Lawrence Durrell and Henry Miller: A Private Correspondence. New York: Dutton, 1963.

Mass-Mediated Fantasies of Feminine Conquest, 1930–1940

Robin Pickering-Iazzi

In November of 1997, Oscar Luigi Scalfaro, then president of Italy, made a historic trip to Ethiopia bearing an official denunciation of Italy's war against Ethiopia (1935–36) and the country's colonial past. Covering this major event, the weekly magazine *Gente* (People) published a suggestive report that takes a retrospective look at Italian colonialism that should give readers pause. Contradicting the contrite tenor of the article's headline, "In Addis Ababa the President of the Republic Acknowledged the Errors of Colonialism," the subhead jumps off the page in block letters printed in bold black typeface that is nearly three times as large. It reads "LITTLE BLACK FACE, 1936 BROUGHT YOU ANOTHER DUCE AND ANOTHER KING BUT 1997 BRINGS YOU OUR APOLOGIES" (Dec. 4, 1997, 4–5). Inscribing two contradictory drifts that run throughout the text, the summary of Scalfaro's acknowledgment of Italy's wrongdoing implies a shift in the political perspective on Italian colonial history, while the invocation of "Faccetta nera" ("Little black face") conjures up a familiar figure of cultural fantasies structuring that very history.[1] In fact, the subhead echoes the lyrics of the song popular with Italian soldiers approaching the war-torn Ethiopian shores in the mid-1930s: "Little black face, beautiful Abyssinian woman . . . we will give you another law and another king." By addressing Italy's apologies to "Little black face," a fabrication of the exotic feminine native created by the Italian colonialist imagination, the subhead establishes a sexual system of exchange that, yet again, displaces Ethiopian men.

Within this discursive framework created by authors Mario Cervi and Massimo Borgnis, the promise of the repatriation of the Axum obelisk announced by Scalfaro during his visit suggests a wealth of crucial implications. At the purely symbolic level, the return from Rome to Ethiopia of the massive granite stele, which rises some twenty-four meters straight into the skies, could be read as signifying a transfer of the phallus, a rearrangement of intersubjective colonial relations. Yet, as Jean Laplanche and J.-B. Pontalis advise, the phallus is highly equivocal as symbol and frequently "turns out to be the meaning—i.e. what is *symbolised*—behind the most diverse ideas" (*The Language of Psychoanalysis* 313). In fact, the Axum obelisk has a range of meanings, articulated in debates among Italy's politicians, intellectuals, and the public at large, as Angelo Del Boca illustrates in his salient analysis in the present volume (especially pages ooo–oo). Del Boca informs us, for instance, that Maurizio Gasparri claims the obelisk is part of Rome's urban landscape and represents a phase in Italy's history, but Susanna Agnelli, focusing on the monument's historical and spiritual value for the Ethiopian people, has called for its immediate return.

In addition to these positions, I would like to propose that the Italian state's gesture of returning the stele self-consciously plays upon historic connotations linked with the Axum obelisk to invest it with new meanings, which also serve what might be called a postcolonial politics of disappearance. As Cervi and Borgnis tell us, at the end of Italy's war on Ethiopia in 1936, Mussolini transported the obelisk from the ancient city of Axum, the site of the coronation of Ethiopian emperors, to Piazza Porta Capena in Rome, where it was inaugurated in 1937 as a symbol of fascist Italy's victory and the foundation of the new colonial empire. This particular location is not lacking in significance, for the piazza stands at what was once the main entrance into Rome from the Appian Way, the esteemed consular road leading south. Some thirty-three years later, the obelisk assumed another meaning as a symbol of the Ethiopian state's generosity, when Emperor Haile Selassie stated, "Consider it my gift to Italy" (6). Nonetheless, Scalfaro announced to the Ethiopian head of sate, Negasso Gidada, that the Italians would return the obelisk, an act meant primarily to symbolize that Italy's "Constitution proclaims the repudiation of the war" (4). In Scalfaro's words, this declaration would ideally "have the power to purify the past and to be a firm message of brotherhood and peace" (4). While elaborating on the theme of purification in his speech before the Parliament of Addis Ababa, Scalfaro suggested that the return of the obelisk also testified to reconciliation and "the desire that Italy's friendship toward your people may be so true, so great, so deep that it can overcome every memory of weapons and war, of the oppression of your independence and your freedom, of every offense to man's fundamental rights on this earth" (4).

We should not, however, while acknowledging the amicable sentiment expressed, ignore the way that Scalfaro's statements work through a familiar strategy designed to erase memories of injustice and aggression, which is to say to "purify" Italian history. The removal of the Axum obelisk is also part of this re-visionary project, for it makes a monumental symbol of colonial conquest disappear from the urban face of Rome. Ironically, this plan reenacts the colonial architectural politics of disappearance executed in Ethiopia by the fascist regime in the late 1930s. As Diane Ghirardo explains, "Anything which would remind Ethiopians of the previous government or institutions would disappear" (104). On the one hand, then, the manipulation of the visual culture in Piazza Capena performs an epistemological reorganization that unburdens Italians of a daily reminder of fascist imperial conquest. On the other hand, the "empty space" may invite a form of colonial nostalgia for lost "possessions." I do not wish to suggest that the Axum obelisk should remain in Rome. On the contrary, in view of the concerted efforts by Ethiopian leaders to repatriate the monument, and the popular outcry in Ethiopia, the granite stele should clearly be returned to its homeland without further delay.

While the apologies and desires voiced by Scalfaro aspire to erase Italy's misdeeds from historical memory, at the same time a substantial portion of the *Gente* article, which claims to ascertain what kind of colonizers Italians were, nostalgically rehabilitates myths that make up national Italian colonial identity. Significantly, Cervi and Borgnis recirculate a central premise advanced in colonial discourses produced by proponents of the fascist regime, who argued that Italian fascist colonialism was different from the colonial enterprises of other nations.[2] Cervi and Borgnis forcefully declare, "In comparison with other nations that had colonized Africa, we repeat, there was a profound difference at the popular level. In fact, Italians did not believe in a rapacious form of colonialism, but, perhaps naively and yet sincerely, they believed in a form of colonialism that might offer the opportunity for work and might also be civilizing" (7). Benevolently cloaked in naivete and sincerity, the figure of the Italian colonizer brings the gifts of "culture and progress" (6) and appears worthy of sympathy. Indeed, the authors propose that "national sentiment was conquered by the attraction to exotic adventure" (6). In this manner, the colonizers are cast as the colonized, and therefore seem unaccountable for their actions. Admittedly, the authors note that the war produced acts of aggression, for which Italy, they say, owes apologies. Their final words, however, take the form of an apologia for colonialism. They state, "But to the Italians for whom Ethiopia represented a dream and illusion of their youth, we owe the recognition that their dream was not mean and their illusion was generous in many regards" (7). Shifting attention to Ethiopia as an imaginary product of Italian dreams and illusions, this passage serves up a fantasy of the benign Italian colonial character that epitomizes the displacement of responsibility for the material violence of colonial conquest, a symptomatic tendency examined by Karen Pinkus *(Bodily Regimes)* and Mohamed Aden. Moreover, it demonstrates the tenacious purchase colonial fantasies continue to have on the popular imagination, and the need to place them under critical scrutiny.

In the following study I want to put a different face on the field of inquiry into Italian colonialism by examining the exotic fantasies constituting a feminine colonial imaginary of the 1930s. To do so, I intend to revisit articles of the 1930s published in the Florentine annual *Almanacco della donna italiana* (Italian woman's almanac) and the Milanese monthly *Domus,* as well as the 1934 colonial novel *La sposa bianca* (The white bride) by the popular author Pina Ballario. My investigation will focus on how the representations of the exotic lands and opportunities offered by the Italian colonies design settings and scenarios for the pleasure, desires, and dreams of women among a mass readership. In this regard, the writings in the *Almanacco della donna italiana* (hereafter referred to as *Almanacco*) are especially valuable, because they provide examples of colonial discourses addressed explicitly to women. Although the readership of *Domus,* a publication dedicated to architecture, home design, and interior decorating, was not exclusively female, its pages carry numerous signs indicating that women counted among the major readers. There are advertisements for cookbooks, described as special offers "for *Domus*'s women readers"; ads for feminine beauty products dot the pages; and letters signed by women living throughout Italy's regions pose questions about home decorating. The analysis of the discursive practices employed in representations of the colonies appearing in the press provides a critical context for my reading of *La sposa bianca.* Written by Ballario, a prolific, successful author, this fascinating book makes an important contribution to the colonial novel genre, and, moreover, presents the opportunity to examine fantasies of the exotic frontier, adventure, conquest, and desire fashioned by the female imagination.

As a category of investigation, fantasy has crucial importance for theorizing the relations between national constructions of colonial identity and women's dreams, ideas, and practices in everyday life.[3] Elucidating the relationship between fantasy, the social subject, and material reality, Laplanche and Pontalis state:

> Even aspects of behavior that are far removed from imaginative activity, and which appear at first glance to be governed solely by the demands of reality, emerge as emanations, as 'derivations' of unconscious phantasy. In the light of this evidence, it is the subject's life as a whole which is seen to be shaped and ordered by what might be called, in order to stress this structuring action, 'a phantasmatic' . . . the phantasy structures seek to express themselves, to find a way out into consciousness and action, and they are constantly drawing in new material. (*The Language of Psychoanalysis* 317)

This model highlights the permeability of fantasy structures as sites of exchange between the "inner world" and the "external world" where, in the context of this study, exotic fantasies of the Africas are produced for mass consumption in hit movies, popular songs, novels, posters, and postcards. Moreover, as noted in the preface to *Formations of Fantasy,* edited by Victor

Burgin, James Donald, and Cora Kaplan, fantasy plays a strong role as a mo-
bilizing force (1). It thus provides an important interpretive key for understanding discourses addressed to women, discourses that beckon them
into colonial lands, both literally and figuratively.

While analyzing potential differences and similarities between the discourses produced under the official auspices of fascism and those beyond,
and between fantasies of female and male invention, I plan to work through
several questions. First of all, as Laplanche and Pontalis explain, fantasy, as
an imaginary scene, "is not the object of desire but its setting. In fantasy the
subject does not pursue the object or its sign: he appears caught up himself
in the sequence of images" ("Fantasy and the Origins of Sexuality" 26).
Therefore, how do colonial discourses set the scene for feminine desires
through their representations of the primitive lands of the new Italian empire? What strategies do these texts employ for soliciting women to dwell
upon the Africas, both in the sense of keeping their reflections and dreams
trained upon the colonial territories and in the sense of literally inhabiting
African lands as colonizers? For example, numerous articles invoke East Africa as a dreamscape of feminine mobility, where professional and entrepreneurial opportunities for women abound. And finally, I wish to examine
what the exotic fantasies of the Africas authored by and for women can tell
us about such complex issues as feminine colonial desire, conquest, and
roles in race relations.

MASS-MEDIATIONS OF FEMININE COLONIAL FANTASIES

Reflecting the general expansion of Italian media coverage devoted to the
Africas in the 1930s, the *Almanacco* and *Domus* published an enticing array
of articles on the Italian colonies, giving special attention to East Africa following the war on Ethiopia. Both the rich variety of topics explored and the
representational practices may have worked to engage readers. The writings
invite women, surrounded by the comforts of home, to travel to faraway
lands as they conjure images of undreamed-of sights: enchanting land-
scapes feature vast open spaces, majestic trees, and lush fauna; picturesque
cities and towns are unveiled, boasting magnificent palaces, gardens, and
circular huts with cone-shaped roofs; "primitive" natives wearing colorful
garb and exhibiting unusual beliefs, rituals, and customs nearly come to life.
Significantly, the articles that ethnographers and cultural commentators
published in the *Almanacco* display a prominent tendency toward hyperdescription, as they furnish highly detailed pictures of the colonies and the
peoples inhabiting them. This practice of representation, which Daniela
Curti has examined in relation to the romance novel, fulfills key functions
in these colonial discourses. First, the plenitude of "empirical" information
strengthens the "reality effect" of the images, which are developed from a

particular Western colonialist perspective while promoting a sense of cultural literacy among the readers. Presented as a transparent field of knowledge, the colonies also become a site of female mastery. Second, if, as Curti has suggested, hyperdescription encourages the reader's effortless flights into romantic fantasy, then it could operate in a similar fashion in colonial discourses, facilitating participation in a multitude of exotic fantasies. As a way of focusing this preliminary critique, I will concentrate on two topoi that give rise to female colonial fantasies: the land and home.

Although virtually every article on colonialism published in the *Almanacco* and *Domus* pauses to reflect upon the African lands, two articles warrant particular consideration for the different ways they portray the Italian colonies as a geographic sphere marked for women. In the first text, "La donna italiana e le nostre colonie" (The Italian woman and our colonies), published prior to the invasion of Ethiopia, Mercedes Astuto adapts conventions belonging to the map as geographical discourse. In contrast, in the 1939 article "La donna italiana in A.O." (The Italian woman in East Africa), Ciro Poggiali employs the form of a travelogue. Maps unquestionably serve as crucial sociopolitical tools for constructing the territory of colonial rule and the power relations therein. Furthermore, as Panivong Norindr cogently argues, the map "is also one of the key elements in figuring and shaping . . . [the] desire for adventure, for territorial claims and possessions" (93). In the texts by Astuto and Poggiali, the geography of Africa takes shape through descriptive narrative. Therefore, the analysis of maps and tours in oral descriptions conducted by Michel de Certeau furnishes a useful approach.[4] In his formulation, the ways people chart places and spaces when speaking form two categories, the map type and the tour type. Though both types represent symbolic and anthropological languages of space and may be combined, the map model focuses on seeing what exists; it marks boundaries and produces "a plane projection totalizing observation" (119). In contrast, the tour type describes going, and thereby spatializes actions in a "discursive series of operations" (119). De Certeau's concluding remarks on the difference between the map and the tour modes of description bear upon their respective functions. He states, "Maps, constituted as proper places in which to *exhibit the products* of knowledge, form tables of *legible* results" (121). Tour treatments of space, on the other hand, "tell us what one can do in it and make out of it" (122).

An examination of how the stories about the geographic colonial places and spaces in the texts by Astuto and Poggiali relate to de Certeau's models enables us to theorize the ways each type of representation may operate for women readers. The map has decisive structural and ideological roles in Astuto's article, which, in general terms, aims to provide a forward-reaching historical account of Italian women's enterprises in the colonies. Indeed, the introduction simultaneously traces the lines of history and territory back to the Bay of Assab on the Red Sea and a strip of land bordering it in Eritrea, an area officially declared an Italian colony in 1882. Briefly noting the military actions taken to expand the colony, she then de-scribes its borders, as defined in 1908, and outlines land formations, islands, bodies of water, and major topographical features. Astuto then shifts her attention to the different racial and ethnic indigenous populations within the colonial confines, and creates a portrait of their respective physical features, character traits, kinship systems, and gender roles. By so doing, her text also exhibits a central tendency of colonial discourse, which aims to "fix" or stabilize the native other. The map and anthropological narrative serve as a context for the author's glowing account of the social and entrepreneurial works Italian women have undertaken. Adhering to this same pattern of organization, Astuto also creates maps of Somalia and Libya as ports of entry into her discussions of those colonies. The three map descriptions and accompanying treatments of women settlers clearly enable readers to envision the places, contours, and borders of the geographical space of the colonies and to locate women in it. Such an interpellation makes an appeal to women readers as settlers, and in fact Astuto voices hopes for women's future colonial works, predicting, "What has been done will have great value, even if it seems slight, and will serve to stimulate increasingly greater work" (116). Moreover, given the map's position in the lineage of scientific discourse, this mode of representation delineates the colonial geography as a "proper place" for women, and authorizes the resultant panorama as part of constituted knowledge.

The exuberant essay written by Poggiali exemplifies several traits of de Certeau's tour model, yet it appears tailored to manipulate spaces according to what the author presents as Italian women's desires. From the beginning, where he situates women's travels to East Africa within the context of the regime's project of demographic colonization, which aimed to settle one million Italian women in the colonies, through the final reveries on domestic bliss, Poggiali explicitly addresses and refers to women. Acting as guide, he first paints the East African lands in shades of adventure, as if beckoning his readers to undertake the journey, and he advises them on travel preparations—the special kinds of clothing to purchase, medicines they may need, and so on. As we move into the tour proper, signaled by the subhead "How you get there," the description works through epistemological modalities, brimming with information about means of transportation, the network of imperial roads "willed" by the duce, and the railway system, which has been transformed into a marvel of efficiency through Italian organization. For instance, he notes that one can travel from Italy three days by airplane, the preferred mode of transportation among politicians and industrialists, and disembark in Addis Ababa. But, he alerts us, this means "missing out on great pleasures; missing out on the gradual passage from one continent to the other; missing out on the extremely opportune chance to acclimate your body to confront such different climactic conditions" (58). Thus, it is better to embark on one of the ships leaving from Trieste, Genoa, or Naples and be treated to precious scenic views of both Italy and the Red Sea. Here, as in the sections subheaded "What you find" and "In the wild lands," Poggiali takes readers step by step to cities and special points of interest, with a steady eye to the myriad possibilities for women in colonial territory and with suggestions as to what they can "make out of it." If one follows de Certeau's line of thought, Poggiali's travel story thus serves "as a means of mass transportation" (115), mapping the ways for Italian women to dwell upon the colonies.

Looking more closely at the images of the land fashioned for women readers, the most prominent trait of the African landscape is the heterogeneity of the visual field. Poggiali provides a superb example, reminding the "women destined for East Africa" that the particularity of this immense country lies in "the eclecticism, variety, and universality of its features. It can satisfy every kind of taste, fulfill all desires, yield to the needs of all temperaments. Within its 1,700,000 square kilometers of land (three times the size of Italy, as you know), it summarizes the entire physical world, it brings together almost all of the fauna and almost all of the flora" (56). In a manner typical of colonial discourse, Poggiali presents the conquered land as malleable. Yet here, women settlers will shape it. Using the African lands as a synecdoche for the world, he lays the land at Italian women's feet, and deploys Africa as a floating signifier that can stand for whatever they may desire. Yet Poggiali also designs the landscape as a site to mobilize more specific cultural fantasies. The first glimpse of Africa that he provides pictures the land as a frontier for women. "In its dawning," he tells us, "the colony is the land of the avant-garde, of discovery, of settlement" (53). Thus, the women who sail the high seas and reach the colonies are "pioneers, that is, fighters, even if engaged in the peaceable field of domestic, social, economic, and agricultural battles, for these are battles nonetheless, which involve positions to conquer, to firmly hold, to fortify forever" (54). Although not a product of the female imagination, this construction of the woman pioneer as the subject of a colonial fantasy of conquest creates a model and scenario for female identification. Similarly, in an earlier article, "La donna in Africa Orientale" (Women in East Africa), Silvia Benedettini represents the new empire as a land of female opportunity, announcing, "Today a vast field of action is opening up for Italian women who will go to live in the colonies with their husbands and children, or in order to practice a profession, an apostolate" (400). In contrast to Poggiali, she describes what historical women pioneers have accomplished, and then outlines several areas for female occupational expansion, including such traditional fields as education and nursing, as well as more groundbreaking positions as doctors and business developers. As enticing as such dreams of adventure and socioeconomic mobility might appear, we must keep in mind that, given the multiple components of subjectivity, women readers likely negotiated the representations of the colonies in quite different ways.

Many of the same writings that depict East African territories as a frontier for female adventure and economic advancement also cultivate strong associations between the land and romance. Poggiali, for example, invokes the "splendor of the unknown, of risk, of romantic fantasies" (54) pervading the lands. In some cases, scenes of seduction are staged between the colonial subject and the land. One such interlude occurs in Poggiali's description of the "wild lands." He persuasively explains, "Down there, in the land of Africa . . . [there is] a boundless expanse of vast panoramic spaces, of personal freedom, of being immersed in Nature. Even the most civilized, worldly ladies will unfailingly fall under the sway of its charm" (63). Here, the natural topography, with its wide-open spaces and horizons reaching as far as the eye can see, comes to symbolize seductive freedom. The representations of love for the land fulfill key functions in colonial politics. At first glance, such "love" could appear as merely an involuntary wave of emotion, belonging to the category of so-called natural kinds in Western philosophy. Yet, as the critical studies on affect and cognition by Catherine Lutz and Alison M. Jaggar have demonstrated, emotions are complex sociocultural constructions. Noting cultural differences between the kinds of emotions identified and the meanings attached to them, Jaggar tells us, "If emotions necessarily involve judgements, then obviously they require concepts, which may be seen as socially constructed ways of organizing and making sense of the world" (151). Furthermore, it would be unwise to view emotions as involuntary reactions, since emotions, she argues, "are ways in which we engage actively and even construct the world. They have both mental and physical aspects, each of which conditions the other" (152–53). Thus, portrayals of the relations between Italian colonists and the lands of Africa as spontaneous affairs of the heart create conceptual structures that shape ways of perceiving and perhaps desiring Africa, thereby articulating a calculated project of colonization.

Staging love stories of a different nature, the representations of the African lands as an unparalleled, exotic setting for untold romantic fantasies likewise arouse desires for conquest. Significantly, the love story as narrative centerpiece became a defining convention of the colonial novel of the 1930s, a point to which I will return in my discussion of *La sposa bianca*. Now, however, let's take a brief detour to an intriguing example of the commodification of the colonies as the space for flights of romantic fantasy, in the form of an invitation extended to newlywed *Domus* readers to compete for an expense-paid honeymoon in Tripoli. It would be difficult to think of a more romantic destination for newlywed couples living in Italy in the

1930s. As if attempting to kindle unimagined desires for faraway lands, the author poses a rhetorical question for readers who may be considering the Italian Riviera or Rome: "Why not push on a little further, where the land is still Italian and the horizon opens onto unknown enchantments, as if on the threshold of a wonderland?" (*Domus* 135 [1939]: 84). Although the context for this description is unique, the discursive strategies employed to create an imaginary land of wonders, with an equally imaginary geographic kinship to Italian soil, are typical. As in the articles by Astuto and Poggiali, the description strikes an ideal balance between contrasting elements—the familiar and the unfamiliar, the primitive and the modern. The photo layout accompanying the text gives visual expression to this variety: an aerial view of the urban center of Tripoli (both the view and the city become products of advanced technology) stands in stark contrast to ground-level shots of natives on camels in the desert, the entrance to the ancient underground city, and a quaint Arab home. Thus, for readers who dream of adventure without having to sacrifice comfort, the author promises "Big cities, full-service hotels, perfect roads for your cars guarantee that your exploration won't be a dangerous or insidious adventure" (84). At the same time, honeymooners can savor the exotic, as "a hundred strange sensations that will never fade from memory await you. . . . No aura is more fantastic, no atmosphere is more lyrical than making one's way across the sea . . . to unknown lands, customs, horizons, and skies" (84). Thus packaged, the enchantingly picturesque sights captured by the photographs and descriptive itinerary lure readers into a trip of their dreams.

Another illustration of how colonial fantasies are commodified for potential female consumers is the system of precolonial camps instituted by the National Fascist Party and the fascist youth group Gioventù italiana del littorio in 1937. An announcement published in the *Almanacco* (1939: 74–75) outlines the program, as it invites women to enroll in the camps, located in various parts of Italy. The participants can experience simulated primitive colonial living conditions while preparing for the challenges of frontier life in East Africa by attending courses on such subjects as the history of the colonies, native religions, the defense of the race, home furnishings, gardening, and cooking. The program also includes military training, with marches, instruction in weapon use, and sentry duty. We could read such simulations of colonial living in selected wilderness sites on the Italian peninsula as constructing opportunities for women to bring colonial fantasies to life. The response among women seems hardly negligible. As Silvana Palma reports in *L'Italia coloniale* (Colonial Italy), which makes available unique photographs of women engaged in camp activities, one hundred thousand female students took the courses in 1938. Yet the uses to which women put their knowledge and experience are open to question. By 1939, fewer than ten thousand Italian women had transferred to Italian East Africa, and of those, five thousand settled in the city of Addis Ababa. Nonetheless, pre-colonial camps represent one of the regime's attempts to incorporate women into national fantasies of the fascist empire and colonial identity.[5]

In fact, fascist colonial ideology and practice formulated central roles for Italian women settlers. Most importantly, the women were to provide a so-lution to what the fascist state saw as a dangerous, diffuse problem of mis-cegenation by defending the borders between white and black bodies at the micropolitical site of daily colonial life. Despite juridical prohibitions out-lawing marriage between and the cohabitation of Italians and Africans, An-gelo Del Boca *(Gli italiani in Africa orientale)* reports that some ten thousand biracial children were born between 1936 and 1940 in East Africa. Thus, in the essay "La donna e l'impero" (Women and the empire), Amadeo Fani, the president of the Fascist Colonial Institute, tells the *Almanacco*'s readers, "New duties are incumbent upon our women who, in Africa, where all promiscuity between races must be banished, will be the courageous com-panions of our brave colonists" (129). In addition, Fani crafts the female settler body as a symbol of fecundity, which will make the vast, open African lands fertile. He thereby mobilizes two suggestive tropes. The first concerns the myth of "empty" land, which in colonial discourses awaits the ingenuity of colonizers who finally make it bear the fruits of labor. The second em-ploys mythic, elevated terms to cast women, who are considered reproduc-ers of the race according to the fascist demographic model, as agents of the Roman empire's rebirth.

Fantasies about the exotic frontier have strong links to the notions of set-tlement and home, for in one sense the latter stands as a sign indicating the foreign land has been conquered and colonists have met the challenges testing their mettle. Yet the charged, polyvalent meanings of home are ob-viously complicated by the colonial system of power and dominance struc-turing race relations. For example, in his reading of the indigenous home in Algiers during French rule, Zeynep Çelik notes the diverse functions of the domestic interior for Algerians, which provides a "refuge" from the colonial gaze, a "buffer" and "inviolable space" where they recover identity (87); for colonists looking at the exterior, "the house both nurtured Ori-entalist fantasies and signified opposition to colonialism" (88). Therefore, we might ask, what kinds of dreams, hopes, and desires are built into the plans for domestic dwellings projected onto the colonial landscape in the context of Italian colonialism? How might the pages of *Domus,* showcasing architectural designs, sketches, and photographs of colonial homes, appeal to readers? Furthermore, what can the important series of articles on colo-nial architecture, written by such esteemed architects as Luigi Piccinato and Carlo Enrico Rava, tell us about fascist fantasies of empire building?

The writings Rava published in *Domus,* while contributing to the debates of the 1930s about what Rava called the problem of "colonial architectural politics," lay the theoretical foundations for a "totalitarian concept" of architecture in the colonies as "the highest expression of the Art of Government" (109 [1937]: 23). Indeed, he argues strongly for the creation of a Colonial Council for Architecture, which would oversee all matters concerning colonial construction, and for a "unitary vision" for urban planning that would regulate all forms of building. Although Rava promotes the idea that architects designing plans for the colonies should live on site and gain firsthand knowledge of the local history, culture, geography, climate, and native constructions, he rejects any imitation of indigenous regional or foreign styles. He proposes instead the development of a modernist Italian aesthetic. This paradigm of a colonial architecture manifesting Italianicity and modernist conventions conforms to the dominant notions of empire building, presented by architects working in the rationalist current. Nonetheless, in an insightful study that charts the contradictions between the theories and practices of Italian colonial architecture, Krystyna von Henneberg suggests, "The idea of a single, imperial style may reveal more about metropolitan longings (or self-deceptions) than about actual practices in the empire itself" (377). Although the model of a totalitarian imperial architecture may be little more than a discursive formation, it nonetheless articulates and authorizes a politics of racial power relations, executed through urban design and producing material effects. Not the least among them is the physical displacement of indigenous populations and the disruption of traditional economic systems.

Here, however, I will focus on the way the plans for urban design elaborated by Rava, among others, endeavor to make fascist theories of the prestige and power of the Italian race concrete, and create a cultural fantasy of dominance. As Rava tells the readers of *Domus,* the first and most important principle for city planning is "the separation of colonial architecture into two parts, with indigenous people on one side and whites on the other" (109 [1937]: 25). The borders between the so-called European city and the native city are designed to perform two key functions. Rava presents the geographic separation of the races as a preventive measure against miscegenation, citing the architect Quadrelli's position that "there must be no cohabitation between whites and people of color inside houses" (109 [1937]: 25). The boundaries dividing the city and races must also serve to make the prestige, privileges, and dominance of the Italian colonizers clear. Thus, Rava voices his support for a plan to create a "new downtown area for the Italian city where all of the military and government offices will stand together . . . [which] must be executed according to the criteria of the monumental and grandiose, serving to affirm fascist power" (106 [1936]: 29). Further elaborating on how the sites and construction should manifest Italian dominance, Rava cites one of his former proposals to adapt the French urban design imposed on Rabat to Addis Ababa and create a "City of Government" on the top of a hill, with the governor's palace occupying the highest point: "a really true government acropolis, dominating everything in the midst of vast gardens. The Ghebbi, after all, began more or less with an analogous concept, which is to act upon the native's mentality, making an impression on him with the isolated greatness of power" (106 [1936]: 29).

Rava's representations draw clear boundaries between the Italian and the African indigenous districts, associating the European space with the pleasures of privilege and dominating power. Indeed, the separation of the races and European dominance structure this architect's conception of urban development overall, which privileges city spaces for the staging of colonial power in ceremonies and official functions. Such events are necessary, Rava argues,

> for maintaining the complex, vast ladder of hierarchies that is the foundation of colonial life, with regards to keeping both the privileges, even superficial ones, and the prestige of the race of the dominating people elevated at the highest level in front of the native. As a result, it is necessary for both public and private buildings to be conceived in such a manner as to provide with grandiose generosity for a life of public display. (109 [1937]: 26)

Here, the pleasures borders produce become linked with a vibrant social life of pomp and circumstance.

The possible allure of cultural fantasies of privilege warrants serious critical attention. Diane Ghirardo credits this ideal with contributing to the appeal of settlement in the African colonization program (105). Lending support to this position, the testimonies from Teresa Piacentini, the daughter of a diplomatic minister in Addis Ababa, and Mario Corsi, the son of a colonel, nostalgically recall the special freedoms, prerogatives, and indulgences experienced while living in the colonies. Representing the particular perspective of the upper social echelons, Piacentini remembers:

> My parents knew a lot of people in the city and took me to pay them visits. In general, the homes belonging to influential Italians were very beautiful, real villas, with sprawling gardens that brimmed with the most beautiful flowers. There were always lots of servants, at least two or three Abyssinian boys, dressed in Indian-style pants and a white guru type of jacket, wearing a wide band of cloth wound tightly around their waist. . . . To me, this style of living seemed fabulous compared to my life in Rome, which was much narrower and modest, and for a while I felt as if I were in a privileged position and in a somewhat fairytale-like dimension, where everything was easy, comfortable, and luxurious. (Quoted in Del Boca, *Gli italiani in Africa orientale*, 223)

Resonating with the imaginings, which the press made available, of East Africa as a wonderland, these youthful memories call attention to material comforts such as servants that see to the colonist's every need (a luxury even the middle classes could have at "rock bottom" prices, according to Del

Boca, *Gli italiani in Africa orientale,* 224). Furthermore, as Mario Corsi re-members, life in the colonies presents more freedoms for girls and women, who occupy their time with horseback riding and other sports, social gath-erings for bridge, or dinner parties. For some, Africa is imbued with a lei-surely party atmosphere. Anna Maria Mòglie, whose husband was a banker, writes in her memoir, "Here you live life as if on holiday; you go out, you or-ganize lunches, you go on tours" (23). Although Mòglie comments upon the respect she gains for her native servants, what remains unspoken in such accounts is the way the colonist's freedoms and privileges depend upon and produce socioeconomic structures of oppression of the indigenous African peoples.

Rava's concern about the prestige of the Italian race and the demanding social engagements of colonial life also shapes his plans for residential dwellings. Thus, for the residences of all government officials, Rava dictates, "the question of dignity and prestige of the race must be placed above all else, and every aspect of building must carry its sign" (109 [1937]: 27). Speaking in specifically racial terms, he then cites Quadrelli's position that "the white man's residence must be as comfortable and relaxing as possible, since it represents the only property he possesses in the colony, and to which he has every right, as guaranteed by the prestige of the race" (109 [1937]: 27). Viewed as a crucial factor for the material success of demographic col-onization, the home also functions as a symbol of Italian dominance over "the conquered populace" (106 [1936]: 29). Perhaps heightening the plea-sures gleaned from such descriptions of privilege, architectural sketches and floor plans for colonial homes grace the pages of *Domus.* Despite the linear simplicity of the residential plans, such sketches form complex sys-tems of signification. Mia Fuller's study of colonial architecture, for exam-ple, provides an insightful reading of the sociosymbolic meanings produced by home floor plans that appeared in an editorial titled "Civiltà" (Domus 9, no. 2: 1–3). As she explains, regular floor plans for ancient Roman houses and for modern Italian residences equate civilization with a certain type of housing: "The depicted floor plans are essentially rectilinear and are typi-cal of 'architecture' that evokes both design and symmetry" (399). In con-trast, three irregular, circular sketches form a floor plan displayed, Fuller argues, as "evidence that Ethiopians were barbaric" (399). Furthermore, I suggest, the clean, dark black lines of the floor plans featured in various is-sues of the magazine attract the eye, drawing readers into spaces where they could perhaps imagine themselves. Interesting here is a photo layout in Mariano Pittana's *Domus* article, which features Elena Fondra Asti's home in Asmara (40–45). We see inviting, tastefully decorated interior spaces, and a manicured lawn no less. Yet such dream houses were for the privileged few in Africa, and in Italy, which experienced a housing crisis that lasted long

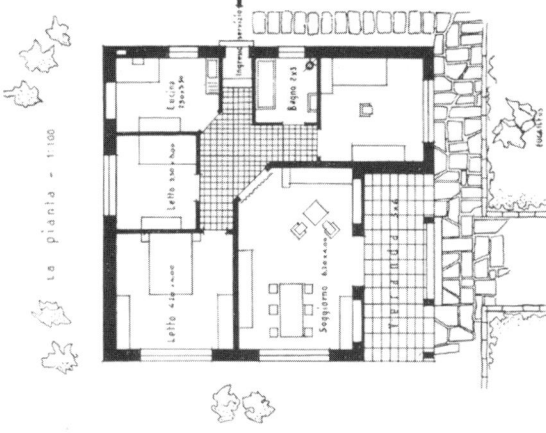

Figure 3. Photo of a *Villetta* designed by the architect Mariano Pittana for the families of Italian officials in Addis Ababa. Copyright Domus Rozzano, Milano.

after fascism. In fact, according to Del Boca, many Italian colonists inhabited makeshift dwellings and huts (*Gli italiani in Africa orientale* 222).

Although Rava refers to women colonists primarily in association with the ways residential building must accommodate their social roles and ease their acclimatization, Poggiali situates women at the center of hearth and home, which he evokes as "that peaceful, restful place, a safe port after a full hard day's work, a little kingdom in which the colonist family feels sovereign" (64). Yet it is interesting how the dream of a secure, tranquil settler dwelling is betrayed by a defensive line; home functions as a haven from labor, but perhaps also as a haven from other, more hostile forces, suggesting an attempt to produce in discourse the stable boundaries and dominance Italian colonialism claims. The image of the kingdom, for instance, evokes the symbolic law of the castle and its associations with hierarchical rule, guaranteed by paternal lineage and protected by borders. The meanings with which Poggiali adorns the colonial home also resonate with Rava's ideas on racial prestige and power. He maintains, for instance, that in the wilderness "every white person becomes sovereign among savage people," (63) and he portrays the family as "a small familial regime" (63). The domestic space thereby becomes a microsite for fascist colonial politics and, as demonstrated by the following example, women appear to be in command: "Every one of our women who has transferred to Africa has felt as if she had to govern a community, even if it were small; and she soon understands that whether the community does well or poorly depends upon her wisdom, her alacrity, and her good will" (64). Poggiali's representations of the Italian woman colonist thereby offer suggestive scenarios of conquest and power, which could hardly be imagined in the daily life of Italy in the 1930s.

LA SPOSA BIANCA: ROMANTIC FANTASIES OF FEMININE CONQUEST

Published in 1934, one year prior to the Italian invasion of Ethiopia, *La sposa bianca* is an important example of women's production of colonial discourses. Ballario, an award-winning author of the 1920s and 1930s with some twenty works of fiction, children's literature, and travel writing to her credit, among which were several colonial novels, enjoyed both popular and critical success. In fact, according to Maria Bandini Buti, the press "had always favorably reviewed her works, and most especially the ones that contribute to the understanding of colonial problems" (56). In *La sposa bianca* Ballario weaves together stories of murder, mystery, and love, all of which she portrays as inextricably linked to the African lands and peoples. The novel incorporates several conventions of Italian colonial literature of the 1930s. These include, for example, the elaboration of a love story that aligns romantic conquest with the conquest of African lands; representations of Italian colonists as agents of civilization; and the figuration of the frontier

as a space for self-regeneration. At the same time, the author crafts complicated images of race and gender that exceed the clear functions the genre
was initially designed to perform. As Maria Pagliara notes in her well-
researched study on the colonial novel, intellectuals and artists working under the auspices of fascism conceived of the genre as a tool that would unite
art and politics, diffusing a national colonial identity among a mass audience. More specifically, she explains, colonial literature would ideally
furnish "the elegant and refined elements of literary mediation, its moral
and formal tension, along with resolutions that would be straightforward
and unproblematic, and quickly grip readers" (365). Despite the clear parameters established for the literary cultivation of the African colonies, the
field became an embattled site, with such figures as F. T. Marinetti, Massimo
Bontempelli, and Margherita Sarfatti entering the fray over the best ways to
reconcile the genre's literary and political aims. A major preoccupation of
such debates is exoticism and the pleasures it makes available, thereby
threatening what some saw as the seriousness and lofty ideals of colonial art
and politics.

In a thought-provoking letter that appears as a dedication in *La sposa
bianca*, Ballario engages with these issues and presents her views on Italian
colonialism. Significantly, she critiques the focus on interracial romance,
evoked as an "idyll of the white officer with the Bedouin woman," caution-
ing that it is a weak "excuse for writing a local color novel." Similarly, she be-
moans the tendency among Italian colonial writers to present a "false, sickly
sweet image of things down there" in a maudlin style. Proposing changes,
she argues that "whoever devotes himself to the colonial problem must aim
for a much more serious scope and speak in real, precise terms about things
in the colonies." Ballario's sobering statements on colonial literature call for
a veracious treatment of life in Africa, a land whose beguiling mysteries and
harsh conditions present life-threatening dangers for all but the strongest.
This aesthetic position reflects her ideas about the Italian empire, which she
takes very seriously. Ballario proclaims, "For us, Africa must not be a land of
quixotic or sensual adventures, but an extension of our homeland, a land
to conquer economically for national riches, tearing bread out of the desert in the name of Rome, which once had its granaries there." Deploying
a strategy that typically operates in fascist colonial discourse, the author
creates a symbolic genealogy linking Italian colonialism of the 1930s with
the ancient Roman empire while voicing a zealous nationalist dream of
conquest.

Ballario's pronouncements on colonial art and practice might lead us to
expect a purely realist story transparently functioning as a mechanism for
the production of fascist colonial ideology. Yet, as the author readily admits,
her novel teems with "imagination." Indeed, throughout the text Ballario
mobilizes diverse modes of fantasy, including reverie, daydreams, and pri-

mal fantasies, which raises important questions. Since this narrative of Africa is fantasized from a woman's perspective, what differences, if any, might sexual difference make in the scenarios? For instance, how might it complicate the seduction fantasy that generally binds sexual and territorial conquest in a racialized, heterosexual economy represented by the Italian male colonist and African female figure? Does the subordinate position of Italian women in patriarchy alter the production of gender and racial categories in any significant ways?

With her opening representation of African space, Ballario immediately draws attention to her tale as a site of artistic invention, which stands in complex relation to both idealized popular images of Africa as a land of adventure and riches and to the actual lands that inspire them. The very first line creates a map, guiding readers into the space of the story as the narrator explains, "On the shores of the Indian Ocean in Italian Somalia, further and further down toward Tanaland, there is a small city we can call Chisimaio, but which isn't exactly Chisimaio, because no one among those who have been there would recognize it from these descriptions" (9). Providing general bearings for the journey, the text charts tangible geographic landmarks of Somalia as an Italian colonial possession, yet the presentation of the city setting refuses the epistemological authority map discourse generally confers. But Ballario does not present her colonial novel as pure fantasy. At several points in the narrative, the author recontextualizes popularized myths of Africa, conjured as characters recall their illusions. For example, early in the story, as Major Emanuele Serristori and Regional Comissioner Aschieri lament the lack of strong colonists to meet the challenges of building an empire, Serristori recounts an exotic cultural fantasy capturing the European urban imagination:

> Romantic, seductive features of African life have been planted in the spirit of the metropolis; dressed in spurs and sun helmet, the colonist is a sort of adventurer who gallops with his whip in hand among a populace of natives bowing in obedience before him. He gets off his horse to stretch out on soft pillows and sip mint tea while the moon winks at the Pario marble fountains. Naturally, he finds gold by the shovelful. People come down here unprepared, with all of their baggage full of dreams and their imagination stuffed with fake images from African films of safaris and adventure. (20)

Made wise by years of experience in the colonies, Serristori focuses on familiar signs and myths—clothing items and a whip, which serve as adornments for a life of luxury amidst submissive, obedient natives—suggesting they are groundless productions of the film industry. Elsewhere, colonial novels and jazz music performed in European variety clubs are credited with feeding the characters' imaginations with wild dreams. As the text works to deconstruct such myths through alternative representations of frontier life and race relations, Ballario claims a stronger purchase on "the real" for her fiction.

The initial depiction of Chisimaio highlights the tension between fantasy and realist strains in Ballario's text. As the author actually creates two visions of the city, its depiction provides a paradigmatic example of empire building as discursive construction. One portrait purportedly describes the place in terms of its recognizable features, with modest homes and peaceful streets. What it still lacks, the narrator tells us, are European-style buildings, wide avenues, tennis courts, worldly women, and dashing officers, all of which appear in the imaginary city of Ballario's design. Moreover, the urban arrangements of gender and race represented in the imagined community both complicate conventions of the colonial novel and intersect to varying degrees with principles of colonialist ideology analyzed earlier. First of all, the opening section of the novel focuses almost exclusively on the Italian community of colonial and military officials and their families, who occupy the European quarter. Apart from Aschieri and Serristori, the main male and female characters belong to a younger generation and appear to partake equally in the socioeconomic privileges their class and race confer. Scenes of sociability picture the merry troupe of young women and officers playing tennis, meeting for dinners, and chatting over cocktails. Somalian characters are for the most part absent from this space and are instead spied in the outlying native district or in the desert beyond. The text thus creates urban racial boundaries that uphold the ideals of Italian prestige and race separation, articulating a project of colonial architectural politics. Furthermore, Ballario's representation of the wilderness, where much of the tale unfolds, devotes sustained attention to the material conditions, beliefs, and politics of Somalian characters. This spatialization of race relations functions as a sociosymbolic mechanism for the production of colonial ideology. From a Western perspective, it aligns the Italian figures with the city as a site of civilization, and the Somalian figures with the wilderness as a site of primitiveness, which, however, will present complex challenges to the process of colonization.

Although colonial literature tends to cast the African frontier as a space for becoming a self-made man, Ballario refashions male and female models typically exhibited in the colonial novel, constructing ample possibilities for identification with active female desires. In general, as Pagliara explains, the conventional male hero displays physical and moral strength and unwavering commitment to establishing order and civilization in the African wilderness. The female figures, indigenous or Italian, perform supporting functions, highlighting the male protagonist's superiority. More specifically, the native female tends to be depicted as a sexual object, either submissively obeying the male or performing an act of betrayal. The European woman represents an obstacle to the colonial mission that the hero ultimately overcomes.

La sposa bianca, however, enacts a woman author's exotic fantasies, and it creates a cast of female characters who exhibit different forms of agency. Giuliana, for example, leads a life of adventure, including hunting, raising wild animals, and overseeing the cotton crops. She is described by Serristori as blond, beautiful, impudent, and audacious. Giuliana embodies modern, assertive female sexuality, which both attracts and threatens, making all of the officers "lose their heads" (27). Paola, Aschieri's daughter, also exhibits modern tastes and independence; she dances the fox-trot, likes jazz, and, significantly, has a talent for breaking horses. Her power of attraction, however, lies not in her physical appearance, but in her sense of ethical and social commitment. She comments, for instance, that "Just serving is not enough . . . one must serve well" (84). Paola also speaks Swahili and demonstrates a valuable knowledge of Somalian customs and politics. In a crucial desert scene she astutely unravels a tale of deceit, thereby saving Afmedò, the bride-to-be of a tribal leader, from the grips of a kidnapper. Ballario's representation of Afmedò Mallim diverges from the dominant model of native femininity. Described as the young daughter of a head "witch doctor" of the Abgal, Afmedò plays a decisive role in the plot and, unlike Galeazzo's nemesis Neber di Lugh, is not presented as an object of male colonial desire. Neber, known to our hero as Abebisc, possesses almost irresistible seductive beauty. In a manner that brings to mind a form of racial, feminine masquerade, Neber performs exotic femininity in order to fulfill her political desires. Belonging to the Tigre race, and a descendant of a long line of royal blood, Neber turns Italian soldiers against their government, and tribal leaders against Italians, in order to recapture Somalian territory and establish her rule. On the one hand, this depiction of indigenous femininity underscores sexuality in a familiar manner. On the other hand, in this white woman's fantasy, the black woman's desires are not aimed at sleeping with the white man, but are inscribed as signs of rebellion against Italian colonial power. Nonetheless, Ballario's representations of racial and sexual difference may work all the more strongly in service of colonialist ideology precisely because indigenous female agency is ultimately punished or recuperated within the colonial economy, a point I analyze more thoroughly below.

Galeazzo Moravia, the male protagonist of the novel and of several pivotal fantasy scenarios, presents a fascinating array of traits that build upon and recast the typology of the colonial hero of the 1930s, destabilizing popularized notions of virile masculinity. Like many of his counterparts in colonial literature, Galeazzo has a strikingly handsome, muscular appearance and a respected family pedigree, although he expresses disenchantment with his earlier life of dissipation and meaningless affairs in the cities of Europe and Asia. Although he had entertained fantasies of Africa, life in the colonies fulfills his need for discipline and a simpler life. And, as Serristori remarks, Galeazzo has "a spirit for heroism and wants to be put to the test" (29). However, Ballario also exposes the hero's fears, insecurities, and flaws, creating a complex model of masculine subjectivity. For example, shortly after his arrival in the wilderness, Galeazzo is overwhelmed by solitude and exclaims "I'm not born for adventure, I'm born for love" (146). And, although he does not shy away from taking command, he defers to Paola's judgment in the desert rescue scene cited above, apparently valuing feminine strength and intelligence. Indeed, setting the romance fantasy in motion, he undertakes a dangerous mission into the African interior largely in order to earn Paola's love.

With exceptional skill, Ballario intricately elaborates the initiation of the romance fantasy, with its complications and deferments, and terms of female and male desire as articulations of colonial politics. The harrowing mission on the African frontier arises because several Italian officers sent to oversee work to cut down the forest near a village at the Lake of the Seven Maidens—in actuality a puddle of putrid water—disappear one by one into thin air, with no outward signs of rebellion among the native population. The next officer must continue the project of cutting the forest to make space for a plantation, since to halt the work would be a show of Italian weakness, tantamount to a victory for the natives. He must also discover the fate of Lieutenant Brancaccio, the last officer sent to the village and, not surprisingly, Paola's fiancé. Paola's response to the news that Brancaccio may be dead incites a conversion in Galeazzo, who, for the first time, becomes aware of a meaningful kind of love. Instantly taking charge of the situation, Paola not only proposes forming a search party, but she insists upon leading it, convinced that she alone can guide the caravan to Brancaccio. Upon realizing that everyone's eyes are upon her, Paola's face transforms, as does the hero's perception of her: "It was just as when a sunny day becomes blanketed by sudden gusts of fog; everything inside her was gray and cold, but the ashes suddenly thrown on the embers did not put out the blaze lit in Galeazzo in the reflection of that ardor" (34–35). Paola's passion endows her with a special beauty of spirit and, as Galeazzo marvels, makes her "a worthy companion for a soldier" (35). As Paola meets his gaze he is beguiled by her eyes, and he volunteers for the mission. Thus begins the romance fantasy, as well as a fantasy of origins, linking Paola with sexual and social transgression. As we discover, Paola has inherited her enchanting eyes from her mother, who brought scandal and tragedy upon the Aschieri family. Involved in an adulterous affair, Paola's mother was killed by her lover, driving Aschieri to move his surviving family to Africa. The linkage between the primal scene of seduction and scandal may function to explain the transgressive elements of Paola's femininity.

Strategically situated between Galeazzo's confession to Paola of the love he feels for her and his departure for the native village, scenes of reverie inscribe the fears and desires elicited in Galeazzo by racial and sexual difference. The sequence runs some six pages and warrants quoting at length. Galeazzo crosses the border separating the European quarter of the city from the indigenous district, drawn by drums announcing the ritual dance of spring. Karen Pinkus's insightful analysis of F. T. Marinetti's *Mafarka le futuriste, roman africain* provides a key to understanding the significance of the construction and transgression of borders. She states, "Textual pleasures reside primarily in the force with which boundaries are drawn and in the extreme tension of the bodies that always threaten to burst forth from some comforting classification" (*Bodily Regimes* 33). As Galeazzo is swept into the crowd, his first reaction is to defend himself from the "swelling, undulating" (89) mass. Yet he becomes mesmerized when a new dance, the dance of hunger, begins and the rhythms of music and bodies change. Interestingly, in this woman's invention of a white man watching black men and women dance, the frenetic bodies prompt Galeazzo to think "I understand why they have good luck with women" (90) and to conjure a memory of a jazz club in Paris: "Blond women and black men: large hands, black and hard as coal, firmly planted on snow-white backs, claiming possession, hot mouths, frank looks, dust, stars, the women's hips moving restlessly from sexual fever, and champagne in the ice buckets" (90–91). The fragmenting of language and bodies here may express the unspeakability of white women's desire for black men. Indeed, the reduction of the women and men to body parts emphasizes sheer carnality, but in a way that denies total union. Furthermore, the reference to the black male hands taking possession of white female backs prompts a defensive positioning, elaborated in Galeazzo's reflections: "We get all wrapped up over dominating them and in reality we are dominated by them; the black man is our shadow; the black man is our master; we copy his customs and barbarousness; it always happens like that among the conquered and the conquerors—and he thought about Rome, crushed and lost to Hellenism, and saw a river of black ink spill over Europe and flood it" (91). At one level, this reversal of power relations between the colonized and colonizers critiques the diffuse commodification of Africa that captured the Italian cultural imagination. Yet it also expresses the threats posed by female desire, as the mixing of white female and black male bodies is linked with the loss of boundaries between bodies of land. Since flowing fluids frequently symbolize the feminine, the metaphor of black ink spilling over Europe combines two powerful markers of difference, femininity and blackness, articulating the fear of assimilation, of becoming black.

Galeazzo is soon drawn back to the sight before him as the sexual dynamics of the dancing change, producing a sense of pleasure in him. Following a sequence in which a young woman skillfully eludes the snares of a young man, "All of the women surrounded him [the native male] and squeezed up next to him, pressing against him, caressing him with their young skin, which was smooth and soft as cloth; they were pure animality, invitation, pleasure, and spasms, slaves to the strength of the male personified by that man who was like a fetish" (92). This suggestive scene of seduction prompts us to ask whether it enacts a white female's fantasy of black female desire or her fantasy of how a white male fantasizes exotic feminine desire. And what might the scene say about an Italian woman's own desires? The depiction follows two currents, as the women perform active roles in the dance yet are characterized as "slaves" to the symbol of male power. What clearly emerges is Ballario's deployment of sexuality as a central determinant of black female subjectivity, which, along with the repeated use of animal metaphors conveying carnality, reinforce the boundaries that colonial discourse constructs between Italian civilization and Somalian primitiveness. Galeazzo's musings in the following passage highlight this point: "Where the black man was not corrupted by contact with the whites, by venereal diseases and alcohol, he still remained a magnificent animal—unassailable and unassailed by wild animal attacks, by terrible African diseases, by the misery of need, by slavery to ambitions" (93). Initially, Ballario introduces a critical perspective on the violence of Italian colonial intervention, which then slips into the native resistance to natural dangers, and then economic and cultural preoccupations. In the process, she creates a myth of the pure native, collapsing differences among indigenous peoples. Her aestheticization of the exotic native produces a static image, evacuated of complex historical and cultural changes. Significantly, as Galeazzo's racial and cultural identity boundaries blur, and he feels as if he were "lost in a black sea" (93), a fellow colonist calls him back to his senses.

The fears and anxieties inscribed in the fantasy sequence examined above foreshadow Galeazzo's affective and psychic experiences of the tropical wilderness, where he falls prey to conspiracies and mystical imaginings, and in many ways Galeazzo comes up wanting in comparison to the traditional colonial hero. An analysis of the thought-provoking plot complications that occur during Galeazzo's many adventures and misadventures goes beyond the range of this study. Therefore, I will focus on elements that are central to the representations of the hero and heroine, and to the romance fantasy. In Ballario's tale, as in many colonial film and literary texts, the tropical forest performs critical functions, and it is encoded with a complex system of diverse cultural and symbolic meanings. When Galeazzo first sets eyes on the forest, he feels as if he were being swallowed up by it and is frightened by the chaotic, twisted roots. If one builds upon the general association of the forest with the feminine and the unconscious, the African forest can be interpreted as symbolizing an uncontrolled, feminized native space. Indeed, the hero perceives the trees as a wall that cuts him off from civilization. At the same time, Galeazzo must master the forest (and his fears) by cutting it down, in order to pass the test of his heroic mission. Obviously, the destruction of the forest makes way for the plantation and the establishment of order and production, symbolizing the sociosymbolic power of colonial rule. For the indigenous villagers, the preservation of the forest, which Ballario represents as a source of magical, mystic power central to their belief system, signifies their victory over the colonizers. It is also significant that the trees and forest appear as horrific, threatening forces that rise up against Galeazzo in his dreams. In the first one, which occurs just after his arrival, he presciently dreams that Paola comes to save him.

Although Galeazzo exhibits commitment to his mission, out of inexperience he makes several nearly fatal egregious errors. He refuses to give money to Saad, a powerful enchanter who incites the villagers to rebel; he pressures the tribal leaders to order their men to cut down the trees; he ignores the friendly warnings of Ben Hamor, Nassib, and then Afmedò's messenger and orders the indigenous soldiers in his command to cut down the forest; and when two of the soldiers are killed, he whips Saad in front of the gathered villagers. This scene begins an incredibly suspenseful series of events that represents the natives' active resistance and rebellion. Although Saad recoils from the first blow of the whip, he then stands in open defiance. All of a sudden Abebisc appears and, when Galeazzo threatens her with the whip too, she tells him to go to hell and strikes a blow on his face with her whip, branding him with a red mark (256–57). Protected this time by the indigenous soldiers, Galeazzo imprisons Abebisc. Though this conflict is quelled for the moment, as tensions again build, Paola, whose arrival has fuelled Galeazzo's fantasies, finally appears with the caravan. However, the hero fares no better in romantic conquest. Paola discovers that her dead fiancé was nothing but a dandy who slept with the native women and carried on an affair with Giuliana, "his true love" and his "white bride," according to a letter Paola finds (289, 293). In a manner typical of romance novels, the successful coupling of Galeazzo and Paola is deferred, and she leaves the very next morning.

In the novel's climax and denouement, Ballario intertwines colonial and romance fantasies, but with an interesting twist. Awakened from his sleep by screams, Galeazzo sees the forest consumed by flames in the distance, as Saad approaches with the villagers. This scene, like the preceding incidents of rebellion, performs an important function in the colonial narrative, exposing conflicts and rebelliousness so that they may then be overcome and pacified. In a violent confrontation Saad cries out, "Death to the white man" (321), causing Galeazzo to aim his gun at the enchanter, in an act of apparent self-defense. But he misses, shooting Abebisc instead. Thus, the black female's active transgression of colonial law is punished by death. Similarly, as Saad then attempts to exact punishment against Galeazzo, yelling "For the death of Neber, death to the destroyer of our race" (322), he too is shot and killed. Not surprisingly, the crowd rebels at the sight of their fallen leaders and attacks Galeazzo, capturing the ill-fated hero. Surrounded by darkness, smoke, flames, and women who sing and dance around him, Galeazzo slips into a dream state in the forest. He senses that "with its roots, the tree was filling up with his blood, dipping into it to water all the sap of the forest that was dying of feverish thirst. It was taking revenge on him: he was flesh, he was blood, he was the victim. Perhaps he was already dead" (329–30). Here again, the narrative marks a slippage. First, the perspective voiced in Galeazzo's delirium conveys a sense of guilt, which might explain the forest's revenge. Then, however, he defensively claims the position of victim. Importantly, the last sight Galeazzo registers in his semiconscious mind is of "big, complicated clouds that made and unmade huge maps" (331) in the sky. This image possibly suggests the loftiness of empire building, but also its ethereal quality, and the instability of territorial borders as imaginary constructions. However, when Galeazzo again awakens, in the comfort of his own bed, "the kingdom is calm and peaceful" (335), as Paola's brother puts it. In point of fact, the hero on the brink of death was saved by Afmedò and Paola.

Although the affairs of the colonial state appear miraculously in order, those of the heart are not. Ballario presents an intriguing reversal in the romantic fantasy, as Paola must now overcome Galeazzo's resistance. When Paola declares her love for him, the tarnished hero can not accept her affections because, he confesses, his mistakes have left him a vanquished man with no self-respect. However, in the euphemistic language of Italian inter-war romance novels, their breaths mingle in the final lines, and Paola proclaims, "I'll stay here with you" (342). This conclusion prompts questions concerning the potential effects this reversal may have on the romantic and colonial fantasies. As Bridget Orr cogently argues, a recurring strategy in colonial discourse is the naturalization of "the violent appropriation of the other's territory . . . through the feminization of the native or exotic culture, often narrativized in love and conversion plots" (155). Ballario's romance plot differs in that the protagonists of the love story are both Italian. Yet the alignment of the stories of sexual and territorial conquest may still function to naturalize the colonial project while upholding the prohibition on miscegenation. We must also remember that in fantasy, the protagonist is caught up in the sequence of images, or in the seduction per se, in which case the reversal that privileges the active female subject may not significantly alter the appeal to female readers. Yet if fantasy functions as a setting for desire, then Ballario's romance scenario clearly maps Africa as a site of feminine desires for conquest. Furthermore, in this romantic tale and the fictions of Africa published in the press, the representations of women as the subjects of adventure, independence, mobility, and desire invent powerful terms of identification. The meanings these texts make available elucidate the need for further inquiry into the colonial imaginary of women's invention and the historically specific ways popular fantasies may articulate Italian politics of gender and race.

NOTES

Among the institutions and individuals who have made this study possible by furnishing key primary texts, I want to thank those at the University of Wisconsin–Milwaukee Interlibrary Loan Office, as well as Maria Pettinato and Manuela Ginepro at the Biblioteca Comunale Negroni in Novara, who generously provided a copy of *La sposa bianca*. I also thank *Italica* for permission to republish portions of this article, which first appeared there in volume 77, no. 3 (2000). Unless otherwise indicated, all translations from Italian to English are my own.

1. For an acute reading of two versions of the lyrics to the song "Faccetta nera" as inscriptions of shifting fascist colonial politics, see Karen Pinkus, *Bodily Regimes,* especially pp. 56–58.

2. In my "Ways of Looking in Black and White," I provide a more detailed examination of fascist colonialism and cultural difference, discourses addressed to women, representations of miscegenation, and female spectatorship. Karen Pinkus ("'Black and Jew'") conducts a fascinating examination of the "discourse of liberal tolerance" constructed in a woman's fantasy, represented in the popular 1934 novel *Sambadú* by Mura. For an engaging treatment of the politics of gender and race in Dutch, French, and British colonialism see Ann Laura Stoler, "Making Empire Respectable."

3. Among the groundbreaking studies that work through fantasy as an integral part of their critical methodology to examine colonial discourses and race, see Panivong Norindr *Phantasmatic Indochina,* and Christopher Lane "The Psychoanalysis of Race."

4. For thought-provoking examinations of feminist approaches to mapping women and space in colonial and postcolonial discourses see *Writing Women and Space,* edited by Alison Blunt and Gillian Rose, as well as *Embracing Space,* by Kerstin W. Shands.

5. See my "Structures of Feminine Fantasy and Italian Empire Building, 1930–1940" for an analysis of women's testimonies about such precolonial camps and their lives in the colonies.

WORKS CITED

Aden, Mohamed. "Italy: Cultural Identity and Spatial Opportunism from a Post-colonial
Perspective." In *Revisioning Italy: National Identity and Global Culture,* ed. Beverly Allen and Mary Russo. Minneapolis: University of Minnesota Press, 1997.
Almanacco della donna italiana (1939).

Astuto, Mercedes. "La donna italiana e le nostre colonie." *Almanacco della donna italiana* (1934): 115–35.

Ballario, Pina. *La sposa bianca.* Milano: La Prora, 1934.

Bandini Buti, Maria. *Donne d'Italia: Poetesse e scrittrici.* Vol. 1. Roma: Tosi, 1946.

Benedettini, Silvia. "La donna in Africa Orientale." *Almanacco della donna italiana* (1937): 399–402.

Blunt, Alison, and Gillian Rose, eds. *Writing Women and Space: Colonial and Postcolonial Geographies.* New York: Guilford Press, 1994.

Burgin, Victor, James Donald, and Cora Kaplan, eds. *Formations of Fantasy.* London: Methuen, 1986.

Celik, Zeynep. *Urban Forms and Colonial Confrontations: Algiers under French Rule.* Berkeley: University of California Press, 1997.

Cervi, Mario, and Massimo Borgnis. "Scalfaro ad Addis Abeba ha riconosciuto gli errori del colonialismo." *Gente* 4 (Dec. 1997): 4–7.

Curti, Daniela. "Il linguaggio del racconto rosa: Gli anni 20 ed oggi." *Lingua letteraria e lingua dei media nell'italiano contemporaneo.* Firenze: Felice Le Monnier, 1987.

de Certeau, Michel. *The Practice of Everyday Life.* Trans. Steven Rendall. Berkeley: University of California Press, 1988.

Del Boca, Angelo. *Gli italiani in Africa orientale: La caduta dell'Impero.* Vol. 3. Bari: Laterza, 1982.

Fani, Amadeo. "La donna e l'impero." *Almanacco della donna italiana* (1937): 129–30.

Fuller, Mia. "Wherever You Go, There You Are: Fascist Plans for the Colonial City of Addis Ababa and the Colonizing Suburb of EUR '42." *Journal of Contemporary History* 31, no. 2 (1996): 397–418.

Ghirardo, Diane. *Building New Communities: New Deal America and Fascist Italy.* Princeton, N.J.: Princeton University Press, 1989.

Jaggar, Alison M. "Love and Knowledge: Emotion in Feminist Epistemology." In *Gender/Body/Knowledge: Feminist Reconstructions of Being and Knowing,* ed. Alison M. Jaggar and Susan R. Bordo. New Brunswick, N.J.: Rutgers University Press, 1989.

Lane, Christopher. "The Psychoanalysis of Race: An Introduction." In *The Psychoanalysis of Race,* ed. Christopher Lane. New York: Columbia University Press, 1998.

Laplanche, Jean, and J.-B. Pontalis. *The Language of Psychoanalysis.* Trans. Donald Nicholson-Smith. London: Hogarth Press, 1973.

———. "Fantasy and the Origins of Sexuality, Retrospect 1986." In *Formations of Fantasy,* ed. Victor Burgin, James Donald, and Cora Kaplan. London: Methuen, 1986.

Lutz, Catherine. "Emotion, Thought and Estrangement: Emotion as a Cultural Category." *Cultural Anthropology* 1 (1986): 287–309.

Mòglie, Anna Maria. *Africa come amore.* Roma: Trevi, 1978.

Norindr, Panivong. *Phantasmatic Indochina: French Colonial Ideology in Architecture, Film, and Literature.* Durham, N.C.: Duke University Press, 1996.

Orr, Bridget. "The Only Free People in the Empire: Gender Difference in Colonial Discourse." In *De-scribing Empire: Post-Colonialism and Textuality,* ed. Chris Tiffin and Alan Lawson. London: Routledge, 1994.

Pagliara, Maria. "Il romanzo coloniale." In *I bestseller del Ventennio: Il regime e il libro di massa,* ed. Gigliola De Donato and Vanna Gazzola Stacchini. Rome: Riuniti, 1991.

Palma, Silvana. *L'Italia coloniale.* Roma: Riuniti, 1999.

Pickering-Iazzi, Robin. "Structures of Feminine Fantasy and Italian Empire Building, 1930–1940." *Italica* 77, no. 3 (2000): 400–417.

———. "Ways of Looking in Black and White: Female Spectatorship and the Miscege-national Body in *Sotto la croce del sud.*" In *Fascism and Film,* ed. Jacqueline Reich and Piero Garofalo. Bloomington: Indiana University Press, 2001.

Pinkus, Karen. *Bodily Regimes: Italian Advertising under Fascism.* Minneapolis: University of Minnesota Press, 1995.

———. "'Black and Jew': Race & Resistance to Psychoanalysis in Italy." *Annali d'Italianistica* 16 (1998): 145–67.

Pittana, Mariano. "Gli italiani in Africa Orientale." *Domus* 146 (1940): 40–45.

Poggiali, Ciro. "La donna italiana in A.O." *Almanacco della donna italiana* (1939): 53–73.

Rava, Carlo Enrico. "Costruire in colonia." *Domus* 106 (1936): 28–30.

———. "Costruire in colonia." *Domus* 109 (1937): 23–27.

Shands, Kerstin W. *Embracing Space: Spatial Metaphors in Feminist Discourse.* Westport, Conn.: Greenwood Press, 1999.

Stoler, Ann Laura. "Making Empire Respectable: The Politics of Race and Sexual Morality in Twentieth-Century Colonial Cultures." In *Dangerous Liaisons: Gender, Nation, and Postcolonial Perspectives,* ed. Anne McClintock, Aamir Mufti, and Ella Shohat. Minneapolis: University of Minnesota Press, 1997.

"Viaggio di nozze a Tripoli e un concorso di *Domus.*" *Domus* 135 (1939): 84–92.

von Henneberg, Krystyna. "Imperial Uncertainties: Architectural Syncretism and Improvisation in Fascist Colonial Libya." *Journal of Contemporary History* 31, no. 2 (1996): 373–95.

Orphans for the Empire

Colonial Propaganda and
Children's Literature during the Imperial Era

Patrizia Palumbo

Despite the important symbolic role played by images of infancy in Western culture, literature for children has long been considered a minor genre. As a result, the cultural location of children and aesthetic works addressed to them have been of only marginal interest in Italian studies, even following the recent turn to cultural studies. And yet cultural materials produced for the young are an essential component of both the invention of collective traditions and a nation's sociopolitical orientation. This is particularly true during an age of totalitarianism and imperialist endeavors such as that which characterized Italy during the years of fascist rule.

The political socialization of youth was at the core of the fascist project after the party assumed power in Italy in 1922. Throughout the *ventennio* the fascist regime systematically fed the youngest Italians with its ideological doctrines by taking control of their schools and their textbooks, as well as the recreative youth organizations and radio programs that provided them with social outlets.[1] Even immediately prior to and after the Ethiopian war, when the fascist government intensified its propagandistic effort, Italian children as well as adults were pervasively exposed to imperialist indoctrination. As Edward Tannenbaum shows, the Ethiopian campaign was the primary topic of discussion in Italian elementary and secondary schools at the time. In 1936, many teachers read an adaptation of the popular song "Faccetta nera" to first graders. They also taught basic notions of "aggressive patriotism" by, for example, assigning their students compositions with titles like "Italy is powerful and feared" or dictation exercises that emphasized the greatness of the Italian nation and attacked other European countries that had joined the embargo against Italy following its invasion of Ethiopia (Tannenbaum 172–73). Even mathematics provided an occasion for imperial propaganda. One of the problems third graders had to solve during this period was "The glorious war in Africa lasted seven months. How many days is that?" (Koon 82). Between 1935 and 1936, moreover, half of the radio broadcasts for children dealt with the Ethiopian campaign (Tannenbaum 161).

Conforming to the dictates of the regime, Italian publishers of children's and juvenile literature filled their lists with texts on the Italian colonization of Eastern Africa just after the beginning of the Ethiopian war.[2] Before that period, although Italy had already had African colonies for four decades, children's literature did not show much interest in Italian colonial endeavors. For example, one of the most beloved authors writing for Italian children of this century, Emilio Salgari, set some of his numerous novels in Africa, but he made no reference to any of the Italian colonial campaigns undertaken during this period. His only novel that hints at the Italian presence in Africa, *Lo schiavo della Somalia,* is his least sensational and adventurous.[3]

The reason for Salgari's avoidance of the Italian colonial setting in his novels certainly resides in the tension between his literary interests and Italian foreign politics. Although, in fact, Salgari believed in white hegemony, the disappearance of the mythical Africa—the subject of his books—as a result of the Italian colonization and incorporation of African lands must have prevented him from utilizing the Italian campaigns in Africa as matter for his exoticizing fiction. Luigi Motta, the most acclaimed of Salgari's followers, also ignores the Italian colonial wars in Africa in his work.[4] Ironically, prominent exponents of fascism later revived Salgari's writings, dubbing him the "prophet of the Italian African destiny," celebrating his writings as precursors of the heroic spirit of fascism, and lauding his passionate animosity toward the English. During the Ethiopian war, in fact, Salgari's works were abundantly reprinted and helped to inspire in young Italian men who participated in the war dreams of an exotic African adventure (Mignemi 57).[5]

A romantic, adventurous spirit also permeates novels written for the youngest Italians between 1925 and 1935 that dealt with the Italian colonial campaigns. In these novels, curiosity about an Africa long fantasized about prevails over interest in concrete aspects of colonial life. In *Il piccolo Brassa: Romanzo coloniale per giovani,* written by Rosolino Davy Gabrielli and published in 1928, for instance, the main desire of the Italian soldiers in Cirenaica is to experience the "spell" of the desert, the oasis, and the nomadic life of the bedouins. The description of the soldiers' adventures in a highly exoticized Africa effectively obscures the gruesome details of their military operations (Scotto di Luzio 200).

Fascist educators and officials, however, were instrumental in the move away from this literary cliché of a mysterious and dangerous Africa; they encouraged Italian writers and artists to represent Africa as a ploughed and cultivated land marked by the dignified white houses of the Italian colonists, the flowing steel ribbons of railroad tracks, and imposing dams. As the governor of Somalia, Guido Corni, argued in 1933, the old "African" novels had to be replaced by ones that would reflect the new "reality" of diligent colonial labor and productivity (Scotto di Luzio 202–3).[6] In 1935, this orientation was supported and promoted by the acclaimed children's author, Giuseppe Fanciulli. In that year, Fanciulli produced a radio program for young children entitled "Coi nostri soldati in Africa Orientale" in order to familiarize the young with the colonial environment. In addition, during this same year Fanciulli published the novel *Dalla Nievole a Bargal: Avventure di un ragazzo nella Somalia italiana* (Scotto di Luzio 205–6). As Adolfo Scotto di Luzio observes in his valuable analysis, in this novel Fanciulli carefully erases the fearful and exotic image of Africa that had characterized much of the previous children's literature and replaces it with a space filled with the reassuring signs of "civilization." In *Dalla Nievole a Bargal,* indeed, the story of father and son's arrival in the colony and their search for a friend is nothing but a pretext to offer a reading tour of the much-celebrated Italian agricultural enterprises where, presumably, the indigenous worked under the supposedly benevolent surveillance of the colonists.[7]

Although a wealth of imperialist fantasies are traceable in Salgari and Motta's narratives, and in texts written for children in the mid-1930s that resuscitated images of imperial Rome, my concern here is specifically the values and the role models propagated by authors of children's literature who, in Fanciulli's wake, responded to the regime's appeal for the creation of a new colonial literature for children immediately prior to or after the formation of the empire.[8] I will first devote my attention to texts that, like Fanciulli's, faithfully reproduced fascist imperial propaganda. Secondly, I will discuss Arnaldo Cipolla's *Balilla regale,* a more complex novel that breaks through what is a relatively homogeneous panorama by articulating skepticism about the dominant myths of Italian imperialism as well as discomfort with contemporary ideals of masculinity. This will also allow me to characterize a children's culture of the period that preserved some autonomy and was not simply a reflection of the pedagogic orientation prescribed by the fascist regime.

Dealing with cultural material produced during and promoted by a totalitarian regime, it is essential not to take popular acceptance and replication of the values promoted by such material for granted. In spite of the combined efforts of the regime and the publishers and authors who supported it, children's colonial literature of the time did not achieve great success among Italian children. According to critics and historians of literature for children, one of the favorite books among children in the 1930s was *Piccolo Alpino,* which dealt with the Great War.[9] In addition, great enthusiasm was aroused by Salgari's novels. Tannenbaum comments that children liked Salgari's adventure stories, American movies, and comics because they "formed a spicy 'counterculture' to the discipline and moralizing they experienced at home, in school and in the *Balilla*" (Tannenbaum 167).

Apart from some marginal references in surveys of children's literature, no critical attention has yet been given to Salgari's "African" texts. As Tannenbaum's observations on the popularity of Salgari suggest, the reason for the exclusion of these "African" texts from national archives cannot be found in the brevity of the Italian domination in Eastern Africa and in the numerical limits of the Italian settlements in that region, although these aspects of Italian colonization may have partially contributed to this cultural selection. Rather, it was the heavily didactic spirit of this literature that compromised its quality in Italian literary critics' eyes and minimized the interest of children, who were already subject in their daily life to intense political indoctrination.

Thus, although we need to be aware of the enormous efforts devoted to the indoctrination of the young into colonial discourses of the period, we must also focus our attention on the multiple counterhegemonic strategies that children of the period employed to negotiate, satirize, and otherwise resist such forms of ideological control. Following the work of Janice Radway in *Reading the Romance* and other contemporary scholars who study the diverse patterns of consumption that characterize communities of readers, we may begin to unravel signs of dissent within literature directed at the individuals to whom Western society most habitually denies meaningful forms of agency: children. Such dissent is particularly important given the central role played by children within the eugenically conceived model of national identity that circulated during the years of Italy's imperial rule.

CHILDREN'S LITERATURE IN THE IMPERIAL CLIMATE

Much of the children's literature of the mid-1930s responded enthusiastically to the fascist imperial appeal and bent deferentially to serve it. This is certainly true of works by Olga Visentini, an authoritative author, critic, and historian of Italian children's literature.[10] Although postwar historians of children's literature do not mention Visentini's obsequious adherence to the fascist regime, the author solemnly expressed her obedience to the dictatorship in her *Libri e ragazzi: Sommario storico della letteratura infantile* by including a propagandistic chapter entitled "Letteratura giovanile fascista." The books praised in her survey of children's literature were those written "nel santo nome della Patria" (in the holy name of the motherland), including works such as *Il figlio di Armonia* and *Bella Italia amate sponde,* as well as the numerous contemporary biographies of Benito Mussolini.[11] Visentini's personal celebration of fascist imperial politics as a writer, however, came only after the invasion of Ethiopia in *Africanelle: Fiabe,* published in 1937. Her embrace of the colonial cause is signified in a few stories of *Africanelle,* in which blond fairies and mermaids depart their idyllic environments in order to find a more "noble mission." In "Mirta's Mission," for instance, the fairy Mirta leaves behind her home of "silvery summits," gnomes, and elves and ends up in a modest Italian home where she helps a child to write a letter to his father, who is laboring in Eastern Africa to build the imperial infrastructure (137–45). The same pedagogical change is dramatized in Visentini's "The Goblin on the Roof," in which the goblin Aldanè interrupts his trip to a fairyland and, with other fabulous creatures, provides a child with the uniform he needs to march with other children in Rome after the declaration of the Italian empire (157–65). Visentini's adaptation of classical fairy tale structures to the ideological ends of the Italian fascists may usefully be compared with the use of such tales by the Nazis to socialize children into the party's images of the stable German family and *Heimat*.[12] The feudal world picture made available in classical fairy tales could be woven seamlessly into fascist models of individual and familial subservience to the nation and race in an imperial context. The popularity of the genre was thought to enable the propagandist writer to lead his or her reader into accepting a new message veiled by a familiar imaginary world.

Besides Visentini's *Africanelle,* the series of books for children that publishers rushed to put on the market at the time were texts that recalled the history of Italian colonialism since its inception: the formation of the Eritrean colony, the war against Ethiopia, and the exploration and commercial penetration of the colonies. Exemplary texts of this genre include, respectively, *Volontario in Africa, Piccolo legionario in Africa Orientale, Genietti e sirenelle in Africa Orientale,* and *Balilla regale.* Since these works are now out of print and are unlikely to be familiar even to most specialists in Italian children's literature, I will briefly describe these books before engaging in a more detailed discussion of the major themes that appear in each.

Volontario in Africa: Racconti di guerra per ragazzi—signed by its author with the militaristic nom de plume Tenente Anonimo—illustrates the heroism of a now-aged Italian soldier during the conflicts that led to the creation of the Eritrean colony in the last century. Motivated by the transparent intention of justifying the imminent invasion of Ethiopia, the author depicts the Abyssinian population as brutal, fearful, and mischievous.

Salvator Gotta's *Piccolo legionario in Africa Orientale* adopts a wider propagandistic scope.[13] In this ambitious novel Gotta narrates the story of an Italian boy, Pierino Marra, who leaves his house in France to follow his father, who is fighting as a volunteer in the Ethiopian war. The French setting of the first part of the novel allows the author to vilify frequently one of the nations carrying out sanctions against Italy. The selection of France as a setting for the novel must have been influenced also by the presence there of a significant Italian community. Furthermore, France presumably was targeted because it was the residence of many antifascist Italian expatriates.[14]

The author of *Genietti e sirenelle in Africa Orientale* also resorts to an ideologically charged pseudonym to sign this and all his works for children: the

pen name Nonno Ebe is clearly informed by the fascist familial and sentimental discourse. In *Genietti e sirenelle,* Nonno Ebe, a very prolific children's
author as well as a voluntary soldier in the Ethiopian war, tells about the military and moral contribution made by fairy-tale creatures to the cause of the
Italian soldiers in Eastern Africa.

All these texts faithfully replicated the ideas propagated by fascist imperial propaganda concerning both the cause and the effects of the Ethiopian
war. They also provided role models for boys and girls that were intended
to prepare the youngest generation for colonial enterprises and settlement.
In addition, they included long digressions on the "history" and on the
physical environment of Eastern Africa, digressions that often incorporated
figures and events from the Italian campaigns in the region.

One of the few exceptions to this uniformity of purpose is constituted by
Balilla regale: Romanzo africano per giovinetti. As I will show, its representation of Italian colonialism is much more complex than that provided by the
other texts discussed above. *Volontario in Africa, Piccolo legionario,* and *Genietti e sirenelle* simply depict a Manichean world in which brave Italian soldiers
were fighting a necessary war against an evil and uncivilized enemy, a representation that *Balilla regale* destabilizes in a particularly interesting manner. Although the book's great divergence from the imperial fascist propaganda make its publication seem surprising at first, its publication actually
confirms that fascist censorship, like many of the directives of the party, was
not always consistent, efficient, and infallible.[15]

The author of *Balilla regale,* Arnaldo Cipolla, was born in a family with a
strong military tradition. He went to Africa first as a legionary in the Congo
and later as an explorer and a correspondent for several Italian daily papers.
Although Cipolla wrote several works of juvenile fiction set in Africa, *Balilla
regale* is his only book for children that refers to Italian colonization. In doing so, it disavows the military past of the author and in general contradicts
the fascist ideals to which Cipolla had declared himself loyal. This intricate
novel recounts the numerous adventures in Eastern Africa of Omar, the
child of an Italian explorer and an African queen, and of Irenetta, the
daughter of an Italian entrepreneur who meets Omar on her way to establish an Italian colony in Africa.

BOYS, GIRLS, EMPIRE, AND MAMMA ITALIA

Like nationalism, its derivate, imperialism, is gendered. Indeed, as Deniz
Kandiyoti has argued, control of women is central to processes of national-
ization and ethnicization (376). In times of social stress or upheaval such as
those that in general accompany imperial projects, in fact, the female element of the nation is usually confined to a symbolic role and excluded from
political agency. As Elleke Boehmer suggests, by contrast, the male role is

"typically 'metonymic'; that is, men are represented as contiguous with each other and with the national whole" (7). They, in other words, are ascribed active roles in constituting the nation. Although a number of critics have discussed the implications of this gendering of the nation for women, perhaps the most useful approach for our purposes is that of Anne McClintock. In the course of a fascinating discussion of the way women have been implicated in nationalist discourse, McClintock argues that icons of familial or domestic space have been a particularly crucial site for controlling women's access to the public sphere of the nation (352–60).[16] Yoked to social Darwinist evolutionary models, national identity came in the late nineteenth century in Europe to be represented in terms of the family tree, an image that equated racial identity with "anatomically distinct family types, organized into a linear progression, from the 'childhood' of 'primitive' races to the enlightened 'adulthood' of European imperial nationalism" (359). At the same time, the patriarchal structure of the bourgeois family was universalized, placing the domestic sphere into which women of the time were consigned outside history and mutability.

If the Janus-faced character of national identity—which looks simultaneously to a mist-shrouded past and toward the glorious future—has often had a deleterious impact on women's rights as citizens of the body politic, what effects has this representation of the national in terms of familial space had on children? Many of the same anxieties that arise concerning the identity and agency of women in the context of imperial nationalism also surface concerning children. For not only are children potent symbols of collective identity, they are also powerful icons of the nation's future. Yet, as McClintock's discussion of the Darwinian family tree suggests, children are also disturbingly unevolved representatives of the national family. Occupying a position in this evolutionary schema that equates them with the colonized, children may be seen as particularly vulnerable to the forms of moral and physical degeneration that colonial discourse often ascribed to the colonized. As a result of this liminal position, children are at the center of moral panics concerning the moral stability and reproductive potential of the community. Moreover, unlike women, who tend to be accorded some of the rights of citizenship in exchange for loyal service during times of collective upheaval, children are seldom accorded any rights of access to the public sphere. As a result, children are represented as at once totally central to and as absolutely marginal to national imperial identity.

The complex effects of such representations of the familial space of the nation are evident in the Italian children's literature of the mid-1930s. Although a fixed line cannot be drawn between literature for girls and boys— girls may have had access to stories addressing boys—a firm distinction is found in the gendering of roles, factual and metaphoric, found in literature for children set in a colonial environment. In the texts written in response to the Ethiopian war and the formation of the empire, girls are either absent—as in the case of *Volontario in Africa* and *Piccolo legionario in Africa Orientale,* in which no feminine figure is either included or addressed—or represented as a means of cultural transmission. In such cases, girls are portrayed as embodiments of continuity and of national integrity, in other words, of conservative principles that militate against any form of agency among young women. Indeed, when in these narratives girls are called to be part of the national colonial project, they are socially static and no real evolution occurs in them from the beginning of the stories to the end. The stories narrated in these works focus instead on the social transformation of boys: on their evolution into brave soldiers and conquerors and, in the case of indigenous Africans, on their liberation from misery and slavery. Regularly, in fact, the function of the African boys is that of faithful helpers of the Italian colonial enterprise. As a result of such loyalty, these boys are offered access to Italian civilization. In other narratives, the painful condition of the African child as a slave, orphan, or homeless child provides a moral justification for the Italian invasion. The Italian boys are, in contrast, the makers and defenders of national greatness. They incarnate the proclaimed modernizing spirit of the colonial "mission," as well as the ideals of bravery and athleticism that fascism aimed at inculcating in them through its propaganda apparatus.

Extraordinary physical vigor and technological superiority are at the core of the first part of *Genietti e sirenelle,* in which the function of its acrobatic protagonist, the *genietto* Nano 48, is to demonstrate the military advantages that Italian technology provides.[17] Thanks to his dexterity in controlling emblems of modernity as diverse as planes, radios, and motor vehicles, Nano 48 is able to coordinate the Italian colonial forces, which then annihilate their enemies with extraordinary rapidity. Nano 48's actions dominate the scene; they are a solo performance of exterminatory technological bravura. An essentially similar role is that of Pierino Marra in *Piccolo legionario.* In the novel, little Pierino's first mission is to maintain the technological disparity between the Italians and Ethiopians by ensuring that a load of weapons, which the hated French plan to sell to the Ethiopians, never reaches the enemy. In addition to his courage, which allows him to thwart the French plan, it is his technical dexterity that is emphasized in the novel. Pierino is also the son of an engineer. He knows how to handle and use explosives and how to repair the engines of motorboats, and he is capable of learning in no time how to use a machine gun to slaughter his Ethiopian adversaries.

As Michael Adas has pointed out in *Machines as the Measure of Men,* technological advancement formed an integral element in arguments concerning the broader civilizational superiority that legitimated European colonial expansion since the nineteenth century. European technological pride was obviously manifested even in children's literature: the stories of the exploits of "heroic" British aviators on colonial missions that have proliferated since the beginning of the twentieth century constitute a good example of the value attached to technology by European imperialists of the day.[18] However, the "belatedness" and limited extent of Italy's industrialization and its colonial enterprises, in comparison to the two major colonial powers, confer a megalomaniac mode to the literary representation of Italy's national and technological strength that diffuses and counteracts fears of inadequacy at an international level. Nano 48's distinct trait, for instance, is a Napoleonic pose that accompanies every planning phase of his military life.

Volontario in Africa and Piccolo legionario in Africa Orientale are war stories that, conforming to a longstanding tradition of the gendering of the public and private sphere, were certainly addressing an audience of young boys in order to instill military spirit and national pride. In contrast, Balilla regale, Genietti e sirenelle in Africa Orientale, and Africanelle catered to girls as well. In Balilla regale, Irenetta and Omar are both enjoined by Cipolla to build a "nuova Italia" in Africa. Similarly, the involvement of both female and male imaginary creatures—although in different degrees and forms—in the conflict between Italians and Ethiopians is represented by Nonno Ebe in Genietti e sirenelle in Africa Orientale. In all these works, girls are the bearers of the national honor and its boundary markers, preserving the integrity of the fatherland in a metaphoric role that is visibly signified in Genietti e sirenelle.

In the first part of his book Nonno Ebe deals with the genietti. With disproportionately large heads because they have "a lot of brains," the genietti are defined as the embodiments of boys' intelligence (59–60). As I previously argued, genietti and Nano 48 in particular provide models of technical mastery and virile heroism to the future "legionari imperiali." In the third part of his book, in which the Italian soldiers have already prevailed over the African adversary, Nonno Ebe turns to the little sirenelle, creatures who are the graceful priestesses of national rituals. After receiving the news of the Italian advance in the area of the lake they inhabit, the sirenelle rush to sing praises to the Italian soldiers and to wear the Italian flag:

> Ad un ordine della regina tutte le sirenelle e le sirene si vestirono dei colori italiani ed in breve sull'immenso Lago Tana una bandiera dai colori italiani occupava chilometri e chilometri di superficie acquea. (86)

> [At a command of the queen all the little sirens dressed in the Italian colors and, shortly afterwards, on the immense Tana Lake, a flag with the Italian colors occupied kilometers and kilometers of watery surface.]

These little female creatures are "natural," ahistorical; their origins go back to a mythical time, as does the motherland they stand for. By contrast, genietti, their male counterparts, are "historical" figures whose past is proudly traced in the narration by their leader:

eravamo presenti quando, il primo marzo del 1896, le orde scioane di Menelik attaccarono le colonne dei valorosi comandanti . . . ed abbiamo visto con
quanto valore ed eroismo i soldati bianchi e neri dell'Italia hanno combattuto
(20–21).

[we were here on the first of March 1896, when Menelik's Scewan hordes
attacked the columns of valiant commanders . . . and we saw with how much
valor and heroism the white and black soldiers of Italy fought.]

Genietti are agents of historical transformation. And, as I previously stated,
Nano 48 is represented as making a particularly valiant contribution to the
Italian military success in Ethiopia and to the consequent formation of the
empire.

Boys' social mobility and the correlative metaphoric fixity of girls in this
imperial imaginary is well exemplified in *Balilla regale*. Irenetta, the daughter of an Italian entrepreneur, is journeying with her father in Eastern Africa toward the kingdom of Ghera, where a new Italian colony will be
founded. In a port on the Red Sea she meets the lovely boy, Omar, who is
initially presented as a *meticcio,* or a mixed-race child. Omar's sole dream is
to reach the Italian shores to find his Italian father. It is through his devotion and through his demonstration to Irenetta of physical strength and
moral nobility that, in the beginning of the novel, Omar proves himself worthy of being included in the Italian national body. As a result, Omar is allowed to journey to Italy on board the ship of Irenetta's father. Later, after
Omar has successfully endured a series of trials and has gained the recognition of Irenetta, his new goal is to protect the physical integrity of the little
girl, which, if preserved, will guarantee the Italian presence and continuity
in Africa. Because of her tender age, Irenetta is indeed the perfect incarnation of imperial Italy in the making. Omar's longing for the grandeur of
Italy is therefore figured by his courtly love for little Irenetta.

The homogeneous character of representations of girls in the children's
literature of the imperial age is confirmed by Visentini's *Africanelle.* The first
fairy tale of the collection, "The Olive Grove in the Sands," attempts to sustain the morality of the Italian colonization of Somalia. Indeed, Italian expansion through conquest is represented as the peaceful journey of the diligent Italian people in search of land to cultivate. The protagonist of this
fairy tale is Fioralisa, the daughter of an Italian explorer. During her father's exploration of Somalia, in which she does not seem to participate, she
meets a little Abyssinian orphan kept as a slave by a cruel local *ras,* or chief-
tain. The encounter of the two children is very brief, but they meet again at
the end of the story, when Fioralisa welcomes Red Assam to her father's
house. Here, the boy will live next to the Italian laborers and be able to learn
how to turn the desert land of his country into olive groves. The metaphor
contained in the story could not be more transparent: the Italian nation lib-
erates the Abyssinians and provides them with a civilized manner of living.

The metaphoric role of girls is even more tangible in another fairy tale of *Africanelle*, "Reginetta Imperiale." Its protagonist, Imperiale, a fairy wearing the Italian colors, cheerfully labors day and night for the well-being of her empire. Both "Reginetta Imperiale" and "The Olive Grove in the Sands" make clear that Visentini, who, as I mentioned earlier, was a writer as well as an educator, fully subscribed to the imperial propaganda that the fascist regime addressed to schoolchildren. A reader for fourth graders in the state-controlled schools exemplifies this political indoctrination. In this text, the war against Ethiopia is presented as the duty of a nation intending to help a country where "there were slaves to liberate, children, men and women to clothe, diseases to cure" (Tannenbaum 82). Children, in other words, learned that the Italian colonial war was a humanitarian effort, the highest expression of a compassionate and motherly nation.

Naturally, this sentimentalized representation of the nation was an effective means of indoctrination, particularly with the youngest children of both sexes, who could identify with the neediness and dependency of the youngest Ethiopians and who had not yet developed strong ties other than familial ones. The position of Italian girls in relation to the motherland was, however, complicated by the dominant gendering of social roles. As many studies of the fascist school programs have shown, girls were inculcated with "motherly sentiments" from their earliest days in the state-controlled schools. In addition, the "recreational" organization Piccole Italiane, which was attended by the youngest girls, greatly contributed to this indoctrination. In the statutes of this organization, indeed, "la patria" is represented as "la mamma più grande, la mamma di tutti i buoni italiani" (Koon 96–98). As an emancipated and wealthy Englishwoman traveling in Italy in the early 1930s reports, among the activities conceived by the organization for Italian girls were doll drills in which the little Italians publicly simulated "maternal" gestures (Hamilton 35–40). Because of this orientation of girls toward motherhood and the equation of mother with nation, the little potential Italian mothers were the ideal signifiers of the expanding nation, which, as I argued above, is perfectly exemplified by Irenetta of *Balilla regale*.

However, in addition to providing a symbolic figuration, children's literature of the time offered Italian girls models of feminine virtue that they could emulate in the colonial environment as future settlers. In "Reginetta Imperiale," for example, Visentini turns the symbol of the maternal nation of the first story of the collection, "The Olive Grove in the Sands," into a domestic figure that performs simple daily rituals:

Raccoglieva in un gran cesto ora i petali delle rose, ora le foglie odorose, o i datteri zuccherini, o i grappoli di banane. . . . Vedeva la fatina premer i fiori, distillarne le essenze, riporle in certe boccette. . . . Per quei bambini Imperiale apriva le boccette colme delle essenze dei fiori risparmiate nella buona sta-

Figure 4. Elementary school notebook. Courtesy of
Adolfo Mignemi, Novara.

gione, toglieva il coperchio ai barattoli colmi di marmellata di dattero o di banane perché i piccini vi tuffassero i chucchiai e le dita. (102)

[She would gather in a big basket now rose petals, now fragrant leaves, or the
sugary dates, or banana tufts. . . . She would see the little fairy squeezing flow-
ers, distilling essences, putting them in certain vials. . . . For those children,
Imperiale would open the vials filled with flower essences saved in the warm
season, would remove the tops from the jars full of date or banana jam so that
the little ones would plunge in their spoons and their fingers.]

"Reginetta Imperiale" turns the African land into a manicured garden where
Imperiale gathers succulent fruits and herbs to feed the orphaned indigenous children and where diligent domesticity is enlivened by Visentini with

exotic diversity and plenty. Conversely, the tropical produce is familiarized by being incorporated into the reassuring Italian decor signified by glass jars and vials.

This image reflects interesting pedagogic elements that need to be discussed and contextualized. Christian ideals, and, in particular, humility and charity, certainly inform all of Visentini's *Africanelle.* In "Reginetta Imperiale" Imperiale, in spite of her high status, works incessantly to feed the famished Abyssinian children. The other little protagonists of Visentini's stories are equally humble and charitable: they include Fioralisa, who introduces the Abyssinian orphan to edifying Italian values, and the fairies who assist the poor Italian children. Furthermore, humility is embodied in the very title selected by the author for her collection, the diminutive term *Africanelle.*

Within this Christian pedagogical framework, however, Visentini makes some distinctions in dealing with the colonial subject. In "The Olive Grove in the Sands," for example, Visentini intends Fioralisa, a model of rectitude and hard work, to serve as a model for the daughters of laborers, who were being encouraged to emigrate by fascist propaganda. The values cherished in them and their families by Visentini are modesty and diligent labor. Fioralisa and the Italian colonists simply work, and work is their happiness.

Although, as I said, Imperiale is also animated by the same Christian virtues, her story presents an element of leisure that is not evident in "The Olive Grove in the Sands" and that points to the picturing, on Visentini's part, of a different audience. Baskets of roses and jars and vials of flowery essences redesign in the colony an Italian bourgeois interior in which domesticity is a cult and charitable work a redeeming and pleasurable pastime. Visentini thus reveals her desire to appeal to girls from two different social groups, the working class and the middle class. At the same time, though, she aspires to create for both of them a pastoral picture of colonial living in which tensions and economic disparities are smoothed away by a common involvement in a Christian mission sanctioned by the presence of the indigenous orphans.

Visentini's charitable sensibility also shows that she inherited some of the piousness and sentimentalism that had characterized the children's literature of the nineteenth century, a mode that culminated in *Cuore* and *Pinocchio. Cuore,* in particular, was often the object of harsh criticism from fascist intellectuals and educators, who rejected its tearful and pathetic ethos in favor of the "male vigor" of the new fascist pedagogy (Scotto di Luzio 146– 47). In spite of this, in the 1930s *Cuore* was, together with Salgari's novels and *Piccolo Alpino,* among the most beloved literary works for children (ibid. 149). Not only did fascism fail to extirpate *Cuore*'s tearful spirit, but sentimentalism came to permeate fascism's official pedagogy as well as the works of its declared supporters. Such sentimentalism was particularly evident in girls' education. The emphasis on the goodness of Italian children and on the tender mother nation was in the statute of the Piccole Italiane alone; nevertheless, it still survived in boys' education as well. The image of poor Abyssinian children was, for example, often used in imperial propaganda directed at boys, too. Another manifestation of the legacy of the nineteenth century's pathetic ethos in children's literature is the figure of the orphan, present both in Visentini's fairy tales and in the contemporary works celebrating the empire, to which I now turn.

ORPHANS FOR THE EMPIRE

Whether the protagonists of children's literature written during the mid-1930s are boys or girls, their mothers are always deceased before the narrative begins. As mentioned above, the bulk of this literature deals with Italian exploration and subsequent military campaigns in Eastern Africa rather than with the daily life of the Italian settlers. Such narratives are therefore antithetical to the depiction of a domestic and familial life that would have required the figure of the mother. Actually, although Italy had already had African colonies for four decades, rare are the texts for children that portray the life of the Italian settlers. In this respect, it is essential to recall that, in spite of the fascist discourse presenting the expansionistic Italian campaigns as providing an outlet to an overly populated nation, the Italian population in the African colonies was always quite sparse. This is particularly true in the case of women.[19] This paucity of Italian civilians in the colonies and the brevity of Italian domination in Eastern Africa partially explain the dearth in Italian literature of fictional works representing the daily life of Italian settlers, both in adult literature and in that for children. Even Italian colonial cinema limits its horizon, for the most part, to Italian military enterprises or to erotic and commercial adventures.[20]

In children's literature of the imperial period, however, the orphanhood of the Italian protagonists is also the prerequisite for adventure. It frees them, that is, of the sentimental ties that would impede their departure from home. For example, having lost his mother, Pierino Marra of *Piccolo legionario* can throw himself into his search for a father who has joined the Italian soldiers in the Ethiopian war as a volunteer. Similarly, the motherless Irenetta of *Balilla regale* can follow her father in his financial adventure in Africa. The same is true for Fioralisa of "The Olive Grove in the Sands" in *Africanelle;* the little Italian girl accompanies her father in his exploration of Somalia. If the motherlessness of Italian boys and girls in these children's stories allows them to leave the domestic space of Italy and to participate in the colonial adventure, the motherlessness of the many indigenous children in Visentini's fairy tales serves as an ethical foundation for the Italian colonial endeavors. It also incarnates, as I will show, the fantasy of a virgin land, of a blank space upon which the author can project her values.

In "The Olive Grove in the Sands," the Somali orphan Red Assam is taken from his mother at a tender age to be sold as a slave to a ruthless *ras* who entrusts to him his flock. In one of his solitary peregrinations as a shepherd, the orphan meets a sorcerer who predicts that he will find peace when he sees "the sands of the desert verdant with trees" (4). Instead of going back to his hut, Red Assam decides to venture away to find the prodigy foreseen by the sorcerer. One day, lying on a dune, the little boy sees an Italian girl with dazzling blond hair who overwhelms him with her grace. After this brief encounter with Fioralisa, he wanders for years through mountains, forests, and deserts. At last he finds himself back in the region of his birth where, instead of the arid land he was familiar with, there is an expanse of silvery olive trees. At the edge of this olive grove is the white house of the little Italian girl he met long before. She has now turned into a beautiful young woman.

This story, in particular, contains a significant misappropriation of the structural form of popular fairy tales, a field of expertise for Visentini. This misappropriation reveals Visentini's inability to fully reconcile popular tradition with colonial ideology. In spite of the many significant cultural and historical differences among fairy tales, the *fabula* of each, the basic plot that underlies each tale, shares structural similarities. The prototypical young protagonist of such tales always has to go through a series of trials before getting the final reward (a bride or a kingdom, for example) and being reintegrated into society, or whatever other form his social transformation takes. Although Visentini suggests in her title—*Africanelle: Fiabe*—that the form of her stories is that of popular fairy tales, she can't help defusing the happy ending that her story sets the reader up to expect. Red Assam's final compensation is not Fioralisa, the beautiful daughter of the Italian explorer, but a less palpable prize: access to the values of the Italian colonists, the most paradigmatic of which is a diligent work ethic. At the end of his story, Red Assam is in fact shown the green olive grove cultivated on Somali desert land by the hard-working Italians. The celebrations that usually are found at the closing of fairy tales are negated in the unrepresentable scene of the encounter, announced in the text by Fioralisa, between the young Somali man and her Italian father:

> Vuoi entrare? Conoscerai mio padre,—gli disse gentilmente Fioralisa; ed egli oltrepassò la soglia della dimora bianca, mormorando una parola: "Lavorare" con la trepidazione con cui avrebbe pronunciato una formula magica per entrare nel regno della felicità. (11)

> [Do you want to come in? You will meet my father—Fioralisa kindly said to him; and he went beyond the threshold of the white abode, muttering a word, "Work," with the trepidation with which he would pronounce a magical formula to get into the realm of happiness.]

Although Red Assam's race annuls his narrative potential, his status as an orphan makes him the most malleable of propagandistic materials. Indeed, this status deprives him of his history and tradition, providing the author with the ideal matter to mold. His cultural blankness is a sort of utopian space where the presumed values of the Italian settlers divulged by the author will not collide with his own cultural values, which were never, of course, transmitted to him by his missing family.

RACIAL AMBIGUITY AND THE FOUNDATION OF A NEW NATION

Presented in the beginning of the novel *Balilla regale* as a *meticcio* child, Omar comes to provide the Italian girl Irenetta with access to Africa by describing the land to her, taming the wild beasts that populate it, and escorting her to her destination, a region in Eastern Africa where her father will found the "nuova Italia." The *meticcio* boy is therefore represented as an intermediary between the colonizing nation and the colonized, in a manner that accords with theories elaborated in the colonial period about children born from the union between Italian men and indigenous women.

The *meticcio* Omar seems at first to conform to ideas circulating among anthropologists, missionaries, and colonial officials in the first decades of the century and then disavowed by the racial legislation of 1938. In short, it was believed by some that mixed-race people, because of their intermediate position, could serve the colonizer's interests.[21] First of all, the *meticcio* was thought to belong to the two cultures involved in the colonial encounter, the Italian and the indigenous. It was also believed that, in genetic terms, *meticci* children demonstrated their Italian fathers' intelligence and their indigenous mothers' physical strength and adaptability to the African physical environment. These were ideas that *Balilla regale*'s author, Arnaldo Cipolla, an educated man with a long-term interest in the African continent, must have been familiar with.

In Cipolla's novel, however, the narratological position of the *meticcio* boy, that of protagonist, is not motivated by the services he offers to the Italian nation. On the contrary, later in the novel Omar's status and racial connotation turn out to be different from that of the mendicant *meticcio* who introduces the superior Italian "race" to their new dominions. As I suggested earlier, *Balilla regale* differs from the highly propagandistic children's literature of the time. Its publication is, in fact, evidence that fascist censorship and directives were not very consistent during the period of the regime's power.

In this novel Cipolla seems to fantasize about an alternative to the actual events of Italian imperialism in Eastern Africa and, in general, to undermine the militaristic spirit of the fascist regime. A look at the plot is enough to indicate its surprising diversion from the expansionistic politics of fascism. Although at the beginning of the novel reaching the shores of Italy and finding his Italian father is the protagonist's only dream, this objective is later deferred and he decides to escort the Italian expedition to their final destination. During the period that Omar is traveling with the Italians, his father has returned to stay with his wife, the queen of Ghera.[22] It is at this point that Omar and the reader also learn that his father had departed from Africa long before to fight for the independence of Ghera, and that "Il congresso Romano," an imaginary Italian political organ, has granted it. At the end of the novel, Omar receives the crown and the newly independent kingdom, which hosts "la nuova Italia," constituted by Irenetta, her father, and his retinue and attendants.

Unlike Tenente Anonimo and Salvator Gotta, Cipolla does not represent the African population in derogatory terms that would help to justify Italian domination. On the contrary, Cipolla describes the wonder of the European explorers who discover Ghera's physical beauty and the elegance and cultural cultivation of its people. He then elaborates a theory of the common origins of the European explorers and the people of this fictional kingdom. Their common genealogy is explained to the Italian explorers by the old king of Ghera:

> Spero che voi, scienziati ed esploratori, non vi meraviglierete apprendendo che 2145 anni or sono all'epoca del massimo splendore della Grecia, quando la Sicilia, la Calabria, la Magna Grecia infine, erano colonie fiorentissime dell'Ellade, ci fu qualcuno che propugnò l'idea di rimontare, sino alle origini, il corso del Nilo. (76)

> [I hope that you, scientists and explorers, will not be surprised to learn that 2,145 years ago, or at the time of the highest splendor of Greece, when Sicily, Calabria, and finally Magna Grecia were flourishing colonies of Hellas, there was someone who championed the idea of ascending the Nile.]

The king's theory has, interestingly, some "scientific" basis. Since the turn of the century, in fact, anthropologists had debated the origins of Eastern African populations.[23] English and American anthropologists, in particular, argued that the "finer" features of the Ethiopians testified to their Caucasian origins.[24] The common descent theorized by Cipolla, however, does not by itself represent an anti-imperialist stance. The common origins of the Italian explorers and the inhabitants of the kingdom of Ghera might have served, in fact, to reiterate European superiority. The refinement of the inhabitants of Ghera, and the superiority of their civilization in relation to the darker and autochthonous populations, might ultimately be represented as a product of their racial kinship with the Caucasians.

What actually makes *Balilla regale*'s political stance ambiguous in relation to fascist imperialistic politics is the independence granted in the novel to the kingdom of Ghera by the Congresso Romano. *Balilla regale*'s ambiguity manifests itself also and in particular with the incorporation of "la nuova Italia" into the kingdom. While obtaining the independence of the ancient kingdom of Ghera from the Congresso Romano, Omar's father also negotiates for the kingdom to be recognized as the "estremo vertice dell'espansione italiana del Continente Nero" (extreme limit of Italian expansion in the Black Continent) (223). As I previously noted, "la nuova Italia" was to be founded within the borders of that kingdom. Since independence has been granted to the hosting kingdom, "la nuova Italia" implicitly acquires a form of autonomy from the Italian nation. In fascist discourse, moreover, the new Italy was the Italian nation transformed and revitalized by the fascist revolution. Giving the same appellation to the Italian colony—founded within an independent African kingdom—seems to suggest the fictional creation of an alternative nation. This speculation is, in addition, corroborated by the values and the model of masculinity incarnated by Omar, which, as I will show, are consistently antithetical to those promoted by the fascist regime.

The first element in the novel that suggests Cipolla's ideological ambivalence, however, is his representation of race. Indeed, Cipolla plays with racial ambiguity throughout his novel. As I stated above, in the beginning of *Balilla regale*, Omar is presented as a *meticcio*. Later, however, his origins are revealed to be Caucasian. Biraciality is suggested again in the last pages of the novel. There, Mesfun, the queen of Ghera, and her son Omar descend into the cavern beneath their mansion, where the kingdom's archives are secretly kept:

> Una serie di sale si susseguiva dove erano conservate le memorie più gelose di Ghera . . . i manoscritti vetusti, dai primi laconici diari di viaggio della spedizione dei greco-italici alle decisioni determinate dall'arrivo degli europei venuti dal mare. (227)

> [A series of rooms where the most jealous memories of Ghera were conserved . . . the ancient manuscripts, from the first travel journals of the Greco-Italian expedition to the decisions determined by the arrival of the Europeans come from the sea.]

The final racial clarification is reflected in the following scene:

> Mentre sfogliava i libri, sotto la luce delle lampade, nella casa antichissima, il suo viso bruno morso dal sole d'Africa, diventava chiaro, roseo. (227)

> [While he was glancing through the books, under the lamp light in the ancient house, his face, burned by the African sun, turned light, rosy.]

At first it seems that Omar turns white by being exposed to documents attesting to his European origins and that the darkness of his face was just the result of the hot rays of the African sun. Then racial traits are mixed again by the author in the image that follows the one above:

> Se il muezzim ritornerà non mi riconoscerà più davvero—diceva il giovinetto guardandosi nello specchio, mentre sua madre gli accarezzava teneramente i capelli ricciuti. (227)
>
> [If the muezzin comes back, really he will not recognize me—the young boy said, looking at himself in the mirror, while his mother was tenderly caressing his curly hair.]

Although his face is whitened to the extent that he is afraid he will not be recognized, his hair is curly. Certainly, white children's hair may be "ricciuto," curly, but in this context this physical trait suggests racial hybridity.

After all, racial separation is not seriously encouraged by the author. When, in the opening of the novel, Omar is still believed by Irenetta and her father to be of mixed race, an erotic tension develops between the two children:

> Omar fu trattenuto a bordo e invitato a pranzo alla tavola di Guaitana Salin. Irenetta lo volle seduto di faccia. La giovinetta che non gli staccava gli occhi di dosso era giunta a dirgli che lo preferiva così bruciato dal sole che non bianco. (25)
>
> [Omar was kept on board and invited to lunch at Guaitana Salin's table. Irenetta wanted him sitting in front of her. The young girl, who couldn't keep her eyes off him, went as far as to tell him that she preferred him so burned by the sun rather than white.]

As the above paragraph shows, however, Omar's presumed black heritage is prudently toned down by Cipolla at this early point in the novel. Irenetta never declares that she loves Omar specifically because of his biraciality. Indeed, Irenetta represses her knowledge of Omar's mixed-race identity by ascribing his dark complexion to a nongenetic factor: "bruciato dal sole" (burned by the sun). In addition, Cipolla never mentions the race of Omar's mother and avoids defining Omar as *meticcio*, before, that is, he reveals that all the inhabitants of the kingdom of Ghera are of European origins.

In addition to problematizing the racial identity of Omar, Cipolla attributes to the young boy an anachronistic form of manliness. In spite of the fascist appellative of *Balilla* granted to him in the novel by the enamored Irenetta, Omar provides a model of masculinity that is almost antithetical to that which the Opera Nazionale Balilla tried to inculcate in its young members. As has been well documented, the primary task of this youth organization was to create "fascist soldiers" who would preserve the new fascist Italy and provide its military strength. Indeed, the military was actually given control of the Opera Nazionale Balilla. Indeed, As Koon indicates, the prime minister chose the central council and the president of this organization from the ranks of the fascist militia (94).

Through protecting Irenetta in her journey to the foundation of the "nuova Italia," Omar certainly helps to preserve the Italian nation and thus to assure the reproduction of future Italian generations in the colonies. However, Omar is not representative of the martial spirit that was inspired in the Italian fascist children of his age. In the novel, Omar's manliness and the bravery that, according to fascist discourse, accompanies it are not tested and proved through violent actions and rituals such as war and hunting. In *Balilla regale,* enemies, such as the marauders he comes across while accompanying Irenetta and the other Italians through the desert, are neutralized by Omar with his shrewdness and rhetorical skills (91–93). In the novel, moreover, there are no safari scenes in which Omar might demonstrate his courage; hunting is even criticized as a practice dictated by cruelty and greed (102). This stance further distinguishes Cipolla's work from more orthodox fascist texts. In novels such as *Africa mia! Un balilla nell'Oltre-Giuba,* for example, hunting figures as one of the testing grounds of the Italian protagonists' virile heroism as well as the means, as Scotto di Luzio points out, to locate fascist colonization within an aristocratic European tradition.[25]

Although Cipolla describes his *balilla* as "regale," Omar's gentility is not a sign of continuity between the fascist colonization and the "greatest" European colonial legacy. First of all, Omar is not a colonizer, and his racial identity is obdurately hybrid, at times *meticcio,* at times white. With the word "regale," rather, Cipolla undermines the aura of prestige constructed for the *balilla*s. He creates, in fact, a distinction between the ordinary Italian *balilla*s—who "believe, obey, and fight" with little thought—and a more noble youth who is above such uniformity and does not subscribe to the militaristic spirit of the former. The inhabitants of Ghera, where Omar comes from,

> Non avevano mai manifestato nessun desiderio di allargare i confini del regno, si limitavano a difendersi se erano assaliti. Ignoravano insomma la passione della conquista. (72)

> [Had never manifested any desire to enlarge the borders of the kingdom; they would just defend themselves were they attacked. They ignored, in short, the passion of conquest.]

This anti-imperialist model, nonetheless, had never been sustained by Cipolla before. During his long career as a correspondent in Africa, Cipolla was significantly uncritical of Italian expansionistic politics. The following are, for example, his reflections after the 1908 battle of Gilib between the Italians and the Somali rebels:

Io non so se tu abbia mai provato quella pietà che prorompe dall'animo dell'uomo civile dinanzi agli effetti di un combattimento fortunato sui neri. E' un sentimento che non attinge certo la sua ispirazione dalla magniloquenza delle affermazioni imperialiste, ma non ha nulla a che fare col pietismo falso dei popoli imbelli. Deriva dal paragone dell'abisso esistente fra i nostri mezzi di conquista e quelli con i quali i neri si difendono. (Del Boca, *Italiani in Africa Orientale,* vol. 1, 816)

[I don't know if you have ever felt that piety that comes out of the soul of the civil man before the effects of a lucky combat over the blacks. It is a feeling that certainly does not draw its inspiration from the magniloquence of the imperialist affirmations, but neither does it have anything to do with the pietism of unwarlike peoples. It derives from the comparison of the abyss existing between our means of conquest and those with which the blacks defend themselves.]

In this statement Cipolla makes clear that he supports the Italian repression of the Somali rebellion and consequently the Italian domination of Somalia. He also takes care to identify himself with the presumed imperialistic spirit of the nation and to separate the martial spirit of Italians from the unwarlike tendencies of other unspecified nations.

Balilla regale is therefore the sole place where the "affermazioni imperialiste" of cultural and racial superiority are, if not clearly rejected, notably destabilized. The racial ambiguity of the book's protagonist reveals Cipolla's fascination with the racial and cultural other and distinguishes his work from numerous contemporary portrayals of the Eastern Africans as cruel and uncivilized.

In the colonial children's literature of the mid-1930s, *Balilla regale* also stands out for its conception of technological progress. As I previously argued, in *Genietti e sirenelle* and *Piccolo legionario in Africa Orientale,* imperialism was represented as the necessary consequence of the Italians' technological superiority. In *Balilla regale,* by contrast, the technological superiority of the kingdom of Ghera makes expansionistic politics obsolete. This is how its old king describes Ghera's more advanced civilization to an Italian explorer:

Conosciamo la radiotelegrafia da tre secoli, il vapore da sette, i motori a scoppio e la fotografia da quattro. Siamo stati in comunicazione con il pianeta Marte. (78)

[We have known radiotelegraphy for three centuries, steam for seven, engines and photography for four. We have been in communication with the planet Mars.]

Obviously, this sophistication is reflected also in the Gherans' arsenal. However, as the king explains, since the fame of their military invulnerability has started to spread, the Gherans have begun destroying part of their arsenal, including the machine of "invisible rays that turns men into ashes"—an obvious reference to the chemical weapons used by the Italians before both the Ethiopian war and the publication of Cipolla's novel (81).[26]

The Gherans' destruction of their arsenal is motivated by concerns that go beyond the national boundaries. Replying to the Italian explorer's disapproving exclamation over the elimination of their arsenal, the king says:

> Un delitto? E' una prova di amore per il genere umano. . . . Se le macchine fossero cadute in mano vostra, se molti dei nostri segreti si divulgassero, l'umanità correrebbe il rischio di sopprimersi in poche ore. (81)

> [A crime? It is a proof of love for humanity. . . . If the machines had fallen into your hands, if many of our secrets had been divulged, humanity would run the risk of being exterminated in a few hours.]

The Gherans' support of universal disarmament must have been disorienting for the *balilla*s explicitly addressed by the author in his title, who had been encouraged to believe in the dynamic revolutionary spirit of fascism. In the novel, indeed, the Gherans' antimilitaristic stance necessarily places fascist Italy in a backward position in relation to their kingdom.

As I have already argued, the kingdom of Ghera is not represented by the author as a civilization external to the Italian that fascist Italy had to confront. The Gherans are said, in fact, to descend from explorers coming from what was at the time of their journey the Greek-ruled island of Sicily. Consequently, this genealogical link promotes an interpretation of the kingdom of Ghera as a more advanced stage of civilization that fascist Italy will have to go through. At the same time, nevertheless, it undermines the credibility of contemporary fascist militarism and imperialism by presenting such values, albeit indirectly, as a phase that will have to be overcome and whose end will signal the beginning of a utopian life for the fascist man. In the higher state of civilization that Ghera represents, happiness reigns:

> le malattie sono ignorate. Gli uomini muoiono vecchissimi e sino a ottanta o novant'anni fanno la vita dei giovani. Quando si sentono presso alla fine i vegliardi dicono: "Ho molto sonno!" e si spengono senza sofferenza. (79–80)

> [Diseases are unknown. Men die very old and they live like young people until they are ninety years old. When they feel close to the end the old say: "I am very sleepy!" And they die without suffering.]

As this passage indicates, the antimilitaristic stance of Cipolla's novel does not prevent the author from appealing to a young generation fed on ideals of virility and athleticism. The very title of his novel, *Balilla regale,* also suggests that the author is aiming at a sort of ideological compromise, pointing as it does to an esprit de corps and to social distinction. Finally, Omar's racial fluidity reveals the tension between Cipolla's Africanism and the Italian imperialism that, as a journalist, he documented for decades and approved of as a loyal fascist follower.

The ideological indoctrination to which Italian children were subjected during the 1930s was not simply passively absorbed by them. Fascist schools, youth organizations, and a complacent popular culture, for example, failed to succeed fully in inculcating motherly attitudes in girls. The results of a survey conducted among girls between six and eighteen years of age in 1938 reveal that the majority of the interviewees lacked any interest in domestic work and did not aspire to marriage and family.[27] Boys, for their part, did not all uniformly identify with the military culture to which they were exposed during the *ventennio*.[28]

The imperialistic propaganda, in particular, disseminated by fascist education and by many of the "African" texts for children was met with resistance by young Italians since, I would suggest, they could not identify with the complexities of its discourse. The "Africa" of Salgari's novels, which clearly exercised a powerful pull on the fantasies of Italian children during the period, figured visibly as the land of exciting and liberating adventure. By contrast, the Africa found in children's literature and imperial propaganda of the mid-1930s was the object at once of desire, contempt, and compassion. It was a multifaceted, highly conflictual site that must have disoriented the members of the young Italian audience it had been pictured for. Furthermore, attempts by authors like some of those whose work I have surveyed here to create a more realist image of a colonized and Italianized Africa contributed to the propagation in children's literature of oppressive ideals of order, discipline, and diligent labor, which must have deterred Italian children's interest in the subject.

The children's literature of the imperial period is perhaps the ideal means to cast light on the Italian nation as a colonial power. The cultural intricacy and ideological contradictions of the colonial discourse circulating in such literature illuminate, in fact, the national uncertainties about the Italian involvement in the African continent. Furthermore, its relevance for our understanding of colonial discourse during fascism necessitates a revision of such literature's traditionally marginal position in scholarly work on Italian culture. Children's reception of such literature, finally, demonstrates the active participation of children in the formation of the national archives and places them in a position less peripheral than that accorded to them in general by cultural critics.

NOTES

1. On young people's socialization during fascism in general see Tracy Koon, *Believe Obey Fight.* For an exhaustive history of the Operazione Nazionale Balilla, see in-

stead *L'Opera Nazionale Balilla e l'educazione fascista.* Radio programs for children are described by Alberto Monticone in *Il fascismo al microfono,* 99–100.

2. Cf. Adolfo Mignemi, *Immagine coordinata per un impero,* 56. Because of the great variety of the cultural documents taken into consideration by Mignemi, his book constitutes an essential and excellent panoramic view of Italian imperial propaganda and imagery.

3. On images of Africa in Emilio Salgari, see Tundonu Amosu, *The Land of Adventure,* 34–45.

4. Luigi Motta's work is dealt with by Antonio Lugli, *Libri e figure,* 156–57.

5. Fascism's instrumentalization of Salgari is amply discussed by Adolfo Scotto di Luzio in his indispensable analysis of the Italian publishing world and literature for children during the *ventennio, Appropriazione imperfetta.*

6. Colonial literature for an adult audience was at the center of a literary debate in the 1930s that involved a great number of literary figures, including Marinetti and D'Annunzio. This debate is discussed by Giovanna Tomasello in *La letteratura coloniale italiana dalle avanguardie al fascismo.*

7. Documents reveal that the working conditions for the Somalis were drastically different and that forced labor was a common practice in Somalia. On this matter, see Del Boca's *Gli italiani in Africa Orientale,* vol. 2, 78–84 and 203–8.

8. On the wealth of texts, such as *Da ragazzi a uomini* by Camilla Del Soldato, that dealt with the greatness and legacy of the Roman empire, see Antonia Arslan, "Le istituzioni culturali e l'organizzazione del consenso."

9. *Piccolo Alpino* was first published in 1926. It sold 400,000 copies in ten years and came out in fourteen different editions. Cf. Lugli, *Libri e figure,* 174.

10. Biographical and bibliographical information on Olga Visentini are provided by Duilio Gasparini in *Olga Visentini.*

11. The many well-known postwar historians of Italian children's literature that I consulted avoid the delicate subject of Visentini's support of fascism and the regime's imperialistic politics. I would like to mention at least Enzo Petrini, Mario Valeri, Ernesto Monaci, and Aldo Cibaldi. Not even Gasparini refers to the fascist parenthesis of Visentini in his monograph. The only exceptions are constituted by Mignemi and by Antonio Faeti's "Una settimana con molte domeniche," 54–55.

12. Cf. Jack Zipes, *Fairy Tales and the Art of Subversion,* 134–69. Fairy tales were manipulated also by French authors during the period of the Vichy government in France. On the use of fairy tales as a means to politicize children in Vichy France, see Judith K. Proud's *Children and Propaganda: il était une fois.* . . .

13. Gotta is also the author of the fascist hymn "Giovinezza Giovinezza."

14. A cogent history of Italian antifascism in France is provided by Simonetta Tombaccini in *Storia dei fuoriusciti italiani in Francia.* In this book Tombaccini deals, admittedly briefly, with Italian immigration into France. She says that around the second half of the nineteenth century, "France, already hit by a fall in the birthrate, started to resort to Italian labor in order to sustain the industrialization process."

15. The inconsistencies and fallacies of fascist censorship in general are portrayed by Maurizio Cesari in *La censura nel periodo fascista.*

16. For more on the centrality of ideals of masculinity to fascist ideology, see George Mosse, *The Image of Man.*

17. As Nonno Ebe indicates on page 59 of *Genietti e sirenelle, genietti* are a manifestation of divine intelligence.

18. An illuminating survey of British flying stories is provided by Dennis Butts in "Imperialism of the Air: Flying Stories 1900–1950."

19. On the demographic limits of Italian colonization in Eritrea, see Negash Tekeste, *Italian Colonialism in Eritrea, 1882–1941*, 51. On fascist population strategies in Ethiopia and their results, see Del Boca, *Gli Italiani in Africa orientale*, vol. 3, 154–227. The Italian presence in Libya is discussed in Juliette Bessis, *La Libia contemporanea*.

20. For a general profile of Italian colonial cinema, see Gian Piero Brunetta, *L'ora d'Africa del cinema italiano*. Illuminating, in this respect, are the contributions of Bertellini and Boggio on colonial cinema in this volume.

21. On the different theorizations of *meticcio*, see Barbara Sòrgoni in her "La zona grigia."

22. The kingdom of Ghera had been immortalized by members of early Italian expeditions to Africa. Their adventures and misadventures in this kingdom are narrated, for example, by Augusto Franzoj in *Continenete nero,* and by Antonino Cecchi, who was held as a prisoner by the queen, in *Da Zeila alle frontiere del Caffa*. This is the exploration literature that certainly nourished Africanism of educated Italian men from Cipolla's generation.

23. The various anthropological assumptions are discussed by Sòrgoni, "La zona grigia," 38–52.

24. Ibid., 39.

25. "The heroic epic of hunt" and its ideological implications are interestingly analyzed by Scotto di Luzio, 208–9.

26. On the use of chemical weapons in colonial military operations see Del Boca's "I crimini del colonialismo fascista," 237–40.

27. Cf. Piero Meldini, *Donna, sposa e madre*, 126–27.

28. On the unsuccessful fascist military indoctrination of Italian youth, see Tannenbaum, *The Fascist Experience*, 125.

WORKS CITED

Adas, Michael. *Machines as the Measure of Men: Science, Technology, and Ideologies of Western Dominance*. Ithaca, N.Y.: Cornell University Press, 1989.

Amosu, Tundonu. *The Land of Adventure: The Representation of Africa in Emilio Salgari*. Lagos: Istituto Italiano di Cultura, 1989.

Arslan, Antonia. "Le istituzioni culturali e l'organizzazione del consenso." In *Immagine e popolo e organizzazione del consenso*. Venezia: Marsilio, 1979.

Bessis, Juliette. *La Libia contemporanea*. Soveria Mannelli, Catanzaro: Rubettino, 1991.

Betti, Carmen. *L'Opera Nazionale Balilla e l'educazione fascista*. Firenze: La Nuova Italia, 1984.

Boehmer, Elleke. "Stories of Women and Mothers: Gender and Nationalism in the Early Fiction of Flora Nwapa." In *Motherlands: Black Women's Writing from Africa, the Caribbean and South Asia*, ed. Sysheuka Basta. London: The Women's Press, 1991.

Brunetta, Gian Piero. *L'ora d'Africa del cinema italiano: 1911–1989.* Roma: Materiali di lavoro, 1990.

Butts, Dennis. "Imperialism of the Air: Flying Stories 1900–1950." In *Imperialism and Juvenile Literature,* ed. Jeffrey Richards, 126–43. Manchester: Manchester University Press, 1989.

Cecchi, Antonino. *Da Zeila alle frontiere del Caffa.* Roma: Loescher, 1885–87.

Cesari, Maurizio. *La censura nel periodo fascista.* Napoli: Liguori, 1978.

Cipolla, Arnaldo. *Balilla Regale: Romanzo africano per giovinetti.* Milano: Casa Editrice "Est," 1935.

Del Boca, Angelo. "I crimini del colonialismo fascista." In *Le guerre coloniali del fascismo,* ed. Angelo Del Boca. Roma-Bari: Laterza 1991.

———. *Gli italiani in Africa Orientale.* Roma-Bari: Laterza, 1992.

Faeti, Antonio. "Una settimana con molte domeniche." In *Conformismo e contestazione nel libro per ragazzi: Storia e sperimentazione.* Bologna: Cappelli, 1979.

Franzoj, Augusto. *Continenete nero.* Novara: Istituto Geografico De Agostini, 1961.

Gasparini, Duilio. *Olga Visentini.* Firenze: Le Monnier, 1968.

Gotta, Salvator. *Piccolo legionario in Africa Orientale.* Milano: Baldini & Castoldi, 1936.

Hamilton, Cicely. *Modern Italy as Seen by an Englishwoman.* London: J. M. Dent & Sons, 1932.

Kandiyoti, Deniz. "Identity and its Discontents: Women and the Nation." In *Colonial Discourse and Post-Colonial Theory: A Reader,* ed. Patrick Williams and Laura Chrisman. New York: Columbia University Press, 1994.

Koon, Tracy H. *Believe Obey Fight: Political Socialization of Youth in Fascist Italy, 1992–1943.* Chapel Hill: University of North Carolina Press, 1985.

Lugli, Antonio. *Libri e figure: Storia della letteratura per l'infanzia e per la gioventù.* Bologna: Nuova Universale Cappelli, 1982.

McClintock, Anne. *Imperial Leather: Race, Gender and Sexuality in the Colonial Contest.* New York: Routledge, 1995.

Meldini, Piero. *Donna, sposa e madre.* Torino: Elle Di Ci, 1995.

Mignemi, Adolfo. *Immagine coordinata per un impero.* Torino: Gruppo editoriale Forma, 1992.

Monticone, Alberto. *Il fascismo al microfono: Radio e politica in Italia (1924–1945).* Roma: Edizioni Studium, 1978.

Mosse, George. *The Image of Man: The Creation of Modern Masculinity.* New York: Oxford University Press, 1996.

Nonno Ebe. *Genietti e sirenelle in Africa Orientale.* Milano: Carroccio, 1942.

Proud, Judith K. *Children and Propaganda: il était une fois . . . : Fiction and Fairy Tale in Vichy France.* Oxford: Intellect Books, 1995.

Radway, Janice. *Reading the Romance: Women, Patriarchy, and Popular Literature.* Chapel Hill: University of North Carolina Press, 1991.

Scotto di Luzio, Adolfo. *Appropriazione imperfetta: Editori, biblioteche e libri per ragazzi durante il fascismo.* Bologna: Il Mulino, 1996.

Sòrgoni, Barbara. "La zona grigia." In *Parole e corpi: Antropologia, discorso giuridico e politiche sessuali interrazziali nella colonia Eritrea (1890–1941),* 203–28. Napoli: Liguori, 1998.

Tannenbaum, Edward. *The Fascist Experience: Italian Society and Culture 1922–1945.* New York: Basic Books, 1972.

Tekeste Negash. *Italian Colonialism in Eritrea, 1882–1941: Policies, Praxis and Impact.* Uppsala, Sweden: Uppsala University, 1987.

Tenente Anonimo. *Volontario in Africa: Racconti di guerra per ragazzi.* Milano: La Prora, 1935.

Tomasello, Giovanna. *La letteratura coloniale italiana dalle avanguardie al fascismo.* Palermo: Sellerio, 1984.

Tombaccini, Simonetta. *Storia dei fuoriusciti italiani in Francia.* Milano: Mursia, 1988.

Visentini, Olga. *Africanelle: Fiabe.* Torino: S.E.I., 1937.

Zipes, Jack. Fairy Tales and the Art of Subversion: The Classical Genre for Children and the Process of Civilization. New York: Routledge, 1988.

PART III

The Colonial Production
of Africa and the Silent Scene
# of Decolonization

Colonial Autism

Whitened Heroes, Auditory Rhetoric, and National Identity in Interwar Italian Cinema

Giorgio Bertellini

Wireless is one person speaking without hearing
and all the rest listening without being able to speak.
RUDOLPH ARNHEIM, *Radio, 1936*

Most studies devoted to "cinema during fascism" allege that they address the film production of the *ventennio,* the twenty years of Mussolini's power. However, they don't really do so. What they most commonly, if not exclusively, address are the *sound* film productions released after 1930–31—just a few years after the beginning of the Italian radio days.[1] The authors of these studies seem to think that a few introductory paragraphs on the silent films of the 1910s and 1920s are enough. All too often and without an explicit acknowledgment, films produced after 1930 are considered the only films made under the Italian dictatorship worth studying. The 1920s are treated as an irrelevant black hole, separating the historical epics and the diva films of the 1910s from the early sound works of the 1930s.

Although debatable, such a historiographical oversight is not entirely arbitrary. First, the 1920s witnessed a remarkable dearth of national film production. The financial failure of the national trust the Unione Cinematografica Italiana (U.C.I.), which was established to tame foreign competition but which sank due to the sharp increase in management costs and the lack of a solid industrial culture, brought national film production to its lowest levels ever.[2] Between 1920 and 1931, 1,316 feature films were produced. This number is deceptive, however, since 1920 saw 415 films produced, and only 2 were produced in 1931.[3] In addition, during this period films ended up being accumulated as stockpile rather than being exhibited as cultural products and artistic works. We should not be surprised to learn, therefore, that because of these practices many talented actors and directors emigrated abroad.[4]

Secondly, and perhaps most decisively, throughout the 1920s the fascist regime failed to take firm, hands-on control of the national film industry, as it did in the 1930s. In contrast with the systematic manipulation of mass media within other totalitarian regimes, such as Nazi Germany or the Soviet Union, the fascist government's delay is quite remarkable and still not fully accounted for. Only in 1929 were initial steps taken to regulate the industry, and even these were not part of a systematic and well-thought-out plan. Instead, they were mainly defensive and protectionist measures instituted to contain the massive presence of American and German film companies.[5] Because post-1945 studies of fascist cinema, both in Italy and in the United States, have granted politics a primary critical sovereignty, more recent film scholars working on the Italian cinema of the interwar period have tended to mainly deal with the national film productions of the 1930s and early 1940s. By focusing on the years in which fascist control of the film industry appears to be documentable, recent scholarship has engaged in uncovering the specifics of the regime's media manipulation and of filmmakers' ideological allegiances. Within this historiographical perspective the 1920s seemed a rather opaque or, at best, marginal realm of inquiry, deserving only quick overviews of nonfiction productions.

Still, the critical dismissal of Italian cinema's least productive decade and the overpoliticization of the historiographical framework are critical methodological decisions begging fundamental questions. What would we learn about the cinema of the 1930s and early 1940s, and thus about the aesthetic practices in "cinema during fascism," if we were to take into full account the silent film productions of the 1920s? Specifically, how does a more comprehensive and long-term assessment of silent film aesthetics affect our understanding of the challenges faced a few years later by fascist Italian cinema? Furthermore, what transformations of film culture and linguistic communication did cinema's transition to sound entail? In light of the historical deficiency of a national spoken language, how did cinema evolve to meet the aesthetic challenge of sound films?

To address these questions, I would like to examine two specific and apparently unrelated phenomena: the transformation of a silent film character after 1915 and the sound score of two 1936 colonial films. Specifically, I shall discuss the radical narrative *recharacterization* of Maciste, the African slave of *Cabiria* (Itala Film, 1914), from the mid-1910s through the mid-1920s. Beginning in 1915, in the aftermath of Italy's military campaigns in Northern Africa, Maciste became a national hero. Replacing his African darkness and exoticism with an equally mighty, heroic, but whitened and fully Italianized identity, he developed into a patriotic "strong man." Initially a fascinating secondary black character from a historical epic, he became the white protagonist of a modern film serial. In other words, Maciste's character and narrative transformation ran parallel with his racial mutation. By becoming white and Italian, Maciste denied any narrative and visual significance to the black epic hero of *Cabiria*. His repeated appearances in a patriotic serial disclose a distinct solipsism.

In this chapter, I shall also discuss the use of sound and spoken language in two 1936 "Imperial films," Augusto Genina's *Lo squadrone bianco* (Roma Film) and Mario Camerini's *Il grande appello* (Artisti Associati). The same anxieties about an encounter with the African other and a colonial self came forth in the sound period, and their aesthetic expressions were tied to Italy's enduring difficulty in developing cultural and linguistic unity. In Genina's film, the main characters, two military officers dispatched to a colonial outpost, hardly speak to each other. In contrast, a profusion of languages and dialects is contrasted with a young hero's perfect Italian utterances in Camerini's film.

I contend that these two distant instances, with their different aesthetic natures (silent and sound), address the same problems in Italian colonial culture: a remarkable uneasiness about confronting the African antagonist, the colonized other, and an inner conflict centered on dilemmas of self-representation. Similar to the processes through which the "West perceived, configured, and silenced the Orient," in Edward Said's words, and through which "whiteness emerged in American literature," in Toni Morrison's, Italian hegemonic culture instituted the identity of the "colonial alien" by juxtaposing it with a commanding self. Africa became a distant, inharmonious space inhabited by exotic, nonwhite bodies speaking a dissonant, mysterious tongue. In this cultural dynamic, the "other" is not allowed autonomous space, image, or voice, and the recognition of similarities and the acceptance of differences are produced by silent and sound films' narrative structure and audiovisual expression with the sole purpose of fostering a clearer national *awareness*.[6] I describe this process as an *autistic* one. In both Maciste and the sound films, the "other" is eagerly employed, absorbed, and denied to construct and assert a firmer, more organic and effective self-representation. Traditionally speaking, broad historical rationales have been put forward to explain this attitude. In comparison to other nations with aggressive imperialist politics dating back to the second half of the nineteenth century, Italy's encounter with and acknowledgment of the African "other" in cultural representations occurred rather late, and thereby conveyed a sense of urgency. As Karen Pinkus has remarked, "blackness did not become a repository for any *particular* fantasies or cultural position in Italy until the Libyan conquest of 1911."[7]

By resorting to the concept of "autism," however, I do not intend either to psychoanalyze the state of national culture and identity, or to uncritically plunge into the common, defensive historiographical model of Italian colonial enterprise as childlike, "innocent," and backward and not fueled by the grave imperialist spirit of more "serious and mature" nations such as France and Britain.[8] By using the term "autism" when examining Italian fiction films, I mean to refer to a self-centered cultural and ideological set-up, which often denies narrative and visual relevance to the "African other" and conceals the profound daily challenges of the colonial enterprise, preferring instead to withdraw into a self-absorbed exploration of personal identity, embedded with fantasies of power and authority, and pubescent aspirations to adulthood. With the arrival of sound, these phantasmatic endeavors displayed an aphasic hesitation in the mastery of the Italian tongue and thus a vocal difficulty in articulating a confident, untroubled possession of national selfhood. My attempt here is to call attention to the inclination of Italians to look inward toward their national identity, and to trace the emergence of this inclination in the cinema of both the 1930s and the 1920s.

The theory and practice of nationalism and imperialism generally allow "colonizing nations" to imagine themselves unified, empowered, and hegemonic. Since the end of the nineteenth century, the notion of "Italianness" has been a *questionable* concept for compelling historical reasons: deep internal tensions and divisions (for example, the Southern question and brigandage), mass emigration, repeated military defeats on international fronts, and weak cultural practices of mass politics and national bonding. The various efforts to create a nationalistic ideology through architecture, public parades, festivities, and official hymns were badly formulated because of the state's inability to perform a real cultural and economic unification beyond the mere rhetoric of territorial unity.[9]

Although quite responsive to the patriotic impulses and mannerisms of anniversaries, public ceremonies, and contemporary literary, theatrical, or artistic productions, silent Italian cinema displayed what one may term an "antiquarian solipsism." Beginning in the nineteenth century, the fascination with Roman antiquity was catalyzed by the process of political unification. "New-emerging nations," as Benedict Anderson has noted, "imagined themselves antique. [Thus] 'Antiquity' [was], at a certain historical juncture, the *necessary consequence* of 'novelty'".[10] In early twentieth-century Italy, little space was left for anything but forms of self-representation.

At the time of the war with Libya, apart from the "scientific documentaries" shot by Luca Comerio, Italian films did not concern themselves with the political and social problems of North Africa.[11] Instead they often displayed their solipsistic refusal to directly engage with the "colonial subject" by framing the whole colonial experience within a rhetoric of "antique," epic, and adventurous narratives, advancing such values as honor, sacrifice, and physical perfection. From its beginning in 1905 to the rise of feature films in the early 1910s, Italian cinema showed a special fondness for historical re-enactments, quite often with patriotic overtones, by developing ambitious but popular adaptations of high-brow literary texts.[12]

Such "antiquarian solipsism" became even more evident when films staged encounters with the African "other" within the culturally sealed and morally safe contours of Rome's glorious history and civilization. Capitalizing on the attraction for historical epics widely circulating among international literary circles—from Shakespearean dramas to the historical novels of Lew Wallace, Edward Bulwer Lytton, and Henryk Sienkiewicz—and on the tradition of popular amusements such as the circus, pyrodramas, and even museums, Italian cinema of the 1910s narrated proud tales about Rome's founding civilization, predestined imperialism, and the unparalleled refinement of its glorious culture. Also, Italian historical films exposed the unique combination of Rome's pagan but advanced humanism with Christian virtues—e.g., *Quo Vadis?* (Cines, 1913), *Spartacus* (Pasquali, 1913)— and emphasized Rome's moral superiority even when exhibiting the fascinatingly exotic cultures of Egypt or Carthage in such works as *Antony and Cleopatra* (Cines, 1913) and *Cabiria* (Itala, 1914). These films became enormously popular internationally and helped nurture a patriotic pride in the domestic scene.[13] More importantly, they became training grounds for the refinement of a nationalistic ideology that, through the cinematic medium, could reach vast and diverse audiences through the highly spectacular attractions of its colossal mise-en-scène. These aggressive formulations of national identity played a part in excluding realism from the expressive venues of the nation's self-representation as they paralleled and broadcast the state's imperialistic ambitions.[14]

The First World War and the ensuing economic crisis halted the manufacture of these spectacular films. The genre crossbred with the emerging international format of serial productions. However, in contrast to French serials like Louis Feuillade's *Fantomas* (1913–14) and *Les Vampires* (1915–16), which were based on detective stories relying on endless stratagems and narrative surprises and cast numerous female characters, the Italian serials displayed images and stories of strong men *(uomini forti)*—such as Ajax, Maciste, Saetta, and Ursus—engaged in spectacular physical performances. Recently termed "athletic-acrobatic," this film genre dominated Italian film production from the mid-1910s to the mid-1920s, lasting longer than any other genre, including the aristocratic diva melodramas in vogue from the mid-1910s.[15]

What is most remarkable about characters like Maciste, Saetta, Ausonia, and Cimaste is not only their displays of sheer force and endurance, which, as has often been remarked, anticipated the fascist deployment of images of male strength and power.[16] What is striking is also their intertextual biographies and their narrative and visual trajectories as characters throughout their film career. In a few instances, the characters present a remarkable tension between, on the one hand, their early identities as foreigners, *other* than Roman or Italian—i.e., "darker" slaves subject to Italian white masters—and, on the other, their progressive development into Italian heroes or, better, white masters themselves.[17] In *Quo Vadis?* (1913), the overlapping of religious and political themes turns Ursus, the giant non-Roman protector of the female protagonist, into a domestic hero, while the Thracian Spartacus in *Spartacus* (1913) becomes a *bersagliere* (Italy's characteristic guardian of public order) in *Il romanzo di un atleta* (Film Artistica Gloria, 1915) and a marine officer in *Il marchio* (Jupiter Film, 1916).

The case of Maciste is, of course, most representative.[18] In *Cabiria,* he is a Roman centurion's black slave who fights for the Romans against the Carthaginian enemy. Yet just a little more than a year later he is turned into an Italian hero in such films as *Maciste alpino* (Itala Film, 1916) and *Maciste poliziotto* (Itala Film, 1918). His racial otherness is rapidly tamed not only ideologically—he appears fully integrated into Italian society—but also physically: his blackness has been utterly erased. In the former of these films, he plays the role of the most representative member of the Italian army, an alpine soldier, while in the latter he is transformed into a policeman. His inclusion in the ranks of the national army and the forces of public order is quite telling of his radical racial and political absorption.[19]

Between the mid-1910s and the mid-1920s, Maciste was the protagonist of countless films that located him at the center of the Italian, Christian, and Western public spheres, from which *other figures* became alien and exotic.[20] After completing in Germany a film called *Maciste e il cofano cinese* (1923), Maciste-Pagano traveled back to Africa to film Mario Camerini's *Maciste contro lo sceicco* (1926) for the Italian company Fert. In Africa, he confronts a sheik in what could genealogically be regarded as a fight against his former racial incarnation. The same year, in *Il gigante delle dolomiti* (S.A. Pittalunga, 1926), he is coded as an Italian superhero, further distancing him from his African intertextual heritage.

The extent to which national symbols, engagements, and geographies caused Maciste to transform after 1914 is striking. Following Ella Shohat, one can argue that his films are essentially "rescue fantasies" that manufacture a role for the Western male as *liberator* from oriental aggression and thus provide a justification for colonial domination.[21] Still, I would like to emphasize this very dynamic of *becoming* a Western, patriotic hero. The trajectory by which Maciste's nationality and color are radically altered, while his primitive strength and generosity are maintained, is particularly striking. Between the mid-1910s and mid-1920s, silent film renderings of the Roman empire minimize, both visually and narratively, contact with the *other.* Instead, exclusive interest in the national hero and his environment takes central stage. With this shift appears a constant exhibition of antique decor and military triumph representing both past and present symbols of power and sovereignty. This process of painting Maciste as an indigenous hero in the artificial light of both national and military unification as well as racial and cultural primacy entrenches in these films a sense of nationalistic solipsism.

Furthermore, in the serials centered on the *uomini forti* like Maciste, there is no real violence: confrontations, duels, and battles are somewhat harmless and even cartoonish. The enemy is quite often injured but rarely killed.[22] The athletic routines of the circus—especially physical comedy—and sports such as boxing frame these adventures of strength and physical stamina. Audiences simply do not see the full consequences of the heroes' tough and dominating gestures. Not by chance did the film periodicals refer to these characters as the "good giants" *(i giganti buoni)*.[23] When one examines the Italian colonial experience, this type of appraisal inevitably resonates with the familiar, all-forgiving representation of Italians as good-natured people *(Italiani brava gente),* which functioned to mask and anaesthetize a guilty imperialistic conscience.

The Italian epic-athletic genre competed both nationally and internationally with the lighthearted adventures of Douglas Fairbanks in *The Mark of Zorro* (Douglas Fairbanks Picture / United Artists, 1920), *Robin Hood* (Douglas Fairbanks Picture / United Artists, 1922), and *The Thief of Bagdad* (Douglas Fairbanks Picture / United Artists, 1924). And like Fairbanks's films, the Italian ones in the long run showed a similar lack of serious dramatic dimension: they increasingly became more athletic than epic. In the end, silent Italian cinema resorted to the aesthetically stylized mannerisms of Maciste's his fellow heroes' spectacular adventures while safely rendering an amusing portrait of colonial aspirations and nationalistic pride.

As I hope to have made clear by now, the 1930s should not be regarded as the only testing ground to discuss the relations between Italian film culture and the government's colonial enterprises. Beyond common allegations of escapism and propaganda, in fact, there are a number of questions related to the international development of stylistic conventions and communicative practices that the 1920s, and specifically the late 1920s and early 1930s transition to synchronized sound, pose to the scholar of Italian cinema under fascism. The transition to sound, an industrial, linguistic, and aesthetic innovation, affected film production in other countries in more or less the same period, but it posed very specific challenges in Italy.[24]

From the early 1930s, in fact, reproduction of sound and the regime's more systematic control over the medium directed cinema to a different aesthetic and social task. The modern necessities of a "patriotic and realist cinema" necessitated major readjustments to the modes and contents of cinematic communication. Films had to develop a closer, yet still official, kinship with Italy's everyday life, people, and stories. In particular, cinematic rendering of national pride during the 1930s had to devise a realistic auditory aesthetic. Realism, until then best embodied in the vernacular tunes and dialogues of novels, stage plays, and even some films containing highly regionalized characters as in Neapolitan cinema,[25] was forced to strive for a national intonation. The challenge, as Giulio Bollati put it, was whether "there existed an Italian way to modernity."[26] If the visuals of such new poetic practices were not too difficult to render or command, the aural dimension proved highly problematic: the nation lacked a single spoken language, an issue Antonio Gramsci has famously addressed in his discussions on *la questione della lingua*.[27] What should a conversation among common people in a verisimilar Italian story sound like? What lexicon or accent would be appropriate for a young housewife or an aged blue-collar worker? What kind of dialogue could have been expected from a peasant?

These important aesthetic challenges, related to the communicative conundrum of an aural realism, have not been addressed by mainstream film historiography informed by neorealist films and poetics. In films of the 1930s, hearing common people talking in Italian was still not as familiar as seeing them speaking. Their utterances struggled to adopt a verisimilar mode. Although the intention was to create a "realistic effect," the opposite was achieved. The secularity of their verbal exchanges challenged the medium's capacity for universality and threatened cinema's potential for aesthetic realism. I would argue that the issues of *orality* and *aurality* represent fundamental dimensions of the expressivity of Italian cinema in general. Although these issues introduce important critical tools for examining the cinema of the fascist period, I believe they exceed the aesthetic and communicative predicaments of the 1930s and 1940s.[28] I would contend that these aesthetic dimensions also informed the expressivity of other periods of Italian cinema, from the "operatic" acting style of the silent divas and the multidialect makeup of *Paisà*'s sound score to Visconti's operatic narrations (e.g., *Senso* or *Death in Venice*), from Antonioni's logophobic cinema to the subproletarians' playful dialogues in Pasolini's early films.

During the fascist regime, at issue, of course, was whether a "national reality," or a reality that would have symbolically appeared as "national," was *there* to be captured, both visually and aurally, or instead had to be somehow invented. The cinema of the period, in fact, participated in the public circulation of an "invented," compromised, yet highly literary national tongue. Films were part of a larger arena of modern cultural phenomena, which included radio broadcasts (especially Mussolini's speeches), dramatic theater, and the linguistic transformations of stage comedy—from the late *café-chantant* and *rivista* to early forms of *avanspettacolo* preceding, in some theaters, the screening of a film—as well as mass journalism, operas, and modern *canzonette* (popular light songs).[29]

With the arrival of sound, the representation of "Italianness," generally speaking, departed from models centered around visual antiquity—with the single and late exception of *Scipione l'Africano* (E.N.I.C., 1937), by Carmine Gallone. In the early 1930s, popular melodies and songs became a necessary and easily exploitable texture of filmic expression: *canzonette* and famous arias of operas *(contrafacta)* were widely adopted as narrative devices and musical accompaniments. Their use enabled both new commercial possibilities and ideological underpinnings. Gennaro Righelli's *La canzone dell'amore* (Cines-Pittalunga, 1930), the first Italian sound film, mixed wordy and literary dialogues with jovial tunes. Alessandro Blasetti's *Terra madre* (Cines-Pittalunga, 1931) and *Resurrectio* (Cines-Pittalunga, 1931) praised workers' and peasants' musical folklore as refreshing and uncontaminated—without, however, employing authentic vernacular songs. Other films literally staged the effort to master a national linguistic articulation on both casual and conventional registers. Remarkable, although uncommon, in this sense were Nunzio Malasomma's *La telefonista* (Cines-Pittalunga, 1932), which told a love story through phone conversations, and Alessandro Blasetti's *1860* (Cines-Pittalunga, 1934), in my opinion one of the most interesting films in this regard. The peculiarity of Blasetti's film lies in the narrative and ideological appropriation of a Sicilian peasant's actions, identity, and dialect—while Garibaldi appears briefly in utter silence—and in a recurring competition between regional songs, culminating in a final chorus in which all the various characters intone the national anthem, "Fratelli d'Italia," as they come to liberate Sicily.

Within our analysis of cinema and colonialism, of great speculative interest are two films produced in 1936, the very year Italy invaded Ethiopia: Augusto Genina's *Lo squadrone bianco,* which is actually set in Libya, and Mario Camerini's *Il grande appello.* By granting very little visual space to the enemy, both films maintain a solipsistic tone as they tell stories of problematic relationships between fathers and sons, either real or figurative. Both plots begin as highly conflictual family affairs that end up being redeemed by the experience of war.

Winner of the Coppa Mussolini at the 1936 Venice Film Festival, and freely adapted from a French novel set in Algeria by Joseph Peyré, *Lo squadrone bianco* is the story of an Italian military outpost in the Libyan desert. The squadron of the title is a visual and racial oxymoron. Composed of troops of native Arabians, whose typical all-white Saharan apparel contrasts with their darker complexions, the squadron is led by an Italian commander, Captain Sant'Elia (Fosco Giacchetti), a solitary and reserved, almost aphasic, officer.

Figure 5. Silent dialogue between Captain Sant'Elia and Lieutenant Ludovici in *Lo squadrone bianco* (1936), starring Fosco Giachetti and Antonio Centa. Courtesy of Museum of Modern Art / Film Stills Archive, New York.

Lo squadrone bianco has as a decidedly misogynist opening: a young officer, Lieutenant Ludovici (Antonio Centa), leaves the city and decides to enlist at a desert station because he has been rejected by Cristina (Fulvia Lanzi), a rich, moody, and selfish woman. At the military outpost he encounters Captain Sant'Elia, an uncommunicative, rugged, and authoritarian figure, a champion of dedication and integrity who is visually presented in a "posterlike statuesque pose . . . a true fascist body in a state of preparedness for war." [30] At first, the captain realizes that the young lieutenant has come to the desert not because of an ideological commitment, but only for private, emotional reasons. For the captain the young officer lacks military vocation, character, and even a sense of worth. Sant'Elia's arguments with the "spoiled" Ludovici over military rules and personal commitment are constant.

An unexpected mission in the desert against the local rebels proves a turning point. The long, excruciating excursion into the desert deeply affects Ludovici who, although exhausted, gathers his energies and manages to survive, showing a surprising strength of will. The captain, who has been attending to the lieutenant's health like a paternal figure, is impressed. In the name of mutual respect, "father" and "son" can finally initiate some form of dialogue. Slowly, Ludovici becomes a different person. When, Sant'Elia is killed during the ensuing battle, the lieutenant's transformation progresses. After burying the father-captain, he takes command of the white platoon and leads it back to the fort. Now a mature and committed officer, he has become what Sant'Elia was: a devoted, dutiful, and aphasic officer. When Cristina arrives at the outpost to beg Ludovici's forgiveness and promise him her love, he rejects her affection and warns her that he is no longer the same person. His identity and destiny are now bound to the desert, its silence, and its heroes.

What is particularly interesting in the film is not just the narrative of conversion, that is, Ludovici's search for personal identity and respect through discipline, sacrifice, and death, but also the way in which these concepts are rendered through cinema's audiovisual expressions. Repeatedly we see scenes in which appear long rows of black soldiers, dressed entirely in white and riding white dromedaries. These scenes are framed as extreme long shots, multiplied through different viewing angles, and intercut with images of a stark white sky. These austere but lengthy sequences, accompanied by the symphonic melodies of Antonio Veretti, constitute a sort of operatic pageant and religious procession, headed by the "priest" and master of ceremony Sant'Elia, whose name has an obvious religious connotation. Once grown into adulthood, Ludovici assumes the same public but mute leadership position once occupied by Sant'Elia. What these images of solitary command and control compose is an operatic and ritualistic fantasy of personal exploration and identity, set in a desolate but monumental elsewhere.

The non-diegetic symphonic music, combined with the diegetic silence of *all* characters, accompanies and enhances the transformation of their excursion through a rite of passage. The result is that the desert is not even exotic anymore. Instead, it is a homosocial and racially indifferent training ground for a white male's identity formation and development into adulthood. By contrast, Cristina is coded as a harmful seductress, despite her late conversion, and is left in the margins. In a manner similar to the way that gender difference is brushed aside in the film, racial diversity also succumbs to a removal: the two white protagonists' personal turmoil is metamorphosed into the astonishingly vast but voiceless landscape. The desolate setting, an objective correlative of their inner life, is closer to the abstract idea of the desert in religious imagery as a site of utter isolation and a catalyst for superior epiphanies and personal transformation. The elegiac sequence in which Sant'Elia pays homage to a fallen officer is most symptomatic of this inward movement. Alone, separated from the rest of the platoon, Sant'Elia

Figure 6. Lieutenant Ludovici (Antonio Centa) alone in the desert in *Lo squadrone bianco* (1936). Courtesy of Museum of Modern Art / Film Stills Archive, New York.

remains silent in front of his own male hero. The ensuing burial site then works as a dramatic prolepsis. The relationship between the two men is cemented when the lieutenant himself takes the place of the fallen "hero." Not only is there narrative and thematic similarity in the two deaths, but the same obsessive sound is played in the background, identifying the same inward development of the characters.[31]

The "autistic" distance from the surrounding environment, or at least the divisive suspension between the personal and the historical, the illusory and the real, is also embodied by the denial of any voice and autonomous existence to the obedient Arab troops. They do not seem to have any voice or any will, except that of their white commanders. All they do is witness the officers' conversation. Even Cristina is turned into a passive spectator, waiting for orders and then executing them when received. As in a dream of personal mastery, the troops' blackness is made invisible or, as the title suggests, erased and whitened, so that they become more subservient to the white male hero's "centripetal" ego.[32] By the end of the film, this courageous "white squadron" has become a visual accompaniment and a piece of scenery, surrounding someone else's inner search.

Mario Camerini's *Il grande appello* is the story of a middle-aged man, Giovanni Bertani (Camillo Pilotto), who runs a hotel named Oriente in Djibouti (East Africa) in the period of Italy's war with Ethiopia. His mistress, a younger Spanish woman (Lina Da Costa), is coded as a darker, rowdy, and deceitful orientalist figure. She and Giovanni do not just run the hotel, but they also smuggle arms to the Abyssinians, the Italian enemy. In addition, she also conducts her own business with sinister foreign figures that often stop by the hotel. As the story progresses, Giovanni begins to have serious doubts about the soundness of his financial dealings. Ideologically, the film singles out the young Spanish woman's personal greed to compensate for Giovanni's moral corruption and to indicate his capacity for redemption. Although she may appear "as fascinating as the African landscape she is fused with,"[33] in the end she embodies Giovanni's degeneration and loss of identity. By distancing himself from her, Giovanni shoulders the ideology of the film as he rejects corruption and treason for moral and spiritual renewal.

More than his recognition of his mistress's clandestine smuggling, Giovanni's unexpected encounter with his "chaste" Italian son, Enrico (Roberto Villa), is what prompts his radical transformation. When he is informed that his former wife is dying and that twenty years ago she had secretly given birth to their son, Giovanni is caught by surprise. He immediately decides to visit the son, who is a radiotelegrapher and a soldier in the Italian army, temporarily stationed at Addis Ababa. Giovanni's initial intention, however, is to convince the son to leave the army and to join forces with him in his business activities. When the two meet, the son is disturbed and saddened by his father's plan and vehemently tries to explain how committed he is to his service. Enrico's rejection of the plan becomes violent after he discovers his father's participation in the smuggling of arms to the Abyssinians. Their first meeting ends with an angry separation. Eventually, however, that encounter becomes the basis of Giovanni's inner transformation: his encounter with the other Italian soldiers of his son's company and his growing desire to sustain and preserve his newly found family act upon his conscience. When he later learns that his son has been injured on the battlefield, he finds an opportunity to redeem himself. He launches his own war against former business companions and ends up sacrificing his life, but regaining his son's respect.

The narrative of the film, which was written by novelist Mario Soldati, who later became a film director, may appear as simply one more story of moral conversion and national reconciliation. Set in a familial and homosocial context, the film relies on melodramatic and misogynist polarizations, such as betrayal versus loyalty, temptation and corruption versus discipline and integrity, and the foreign, pernicious woman versus the virtuous son. Yet, despite the dramatic quality of these conflicts, the most interesting element of the film is the singular linguistic fabric of its sound score.[34]

The dialogue in the first sequences at the Hotel Oriente is disorienting, although it did not represent a *unicum* in Italian cinema. Other Italian military films of the period mixed dialects and other linguistic modes. Notable among these are *Scarpe al sole* (1935), *Il piccolo alpino* (1940), *La nave bianca* (1941), *Bengasi, Giarabub, I tre aquilotti,* and *Alfa Tau,* all made in 1942, and *Quelli della montagna, Marinai senza stelle,* and *Gente dell'aria,* made in 1943.[35] At the beginning of *Il grande appello,* we are presented with a Babelic environment: it is possible to hear German, French, Spanish, Italian, and a few indigenous idioms in the soundtrack. Giovanni himself alternates frequently between Spanish and French, speaking Italian only when someone speaks Italian to him. His Italianness is thus presented more as a provoked and interpellated reaction rather than a spontaneous expression. The reason for this cultural displacement, it seems, is because he has spent the preceding eighteen years traveling abroad. While boasting that his name is still know in all the places he has been, such as New York, Shanghai, Brazil, and Australia, he astonishingly pronounces his own name the "wrong" way—with a French accent. The change in the accent, from Bertàni to Bertanì, alarmingly signals that he has lost contact with his original Italian identity. Without a country, the film appears to suggest, Giovanni has lost his dignity and integrity.

In a remarkable scene, an Italian journalist working in the hotel lobby types an article for an Italian newspaper, *La Gazzetta del Popolo.*[36] While the background is filled with the sounds of loud conversations in different languages, the journalist asks Giovanni if he knows when the Italian radio bulletin *(comunicato italiano)* is being broadcast. Giovanni babbles in a mixture of French and Italian, but ultimately he does not answer. Appealing to Giovanni's national identity, the journalist then inquiries: "But aren't you Italian?" *("Ma non è italiano Lei?"),* to which Giovanni does not answer. A second interpellation of patriotic demeanor occurs shortly afterward. When the war report is finally broadcast, the newspaperman positions himself in front of the radio and increases the volume in order to drown out the foreign crowd. He then invites Giovanni to listen to the latest developments in the Italian war effort. In the early part of the film, these repeated requests of national allegiance leave the self-absorbed hotel owner puzzled.

A similar verbal appeal occurs when an Italian sailor informs Giovanni of the death of his former wife (whom he incidentally denies ever having married) and of the whereabouts of his son. The initial dialogue between Giovanni and the sailor emphasizes Giovanni's indifference to his Italian heritage. The dialogue goes as follows:

Sailor: Excuse me, the boss?

Giovanni: C'est moi

    Sailor: Are you Mr. Giovanni Bertàni?

Giovanni: Oui, Jean Bertanì

    Sailor: Bertàni or Bertanì?

Giovanni: Oh, . . . Bertàni or Bertanì, that's just the same.

During his trip to meet Enrico, he insists on pronouncing his name in the French way, while officers and soldiers keep "correcting" him. Taking an example from what Arnheim wrote about the "one-sidedness" of radio broadcasting, we can say that Giovanni appears to practice the "art of not listening in."[37]

Other linguistically formulated requests of patriotism await Giovanni. When he arrives at the Italian camp to meet his son, he is exposed to a variety of Italian dialects: soldiers are speaking loudly and joking in their local Genoese and Venetian dialects. Interestingly, the emphasis on their different vernacular speech, which betrays their lower-class backgrounds, underscores both their industrious and harmonious communality and their patriotic authenticity—in the best spirit of the cultural ideology of *strapaese*, which equated local popular traditions with genuine Italianness. Despite their regional idioms, all these soldiers face the identical challenges and dangers of the war. Not by chance, in Giovanni's presence they all start singing the famous fascist hymn *Giovinezza*.

Under these pressures, Giovanni meets Enrico. At first the encounter with his son, who thought his father was long dead, is heralded by the soldiers of the camp, who cheer the guest and prepare a party to celebrate the family reunion. Giovanni overcomes his initial embarrassment when he begins to remember the lines of an old popular song. Shortly, the entire company joins in. When father and son are finally alone for the first time, however, their stark differences emerge. The son has well-thought-out plans to join the national aviation force to better serve the country. He expresses his clear disinterest in helping his father with his business in Djibouti. Rejected, Giovanni resorts to a few French expressions and dismisses his son's patriotic idealism. The final separation occurs when Enrico learns about Giovanni's arms trafficking. The dramatic rupturing of their relationship is a turning point for Giovanni. At that moment he begins his "conversion" to fatherhood and patriotic citizenship.

Giovanni's return to Djibouti reveals the extent of his transformation. He pretends to continue smuggling arms to the Abyssinians, although secretly he is really betraying them. Dressed as one of the Abyssinians, he attacks them with the very arms he has sold them. In the ensuing battle, he is wounded. In a lingering close-up, Giovanni looks up at the sky, filled with Italian

planes—truly a fascist colonial obsession—and twice utters the only name
that reconnects him with his son: "Italia." The final image shows him close
to death, with an Italian flag visible in the background.

As the film ends, the effect of hearing regional vernaculars in an Italian
colonial outpost in Africa cannot but call attention to the problematics of
an "imperialist presence and identity." The soldiers care about each other
and joke, sing, and work together, but they do so by constantly drawing on
their various dialects. Their unity is not located in an imaginary colonial
consciousness, but in their microcultural differences; their localism is what
makes up their Italianness. Within the film's ideological framework, region-
alism and localism constitute the domain generating an "authentic" Italian
popular identity. Yet the film also endorses a more modern expression
of Italianness, devoid of vernacular connotations. It does so in the association of characters somehow related to mass media or communication with
a "purer" version of the Italian idiom. These characters, from the press journalist and the radio announcer to Enrico who, as we noted, is a radiotelegrapher, all speak without a recognizable regional inflection. Outside these
different configurations of Italian allegiance, vernacular and retro or national and modern, is Giovanni. Distant from his regional origins and un-
interested in Italian written or broadcast news, he has become disengaged
from any linguistic facet of Italianness.

Interestingly, screenwriter and novelist Mario Soldati, interviewed by film
historian Jean A. Gili, commented on the film's linguistic richness and complexity by noting:

> Camerini and I wrote the screenplay. Although it is a bad film, I put in it a few
> things I really cared about: I understood that the strength of Italy was in the
> dialects. In the film then, the truck drivers are from Genoa, the soldiers from
> Brescia, and an officer of the commercial marine is from Genoa too. Camerini
> and I chose a number of nonprofessional actors. Overall it is a film in which
> nobody speaks of fascism or Mussolini, and yet it is still a propaganda film.[38]

In the end, the film did not obtain considerable support from state dis-
tributors and exhibitors because it was not deemed propagandistic enough.
The ambiguous and problematic drama of reformation in *Il Grande appello,*
released at the time of the colonial campaigns, did not turn out to be an
effective one. Although we cannot rely on specific studies of spectators' reactions, it is likely that the centrality of a disengaged anti-hero like Giovanni
depressed instead of heightened the film's ideological purpose.

As homosocial dramas of conversion, these two films do not display, from
the very beginning, gestures of heroism performed against the enemy. Instead, the films' male protagonists need the entire narratives to overcome

moral ambiguity, personal uncertainty, and excessive individualism. In order to become fascist or Italian heroes, these characters somehow had to train themselves by taking a political stance against women, the African enemy, and, most importantly, their own narrow egotism. The war is against not only immorality and barbarism but also personal, selfish isolation, which, if unchecked, will lead to inevitable disintegration.

The victories of the protagonists are the result of the internal dramas of a sealed conscience. The risk of autism is the worst threat to the protagonists' ultimate self-realization. The training opportunities for such radical transformations are a process of identity making, embodied in passages from blackness to whiteness, from exotic strength to national heroism, from silence or Babelic confusion to linguistic mastery. The circus arena, the sport stadium, the later African war campaigns, the Dolomites, and even the modern media provide an opportunity to expose the still capricious and reluctant male protagonist to real deeds of bravery and heroism. In the end, fascist nationalism is essentially a male, solitary affair. The protagonist's route to heroism need not intersect with an enemy to compete against. Instead, it surfaces as a slow, uneasy acquisition of patriotic identity and speech, a transformation with which it may have been hard to identify.

NOTES

I would like to thank Paul Sellors and Ingalisa Schrobsdorff for their precious comments on earlier drafts of this chapter. Unless otherwise noted, all translations are my own. Whenever possible, I use the available English title of the films mentioned here. This chapter is dedicated to Giuliana Muscio, exemplary film historian.

1. For instance, in her remarkable study on theatricality in Italian cinema during fascism and referring to one of her previous works, Marcia Landy writes, "In *Fascism and Film* (1986) I examined the character and contributions of Italian sound cinema during the twenty years of the Fascist regime" (Landy 1998: xi). Although the earliest broadcasts in Italy occurred in 1924, the fascist regime began to systematically control and make use of the medium in 1928, by instituting a state radio broadcasting agency, EIAR (Ente Italiano per le Audizioni Radiofoniche).

2. In his history of Italian cinema, Gian Piero Brunetta summarizes the reasons for the crisis (1993: 245–94). For a general overview of the film production of the 1920s, see Aldo Bernardini and Vittorio Martinelli (1979). Consider also the insightful essay by Mario Quargnolo (1964). According to Aldo Bernardini, the total number of films produced in the 1920s (inclusive of shorts, which constituted the majority of the yearly output) varied as follows: 786 in 1920, 695 in 1921, 298 in 1922, 250 in 1923, 142 in 1924, 78 in 1925, 64 in 1926, 50 in 1927, 65 in 1928, 43 in 1929, and 20 in 1930. Cf. Aldo Bernardini (1991: 1112). The archival records are even more disheartening. For a fairly accurate account of Italian films of the 1920s preserved at national and international film archives, see Riccardo Redi (1999: 229–33).

3. When compared to the distribution of French and American films within the

Italian market, the circulation of domestic productions was notably low; domestic films steadily accounted for 20 percent or less from the mid-1920s to the late 1930s. Bernardini's systematic study slightly corrects James Hay's charts without contradicting his overall assessment. Cf. James Hay (1987: 252, appendix B).

4. Among them were both young and experienced directors such as Nunzio Malasomma, Carmine Gallone, Mario Bonnard, Augusto Genina, and Guido Brignone, as well as prominent actresses such as Carmen Boni, Maria Jacobini, Marcella Albani, and Clara Galassi. On the topic, see Vittorio Martinelli (1978) and Martinelli and Quargnolo (1992: 131–69). After the extraordinary global successes of pre–World War I film distribution, the postwar years witnessed surprisingly scant interest and effort in exploiting films' commercial value, both domestically and internationally. The only figure with some business expertise was the highly capable manager, Stefano Pittalunga, who before dying prematurely helped restructure and adjust Cines, together with other film companies, to the sound system.

5. The first step was the establishment in 1929 of ENAC (Ente Nazionale per la Cinematografia), a state-assisted financial organization designed to negotiate joint marketing and distribution rights between Italian and foreign producers. Unsuccessful, ENAC was replaced in 1933 by a system of direct government control, implemented through the Ministry of Popular Culture. Although national productions were funded, fewer and fewer foreign films were authorized to circulate, and they could do so only after being dubbed. In 1938, the so-called Alfieri law virtually prohibited the distribution of American films. For a brief discussion of fascist cultural policies on national and international film distribution, see James Hay (1987: 66–72). For a rare examination of the circulation of foreign films in Italy during fascism, read Mario Quargnolo (1986). About the state intervention in the film industry, see Jean A. Gili (1981).

6. On this cultural process, see Richard Dyer (1997: 1–40, especially 13). The references to the work of Said and Morrison are, respectively, Said (1978) and Morrison (1992).

7. Karen Pinkus (1995: 29; emphasis in the original), but all of chapter 2, on advertising black bodies during the African campaigns, is fundamental.

8. This kind of contention is often coupled with two other quite problematic theses that, by the same token, I am not interested in emphasizing here. The first one is the inferiority that Italians feel in relation to other countries. The second stresses an Italian apathy about the colonial experience. Karen Pinkus has best explained this stance when writing about "colonial innocence" in her *Bodily Regimes*: "the Italian Empire tends to emerge from various histories as a sort of good-natured, almost pathetic occupation of unfertile lands, a last minute attempt on the parts of *Italietta* to catch up to its neighbors. Culpability is blurred since little planning was given to the economic consequences of capturing a relatively unproductive desert state in East Africa, which, after all, was essentially 'the only land available' by the time Mussolini resolved to engage in a total war." Karen Pinkus (1995: 22 ff).

9. As historian Emilio Gentile best put it, "the most likely reasons for the liberal failure were the lack of organizational support, of any real, collective enthusiasm, of a *democratic sensibility* in regard to mass action, and the liberal culture's failure to conceive and set in motion a mobilization of the masses through the systematic use of ritual and symbol. Here, a fundamental diffidence toward the masses seen as dan-

gerous, even explosive, human material, full of seditious energy, kept the country's liberal, rationalist leaders from any steady and convinced commitment to mass politics." Emilio Gentile (1996: 11–12).

10. Benedict Anderson (1991 [1983]: xiv; emphasis in the original).

11. Comerio was the only state-authorized cinematographer allowed to accompany Italian troops in Libya. For his filmography and a general discussion of his work both as a photographer and a filmmaker, see Luca Manenti, Nicolas Monti, and Giorgio Nicodemi (1979: especially 46–60; filmography 104–6).

12. For instance, the very first Italian fiction film was an edifying exaltation of the Risorgimento, titled *La presa di Roma: 20 settembre 1870* (The taking of Rome: September 20, 1870) (Alberini-Santoni 1905). The seven scenes of this film visualized a crucial event in Italian history: the seizure of Rome by the newly formed Italian army and the election of the city as the nation's capital. The film's plot literally paraphrased the lay and monarchic historiography of Italy's ruling bourgeoisie. A discussion of the film is in Aldo Bernardini (1983: 118–27).

13. I have discussed Italian cinema's commercially successful exploitation of antiquity and the Roman past in G. Bertellini (1999: 227–65). For an examination of the impact of historical films in Europe, see Vittorio Martinelli (1992). A remarkable study on Italian historical films is Maria Wyke (1997).

14. G. P. Brunetta has shown how the most important production house of the time, Cines (Rome), was financially dependent on Banco di Roma, a banking institution controlled by leading national industrial groups and by the government. Not surprisingly, Cines's historical-spectacular productions were timed to coincide with the Italian 1911 military campaign in Libya, which occurred under the imperialist pressures of industrial and commercial interest groups. The construction and shaping of a proud national ideology through propaganda was then a compelling cultural necessity that affected from within the emerging film industry. See G. P. Brunetta (1993: 170–71). An insightful examination of *Romanità* in *Cabiria* and other silent historical films is in Giovanni Calendoli (1967: 63–111). A fundamental discussion on the nationalistic ideology of the historical films of the 1910s is Alphonse Cugier (1979: 120–30).

15. For an overview of serial production in Europe and in Italy, read Monica Dall'Asta (1999: 277–323). Italian cinema also produced serial thrillers such as those with Za-La-Mort (1914–18) as protagonist, but their success was a replication of French models and did not initiate a lasting domestic production. The term "athletic-acrobatic" was coined by film historian Mario Verdone (1971).

16. See on this subject Renzo Renzi (1975).

17. Useful filmographies of the genre are in Vittorio Martinelli and Mario Quargnolo (1981). For more specific analysis of the genre's cultural reverberations, see Alberto Farassino and Tatti Sanguineti (1983) and Monica Dall'Asta (1992).

18. The very name, "Maciste," was one of D'Annunzio's few actual contributions to the film, despite the fact that Itala Film advertised that the famous Italian *vate* had written the film's story and dialogue. Evidence documenting D'Annunzio's choice of the name "Maciste" exists, although it was the director, Giovanni Pastrone, who racialized the character. In a letter sent between August and early September 1913 by Giovanni Pastrone to Gabriele D'Annunzio, Pastrone comments on the names devised by the Italian poet for *Cabiria*'s characters. "I would like to thank you for

your notes and for the names, which I esteem splendid. Allow me only to remind you that in *Quo Vadis?* there is a character named *Eunice.* Don't you fear for our *Eunoa?* *Maciste* is well picked, but we would need to find for him a different nationality. I made him mulatto." The letter, part of the "Correspondence between Giovanni Pastrone and Gabriele D'Annunzio," is preserved at the Fondazione "Il Vittoriale degli Italiani" (Gardone Riviera) and has been published in Paolo Cherchi Usai (1986: 75).

19. Interestingly, Dall'Asta has argued that what is most typical of Italian serials is the process of identification with the actors or actresses more than with the characters they play. Bartolomeo Pagano, who played Maciste, had been a dock worker. His distinctive working-class background, in conjunction with his screen persona, made him widely popular with Italian audiences. Cf. Dall'Asta (1999: 313).

20. In *Sansone contro i filistei* (Pasquali & C., 1918), for instance, the opposition is repositioned in the Middle East, and both Arabs and Jews are cast in this externalized role.

21. Ella Shohat (1991: 43) refers to "rescue fantasies."

22. Martinelli and Quargnolo (1981: 10).

23. For instance, the filmography of Luciano Albertini's character, Sansone, clearly indicates the presence of circus, sport, and even the carnival among the physical and performative references of the genre. Between 1919 and 1921, some of Albertini's films were *Sansone e la ladra di atleti* (Albertini Film, 1919), *Sansone burlone* (Albertini Film, 1920), and *Sansone l'acrobata del Kolossal* (Albertini Film, 1920).

24. Unfortunately, film's transition to sound has not gained appropriate attention within the scholarship of Italian cinema. For general overviews of this topic, see Mary Lea Bandy (1989) and Christian Belaygue (1988). For a summary of the European situation, see Alberto Boschi (1999: 395–427). A rare systematic discussion of the Italian case is Riccardo Redi (1986). I have dealt with this issue in terms of film culture (but not in relation to Italian imperialism) in G. Bertellini (2001).

25. The Neapolitan film company Lombardo Film, for instance, established by Gustavo Lombardo in 1917, avoided the debacle of Italian cinema of the 1920s because it refused to align itself with U.C.I. and its standard productions. As a result, Neapolitan street melodramas, with their vernacular intertitles and their emphasis on songs in dialect, did not fade away in the 1920s. The linguistic policies of fascism and the transition to sound, however, trampled the production of these films. For an overview of Neapolitan koiné in cinema and its relationship to the rest of Italian film production, see Adriano Aprà (1993); for an original discussion of one particular production company, Notari Films, see Giuliana Bruno (1993).

26. Although Bollati never mentions cinema, his essays on photography and Italy's nineteenth- and twentieth-century culture have been a constant inspiration for this chapter. See his "L'Italiano" (The Italian) and "Il modo di vedere italiano (Note su fotografia e storia)" (The Italian way of seeing: Notes on history and photography), both in G. Bollati (1983: 34–123 and 124–78). The two essays had previously been published in G. Bollati (1972: 951–1022 and 1979: 3–55, respectively).

27. Until the late 1920s, in fact, Italy was still a nation where the vast majority of the population spoke local dialects. From the early 1930s, however, the government made strenuous efforts to prohibit the use of local idioms in schools, the press, ra-

dio, novels, and film intertitles, since dialects were deemed to be signs of cultural backwardness and political resistance. As language historian Tullio De Mauro argued, literacy, which had reached an average of 80 percent by 1931, did not imply an actual use of the Italian language, only a potential capacity. Still, in the early 1930s the Southern regions had an illiteracy rate of about 40 percent. (De Mauro 1963: 99 and 91; cf. De Mauro 1991: 135–44). On the Italianization of film titles written in dialect, see Sergio Raffaelli (1992: 64–86).

28. For a discussion of the "operatic" in Italian cinema, and specifically in Blasetti and Visconti, see Marcia Landy (1996: 107–50). On Visconti's use of silence, sound, and music, see G. Bertellini (1997: 11–19).

29. For an analysis of the language spoken on radio programs, see Gianni Isola (1990); an excellent analysis of Mussolini's phonic-rhythmical language (often utterly de-semanticized) is in Erasmo Leso (1978); for the evolution of Italian theater, see Stefano De Matteis (1980); on the visual and musical rhetorics of the state-controlled journalism, see Mario Isnenghi (1979: 175–85); on the nationalistic instrumentality of opera and the vast popularity of songs between the wars, see, respectively, Giovanni Morelli (1996) and Emilio Franzina (1996).

30. Marcia Landy (1998: 195).

31. The value of the film's sound score was noted at the time. Comparing *Lo squadrone bianco*'s music to other films, the composer Antonio Veretti (1937: 307) noted, "Every time the problem emerges in different ways. For instance, in *Scarpe al sole* [ICI, 1935] I composed an atmospheric score, without a single main theme, whereas for *Squadrone bianco* there was the necessity of a single theme, which is the march on the desert."

32. Only one Arab character speaks in the film: the servant and translator El Fennek, played by an Italian actor in blackface, Cesare Polacco.

33. Marcia Landy (1998: 192).

34. The film raised bitter controversy over its narrative strategy of depicting acts of patriotism performed by former smugglers. The criticism—"why this obstinate tendency to have patriotism emerging out of felony?"—was voiced by the film critic of *Il Tevere*, a Roman newspaper, and refuted by Luigi Freddi, head of Direzione Generale di Cinematografia. Freddi publicly defended the film against what he considered the critics' and censors' insensibility, by simply pairing *Il grande appello*'s realism and audacity with renowned masterpieces such as King Vidor's *The Big Parade* (1925). See Luigi Freddi (1994 [1949]: 163–68). For a broader discussion of the relationship between the fascist regime and Italian colonial films, see Gian Piero Brunetta and Jean A. Gili (1990: 50–58).

35. Interestingly, these films show that it is on the front or during military emergencies that the use of dialects holds an aura of authentic Italianness. Cf. Valentina Ruffin and Patrizia D'Agostino (1997: 106 ff).

36. The appellation of *La Gazzetta del Popolo* is possibly a play on and a reference to Mussolini's *Il Popolo d'Italia*, although at the time there were several newspapers in Italy with the same name (in Turin and Padua, for instance). I am grateful to Philip Cannistraro for discussions on this point.

37. Arnheim (1936: 274–75).

38. Mario Soldati in Jean A. Gili (1990: 68).

WORKS CITED

Anderson, Benedict. [1983] 1991. *Imagined Communities: Reflections on the Origin and Spread of Nationalism.* London: Verso.

Aprà, Adriano, ed. 1993. *Napoletana: Images of a City.* Milano: Fabbri Editori.

Arnheim, Rudolph. 1936. *Radio.* Trans. Margaret Ludwig and Herbert Read. London: Faber and Faber.

Bandy, Mary Lea, ed. 1989. *The Dawn of Sound.* New York: MoMA.

Belaygue, Christian, ed. 1988. *Le Passage du muet au parlant.* Toulose: Cinémathèque de Toulouse / Editions Milan.

Bernardini, Aldo. 1983. "La presa di Roma, prototipo del cinema italiano." In *La meccanica del visibile: Il cinema delle origini in Europa,* ed. Alberto Costa, 118–27. Firenze: La Casa Usher.

———. 1991. *Archivio del cinema italiano.* Vol. 1, *Il cinema muto, 1905–1931.* Roma: Anica.

Bernardini, Aldo, and Vittorio Martinelli, eds. 1979. *Il cinema italiano degli anni venti.* Roma: Cineteca Nazionale–CNC.

Bertellini, Giorgio. 1997. "A Battle *d'Arrière Garde:* Notes on Decadence in Luchino Visconti's *Death in Venice." Film Quarterly* 50, no. 4: 11–19.

———. 1999. "Epica spettacolare e splendore del vero: L'influenza del cinema storico italiano in America (1908–1915)." In *Storia del cinema mondiale,* vol. 2, ed. Gian Piero Brunetta, 227–65. Torino: Einaudi.

———. 2002. "Dubbing l'*Arte Muta:* Poetic Layerings Around Italian Cinema's Transition to Sound." In *Re-viewing Fascism: Italian Cinema, 1922–1943,* ed. Piero Garofalo and Jacqueline Reich, 30–82. Bloomington: Indiana University Press.

Boschi, Alberto. 1999. "Il passaggio dal muto al sonoro in Europa." In *Storia del cinema mondiale,* vol. 1, ed. G. P. Brunetta, 395–427. Torino: Einaudi.

Bollati, Giulio. 1972. *Storia d'Italia.* Vol. 1, *I Caratteri originali.* Turin: Einaudi.

———. 1979. *Storia d'Italia: Annali 2.* Vol. 1, *L'immagine fotografica, 1845–1945.* Torino: Einaudi.

———. 1983. *L'Italiano: Il carattere nazionale come storia e come invenzione,* 34–123 and 124–78. Torino: Einaudi.

Brunetta, Gian Piero. 1993. *Storia del cinema italiano: Il cinema muto 1895–1929.* Roma: Editori Riuniti.

———, ed. 1999a. *Storia del cinema mondiale.* Vol. 1, *L'Europa, miti, luoghi, divi.* Torino: Einaudi.

———, ed. 1999b. *Storia del cinema mondiale.* Vol. 2, *Gli Stati Uniti.* Torino: Einaudi.

Brunetta, Gian Piero, and Jean A. Gili. 1990. *L'Ora d'Africa del cinema italiano, 1911–1989: Materiali di lavoro.* Rovereto/Trento: Provincia Autonoma di Trento.

Bruno, Giuliana. 1993. *Streetwalking on a Ruined Map: Cultural Theory and the City Films of Elvira Notari.* Princeton, N.J.: Princeton University Press.

Calendoli, Giovanni. 1967. *Materiali per una storia del cinema italiano.* Parma: Maccari.

Cherchi Usai, Paolo, ed. 1986. *Giovanni Pastrone: Gli anni d'oro del cinema a Torino.* Torino: UTET.

Cugier, Alphonse. 1979. "Discours de l'Idéologie: Idéologie du Discours (A propos des films italiens des années 10)." *Les Cahiers de la Cinémathèque* nos. 26–27: 120–30. Special issue on "Le cinéma muet italien," ed. Jean A. Gili.

Dall'Asta, Monica. 1992. *Un Cinéma musclé.* Disnée, Belgium: Yellow Now.

——. 1999. "La diffusione del film a episodi in Europa." In *Storia del cinema mondiale,* vol. 1, ed. G. P. Brunetta, 277–323. Torino: Einaudi.

De Mauro, Tullio. 1963. *Storia linguistica dell'Italia unita.* Roma-Bari: Laterza.

——. 1991. "Alcuni appunti su Gramsci linguista." In *Gramsci e la modernità: Letteratura e politica fra Ottocento e Novecento,* ed. Valerio Calzolaio, 135–44. Napoli: CUEN.

De Matteis, Stefano, et al., eds. 1980. *Follie del Varietà: Vicende, memorie personaggi, 1890–1970.* Milano: Feltrinelli.

Dyer, Richard. 1997. *White.* London: Routledge.

Farassino, Alberto, and Tatti Sanguineti, eds. 1983. *Gli uomini forti.* Milano: Mazzotta.

Franzina, Emilio. 1996. "Inni e canzoni." In *I luoghi della memoria: Simboli e miti dell'Italia Unita,* ed. Mario Isnenghi, 115–62. Roma-Bari: Laterza.

Freddi, Luigi. [1949] 1994. *Il Cinema: Il governo dell'immagine.* Roma: CSC.

Gentile, Emilio. 1996. *Il culto del littorio: La sacralizzazione della politica nell'Italia Fascista.* Rome-Bari: Laterza, 1993. Translated by Keith Botsford as *The Sacralization of Politics in Fascist Italy.* Cambridge, Mass.: Harvard University Press.

Gili, Jean A. 1981. *Stato fascista e cinematografia.* Roma: Bulzoni.

——. 1990. *Le cinéma italien à l'ombre des faisceaux (1922–1945).* Perpignan: Institut Jean Vigo.

Hay, James. 1987. *The Passing of the Rex: Popular Film Culture in Fascist Italy.* Bloomington: Indiana University Press.

Isola, Gianni. 1990. *Abbassa la tua radio, per favore: Storia dell'ascolto radiofonico nell'Italia fascista.* Firenze: La Nuova Italia.

Isnenghi, Mario. 1979. *Intellettuali militanti e intellettuali funzionari: Appunti sulla cultura fascista.* Torino: Einaudi.

——, ed. 1996. *I luoghi della memoria: Simboli e miti dell'Italia Unita.* Roma-Bari: Laterza.

Landy, Marcia. 1996. *Cinematic Uses of the Past.* Minneapolis: University of Minnesota Press.

——. 1998. *The Folklore of Consensus: Theatricality in the Italian Cinema 1930–1943.* Albany: State University of New York Press.

Leso, Erasmo, et al. 1978. *La lingua italiana e il fascismo.* Bologna: Consorzio Provinciale Pubblica Lettura.

Manenti, Luca, Nicolas Monti, and Giorgio Nicodemi, eds. 1979. *Luca Comerio: Fotografo e cineasta.* Milano: Electa Editrice.

Martinelli, Vittorio. 1978. "I Gastarbeiter fra le due guerre." *Bianco & Nero* 39, no. 3.

Martinelli, Vittorio, and Mario Quargnolo. 1981. *Maciste & Co.: I giganti buoni del muto italiano.* Gemona del Friuli: Edizioni Cinepopolare.

——. 1992. "Cineasti italiani in Germania fra le due guerre." In *Cinema Italiano in Europa, 1907–1929,* ed. V. Martinelli, 131–69. Roma: Associazione italiana per le ricerche di storia del cinema.

Morelli, Giovanni. 1996. "L'opera." In *I luoghi della memoria: Simboli e miti dell'Italia Unità,* ed. Mario Isnenghi, 43–113. Roma-Bari: Laterza.

Morrison, Toni. 1992. *Playing in the Dark: Whiteness and the Literary Imagination.* Cambridge, Mass: Harvard University Press.

Pinkus, Karen. 1995. *Bodily Regimes: Italian Advertising under Fascism.* Minneapolis: University of Minnesota Press.

Quargnolo, Mario. 1964. "Un periodo oscuro del cinema italiano: 1925–1929." *Bianco & Nero* 25, nos. 4–5: 16–32.

———. 1986. *La parola ripudiata: L'incredibile storia dei film stranieri in Italia nei primi anni del sonoro.* Gemona, Udine: La Cineteca del Friuli.

Raffaelli, Sergio. 1992. *La lingua filmata: Didascalie e dialoghi nel cinema italiano.* Firenze: Casa Editrice Le Lettere.

Redi, Riccardo. 1986. *Ti parlerò . . . d'amor: Cinema italiano fra muto e sonoro.* Torino: ERI.

———. 1999. *Cinema muto italiano (1896–1920).* Roma: Biblioteca di Bianco & Nero.

Renzi, Renzo. 1975. *Il fascismo involontario e altri scritti.* Bologna: Cappelli.

Ruffin, Valentina, and Patrizia D'Agostino. 1997. *Dialoghi di regime: La lingua del cinema degli anni trenta.* Roma: Bulzoni.

Said, Edward. 1978. *Orientalism.* New York: Vintage.

Shohat, Ella. 1991. "Imaging Terra Incognita: The Disciplinary Gaze of Empire." *Public Culture* 3, no. 2 (spring): 41–70.

Verdone, Mario. 1971. "Il film atletico e acrobatico." *Centrofilm* 17.

Veretti, Antonio. 1937. *Cinema* 33: 307.

Wyke, Maria. 1997. *Projecting the Past: Ancient Rome, Cinema, and History.* New York: Routledge.

Black Shirts/Black Skins

Fascist Italy's Colonial Anxieties and Lo Squadrone Bianco

Cecilia Boggio

The experience of colonialism since the early modern period has been an experience of disproportions of both numbers and size. The desire to encounter and to master a vast "open" territory, which was in the eyes of the European colonizers grotesquely disproportionate in size and almost unimaginably densely populated, fueled the two most urgent anxieties of colonialism: crowd anxiety and space anxiety. A colony is by definition a human space, even in its loosest meaning of a body of people settled in a new territory. Thus, in the colonial experience, crowds and space are necessarily linked.

In the case of the Italian colonization of East Africa, the anxiety of disproportions of numbers and space assumes a heightened relevance for at least two reasons. From a factual point of view, when Mussolini proclaimed the conquest of Ethiopia and the birth of the Italian empire on May 9, 1936, two-thirds of the Ethiopian territory was still, and would continue to remain, in the hands of the indigenous populations. This is significant to the extent that the "African films" authorized and sponsored by the Italian fascist regime celebrate not so much the actual colonization of the East African territory (in fact, such a colonization never really occurred, at least not in the way that the regime wanted the Italian people to believe), but rather the colonizing power of cinema.[1] The truth is that Italians were controlling Ethiopia only with and through cinematic fantasies. As Ruth Ben-Ghiat has pointed out, these films not only functioned as symbols for taking possession, but they actually took possession of a territory and its subjects in the only way they could, that is, by reproducing them in visual form (109–44). From a more symbolic point of view, crowd anxiety and space anxiety were particularly fueled by the importance attributed by the regime to the acquisition of African colonies. The colonization of East Africa was not only

Italy's attempt to catch up with its neighbors (France in particular) and to end its inferiority complex resulting from its lack of colonies. It was also the solution to Italy's demographic problem and the consequential problem of unemployment and the general discontent that followed.[2] The conquest of East Africa was part of the attempt, which had started with the conquest of Libya in 1911, to construct a new Italian "epic" space. It followed in the footsteps (though in the opposite direction, from Rome to Carthage rather than from Carthage to Rome) of Italy's founding father, Aeneas, and emulated the Roman "epic" conquest of the Republic of Carthage, which gave Rome full dominion over the Mediterranean sea.

The narrative film *Lo squadrone bianco,* directed by Augusto Genina and released in 1936—the year in which the film won the Coppa Mussolini as the best Italian film at the Venice Arts Festival—well represents the Italian "anxieties" about both the African indigenous populations and the vast desert territory. In the film, indigenous crowds and the desert space appear in two aspects: as threat and as promise, as enormous dangers to be controlled and as vast resources to be harnessed. Both aspects require keeping the colonized crowds in check. This is a necessary condition for establishing the perimeter of a stable and consequently manageable colony in an unknown territory that was not delimited or circumscribed by fixed boundaries.

Fascist policy toward the mass-crowd phenomenon is strictly derived from Gustave Le Bon's late-nineteenth-century crowd psychology, and his theories also perfectly fit colonialist discourse. According to Le Bon, crowds are primitive, essentialized, feminized, incapable of reason, fetishistic, and in need of a leader (32). He developed the idea of the "psychological" or "organized" crowd, which could be collectively surrendered to a leader more completely than any singular conscious personality. A random congregation of a group of people without a precise purpose or aim does not make a "psychological" crowd. The main characteristic of this type of crowd is the orientation of feelings and thoughts in the same "direction." The crowd's members become like the cells of a single body, subject to the contagion of every sentiment and act expressed by others. Shedding individual inhibitions, each member becomes enormously suggestible. In other words, each singular conscious personality blends into a "collective mind" (45–46).

Fascist behavior toward crowds derives mainly from Le Bon's theories.[3] This behavior corresponds to the previously mentioned ambivalence in the perception of the indigenous crowds, as either threat or promise, that emerges from *Lo squadrone bianco.* Fascism's intent is to mobilize oceanic "masses" of human beings. This (domesticated) "mass" that fascism outwardly celebrates is Le Bon's "psychological" crowd, or, in Klaus Theweleit's words, the crowd that is "strictly formed, poured into a system of dams" (4). Fascism, however, simultaneously disdains "crowds." The "crowd" that fascism despises is formless, purposeless, and consequently uncontrollable. To this "crowd" fascism attributes "all that is flowing, slimy, teeming" (Theweleit 4), and it is dangerous because potentially rebellious and revolutionary. As an example, a potentially dangerous and corrupted crowd was the masses that the Italian Communist Party organized to protest the Ethiopian campaign and Italian imperialism in Africa. This crowd was frightening because it was seen as "a carrier of political and social anarchy" (Ben-Ghiat 112).[4]

In addition, from Gustave Le Bon comes a confirmation of my thesis that crowds and space are two interrelated phenomena. His theories, summarized in his highly influential book *The Crowd: A Study in the Popular Mind,* were mainly the elaboration of a scientific analysis of the "spatial" event of the Paris Commune of May 1871. These theories, together with the production of a colonialist class and the construction of a colonial space, had considerably fueled the changing notion of space in the second half of the nineteenth century.[5] The Commune was mainly a "spatial" event because of the fundamental role played by the city space in both the disputes and the fighting of May 1871. As Kristin Ross argues, a consciousness of space and the consequent reorganization of its revolutionary potential were essential to the initial success and establishment of the Paris Commune.[6] In a similar way, one can observe that the pairing of crowd and space plays a very important role in any colonial enterprise. A colony is a "spatial" event insofar as it is constituted by a land to be conquered and (a crowd of) people to be subjugated.

There is another reason that one might consider crowds and space as two interconnected phenomena. As I have previously pointed out, keeping colonized crowds in check is a necessary condition for establishing fixed and stable boundaries for the space that colonizers conquer. From this perspective, what seems to be the colonial space of *Lo squadrone bianco,* namely the desert, can be considered the equivalent, in spatial terms, of the rebellious and dangerous crowd that fascism despises and fears. The invisible rebels who threaten the Italian colony and need to be defeated once and for all by the White Squadron share many characteristics with the territory that, perhaps not by chance, they occupy. Indeed, in the eyes of the colonizers, the space of the desert is as illogical, unfathomable, indefinite, and perpetually moving as the "invisible" rebels who threaten the Italian colony of Libya in the film.

My purpose in this chapter is to propose an analysis of *Lo squadrone bianco* based on what I have defined as the Italian colonizers' ambivalent perception of crowd and space as both threat and promise. The title of the film reflects the importance given by the director, Augusto Genina, and the "producer" of the film, the fascist regime, to the White Squadron ("Lo squadrone bianco"). This army of exotically dressed (in the Italians' opinion) "white" soldiers constitutes the visible "psychological" crowd on the screen. Unlike the director, however, I want to focus on the invisible "African" crowd (which is virtually absent from the screen) and the desert space it occupies. Furthermore, I intend to focus on what I consider the antithesis of the African crowd and the desert: the figure of the cavalry lieutenant Mario Ludovici.

The film's narrative can be divided into three sections: the bourgeois prologue, the colonial segment, and the epilogue. The character of Mario Ludovici is the *trait d'union* among them. The prologue involves a traditional story of troubled love set in an urban environment: the prologue ends as Mario leaves the house of his cruel lover, Cristiana, after a violent quarrel. The colonial segment begins with Lieutenant Ludovici arriving at an Italian military outpost in the middle of the Libyan desert and ends with the lieutenant returning from the victorious mission after the White Squadron defeats the indigenous rebels. Finally, the epilogue shows Mario's confrontation with Cristiana and the bourgeois world he left behind. It is during this confrontation that Mario announces his decision to assume the command of the White Squadron and replace Captain Sant'Elia, the fascist hero who had been killed during the final battle against the rebels.[7]

By focusing on the central, and most famous, section of the film, critics have often interpreted the main character, the cavalry lieutenant Mario Ludovici, as the subject of a traditional fascist drama of male conversion. In *Lo squadrone bianco,* the drama is based on the antagonism between Captain Sant'Elia, the psychological "surrogate father," and Lieutenant Ludovici, the "prodigal son," and the triumph of fascist homosocial relations founded on the exclusion of the feminine figure, in this film represented by Mario's lover, Cristiana.[8] Instead, I look at the young lieutenant as "a builder of dams, a constructor of space" (Theweleit 6), as someone who constructs the colonial "outer" space as well as his own "inner" space. In the film, one sees the twenty-three-year-old lieutenant trying to construct a "stable" colonial space. However, the space that Mario tries to build is not merely a geographical space (the desert and its inhabitants); it is also a mental and corporeal space, a metaphorical land to be appropriated and mastered. From this perspective, the colonial segment of the film can be viewed not only as the fascist dream of stable African colonies for the new Italian empire, but also as the main character's attempt to impose fixed boundaries onto his internal space. Indeed, Mario's psychological transformation throughout the film can be read as an internal colonization that presents deep structural parallels with the external historical event of colonization.

"WHITE" SOLDIERS, BLACK REBELS, AND THE ITALIAN FANTASY OF INCORPORATION

In *Lo squadrone bianco* what one clearly perceives is a colonial authority sustained both by its own confidence, that is the confidence of colonialism, and by the use of military force. From this point of view the film presents two different African crowds: the Libyan troops at the service of the Italian colonizers and the dangerous rebels that threaten Italian control of the territory. Although one never gets to see "those damned rebels" ("quei maledetti ribelli"), they form, throughout the film, a quite disturbing image of the colonial encounter between the Italian "black shirts" and the African "black skins." This crowd anxiety stems from the threat posed by a crowd of natives who know how to move around in the desert and are, moreover, invisible. In fact, this unseeable, hostile, and fanatical African crowd cannot be controlled without the use of military force and the infliction of severe casualties on the Italian troops, as the final scene of the film, and sole battle scene, shows. Even during this battle, however, the crowd of rebels remains quite invisible. One does not really see the rebels as a crowd, but only as fragments. Similar crowds—as hostile as those in *Lo squadrone bianco* but not as invisible—emerge from other colonial narrative films of the 1930s. *Luciano Serra, Pilota,* for instance, presents a number of guerrilla warfare scenes between Italians and Africans and a scene where black-skinned Abyssinian men with ferocious expressions assault a train full of Italian soldiers. Likewise, in *Sotto la croce del sud* one sees a large crowd of savage spear-wielding Africans trying to track Simone, the Italian villain, into the jungle.

Lo squadrone bianco portrays not only a rebellious crowd but also a "psychological" crowd, the type of crowd that fascism celebrates. As in the documentaries sponsored by the fascist regime,[9] what one perceives by observing the Libyan troops at the service of the Italian military leaders is a colonial authority that depends on a cultural sovereignty that seems to be induced by a state of fascination akin to that of hypnosis. As the battle scene of *Lo squadrone bianco* demonstrates, a crowd can be defeated only by another crowd. However, a crowd is, instead, easily persuaded by a single individual, a small group of people, or an idea. Garth Jowett and Victoria O'Donnell define persuasion as "a complex, continuing, interactive process in which a sender and a receiver are linked by symbols, verbal and nonverbal, through which the persuader attempts to influence the persuadee to adopt a change in a given attitude or behavior because the persuadee has had perceptions enlarged or changed" (24). As a consequence, a fundamental element of persuasion can undoubtedly be what Le Bon calls "prestige," a word that is repeated over and over not only in the documentaries but also in Mussolini's speeches *(prestigio).*[10] With "prestige"—the display of a high degree of self-confidence—the colonizer is able to wield a (presumed) cultural and racial supremacy in such a way as to dominate the minds of the colonized. According to Le Bon, moreover, colonial troops, being black, "had practically no mind at all, so the orders of their officers could pass almost directly into their consciousness" (50). Thus, the troops are easy to influence and manipulate.

A confirmation of the importance for the colonizers of exerting "prestige" on the colonized comes from a conversation that Captain Sant'Elia has with one of his officers concerning Lieutenant Ludovici. Although he expresses doubt about having to undertake a mission in the desert with a totally inexperienced lieutenant, he maintains that "Qui è la suggestione e l'esempio del capo che conta, non il taglio dell'abito" ("The cut of the shirt is not important here. What really counts here is the suggestion and the example of the chief"). This form of psychological domination, as Le Bon remarks, entirely paralyses the critical faculties of the subjugated and fills their souls with astonishment and respect (130). As a consequence, the Libyan native troops seem most of the time to be hypnotized by the colonizers' "prestige," usually personified by the leader. For this reason they can be described as dormant or, as Elias Canetti puts it, as a "stagnating" crowd, that is, a passive, closely compressed crowd that keeps still because it is not quite sure of its unity (34). This state of hypnosis is conveyed in the film not only by the "white" squadron's total submission to the orders of its "white" leader, Captain Sant'Elia, but also by the scenes of the White Squadron's procession in the desert. The scene of the camel-riding troops slowly advancing across the dunes is accompanied by the music of bagpipes and is intercut with backlit images of the sky, the horizon, and the broad desert. In these scenes the movement and trajectory of the White Squadron indeed appears unconscious.

Lo squadrone bianco is the only "African film" of the 1930s filmed on location in the Libyan desert. Since the Italian conquest of Libya happened in 1911, why shoot a film in Libya in the heyday of the Ethiopian campaign? The decision to film in the Libyan desert may have been made for practical reasons. From the proclamation of the Italian Empire of Ethiopia in 1936 to its end in 1941, the Ethiopians had been in a state of perpetual revolt. The insurgent populace led Mussolini to practice a "policy of terror" ("una politica del terrore"; Rochat 168), to which the indigenous populations often responded by massacring the Italian settlers. It would thus have been too dangerous to film in Ethiopia. Moreover, the decision to film in Libya could also be related to the notions of "blackness" that were circulating in Italian culture in the early twentieth century. First of all, the Africans that one sees in the film are Libyans—light-skinned African Arabs—with much more "Aryan" bodies than the Ethiopians—dark-skinned sub-Saharans— against whom the Italians were fighting at that time. The different "degree of blackness" of Ethiopians and Libyans played a fundamental role in the Italian construction of the black "Other." From this point of view, the light-skinned Libyans who, moreover, wear white uniforms, serve the significant purpose of helping in the creation of the "exotic Africa." In other words, as Karen Pinkus maintains, what would most appeal to colonizers is not the quality of blackness but the aestheticization of blackness because it helped normalize white domination (37).

Two other sequences of *Lo squadrone bianco* help in the construction of the "exotic Africa" for the genteel Italian public.[11] One perceives exotic African objects and drawings in Cristiana's apartment in the "bourgeois" prologue of the film. Her apartment, whose interior decoration is extremely rationalist and functional, gives a glimpse of one of the ways in which exotic cultures can be consumed. When the camera follows her while she walks from the living room to her bedroom, she seems to guide the viewers on a tour of her collection of African art. African objects are exhibited as if they were in a museum. Particularly interesting is the wall that divides the living area from the sleeping area of the house. Whereas the lower part of the wall is made of bricks, the upper part consists of a glass cabinet very similar to a museum display cabinet containing African artifacts.

Exoticism also informs the behavior of the group of eighteen tourists (of whom Cristiana is one) that in the film's epilogue arrives at the fort and witnesses the return of the White Squadron from its mission. One of the tourists, after having himself photographed in front of some palm trees, comments that the story of the squadron mysteriously lost in the desert that finally returns led by only one officer sounds "really novelistic" ("La storia dello squadrone perduto misteriosamente che ritorna con un solo ufficiale, sembra proprio un romanzo!"). Their involvement in an African "fictional" adventure (as characters who witness the return of the mysterious lost squadron) as part of their cruise package offers them (and the viewers) the vicarious experience of participating in the exotic life of the colony in more than one sense. Not only does the experience indulge the senses so that the visitors can feel the African "poetry, warrior strength, and epic" ("la poesia, la forza guerriera, l'epopea, l'Africa"), as one of the inhabitants of the fort claims, and offer pleasure, but it also attempts to transform the visitors and make them into Italian colonizers. Secondly, the Libyans' lightly colored bodies arouse a certain degree of "comfort and domesticity" that, in the eye of the white public, has the function of normalizing white domination and helping the construction of an optimistic, albeit fictional, colonialist vision. This is so because North African bodies did not have the same physiognomical "deformities" as sub-Saharan African bodies. Features such as a flattened nose, an angular skull, enormous development of the maxillaries and the zygomata (prognathism), fleshy lips, tufted and wiry hair and darker pigmentation of the skin were, according to the so-called racist scientists of the fascist regime, atavistic, that is, belonging to primitive humanity, and shared by animals (such as apes), Negroes, and criminals.[12] Upon careful analysis, one realizes that the only Libyan character that really communicates with the "white" officers, El Fennek (played by the Italian actor Cesare

Polacco), has a painted face and speaks Italian like a stereotypical African, that is, using only verbs in the infinitive mood. Captain Sant'Elia appoints the "civilized" El Fennek as the young lieutenant's orderly ("attendente") because he is the only Libyan soldier who speaks "an understandable Italian" ("un italiano possibile"). He is a soldier who also, when it is needed, serves cups of coffee in the morning and often reassures the Italian soldiers that they are all "in the hands of God" ("siamo nelle mani di Dio").

The character of El Fennek should not be overlooked. On the contrary, he should be given particular consideration because he represents one of the (stereo)typical images of Italian colonialism in Africa, the *ascaro*. The Arab word *ascaro* means "soldier." In the context of Western colonization *ascaro* refers specifically to the indigenous soldier in the Italian colonial troops in Eritrea, Somaliland, and Libya. From the white uniforms that the *ascari* wore comes the most literal meaning of the title *Lo squadrone bianco*. Particularly during the fascist era, it was in the image of the exotic "white" *ascaro* that Italy celebrated its colonial authority and its civilizing capacity. This image often appears in colonial political journalism and documentary images such as newsreels, photo essays, and ethnographic exhibits. In the transformation of the seminaked savage warrior, primitively armed and cruel, into a soldier wearing a uniform—a white uniform—and subject to discipline and fighting in the service of "civilization," Italy celebrates with paternalistic superiority not so much its capacity to dominate but rather its capacity to "elevate" uncivilized people. It then uses the image of this "white" soldier to justify and legitimize its expansionistic campaign in Africa. The *ascaro*, in other words, fits Homi Bhabha's idea of "colonial mimicry," an action of reform, regulation, and discipline. Mimicry, as an effect of persuasion through "prestige" exercised by the colonizers on the colonized, is one of the most effective strategies of colonial authority. As Bhabha points out in "Of Mimicry and Man," colonial mimicry is "the desire for a reformed, recognisable Other, as a subject of a difference that is almost the same, but not quite," to which I would also add "and not white." Colonial mimicry, as a consequence, "appropriates" the Other while pointing at it as the locus of the "inappropriate" because it is "the representation of a difference that is itself a process of disavowal" (86). Thus mimicry, while constructing a fantasy of incorporation that is a collective experience of "nation-ness" (Anderson 4), at the same time visualizes power. In *Lo squadrone bianco* the ambivalence of colonial mimicry is acted out not only by the *ascaro* El Fennek but also by the "psychological crowd" on the screen, the White Squadron, which is indeed a troop of *ascari*.

In what follows I will focus on the crowd of indigenous rebels that constitutes a threat for the Italian colony of Libya and that, contrary to the White Squadron, is virtually absent from the screen: absent, but not nonexistent. Although invisible, this threatening crowd is very much in evidence in the speeches of the Italian officers at the fort. Moreover, this crowd is also present in its spatial representation: the vast open space that it occupies, which seems to be the colonial space of the film, the desert. I argue that in the film the illogical, unfathomable, and perpetually moving desert is not only a geographical space and a symbol for the crowd of African rebels, but it is also the main character's mental and corporeal space, his erupted 'interior," as he physically engages with the geography of the colony.

COLONIAL AND PERSONAL SPATIAL GEOGRAPHIES

The first futurist/ic sequence is of fundamental importance not only for the economy of the film, but particularly for my reading of Lieutenant Mario Ludovici's colonial adventure in the Libyan desert as a "spatial story" (de Certeau 111).[13] The film begins with a shot of a speeding car in the darkness from the driver's point of view, which, incidentally, invites the spectators to fully involve themselves in what they are going to watch. Then, there is a close-up shot of the driver, Mario, hurtling forward. He seems entrapped not only by the rigorous framing of the camera but also by the frame created by the windshield of his car. Entrapped by whom or by what? One sees the road, the headlights in the foggy night, and a level crossing. Then, after an abrupt break, Mario's situation suddenly becomes perfectly clear: he is entrapped in a glamorous bourgeois world and in a relationship with a well-off woman, Cristiana, who plays with him according to her moods. At times she seeks him out and at times she sends him away. Another abrupt break and now Mario, his image portrayed in a series of alternating cuts and then superimposed on a speedometer and then on a clock, is once again in his car racing in the darkness. In the next scene, one sees Mario in Africa where he arrives at night and gets out of a truck. This change of setting—from Mario racing in his car in Italy to his arrival in the Italian military outpost in Libya—is the result of a sudden cut in the editing. As a consequence of this cutting, Mario looks like someone who has been taken to the Libyan desert by a time machine rather than someone who has explicitly requested—as the film suggests—a transfer to a camel unit in the new Italian colony of Libya. Later in the film, Captain Sant'Elia will confirm the hypothesis that Mario seems to have been taken to Africa by a time machine when he angrily says of Mario: "These people tormented by who knows what. These people who jump into the water without being able to swim. What does he think he has come here for? To be an officer or a man fallen from the moon?" ("Questi tormentati da chissà che. Questi che si buttano nell'acqua senza saper nuotare. Che cosa crede di essere venuto a fare qui? L'ufficiale o l'uomo della luna?").

The pace of the editing of the colonial segment of the film is considerably different from that of the prologue. The sequences of both the White

Squadron's procession in the desert on the rebels' trail and the life of the soldiers at the Libyan fort are edited according to a very slow rhythm, with long takes. The prologue, on the other hand, depicting a bourgeois and urban life, is rapidly edited with many quick cuts and brief shots. If both Mario's agitated behavior and the fast editing of the opening sequence provoke a certain degree of disorientation in the viewers, it is because the film begins to portray the main character's anxiety about the space in which he finds himself entrapped. To begin untangling Mario's anxiety I borrow Kathleen Kirby's inherently spatial notion of "disassociation," which she believes refers

> not only to a detachment of subject from the world, but also to the deterioration of the internal ordering of subjectivity. . . . The internal-external relation breaks down, resulting in a degeneration of interior organization, and finally—one could imagine, in advanced stages—in a confusion of the external order too. . . . Foundations and frameworks crumble and things loop and circle and shift and spin: the inside flies to pieces and explodes outward, the outside melts and fragments, and elements from both sides drift freely across and indifferent boundary. (101–2)

This definition of "disassociation" is an interesting starting point for my analysis of Mario Ludovici as a constructor of both the colonial "outer" space and his own "inner" space. It suggests the necessity of an imbalance between internal and external space or, more specifically, between the internal space of the subject and the external space that the subject occupies. Indeed, Kirby's definition of "disassociation" seems to perfectly summarize Mario Ludovici's "spatial story."

In the crucial scene of the prologue, Mario bursts into Cristiana's apartment and, after a short and very intense quarrel, he almost strangles her. After that, one sees Mario racing in his car into the darkness and then suddenly arriving at the fort in Libya in the middle of the night. It is precisely at this point in the narrative that I see the sand of the desert, as well as the African rebels, turning into an embodiment of Mario's erupted "interior." The pivotal moment of the transformation is the aforementioned violent confrontation between the two lovers. In contrast to the traditional interpretation of this film—according to which Mario's "conversion" begins when he starts to become sick and loses consciousness in the middle of the desert—my reading of the film in psychoanalytic/cinematic terms places Mario's so-called conversion at the scene of the quarrel. Kirby suggests that a subject's "disassociation" from the outside may well come from being stuck in a situation or place that is at odds, sometimes violently, with the subject. I argue that it is during the violent confrontation with Cristiana that Mario, the subject, starts to disassociate himself from a hostile environment—the bourgeois world with its strictly assigned social order—in which he feels out of place. In psychoanalytic terms, this disassociation results in Mario's unconscious bursting the banks of the bourgeois-encoded forms of desires and fears. The products of the unconscious emerge no longer in the form of compromise formations but as "a product of the body, a substance which, once released, becomes ungovernable, combining itself with uncontrollable external masses and laying waste the boundaries of the body" (Theweleit 7). Not only does the internal space of the subject degenerate, break its boundaries, and explode outward, but it also blends with the external space so that the distinction between inside and outside ceases to exist. As a consequence, Mario begins to perceive the repressed production of his unconscious in a thoroughly objectified form: the colonial space.

What I have just described can be seen very clearly in cinematic terms beginning with the violent confrontation between Mario and Cristiana. When the quarrel between the lovers reaches its climax, Mario aggressively warns Cristiana that soon he will no longer be able to control his actions: "Be careful, Cristiana. I feel that I could do anything. Do you understand? Anything! I'm afraid of myself" ("Bada, Cristiana, mi sento capace di tutto. Capisci? Di tutto! Fo' paura a me stesso"). At this point the camera moves away from the lovers and focuses on the shadows on the wall behind them created by the African objects elegantly displayed in Cristiana's living room. These shadows are magnified to cover almost the entire wall. The walls of the room serve as a screen for the projection of a different story from the one that is told in Cristiana's living room. The "external" story shows that the love relationship between Mario and Cristiana is coming to an end. The gigantic shadows on the wall, on the contrary, tell Mario's "internal" story. Since in the next scene Mario will be arriving in Africa, the shadows seem to entice him away from the closed space of the bourgeois world out into the exterior, the colonial space. The boundaries that encode the bourgeois forms of desires, and of desiring, can no longer accommodate Mario's unconscious, and consequently it erupts without him being able to control it.

The black shadows on the wall can be perceived as Mario's "primitive" force that erupts from within and expresses itself as a separable entity completely divorced from his body. At this point, however, Mario has not yet realized what is happening. During the whole scene the shadows are behind him: he cannot see them. From my perspective, these shadows represent the need of Mario's inner drives to express themselves as an entity separate from the body. This need becomes the first and foremost justification to see both the display of primitive art in Cristiana's living room and the "primitive" African crowds in the "primitive" colonial territory of Libya/Ethiopia as an embodiment of the young lieutenant's "interior." In a previous scene Cristiana describes Mario as "exasperating" ("esasperante") and as someone who has "no limits"—or boundaries—because "he is too much in love" ("è troppo innamorato"). Her language of excess seems to signal that Mario's

Figure 7. Frame enlargements from *Lo squadrone bianco* (1936).

unconscious threatens to burst out. Immediately afterward, at the climax of the quarrel, one sees this happening, but Mario will fully realize it only after his arrival in Libya. There, he will perceive his "inner life" reified in the dangerous, savage rebels and the ungovernable space of the desert. Once at the fort the young lieutenant starts to hear other officers talking about the "damned rebels," but nobody, neither Mario nor the viewers, ever sees them. The crowd of African rebels in this film is not really a collection of human faces and forms but, rather, a sort of crowd effect created by the sand of the Sahara desert. This could be seen as an addendum to Elias Canetti's observations about "crowd symbols." Sand, according to Canetti, is a "crowd symbol," a collective unit that is not made up of men but is felt to be a crowd (75). In other words, one can argue that Mario's unconscious undergoes a further transformation—or conversion—as he physically engages with the geography of the colony. The colonial territory becomes a corporeal territory formed by Mario's erupted "interior."

The sand of the desert is a "crowd symbol" because it shares many characteristics with a crowd of enemies. These common traits illuminate the development of the narrative in *Lo squadrone bianco*. The sand of the desert, similar to the crowd of indigenous rebels, is hostile and aggressive. This is so not only because of its vastness and apparent boundlessness, but also because it consists of innumerable, small, homogeneous particles that present to man an almost unbeatable power. According to Canetti, "sand suffocates man as the sea does, but more maliciously because more slowly" (87). During the first of the two sandstorms that complicate the White Squadron's pursuit of the rebels, El Fennek tells Mario of the dangerousness of the sand. In broken Italian he advises Mario not to open his mouth until the end of the storm in order not to be consumed by the sand: "Close your lips, do not breathe sand. Sand consumes man as it consumes stones" ("Chiudi labbra, no respirare sabbia. Sabbia consumare uomini come consumare pietre").

Mario's relationship to the sand of the desert anticipates, in a sense, the struggle he will wage against the rebels in the only battle scene of the film, when the squadron finally has to confront the rebels. Moreover, the sand, and more specifically the sand in the form of a storm, creates throughout the White Squadron's mission in the desert an atmosphere that is typical of guerrilla warfare. Traces of the rebels appear and disappear, tracks shift constantly and sometimes are lost in the sand, and the fear of an uncontrollable and unexpected encounter with the enemies never leaves the soldiers. In my reading of the colonial segment of the film, the qualities that I have attributed to both the enemy and the landscape in guerrilla warfare correspond to the qualities of Mario's erupted "interior." By remaining almost invisible and, at the same time, by moving in the desert in an unpredictable and apparently confused way, the armed enemies, together with the (outer) space that they occupy, become a particularly intense embodiment of the inner space of Lieutenant Ludovici.

Mario constructs the external world—the space "to be colonized"—in the image of his own inner body. Viewed in this way, the battlefield, the place of violence and the site of direct confrontation with the rebels, becomes the locus of the reconstruction of Mario's inner body's boundaries. This explains why Mario after recovering from the fever no longer behaves as a novice at the mercy of his superior, Captain Sant'Elia, but suddenly becomes eager to fight. When Captain Sant'Elia announces that the squadron is finally getting close and will soon reach the rebels, Mario enthusiastically says, "So we will fight!" ("Allora ci batteremo!"). He has come to realize that he needs to rebuild the dams for his inner body, and in order to do it he must confront the "mass" of his erupted "interior." This is the same logic that propels the fascist male soldier, according to Theweleit, to actively seek a proximity to the "mass" of enemies (33). Immediately after the beginning of the battle a sandstorm rises so that, once again, the rebels are hardly visible. The camera shoots close-ups of individual soldiers firing their rifles so that not only are the rebels not portrayed as a crowd but, moreover—and probably as a result of a blinding sandstorm—one is not able to clearly discern who are the rebels and who are the White Squadron soldiers. This is the ultimate example of what I have described as the breaking down of the boundaries between internal and external space.

During the battle one sees Mario courageously helping the wounded soldiers and firing on the rebels. Then the scene abruptly shifts to the tranquil life at the fort, where soldiers and tourists are anxiously awaiting the return of the missing squadron. During the battle scene the camera seems to convey the idea that Mario is not only at the center of the fight but that he is also at the center of his erupted unconscious. It is not so much the mass of dead enemies that he wants to see, but rather the mass of his dead desires, that is, of life that has died within his own body (Theweleit 14). He exterminates the crowd of dangerous rebels, and in so doing he creates an empty space: the colonial space is clean, and so is his body. Both the colonial territory and Mario's body are "whole" again.

It should now be clear that my interest does not lie in what causes Mario's unconscious to burst the banks. Whether the relaxation of the boundaries between "inner" and "outer" space is the result of Mario's detachment from the status quo and cultural expectations, or his reaction to oppressive bourgeois social roles, or his disassociation from hegemonic masculinity in favor of (fascist) homosocial relations (male bonding), what is crucial is the breaking down of the boundaries between "inner" and "outer" space. This breaking down occurs when the order of the external space can no longer be accepted by the internal space of the subject; Mario can no longer accept the order of the bourgeois and urban space in which he lives. Moreover, the failure to recognize the "inner" space as separate from the "outer" space could result in the disintegration of the subject in the same way as the breaking down of the stable and fixed boundaries of the colony could result in the disintegration of the colony. Because Mario experiences the "outer" space as his "inner" space, in order to reconstruct the dams of his internal space, and consequently experience it again as separate from the external space, Mario needs to either restore the order of the external space or to construct a new space. The final aerial view of the desert in *Lo squadrone bianco* has precisely the function of showing the restoration of order, and the reconstruction of the colonial space (and of the fascist colonial dream of Mediterranean aspiration). The defeat of the indigenous rebels symbolizes the restoration of fixed and stable boundaries that separate the territory of the colony from the *terra infirma*. In a similar way, Mario's last words to Cristiana after his return to the fort reveal that he has managed to rebuild the dams of his inner space by killing the "mass" of bourgeois desires, which first erupted in Cristiana's apartment, and leave them behind him. He left them on the battlefield together with or, better, *as* the corpses of his enemies, the crowd of rebels, and of Captain Sant'Elia, who was killed "heroically" fighting in the battle. In so doing, Mario constructs a new "inner" space for himself. In the film, Cristiana has come to the fort with the group of tourists to look for Mario, but when they meet, the two former lovers hardly recognize each other. This is because, as Mario tells Cristiana before bidding her farewell, "Mario doesn't exist anymore. He was left down there, under the sand, like Sant'Elia" ("Mario non esiste più. E' rimasto laggiù sotto la sabbia come Sant'Elia").

In destroying the "mass" of desires that erupted from his unconscious, and rebuilding the boundaries of his "inner" space, Mario has undergone a visible transformation. In the narrative of the film, his last words explain perfectly his transformation: the experience in the desert has changed him, and he has become another man and has chosen a different life, a life in which Cristiana no longer figures. He has buried not only the person that he once was but also the body of the "heroic" captain Sant'Elia, and he is now ready to take his place as the leader of the White Squadron and as the commandant of the Italian outpost in the Libyan desert. According to this interpretation, Mario has chosen a colonial military life in the desert over a bourgeois life in the city. In this traditional interpretation of the film, this choice would be viewed as Mario moving away from patriarchy and hegemonic masculinity (that is, marriage and family) and embracing a life of homosocial bonding and of total dedication to the fatherland as a real fascist soldier, just as the fascist hero Sant'Elia dedicated himself to Italy's cause.

From a psychoanalytic perspective, however, Mario's last words, the statement that he managed to bury his own body, becomes more problematic. This is because, in psychoanalytic terms, Mario has performed the impossible. As a matter of fact, his last words express a delusion. In psychoanalysis, to "bury the body" is the equivalent of repression. What is repressed, however, does not disappear from one's psychic life because it still exists in the unconscious and always threatens to return. As a consequence, by burying his own body Mario only represses the bourgeois forms of his desires but does not "kill" them; he makes them disappear, but this does not mean that they no longer exist. On the contrary, it is as if he has run away from them and pretends that they are "dead." Moreover, if one attempts to escape the repressed, what is repressed becomes the very motive behind one's action. Thus, Mario's attempt to escape the repressed by building strong boundaries for his internal space is self-defeating. Inevitably, those same boundaries will limit his freedom of operation and movement and, more specifically, of desiring because they are construed as a denial of desire. In conclusion, Mario will always face the threat of engulfment by the desert, the objectified form of his erupted inner space; in other words, he will end up always being controlled by the body that he has buried.

The end of *Lo squadrone bianco* shows Mario Ludovici's psychological transformation. The colonization of his internal space presents deep structural parallels with the external historical event of colonization. Both the corporeal space, a metaphorical land, and the geographical space, the desert, stand for the same colonial "fantasy of power" that was one of fascism's hallmarks: the appropriation of a piece of African land and the mastering of its inhabitants in order to construct a colony or, even better, a colonial empire, with fixed and stable boundaries.

Lo squadrone bianco, its traditional interpretation notwithstanding, is not simply a film about fascist Italy's colonial aspirations. By focusing attention on the "psychological" crowd of the title, the White Squadron, the film can be read as fascist Italy's colonial *dream* of incorporation. On another level, by focusing on what seems to be the colonial space in the film, the desert with its "invisible" rebellious inhabitants, and their antithesis, Lieutenant Ludovici, *Lo squadrone bianco* can be read as a film that illustrates two aspects of fascist Italy's colonial reality.

After the victory in Ethiopia, culminating in General Badoglio's taking of Addis Ababa on May 5 and Mussolini's proclamation of the birth of the Italian empire on May 9, 1936, fascist propaganda managed to convince the Italian nation that the African colonies were the panacea for all national troubles. The conquest of "a place in the sun" was presented as the solution to all economic and social problems, as it guaranteed a job and wealth for everyone. For this reason, the Italians never colonized the African desert, and they never intended to do so. The film portrays colonial reality by showing the Italians' real intention: to establish a stronghold on the edge of the desert (represented by the military outpost of the film) with the idea of colonizing spaces that could be cultivated or urbanized.

The crucial role played by the desert in the film reveals another colonial reality. Whereas Mario's last words represent a personal delusion, the control of the desert—a space that cannot be controlled and, least of all, transformed into productive land—represents the ideological delusion of fascist Italy. Mario's wish to destroy his erupted unconscious will never be fulfilled, and he will always be controlled by the "mass" that he has buried under the sand of the desert. The fascist regime's aspirations for territorial control and the establishment of stable colonial boundaries in North and East Africa would never be realized in the way that the regime wanted the Italian people to believe. In *Lo squadrone bianco,* the desert and its swift and "invisible" inhabitants represent fascist Italy's colonial anxieties, spatial anxiety, and crowd anxiety. Like Mario's erupted unconscious, these anxieties cannot be "buried," and they often haunt portrayals of the Italian colonial enterprise.

NOTES

1. The genre is normally considered to consist of eight narrative films—*Lo squadrone bianco* (1936), directed by Augusto Genina; *Il grande appello* (1936), directed by Mario Camerini; *Scipione l'africano* (1937), directed by Carmine Gallone; *Sentinelle di bronzo* (1937), directed by Romolo Marcellini; *Luciano Serra, pilota* (1938), directed by Goffredo Alessandrini; *Sotto la croce del sud* (1938), directed by Guido Brignone; *Piccoli naufraghi* (1939), directed by Flavio Calzavara; *Abuna Messias* (1939), directed by Goffredo Alessandrini—and one documentary, *Il cammino degli eroi* (1937), directed by Corrado D'Errico. All of these films were shot in the span of three years, 1936–39. See Jean A. Gili, "Les films 'Africans' et l'exaltation du colonialism," in *L'Italie de Mussolini et son cinéma,* 112–19 (Paris: Henry Veyrier, 1985).

2. With the conquest of Ethiopia Italian colonization entered a new phase. Before 1936, the state had undertaken the so-called "demographic colonization" ("colonizzazione demografica"), particularly in Libya, which was purported to give many

Italian families the by now proverbial "place in the sun" ("il posto al sole"). This program of colonization granted farmland to Italian families in widely dispersed settlements, but without building actual towns. These settlements were, in fact, isolated rural centers along the roads joining major cities. Italian colonial programs changed considerably in the late 1930s. In this new phase, the state made great efforts to encourage all the unemployed from the mainland to move to East Africa in order to lessen the problem of excess labor in Italy. For this reason the state built full-fledged civic centers, similar to those in Italian towns, with schools, churches, Case del Fascio, post offices, carabinieri barracks, first-aid clinics, and housing for officials and civilians.

3. Indeed, Le Bon's ideas found new popularity in interwar Italy thanks to Mussolini, who openly acknowledged his intellectual debt to the Frenchman in speeches and interviews.

4. To spur as many Italians as possible to a mass mobilization against the fascist regime's imperialist aggression in East Africa, Luigi Longo, one of the most active scholars of Italian imperialism at the time and a member of the Communist Party, wrote the article "Per la disfatta dell'imperialismo italiano," published under the pen name Luigi Gallo in the February 1935 issue of *Lo stato operaio* (93–101). The following is an excerpt from the article that helps indicate its content and tone:

> Il fascismo in Africa va a fare una guerra brigantesca, di rapina. Il fascismo e i capitalisti, lavorando per l'asservimento delle popolazioni coloniali, lavorano per difendere gli interessi e i privilegi di un pugno di sfruttatori e di alti gerarchi, gettando nella rovina, nella miseria e nella schiavitù milioni e milioni di lavoratori italiani e coloniali. . . . Noi dobbiamo smontare la demagogia fascista per accelerare la mobilitazione di massa contro il fascismo e la guerra, per allargarla a tutti gli strati della popolazione, per strappare al fascismo gli illusi e gli esitanti, trattenuti lontani dall'azione disfattista e rivoluzionaria contro la guerra da un falso sentimento nazionale e patriottico. Noi vogliamo la disfatta militare dell'imperialismo italiano, perché noi amiamo il nostro paese; perché noi vogliamo salvar il suo popolo dalla guerra; perché lo vogliamo liberare dall'onta e dall'oppressione fascista; perché vogliamo salvarlo dalla catastrofe finale a cui il fascismo lo porta.

> [Fascism is going to Africa to engage in brigandage and robbery. Fascists and capitalists want to enslave colonial populations. By working to defend the interests and privileges of a handful of profiteers and party leaders, they reduce to poverty and slavery millions of Italian and colonial workers. . . . We must dampen fascist demagoguery in order to accelerate a general mobilization against fascism and colonial war. We must convince Italians from all social classes to mobilize against fascism. We must draw away from fascism the dreamer and the hesitant, who do not engage in subversive or revolutionary action against the war because of false nationalistic and patriotic sentiments. We want the military defeat of Italian imperialism because we love our country and want to save it from a war. We want the military defeat of Italian imperialism because we want to save the Italian people from war, because we want to free it from the shame of dictatorial oppression, and because we want to save it from the final catastrophe to which fascism is leading it.]

5. The second half of the nineteenth century witnessed the beginning of the process of what Michel Foucault in the essay "Of Other Spaces" has defined as the "desanctification of space." The separation between the traditional conception of space and the modern conception of space began to occur in the first decade of the

twentieth century, with the development of technology, the avant-garde movements in arts, and the development of non-Euclidean geometries. However, already in the second half of the nineteenth century new ideas about the concept of space and "spatial" events, such as the Paris Commune, began to challenge the popular notion that there was only one space that was continuous, uniform, immutable, static, and at rest, in other words, an "absolute space." This conception had relegated our understanding of space to a passive stage that simply contained human activities. Space was an empty Cartesian plane until it became filled with people, their activities, and culture. The modern conception of space envisions it no longer as a mere container for human life but, instead, something that needs to be constructed, something that is produced by human beings, alone or collectively. This led to an appropriation of space in order to turn the abstract concept of space—the given, homogeneous, empty, and infinitely open space—into a more concrete, delimited, and formal concept of space and to emerging awareness of space as "social practice." Michel Foucault and Henri Lefebvre are two of the leading philosophers who, in recent years, have elaborated on the changing notion of space in the last hundred years. Also Stephen Kern documents the changing notion of space in *The Culture of Time and Space, 1880–1918* (Cambridge, Mass.: Harvard University Press, 1983).

6. In her book *The Emergence of Social Space: Rimbaud and the Paris Commune* (Minneapolis: University of Minnesota Press, 1988), Kristin Ross gives an extensive account of the Paris Commune as "spatial event."

7. Although, as Giorgio Bertellini points out, the name Sant'Elia has a religious connotation, I believe that there is another referent for the character of Captain Sant'Elia: Antonio Sant'Elia, the author of the "Manifesto of Futurist Architecture" (1914). Much praised by futurists and later by fascists as the "inventor" of modern Italian architecture and urbanism, Antonio Sant'Elia, who had died before Mussolini came into power, was virtually transformed into a fascist hero during the *ventennio*. This is so not so much because he had changed the direction of Italian architecture, which was headed "for the cemetery," but because he had sacrificed his life for the fatherland. Sant'Elia died on October 10, 1916, fighting against the Austrians in the offensive against Trieste during World War I. For his heroism and sacrificial death he became a precursor of the legendary *arditi* (shock troops), who had formed the original nucleus of fascism and to which various futurists had belonged. In *Lo squadrone bianco,* Captain Sant'Elia is clearly modeled after Antonio Sant'Elia. Like him he dies fighting for Italy's unredeemed territories. For an extensive explanation of the "legend" of Antonio Sant'Elia see Esther Da Costa Meyer's *The Work of Antonio Sant'Elia* (New Haven, Conn.: Yale University Press, 1995).

8. Although I read the film from a different angle, it is not my intent to discard the validity of this traditional interpretation. For further accounts of the unfolding of the fascist drama of male conversion in *Lo squadrone bianco* see Marcia Landy, "Surrogate Fathers and Prodigal Sons," in *The Folklore of Consensus: Theatricality in the Italian Cinema, 1930–1943* (Albany: State University of New York Press, 1998), 194–97; and Giorgio Bertellini's chapter in this volume.

9. *Il cammino degli eroi*, shot by Corrado D'Enrico in 1937, is the only official documentary of the fascist regime about Ethiopia. There is, however, a recently edited documentary on the Ethiopian campaign, *Maldafrica,* based on footage, most of it previously unreleased, from the archives of the Istituto LUCE.

10. On the notion of "prestige" see also Giulia Barrera's chapter in this volume.

11. For a discussion of other roles played by "exotic Africa" during the fascist regime see Cinzia Sartini-Blum's chapter in this volume.

12. In the Italian context, these physiognomic details correspond to elements of Cesare Lombroso's nineteenth-century criminal anthropology. Later, Lombroso's theories provided the foundations of the documents signed by the so-called racist scientists under fascism. For a detailed discussion of Italian anthropological studies of Africans and the classification of racial types see Barbara Sòrgoni's chapter in this volume.

13. For an account of the influence of the futurist movement on *Lo squadrone bianco* see Vito Zagarrio's "Ideology Elsewhere: Contradictory Models of Italian Fascist Cinema," in *Resisting Images: Essays on Cinema and History,* ed. Robert Sklar and Charles Musser, 149–72 (Philadelphia, Penn.: Temple University Press, 1990). Zagarrio also provides an interesting analysis of *Lo squadrone bianco* in relation/contraposition to the Hollywood film *Morocco* by Joseph von Sternberg (1930) and the French novel *l'Escadron blanc* by Joseph Peyré, which inspired the film *Lo squadrone bianco.*

WORKS CITED

Alessandrini, Goffredo, dir. *Luciano Serra, pilota.* Perf. Amedeo Nazzari, Germana Paolieri, and Roberto Villa. Istituto LUCE, 1938.

Anderson, Benedict. *Imagined Communities,* 1–7. London and New York: Verso, 1983.

Ben-Ghiat, Ruth. "Envisioning Modernity: Desire and Discipline in the Italian Fascist Film." *Critical Inquiry* 23, no. 1 (1996): 109–44.

Bhabha, Homi K. "Of Mimicry and Man: The Ambivalence of Colonial Discourse." In Bhabha, *The Location of Culture,* 85–92. London and New York: Routledge, 1994.

Brignone, Guido, dir. *Sotto la croce del sud.* Perf. Doris Duranti and Antonio Centa. Istituto LUCE, 1938.

Canetti, Elias. *Crowds and Power.* New York: Noonday Press, 1996.

de Certeau, Michel. *The Practice of Everyday Life.* Trans. Steven F. Rendall. Berkeley: University of California Press, 1993.

D'Errico, Corrado, dir. *Il cammino degli eroi.* Istituto LUCE, 1937.

Genina, Augusto, dir. *Lo squadrone bianco.* Screenplay by Augusto Genina and Gino Valori. Perf. Fosco Giachetti, Antonio Centa, Fulvia Lanzi, and Cesare Polacco. CINES, 1936.

Jowett, Garth S., and Victoria O'Donnell. *Propaganda and Persuasion.* London: SAGE Publications, 1986.

Kirby, Kathleen M. "Vertigo: Postmodern Spaces and the Politics of the Subject." In Kirby, *Indifferent Boundaries: Spatial Concepts of Human Subjectivity,* 96–121. New York and London: Guilford Press, 1996.

Le Bon, Gustave. *The Crowd: A Study in the Popular Mind.* Harmondsworth: Penguin, 1977.

Maldafrica. Historical consultant, Angelo Del Boca. Istituto LUCE, 1995.

Pinkus, Karen. "Selling the Black Body: Advertising and the African Campaigns." In

Pinkus, *Bodily Regimes: Italian Advertising Under Fascism,* 22–81. Minneapolis: University of Minnesota Press, 1995.

Rochat, Giorgio. "Le direttive di Mussolini per l'impiego dei gas asfissianti e per una politica del terrore." In Rochat, *Il colonialismo italiano,* 168–70. Torino: Loescher, 1972.

Ross, Kristin. *The Emergence of Social Space.* Minneapolis: University of Minnesota Press, 1988.

Theweleit, Klaus. *Male Fantasies,* vol. 2. Trans. Erica Carter and Chris Turner. Minneapolis: University of Minnesota Press, 1987.

Empty Spaces

Decolonization in Italy

Karen Pinkus

ECLIPSE AS A METAPHOR

In Michelangelo Antonioni's 1962 film *L'eclisse (The Eclipse)*, Vittoria (Monica Vitti) painfully breaks up with her lover and walks lithely through a semi-deserted landscape in the early morning. Passing a strange water tower that resembles a frozen mushroom cloud, Vittoria seems ill at ease with her surroundings. The streets are silent, their black tar and white lines perfectly untouched. The landscape is barren except for a few maritime pines that appear to have been planted only recently. The grass is neatly trimmed and does not overgrow any of its concrete boundaries. The viewer has the sense that this location might be false, a film set. Perhaps it is a real place, but the residents have been cleared out to make room for the filmic apparatus. Perhaps the director wishes to indicate a postapocalyptic state in which the sole survivors are Vittoria, her former lover, and a young boy who suddenly emerges from one side of the frame only to disappear on the other side (is he the hope of the future?). To refer to the aura of the opening scenes of this film merely by reference to Antonioni's signature "alienation" seems inadequate. Something has happened here, or, better, nothing has happened. The emptiness of this location opens up the possibility of an unnamed event in the past. Simultaneously, however, Antonioni's camera posits the more annihilating possibility of a nonevent, a continuity with a past that has always been out of sync with itself.

Although this location is never granted a proper name during the course of *Eclipse,* viewers might recognize Vittoria's home as part of the neighborhood known as EUR (Universal Exhibition of Rome), an acronym that might be said to mime another acronym symmetrically: AOI, or Italian East Africa.[1] As a development, EUR boasts a tangled history linking fascism, co-

lonialism, and the period of decolonization. Set precisely during the years
of the independence of most African states, *Eclipse* is exemplary for my
discussion, just as an "eclipse" seems an exemplary figure for the very idea
of decolonization, and a fitting ending to the present volume. An eclipse
is both a spatial displacement and a temporary/temporal one. The director had already begun work on his new film, focusing on the affective states
of a bourgeois woman whose mother is obsessed with trading on the stock
exchange, when he was asked to photograph a solar eclipse in Florence. He
noted that during the event all motion ceased. He wondered, then, if emotions also stopped, and this became a central figure for the film already in
progress. Although the film was not conceived, then, as a meditation on
race, or even on the end of a historical moment, an eclipse has to do with
the overlapping of dark and light, and so it serves as an apt metaphor for
racial differences. As I will discuss later, it is also a "primitive" phenomenon
that opens itself up to mythologization and arouses atavistic beliefs. It disrupts daily life, if only for a brief period. Finally, as with decolonization, one
can never say when an eclipse truly begins or ends. It is essentially ambiguous and defies perceptual certainty.

In this chapter I am treating an event—tinged with anxious spatiality and
temporality, like a film of Antonioni—that could actually be considered a
nonevent. This nonevent is, precisely, the cultural effects of decolonization
in Italy. The term nonevent suggests, indeed, that the lack of any traumatic
severing of Italy's colonial appendages has contributed to the lack of a full-
scale national reevaluation of the country's colonial past. In a more strictly
political-historical context, Angelo Del Boca argues a similar position in this
volume. Indeed, it is the vagueness of a "postcolonial politics of disappearance," as Robin Pickering-Iazzi suggests, that has allowed political parties to
continually defer the return of the Axum obelisk, precisely the kind of symbolic gesture that might be said to indicate a definite terminus to Italy's colonial era.

Even throughout the 1940s and 1950s, the decades of European re-
alignment, only a relatively small sector of the Italian population concerned
itself with the African question. One might say that within the spaces of the
Italian peninsula, there was a lack of knowledge about Africa, and a forgetting of what was known.[2] In the years immediately following Italy's withdrawal from Africa, cultural energies were shifted to *other* geopolitical regions (and indeed, in time, to the very idea of *outer* space);[3] economic and
libidinous investments were withdrawn from Italian East Africa; and the
colonialist enterprise was quickly demonized as a fascist enterprise. A relatively rapid expurgation of Italy's presence in Africa has been facilitated
by a certain ideological tendency to ignore earlier manifestations of colonialism, making Italian colonialism virtually coincident with fascism. If Italy
lacked a "democratic" model for colonization like that of Britain and France,

then colonialism found itself subject to the same fate as fascism, bracketed off in the national psyche as an anomaly. Without any significant emigration of black labor to the space of peninsular Italy, it seemed a relatively simple matter to truncate the discursive flow of "racist science" of the prewar period.[4] In comparison, without the kind of organized torture that shaped Algeria into a space for the exercise of expertise by the new French "organization man," AOI, now carved up, failed to capture headlines. Italians stopped talking about race as their own whiteness became normative, internalized as a nonissue.[5]

My thinking in this essay takes its primary inspiration from *Fast Cars, Clean Bodies: Decolonization and the Reordering of French Culture,* in which Kristin Ross writes of the phantasmagoric effect of the splitting of France from Algeria (that is, the splitting of France from "itself," inasmuch as Algeria was profoundly part of France) beginning in the mid-1950s.[6] Of course, we would not expect to make direct parallels with the French situation, but the phenomenon of decolonization in Italy certainly deserves to be studied, particularly since we know that the years in question witnessed a superficial retooling and renaming of certain institutions and individuals of fascism that continued to operate in a nearly uninterrupted fashion.[7] Moreover, if the imperial moment in all of its monumental symbolic potential can indeed be considered the height of consent to fascism, as echoed in the work of Giorgio Bertellini, Cecilia Boggio, and others in this volume, then we would expect to see some cultural countereffects in its withering away.

My interest, then, lies not specifically in the politics and policies of decolonization in Ethiopia, Eritrea, and Somalia (dealt with most extensively in volume 4 of Angelo Del Boca's *Gli italiani in Africa orientale,* aptly subtitled *Nostalgia delle colonie*), but rather in reading the very absence of traces of the colonial in the recoding of urban and neobourgeois space in Italy itself after the war. The colonial problem had always been a spatial one, at least in part. The fantasy of endless and boundaryless territory fueled much of the consensus to a European presence in Africa. Propaganda and "information" about demographics and the colonial enterprise had often been figured in spatialized terms. These terms remain fantasized inasmuch as few Italians ever visited AOI or experienced its peculiar spatiality. What happens, then, as Italian culture begins to eclipse a "consciousness of race" with a new "consciousness of space" on the peninsula? In part, the coincidence of the withdrawal from Africa and the radical readjustment of place and space in Italy could be considered purely coincidental, and thus without any apparent correlation. In part, though, Italy expressly confronts the very serious postwar housing crisis by "colonizing" its own deserts on the outskirts of the major cities, rapidly developing industries, and engaging in ambitious road-building projects, all significant elements of the colonial enterprise. The rhetoric surrounding the groundbreaking north-south highway, the

autostrada del sole, begun in 1956, resounds with colonialist clichés about uni-
fying tribal entities, collapsing spatio-temporal zones, and penetrating the
hinterland.[8] It is by confronting questions about the new spatial organization in Italy that we may find clues about the no-place of decolonization.

We would not expect to find, then, an explicit "whitening" of Italy after its effective withdrawal from Africa, as Kristin Ross has documented in
France. The elaborate rhetoric of racial difference developed during the
1930s through visual and verbal campaigns, in the daily newspapers as well
as in more focused periodicals such as *La difesa della razza,* simply disappears
from public life, supplanted by a vocabulary of foreign words (imported
into Italy with gusto now that the ban imposed by Mussolini has been lifted)
such as "trusteeship" and "protection." As in France—but to a degree that
was certainly more extreme—Italy in the postwar period focused on west-
ernizing itself according to the American model. The cultural results of
Americanization are well known and cannot be fully developed here.[9] The
most powerful illustration of this ideology was the planning of EUR as
the opening up of Rome to the sea. However, by the period just before the
"boom" such images vanish, to be replaced with another series concerned
with measuring Italy favorably against Eastern, "despotic" modes of production and the lack of consumer goods behind the iron curtain.[10]

Put in more broadly symbolic terms, Italy was colonized by America at the
very moment that it silently slunk away from its colonies. The rhetoric of
restitution and rebuilding that Italian politicians from a wide spectrum of
parties developed paralleled that of the Marshall plan and other modes
of aid to, or trusteeship of, Italy itself. Nevertheless, although decolonization meant that fascist colonialism had to be exorcised, the new antiracist
and "benevolent" talk of an Italian presence in Africa was still highly nationalist, formed out of the struggle for power against the four superpowers
after the war. Ultimately, however, such discourse remained at the level of
public policy or specialized speech. At the same time, at home the new frontier was the desert space of the formerly rural Italy, especially the territories
close to large cities, that then needed to be developed to house the expanding population.

PERIPHERAL SPACE

Antonioni's *Eclipse,* much of which was filmed in the peripheral town of
EUR, was made at the end of the period of Italian decolonization, after
many of the African states (including Somalia) had achieved their nominal
independence. The economic boom was already underway, but its effects
had not yet been fully experienced. EUR was originally a fascist urban project, built on a vast area of previously undeveloped (or uncolonized) land located between Rome and the sea. The project was conceived to commemo-

rate the five-year anniversary of the foundation of the empire in Addis Ababa, but plans were later deferred, and rhetoric was realigned to present the exposition as a celebration of the twentieth anniversary of the march on Rome. The site was to be called E'42, a name that was changed by popular referendum after the war. Thus EUR has a complex and ambivalent history. It was intended to serve a double function: first, it was to serve as a vast display of urban ingenuity and as a site for an exposition directed outward to the world. Later, it was to be converted into a habitable (national) space. It was also inherently tied to Italian colonialism, a conceptual and psychological reflection of what Italy aspired to achieve in its empire, as Mia Fuller has explored in an article drawing parallels between the plans of EUR and the plans for colonial Addis Ababa.[11] Both zones were to be planned on virgin soil (in the case of Addis Ababa, this was not strictly true, but fascist rhetoric made it seem as if the inhabitants of the existing town had been incapable of forming any kind of urban organization before the intervention of whites). And both plans featured a central, triumphal axis with living quarters occupying designated lateral zones. In the case of Addis Ababa, the residential areas were to be segregated, and the indigenous people were to inhabit semipermanent huts in areas outside of the imperial zone, but not so far off to the margins as to be "off the map."[12] The plan for the Ethiopian capital would have been "regular," as opposed to the real and hybrid lived spatiality of colonial cities such as Alexandria (described by Lucia Re as "anarchic and chaotic, with frequent compromises, infractions, and mixed or unorthodox usages of buildings" in her chapter in this volume). In fact, there was not enough time to build Addis Ababa; and by the period of the economic boom, the imperial trajectories inscribed in EUR had been suppressed in favor of new ones. The exposition of 1942 never took place, but the town managed to repress this historical "failure" and to re-present itself as a successful community. I am, naturally, more interested in the experience of navigating the spaces of EUR after its originative function was made impossible, and after its immediate colonialist referents have faded to some degree.

During the postwar period, EUR became increasingly plausible as a suburban residential community, especially due to the development of new train lines linking it (as well as areas such as the ancient port town of Ostia) to the center of the city. Favoritism shown toward certain builders and speculators led to widespread investment in the infrastructure of EUR and other locations along the same trajectory, to the detriment of poor peripheral suburbs that cropped up in other directions. The apparent cleanliness, safety, and verdancy of EUR are also, then, latent symbols of the corruption that characterized development in Italy in the 1950s and 1960s. By the time Antonioni filmed there, EUR, the "quartiere-giardino" (garden city), had become the kind of purely rational space for gracious living that an avant-garde group like the Situationists might have wished to undermine.[13] In the early 1960s, just around the period of Antonioni's eclipse trilogy and the end of the Algerian war, the Situationists fought against the "benign professionalism of architecture and design," which they understood as leading to "a sterilization of the world that threatened to wipe out any sense of spontaneity or playfulness."[14] There is no question that the calculated geometry of EUR's architecture provides an ideal background for Antonioni's particular cinematic-spatial idiom.[15] As various critics have noted, the director has demonstrated a strong interest in filming his subjects against rectangular frames that appear to box them in, and in filming them against unusual and disturbing structures that the viewer cannot immediately embrace. And it should be noted that he privileges the more modern and characterless residential sites over the monumental. Antonioni's EUR is virtually and spiritually empty. At the same time, during the postwar period EUR still retained some of its aura as a model city like Levittown or the San Fernando Valley in the United States, a space that had the potential to transform social life. This potential redeems the city from becoming a mere vacuous monument to triumphalist rhetoric. Historically, EUR was (imperial) Rome, an oasis sprung up in a desert six kilometers from the city, a mirror of the *Urbs* (its dimensions corresponding to those of the center of the city, from the Piazza del Popolo to the Piazza di Spagna), but cleaner and purged of urban blight.

What is most important to keep in mind is the sense of no-where generated by Antonioni's EUR, not only in its marble whiteness and symmetry, but in the lack of crowds that have signified urbanity since the early years of cinema (think of Alberto Cavalcanti's *Rien que les heures,* or Walter Ruttman's *Berlin: Symphony of a Great City,* and so on). Indeed, it is possible to think of EUR as the kind of space that was to be filled with triumphal crowds, to be marched on, like Addis Ababa. (It is significant, then, that Italy never truly managed to establish a "domestic" space in Africa, where such marching-on would cease, giving rise to segregated but normalized living quarters.) Antonioni's uneasy camera makes clear the awkwardness, and even the impossibility, of navigating such a space in peacetime.

The character of Vittoria, blond and slender, might well have been born the year of the Italian conquest of Ethiopia. She would have no memory of the campaigns. Rather, she belongs to a generation that may have internalized certain of the fascist racial ideas. In any case, Vittoria suffers a crisis of emotions, not a social crisis. If Vittoria (or the film) suspends her rigorous alienation long enough for the introduction of nostalgia, it is certainly not nostalgia for the colonies (to invoke Del Boca's title) or for fascist rigor. In one scene, for instance, Antonioni allows his camera a moment of sentimentality as it pans across a series of framed snapshots in the home of Vittoria's mother. One of the photographs hints at the rural poverty of the family's past, but we are not allowed to look long enough to decide if we are seeing a picture of Vittoria's mother, as a child with her parents in the years before the war, or of Vittoria herself with her parents. This lack of concrete information is typical of Antonioni's semiotics, as if he wants us to avoid constructing a particular history for the character and instead to focus on the general signifier of "backwardness" that stands as an alibi for the unbridled greed of Vittoria's mother in the stock market. I call the function of the photograph "nostalgic" in the sense that it represents a place to which one might not wish to return, but to which one is also inevitably drawn, and this is also the sense in which I understand a potential nostalgia for the colonies that is absent from this film. In other words, Vittoria's nostalgia bears the same aura as a potential nostalgia for the colonies, but it is transferred to Italy itself. When Vittoria's supple body moves through EUR, the shot does not explicitly refer back to the earlier virility that haunts the town, but her body cannot help but be framed by the fascist past, inscribed within its codes. Vittoria—Victory—cannot fully escape her name.

Before we continue to examine the scenes of the film that explicitly reference Africa, we need to consider the particular location of EUR in relation to Rome, and the question of spatial mobility that underlies the lack of genuine habit(u)ation in the periphery. In a sense, the single vowel that distinguishes "habitate" (or inhabit) from "habituate" expresses the pathos of modern characters in their inability to genuinely become used to a place rather than merely residing there or visiting. The postwar period, as is well known, meant increased mobility, yet this was not always purely liberating. Workers had to commute long distances to the center of Rome via a series of slow and limited trams, a fact rehearsed in many neo-realist films.[16] In contrast to such lived practices, advertisements show Americanized couples eliding the distance between the crowded center and the rural edges as they hop on a Vespa or Lambretta and head out for an afternoon picnic. Women began to own cars, to drive around the city. There was a certain mobility not only within the city (the *mezzi*), but also from the city to key points (indicated by the practice of referring to "a certain kilometer" from the center such as EUR). Neobourgeois families might own a home in town and a weekend home near the sea. A number of scenes in Fellini's *La dolce vita* (1960) involve movement from the Via Veneto in the center of Rome to peripheral houses.

These spatial modifications would seem to have precisely nothing to do with (de)colonization. What logic would link newly enhanced circulation *(giri)* around the city and just beyond its limits with the expansion into the colonies of a decade earlier? What is important to my thinking is the idea that motion will try to pass itself off as pure motion (a joyride, a spin, a free pass, a road trip), but it is always motion to a place. Motion turns out to be highly regulated, like the *piano regolatore* (zoning) of the roads and of construction in general. In Italy, many of these plans, driving codes, and the very paths of roads themselves are built in layers upon ancient Roman codes. The (re)construction also reflects a transfer of colonialist knowledge and planning to the new Italy. Whether these subtexts contain or retain imperial referents or not, they nevertheless underlie the trajectories of modern mobile subjects. My interest in the "new colonies" around the *Urbs* derives, in part, from Henri Lefebvre's suggestive dialectic between "rigorously formal" codes and users; or rather, between ancient urban codes that are no longer actual, and contemporary productions.[17] It isn't that we should expect to trace directly the means by which new forms of navigating and construing space in Italy come to replace forms of penetration, land reclamation, and attack in AOI. Rather than attempting to lay bare what is clearly a gradual and painful process of replacement and development, we may come to understand something about the conditions of daily life under decolonization by exploring the gaps and overlappings between spaces and subjects, between plans and tactics. (Nowhere is this exploration more promising than in the peripheral zone of EUR.) The logic that links Africa, and racial thinking, with the postwar periphery is a logic of forgetting.

I invoke in this context another film, an exemplary *commedia all'italiana,* released the same year as Antonioni's *Eclipse.* Dino Risi's *Il sorpasso* thematizes mobility in the figure of the car (a Lancia Aurelia B24 Cabriolet) driven by Bruno (Vittorio Gassman). Again, this is not a film that discusses decolonization in any explicit way, nor does it explore "whiteness" (class, above all, is the film's key contribution to a discussion of Italian identity). The opening credits roll over a brilliant scene in which Bruno attempts to find an open store in Rome during *ferragosto* (mid-August holiday). Stopping at a water fountain in a residential district, Bruno spots Roberto (Jean-Louis Trintignant) staring from the only window that is not barred by metal shutters in a nondescript, boxy apartment building. Roberto invites Bruno to use his phone, but the girl Bruno was supposed to meet does not answer. And so their road journey begins. At first, Bruno promises Roberto a drink in the center of Rome, but when the pair find no open bars he suggests lunch at a trattoria near the Vatican. This too is closed, but the search provides an excuse for a cinematic sweep of key sites in the city center, from the Piazza di Spagna to St. Peter's, filmed on location from a speeding platform. Next, Bruno pressures Roberto into trying an outdoor restaurant, Ernestino's, located at the "thirteenth kilometer" of the Via Aurelia. ("We'll be there in four minutes," Bruno promises, although, ironically, the driving scene actually lasts longer than four minutes of real time on screen.)[18] Unlike the *autostrada,* the Via Aurelia—whose ancient origins are signaled by Roberto's references to Etruscan tombs ("Etruscan tombs? Shove them!" Bruno laughs)—is not encumbered by tolls or interrupted (visually) by large overpasses or signs.[19] It is a two-lane highway across flat terrain, perfect for driving fast.

The anxiety that drives the narrative—at least inasmuch as the viewer sympathizes with Roberto's desire to study his law books and pass his exams—is the anxiety of an open-ended road trip away from the city without schedules, road markers, or maps. What Risi shows is that such freedom is actually illusory, a simulacrum of an "original" American-style freedom that itself does not exist. The men stop for gas at a modern service station along the highway. As they walk toward the building, Bruno suggests that Roberto leave behind the codified law of "a thousand years ago" to embark on the new terrain of spatial law *(diritto spaziale)*. The phrase has a ridiculous ring to it, but Bruno has a point. That is, his point reveals the gap between the representational codes of space embedded in Roman law and the sociospatial practices of everyday life in the modern world. It is at this moment that a black woman, clearly a tourist, asks Bruno for directions. Unable to communicate, Bruno simply calls her "pale face," a phrase that he must have heard in American Westerns. Although this brief incident is only one of many in the film meant to depict the mentality of the "new man" of the boom years, revealing his limited ability to extend beyond his own trajectory of acquisition and pleasure and his rather paternal or *"buonista"* (goodhearted) racism, it is, again, interesting because of the linguistic and geographical displacements it suggests. Taken together, the proposition of spatial law and the inability to place the black "pale face" sum up the moment of decolonization in Italy.

Bruno pushes further up the coast to a town near Pisa where his ex-wife lives in a model contemporary summerhouse. She works in advertising, like so many of the modern characters in both French and Italian stories of this period;[20] her ambitious daughter intends to study "public relations" (in English in the original) at Harvard University. Like so many of the "modern" people and consumer goods analyzed by the French philosophical school of "everyday life," these two highly competent women, with their glass-enclosed box of a house filled with the latest appliances, gleaming and symmetrical, are potential ciphers for the forgetting of the African colonies.

And like *Eclipse,* a film that Bruno himself has seen and found boring (although he admits that Antonioni is an admirably fast driver), *Il sorpasso* also includes a nostalgic reference to Italy's rural or preindustrial past. This past—figured in the country estate where Roberto used to spend summers with his relatives—is a place to which it is impossible to return (at least without shattering so many illusions that it is no longer the same place). The narrative grinds to a near stop as Dino Risi also allows his camera to slow down, during the scene when the two men disrupt the sleepy life of the farm near Grosseto. The scene contrasts with the driving scenes, during which the camera is frequently changing angles and keeping pace with or even anticipating Bruno's attempts to overtake the other drivers on the road. *Il sorpasso* is also about redrawing the map of Italy after colonization, a map that is characterized by its relearning of its own national boundaries as absolute limits, and by a series of zigzagging trajectories of increasing speed along a series of familiar paths.

BLACK AND WHITE

At the end of the third scene in *Eclipse,* Antonioni fades to black. The viewer is momentarily disoriented as the director then fades back in, not to light, but to the darkness of a hot night, when Vittoria's doorbell rings. It is her friend, Anita, who cannot sleep because of the heat. The two friends make visual contact with a third woman named Marta, who lives across from Vittoria in her sparse, modernist apartment complex in EUR. A light is coming from Marta's apartment. Vittoria and Anita stand silhouetted in the doorway. It almost appears as if there is no one else in the building (an atomic eclipsing of humanity?). Black and white are used here to indicate nonpresence and presence.

Antonioni continues with a jump cut. Vittoria and Anita have relocated to Marta's apartment, which we first identified only as a square of white light in the complex across the way. It is the kind of edit that calls attention to itself, a radical cut, and it is the first in a series of such cuts. In other parts of the film (as well as in his work in general), Antonioni shows himself to be a master of transitional moments: Vittoria's move from her former lover Riccardo's apartment across the deserted atomic landscape of EUR is painfully slow; and there is an aerial shot of almost unwatchably long duration as Vittoria flies with Anita over Verona. Clearly, then, in the "African scene" it is precisely the temporal eclipses that Antonioni wants to highlight. The effect is disorienting, but deliberately so.

Now settled in the apartment, the three women talk of Africa, as the camera pauses to take in a series of black-and-white photographs tacked to the wall, and then images from a coffee-table book highlighting geographical and ethnic qualities of Marta's native Kenya. Marta spouts a series of banal statements about her country that seem to come directly from a travel guide, like the "ordinary speech" of advertising or the jargon of the new professional cadres that Michel de Certeau cites as central to the "practico-inertness" of everyday life in the postwar period.[21] Vittoria asks Marta about the origin of a large stuffed elephant hoof that serves as decoration (it was shot by her father in her presence). Other black-and-white neo-primitivist decorative items such as an ottoman and a zebra-skin rug appear in the shot as the camera pans across the room.[22] During this visual survey of the apartment's "Africanness," Vittoria and Anita ask Marta if she is afraid of elephants. Marta replies in an annoyed tone, "No, I was born. Ero nata lì. Hai paura te delle macchine?" ("No, I was born. I was born there. Are you afraid of cars?").

The switching between Italian and English in the Africa scene appears particularly important, as I will suggest later. For the moment, though, it is enough to note that the viewer gets a sense of unrootedness, if only because Marta's speech follows a kind of stilted, infantile bilingualism (she refers to her fatherland in her mother tongue, and then to cars in Italian) in which a void is created, the void of an authentic African language—or at least an African idiom—that could be spoken in the space of Europe.[23] The void is filled, temporarily at least, as Vittoria plays a record of tribal music she finds conveniently laid out on the turntable.

The sense of the inadequacy of the spoken idiom is deepened as Vittoria surveys a mountain and we hear Marta's voice inform her, "Quello è Kilimanjaro" ("That's Kilimanjaro"). "Già, le nevi del Kilimanjaro" ("Of course, the snows of Kilimanjaro"), replies Vittoria, framed in an unforgiving close-up against the temporary photographic wall display.[24] Her point of reference is a Hemingway novella (also a 1952 film starring that most American of actors, Gregory Peck), a reference translated into Italian, but then, we recall, Vittoria earns her living as a translator. Translation figures here not as a bridge but as a secondary dislocation, as we may infer from the clicking of the keys of Vittoria's typewriter, which reverberate through the empty space of the apartment in a later scene. Indeed, Hemingway's story is a moral tale about the dangers of forgetting Africa's natural powers. Vittoria's response to Marta's indication of a real African locale thus shows itself to be another dislocation from a genuine "habit(u)ation"—understood as a sustained being-in, as opposed to a circumscribed residence or a violent imposition of self—in (any) one genuine space.

Following Vittoria's close-up there is a cut of such radicalness and momentary disorientation in time and space that the first-time viewer might even imagine that the film's print itself has been damaged. We see, suddenly, a medium close-up of Vittoria, covered in black-face. She wears tribal jewelry and has been costumed in a sheath. She dances on the bed with a spear. Thus the initial shock is twofold. The viewer cannot make the image of the actress coincide with anything seen previously; she is virtually unrecognizable. Once the viewer adjusts to her disguise, we realize that the transition between her two states—the modern, blond, bourgeois Vittoria and the dark, tribal Vittoria—would have taken a significant amount of real time, perhaps as long as an hour. The temporality of the transition has been utterly eclipsed by the edit. Vittoria dances around to the music until the angry moment when Marta decides she's had enough and Vittoria picks up the needle from a small phonograph in the corner of the room, ending the

Figure 8. Film still of African dance from *L'Eclisse* (1962). Courtesy of Museum of Modern Art / Film Stills Archive, New York.

charade. It is only then that we fully realize the pure theatricality of the scene, underscored by the dramatic interplay of zones of light and dark in the apartment.

At the end of the tribal masquerade, the cut that locates the women back in their normal states of dress on the bed, with cold drinks, does not appear nearly as disruptive. At this point, Marta launches into a tirade about racial relations in Kenya with the following exchange:

> *Marta:* They've all got their revolvers. All of them again.
>
> *Vittoria:* All who? The whites or the coloreds?
>
> *Anita:* Non incominciate a parlare in inglese perché non capisco niente [Don't start speaking English because I don't understand anything].

Vittoria's question thus remains unanswered, as Marta describes the terror of being in the white minority in a country of "six million monkeys." There is a high degree of tension in the bedroom, which is, mercifully, interrupted when Marta's black dog escapes and begins to run with a pack of other (black and white) dogs across the black and white lines of the piazza nearby to the building complex. Marta appears only once again in the film, as she leans from a window and shoots a balloon that has floated upward while Vittoria and Piero, the stockbroker, walk past her building. Most of the metal

Figure 9. Film still from *L'Eclisse* (1962). Courtesy of Museum of
Modern Art / Film Stills Archive, New York.

shutters in the building are closed, and Marta appears to be the only sign of
life. This scene thus represents a potential for some playful contact, some
way out of the anxiety of the EUR at this moment. Vittoria laughs, but then
the viewer realizes that her bond with the other woman will never progress
beyond detached amusement. Marta makes no impact. Her presence is
ephemeral and marginal, like the floating signifiers of her Africanness.

Naturally, the entire "Africa" scene disrupts the conscience of the liberal
viewer, not only because of the awkward cuts and the offensive lines uttered
by Marta (to say nothing of the bored responses of Vittoria and Anita—
"They must be very nice monkeys if you stayed there so long"), but also because of the position of the scene in the broader narrative. Overall, the

scene enacts a series of displacements: from Vittoria's apartment to Marta's; from Italian to a mixture of Italian and English; from neobourgeois minimalism to tribalism; from ponderous silence to tribal rhythms and back again. But the most significant dislocation, for our purposes, is one that is not explicitly played out on the screen: the movement from the spaces and histories of Italian colonialism to those of English colonialism. This bears some explanation, for it isn't precisely that Antonioni begins by talking of Italian colonies or even of Italian nationalism only to drop this discourse in favor of an Anglo-centered one. Indeed, one might well argue that the entire film is pan-European in its aesthetic and ideological orientation and is only set in Italy for reasons of convenience. Yet there is something quite specific about the linguistic switches I have mentioned above, just as there is something specific about the reference to the rebellion of the Mau Mau and the threat to white domination in the former British colony. This specificity bears the double signifier of a turn toward and away from Italian Africa. It is as if, for Antonioni, it would be impossible to narrate the story of Italian decolonization itself; as if such a story is always already eclipsed. And yet, it could be argued that *Eclipse* is the most eloquent film about Italian decolonization ever made. Instead, Antonioni chooses as the catalyst for Vittoria's mimicry a European woman, one who is at home no-where and occupies a nontime. ("If Kenya is so bad, then why did you choose to return there to have your baby?" asks Vittoria. "Because Kenya is my home," Marta responds. And besides, there is a very modern hospital. But then she lapses into other reveries, and indeed we see no signs of a child, not to mention the husband who is apparently "away" from Marta's very adult-contemporary apartment.) Marta's estrangement is signified by virtually all of the details of her life: her apartment is decorated with temporary images; she does not work and yet does not live directly from the capital generated by now-outdated colonial labor; she is childless; and, most importantly, she is a woman who has set up home, however provisionally, in the no-place of EUR. She is, in sum, morally and historically distanced from a colonial past that nonetheless remains a part of the nation.

Eclipse is a film in which the alternating rhythms of blackness and whiteness (Antonioni would not use color until *Red Desert* in 1964) are played like piano keys. In the stock exchange, the key locus of the film's social critique, prices of the *azioni* (stocks) appear on a large board, changed by a flipping mechanism that causes a momentary eclipse. The white background is metamorphosed into blackness for a brief interval of suspended time. In one of the last scenes, when the camera revisits the *loci* in the park at EUR that were at one time occupied by the lovers, Vittoria and Piero, Antonioni uses piano music—perhaps even an alternation of major and minor chords—behind the image of the black and white stripes on the nearly deserted streets. We might point to many more examples of such visual and acoustical meditations on blackness and whiteness. *Eclipse* is not an outright political film in any traditional sense. It does not speak openly about race, nor does it attempt to address the moral implications of the boom against the desolation of the postcolonial conditions of Ethiopia, Somalia, and Eritrea (or Libya). Yet there is potential eloquence in the film's silence.

The possibility of speech—the multiple displacements of the "Africa" scene, as well as the introduction of an Anglo-Italianism—should be understood against the peculiar historical circumstances of Italian decolonization. A few notes are in order. First, it should be recalled that even Italy's departure from Africa after the war appeared like a repetition (in very bad faith) of the slinking away from the defeat at Adwa in the late nineteenth century, which, ironically, served as a spur to colonialist impulses in fascist rhetoric.[25] If the fascists justified their aggressive moves in part as a way of "catching up" with the mature European nations, then to some degree, democratic decolonization was also construed in terms of Italy's inferiority, especially inferiority with respect to Britain. Of the four superpowers, the British remained the most adamantly opposed to Italy's continued presence in Africa. Moreover, "democratic colonialism" was dominated by the British model, based on the exploitation of raw materials and markets, as opposed to the Italian model, based on emigration and the need to resolve the unemployment and overpopulation problems. These terms colored the international debates throughout the postwar period.

Certainly, then, the signifier "British post-colonialist Africa" has a particular meaning in Italy. Even Pier Paolo Pasolini, when he began to film his *Notes for an African Orestes,* chose the postcolonial Anglophone countries of Uganda and Tanganyika Tanzania (originally German colonies but under British rule after the war), areas where the effects of modernization were to be felt much more potently than in feudalistic Somalia or Eritrea. The bookstore he films at the University of Dar es Salaam reflects the two poles, Soviet and Chinese Communism versus neocapitalist and Anglo-Saxon cultures. There are no traces of Roman imperialism or Mediterraneanism in the film's meditations on transition and justice. In searching for a musical idiom to accompany his piece he experimented with the African-American jazz of Gato Barbieri. Pasolini, it would seem, deliberately avoids any particular referent to the time and space of the Italian colonies.[26]

The lack of what I have called an "authentic Italian-African" idiom in the period of decolonization cannot be said to have been experienced as such by the majority of Italians. More than any explicit fears about loss of empire, *Eclipse* is haunted by nuclear fear, perhaps related to the Cuban Missile Crisis, which had occurred just prior to production. If anything, this crisis (a word that Antonioni disdained) is alluded to only by a number of ciphers such as newspapers held by commuters with the headlines "The Atomic Age" or "Peace is Weak"; or the final blackout of the film, as the camera pans upward into a glaring white light while the end title emerges out of the light like a secondary effect of an explosion. Viewed in the context of the film's broader themes, and especially after a close reading of the "Africa" scene, such allusions suggest that the theater of global anxiety has been shifted from (quaint, nineteenth-century) Africa to the new stages of the struggles of communism and capitalism.

Indeed, in the scene immediately following the "Africa scene," Vittoria and Anita accompany Anita's husband to Verona to deliver a plane. While waiting at the tiny provincial airport, Vittoria apparently begins to feel an unexpected sense of well-being. "I feel so good here," she says, for reasons that escape the viewer. If Vittoria was unable to feel at home, to "habituate" herself to her own surroundings, for a brief moment, displaced to this strange yet simple location, she at last dwells poetically. But before she makes this explicit declaration, Antonioni films her wandering around, and at one point she stands against the background of a white wall, hesitating before entering a small bar. Two black men sit outside waiting. As the only blacks to appear in the film they are both remarkable and unremarkable at the same time. They appear as merely one of many images of blackness (framed by whiteness) in the film. Yet they are unique precisely because their ordinariness is uncanny in the bourgeois whiteness of the film's state of being.

Do these two black men contribute to Vittoria's momentary happiness? Not directly or in any narrative sense, but filmed as they are against a stark white wall, they point toward a condition of waiting, of suspended time and place. The scene suggests a place and time that are both generically provincial (this is not the center of Verona but an airport, a place of transition) and, in contrast with EUR, nontriumphal, small, built on a human scale. Actually, Verona was a Roman colony. Antonioni's camera lingers on the Roman amphitheater in the town's center as if to emphasize this fact. Because these two men do not appear with any "African" signifiers, they might evoke for the viewer African-Americans, in their condition of waiting for full civil rights, for integration, for power. There are U.S. military planes nearby, so we may assume the men are, in fact, soldiers. In any case, they do not belong in Italy (or better, *to* Italy), yet they are somehow more comfortable there, in their skins, than Vittoria herself. With their calm presence, they contrast with the tribal hysterics of Vittoria of the night before. So I would like to suggest that a cluster of signifiers—suspended, unconstrained time, Africa, African-Americans (or Negroes, to use the term of the period in question), provincial scale—all coalesce in this shot and point Vittoria toward a possible condition outside her constraints. And it is precisely this state of waiting, as opposed to the potential "boom" of the market (the crash scene will follow the Verona scene), of the Italian economy, or of the annihilating atomic bomb that now conditions the temporal state of Italy after decolonization.

In all likelihood Antonioni did not plan to film the black men in Verona but simply found them there. At any rate, the scene is not nearly as calculated as the "Africa" scene preceding it. In an interview on his techniques of location shooting, he once said,

> I arrive on location in a fixed state of "virginity." I do this because the best results are obtained by the "collision" that takes place between the environment in which the scene is to be shot and my own particular state of mind at that specific moment. . . . So, as I was saying a short while ago, improvisation comes directly from the rapport between the director and the people around him, both the usual professional collaborators and the people who just happen to be gathered in that particular area when the scene is being shot.[27]

Antonioni's shooting style—the same kind of improvisation applies equally to place, as he notes—allows us to consider the appearance of the two men as something like the expression of an unconscious desire. Although a culture like Italy that is essentially "white" might exist in a state of the noneventfulness of race, again, Antonioni's reflections on his cinema point out how such a forgetfulness is always significant. Discussing a period in his youth, the director imagined how he would construct a film about the experience of waiting in wartime:

> In that white seafront [Nice], that lonely figure, that silence, there seems to me to be an extraordinary strength of impact. The event here adds nothing: It is superfluous . . . the true emptiness, the malaise, the anxiety, the nausea, the atrophy of all normal feelings and desires, the fear, the anger—all these I felt when, coming out of the Negresco [Hotel], I found myself in that whiteness, in that nothingness, which took shape around a black point.[28]

For Antonioni, making films in black and white in an age of color, the eclipse cannot help but be a key figure, both for the existential condition of his protagonists and for the new conditions of daily life in the period of the boom, conditions of waiting and noneventfulness, which are unconsciously reflective of the state of decolonization.

THE END

At the end of *Eclipse,* night begins to fall. Motion in a central piazza in EUR's residential zone slows. What is clearly the last bus of the day arrives from the city center and its passengers disperse. Then silence descends on this peripheral suburb. In the final sequence of shots—deemed too long by Antonioni's producers—the static camera focuses on sprinklers, a barrel, a fence under construction, rustling trees, streetlights, and so on. The sequence is a visual catalogue of the objects that Vittoria and Piero passed on one of their early dates. We know they have separately decided not to keep their appointment for this evening. The music is a jarring piano piece that must arouse a visual image of both black and white keys being struck. And the viewer is reminded of black and white as a significant trope when the end title struggles to be legible against the white light, the final object of the sequence. There is much to say about this scene, for it is the moment when the film transforms itself into a purely phenomenal visual-acoustical experiment. After the departure of the bus, the only narrative element is the nonevent of the missed appointment between the two lovers. The only characters are the missed crowds of urbanity, the festive masses in other films. Thus the scene works as a series of negations. What is perhaps the most disturbing and unresolved aspect of the scene is the fact that nothing happens. There is only the suggestion of a fading away of affect. In this sense, Antonioni's *Eclipse* offers itself as an ideal figure for decolonization, disturbing, precisely, because of its fading, its ebbing away, without clear boundaries of time or space.

NOTES

1. Most Romans now use the acronym EUR unthinkingly, without considering the complex history of this area first developed for the 1960 Olympics, and which is now home to various government and private-sector offices, condominiums, and a recreational zone. In an early scene, Antonioni films Vittoria as she passes Pier Luigi Nervi's flying-saucer inspired Palazzo dello Sport, created as part of the Olympic building boom.

2. For example, even an intellectual like Antonioni, when asked in an interview about a certain "African aura" that one critic noticed in many of his films, responded with vague inaccuracies and clichés about nonlinear time: "I know Africa very well. I was there as a reporter, even when World War II broke out. I went back later and visited the country [*sic*] extensively for long periods. More than the desert in and of itself, I always felt the need to live in a different historical context, in a nonhistorical world, or in a historical context that is not conscious of its own historicity." Cited in *The Architecture of Vision: Writings and Interviews on Cinema*, Carlo di Carlo and Giorgio Tinazzi, eds. (New York: Marsilio Publishers, 1996), 183.

3. For Italians, as for Europeans in general, space travel was considered a thing of the distant future and an American idea. A conference held in Copenhagen in the mid-1950s concluded that it would not be possible to send a manned mission to the moon before the year 2000. The primary obstacle to space travel was thought to be nourishment (conference participants suggested astronauts could binge before the flight and then starve themselves until their return to earth), rather than engineering. In any case, the rhetoric of outer space that begins to develop in Italy during the postwar period does not significantly draw on a rhetoric of permanent colonization or demographic solutions. See "Didimo: La prima spedizione umana potrà atterare sulla luna per il 2000," *La Stampa*, Aug. 4, 1955: 6. Also see my comments on the reference to "spatial law" in Dino Risi's *Il sorpasso*, later in this essay.

4. The reference to "racist science" is one familiar to scholars of Italian fascism.

It is generally agreed that the discourse of "racist science" was imported, in part or in whole, from Nazi Germany and diffused in publications such as *La difesa della razza*. For the "science" of the fascists see, among others, Luigi Preti, *I miti dell'impero e della razza italiana negli anni '30* (Roma: Opere nuove, 1965); *La menzogna della razza: Documenti e immagini del razzismo e dell'antisemitismo fascista,* curated by the Centro Furio Jesi (Bologna: Grafis Edizioni, 1994). Also see my *Bodily Regimes: Italian Advertising under Fascism* (Minneapolis: University of Minnesota Press, 1995).

5. In this sense, Italians also stopped talking about their own whiteness as they simultaneously turned their gazes from a Mediterranean-peninsular to an Eastern-Western axis. Richard Dyer, who has written eloquently on whiteness as a quality that has normally passed itself off as a nonquality, notes that "the sense of whites as non-raced is most evident in the absence of reference to whiteness in the habitual speech and writing of white people in the West." See his *White* (London and New York: Routledge, 1977), 2.

6. Of course, as Kristin Ross notes, the violence and terror at one time experienced by the French in relation to the Algerian revolution have not meant a sustained engagement with the history of colonialism today, since, by keeping the stories of modernization and decolonization separate, the French could think of colonial history as "an 'exterior' experience that somehow came to an abrupt end, cleanly, in 1962. . . . Having decisively slammed shut the door to the Algerian episode, colonialism itself was made to seem like a dusty archaism, as though it had not transpired in the twentieth century and in the personal histories of many people living today, as though it played only a tiny role in France's national history." See her *Fast Cars, Clean Bodies: Decolonization and the Reordering of French Culture* (Cambridge, Mass.: MIT Press, 1995), 9.

7. On the enduring role of the former colonial bureaucracy in postwar Italy, see Angelo Del Boca, *Gli italiani in Africa Orientale,* vol. 4, *Nostalgia delle colonie* (Roma-Bari: Laterza, 1984), 17: "With the fall of fascism, there comes a tendency to praise all that Italians did there, without any self-criticism. And the men who write the reports that are transmitted to the four great powers are, mostly, the same men who were there under fascism" (translation mine).

8. It is important to note that throughout the 1950s the housing crisis was configured in terms of a debate between nomadism and permanence, echoing a strong tradition in the ideological critique of (especially North) Africa and a justification for colonialism itself. See, for example, the article "Circa cinquantamila persone abitano ancora in grotte, tuguri, capanne e campi di raccolta," *Il messaggero di Roma,* July 29, 1953: 4. For the rhetoric of road building, see Enrico Menduni, *L'autostrada del sole* (Bologna: Il Mulino, 1999).

9. Much has been written on this phenomenon from a historical and cultural perspective. Among others, see Pieropaolo D'Attore, ed., *Nemici per la pelle: Sogno americano e mito sovietico nell'Italia contemporanea* (Milano: F. Angeli, 1991); Christopher Duggan and Christopher Wagstaff, eds., *Italy and the Cold War: Politics, Culture and Society 1948–1958* (Oxford: Berg, 1995); Leopoldo Nuti, *Gli Stati Uniti e l'apertura a sinistra, 1953–1963: Importanza e limiti della presenza americana in Italia* (Roma-Bari: Laterza, 1999); Richard Pells, *Not Like Us: How Europeans Have Loved, Hated, and Transformed American Culture Since World War II* (New York: Basic Books, 1997).

10. For example, in 1954 the son of the Christian Democrat minister Umberto

Tupini organized an extremely dramatic traveling exhibit called "Mostra dell'Aldilà" (Exhibition of the beyond). The "beyond" of the exhibit was not, as might be expected, the afterlife, or even the "beyond" of some Mediterranean frontier, but the "beyond" of the iron curtain. Visitors to the exhibit were shown theatrical displays comparing the inflated prices of consumer goods in Eastern bloc countries versus the prices of the same goods in the West. At the exit visitors were asked to fill out opinion cards, a performative gesture meant to demonstrate to them their right to exercise free speech.

11. Mia Fuller writes of the similarities between the urban projects of Addis Ababa in Ethiopia and EUR in Rome in her "Fascist Plan for Addis Ababa and EUR '42," *Journal of Contemporary History* 31 (1996): 373–95.

12. This zoning policy is echoed in Robin Pickering-Iazzi's chapter in this volume, in which she compares the (missed) monumental gesture of the return of the Axum obelisk to the "politics of disappearance executed in Ethiopia by the fascist regime in the late 1930s." She also cites several articles from women's magazines that support this idea of a segregated and regularized living quarter for whites, obviously key in the propaganda effort to attract women to the colonies.

13. The phrase "garden city" comes from an article on the history of habitation in EUR by Fulvio Irace, "Riguardare l'architettura EUR, 1937–1987," *Abitare* 255 (June 1987): 179.

14. The eclipse trilogy of Antonioni also includes *La notte* and *L'avventura.* For the Situationists revisioning of urban space see Simon Sadler, *The Situationist City* (Cambridge, Mass.: MIT Press, 1998), 5.

15. In many of his films Antonioni has dealt extensively with the uneasy production of architectural spaces by his characters. In fact, an important collection of his essays and interviews bears the title, in English, *The Architecture of Vision.*

16. Moreover, the politics of transport in the period under consideration meant that certain axes—particularly the one leading from the center to EUR and the sea—had received investment capital from a limited number of powerful speculators and were thus privileged over others. In part, this uneven investment can be explained by a tangled web of favoritism that enriched men with the ability to capitalize on the lack of a regulatory plan in Rome and on loose rules for postwar reclamation. For this sad history, see Italo Insolera *Roma moderna: Un secolo di storia urbanistica, 1870–1970* (Torino: Einaudi, 1976).

17. Henri Lefebvre, in *The Production of Space,* trans. Donald Nicholson-Smith (Oxford: Basil Blackwell, 1991), writes that to apply (semiotic) codes derived from literary texts to spatial problems would be "to reduce space itself to the status of a *message,* and the inhabiting of it the status of a *reading.* This is to evade both history and practice" (7).

18. In invoking "the thirteenth kilometer," Bruno points to a kind of local geographical knowledge based on (and yet possibly undercutting) the regulatory plan of the roads, the overarching code of a "planned" Italy.

19. In *L'autostrada del sole* Menduni recounts the fascinating microhistory of these bridge elements, meant to be accessible to traffic in both directions along the highway. The bridges do interrupt the visual flow, the "free-way" of the car's mobility. But they also stand as emblems of a decolonized mentality: they stand for the permanent and mature commitment to "two-way" mobility (from the North to the

South; or the South to the North), as opposed to the one-way mobility of colonialist "penetration" of the hinterland.

20. In works like George Perec's *Les choses*, Pauline Réage's *L'histoire d'O*, and Simone de Beauvoir's *Les belles images*, not only is advertising a field that is wide open to women, but the discourse of advertising (or public relations) is actually linked with an ethos in which gender differences are absolutely minimized and equality between the sexes reaches a state of quasi-utopianism.

21. For ordinary speech and its relation to the language of advertising, see Michel de Certeau, *L'invention du quotidien*, vol. 1, *Les arts de faire* (Paris: Gallimard, 1990).

22. I take a different view from that of Kevin Moore, in "Eclipsing the Commonplace: The Logic of Alienation in Antonioni's Cinema," *Film Quarterly* 48 (Summer 1995): 22–34, where he claims that the interior is authentically African, "like a foreign country" (28). He continues: "Antonioni shoots the scene as though she [Vittoria] were stepping into a picture, going 'through the looking glass' into a foreign world." This also contradicts my point about the abrupt cuts in the scene because it leads us to expect a filmic device, something like an iris-in (a noticeable tightening of the focus) to the picture, or animation from a still shot. Moore does, however, understand the dance that follows as pure desire for difference, and on this point I am in agreement. For neo-primitivism in relation to the politics of architecture in the 1960s, see Sadler, *The Situationist City*.

23. This awkward switching of languages should not be understood, I believe, in the positive sense of a fluidity that also masters multiple identities or opens up new possibilities for self-definition. With regard to race (and gender), this kind of flow has been most aptly explored by Anna Camaiti Hostert in *Passing: Dissolvere le identità, superare le differenze* (Roma: Castelvecchi, 1996).

24. As in the previous note, my reading of the scene departs from one that understands this apartment as a permanent ethos for an African-European identity. Rather, I would say that Marta's apartment corresponds to the typical interior of Antonioni's films. In general, Antonioni's characters are never authentically at home. "I personaggi di Antonioni non 'abitano', ma sono dei veri e propri consumatori di domicili. Come i nomadi, ripetono continuamente l'atto di fondazione, anche se sentimentalmente e culturalmente fanno parte di una società di non-nomadi" (Antonioni's characters don't "inhabit" but are true consumers of residences. Like nomads, they repeat the act of foundation, even if, sentimentally and culturally, they belong to a non-nomadic society). Astrid Vinatzer, "The House of Unease: Habitation in Michelangelo Antonioni," *Abitare* 367 (Nov. 1997): 136.

25. Writing of this departure, Del Boca notes, "Il loro sbarco, frettoloso e in silenzio, ricorda quello, fatto di notte a Napoli, dei soldati italiani caduti prigionieri ad Adua, nel 1896, e ricondotti in patria quasi di nascosto l'anno successivo, dopo le umilianti trattative con Menelik. Anche nel 1943, come nel 1897, l'Africa non è più di moda." *Gli italiani in Africa orientale*, vol. 4, *Nostalgia delle colonie*, 4.

26. Incidentally, Pasolini himself moved to EUR in 1963. The move was probably meant to appease his mother, with whom he shared his living space. EUR would not seem to be a typical *locus pasolinianus*.

27. *The Architecture of Vision*, 28–29.

28. Because the filmmaker works in black and white, it is necessarily these colors (with their racial overtones) that condition his lived experiences. Ibid., 53.

WORKS CITED

Antonioni, Michelangelo. *The Architecture of Vision: Writings and Interviews on Cinema.* Carlo di Carlo and Giorgio Tinazzi, eds. New York: Marsilio Publishers, 1996.

Camaiti Hostert, Anna. *Passing: Dissolvere le identità, superare le differenze.* Roma: Castelvecchi, 1996.

D'Attore, Pieropaolo, ed. *Nemici per la pelle: Sogno americano e mito sovietico nell'Italia contemporanea.* Milano: F. Angeli, 1991.

De Certeau, Michel. *Invention du quotidien.* Vol. 1, *Les arts de faire.* Paris: Gallimard, 1990.

Del Boca, Angelo. *Gli Italiani in Africa orientale.* Vol. 4, *Nostalgia delle colonie.* Roma-Bari: Laterza, 1984.

Duggan, Christopher, and Christopher Wagstaff, eds. *Italy and the Cold War: Politics, Culture and Society 1948–1958.* Oxford: Berg, 1995.

Dyer, Richard. *White.* London: Routledge, 1997.

Fuller, Mia. "Fascist Plan for Addis Ababa and EUR '42." *Journal of Contemporary History* 31 (1996): 373–95.

Insolera, Italo. *Roma moderna: Un secolo di storia urbanistica, 1870–1970.* Torino: Einaudi, 1976.

Irace, Fulvio. "Riguardare l'architettura EUR, 1937–1987." *Abitare* 225 (June 1987): 178–85.

Lefebvre, Henri. *The Production of Space.* Trans. Donald Nicholson-Smith. Oxford: Basil Blackwell, 1991.

Menduni, Enrico. *L'autostrada del sole.* Bologna: Il Mulino, 1999.

Moore, Kevin. "Eclipsing the Commonplace: The Logic of Alienation in Antonioni's Cinema." *Film Quarterly* 48 (Summer 1995): 22–34.

Nuti, Leopoldo. *Gli Stati Uniti e l'apertura a sinistra, 1953–1963: Importanza e limiti della presenza americana in Italia.* Roma-Bari: Laterza, 1999.

Pells, Richard. *Not Like Us: How Europeans Have Loved, Hated, and Transformed American Culture Since World War II.* New York: Basic Books, 1997.

Pinkus, Karen. *Bodily Regimes: Italian Advertising under Fascism.* Minneapolis: University of Minnesota Press, 1995.

Preti, Luigi. *I miti dell'impero e della razza italiana negli anni '30.* Rome: Opere nuove, 1965.

Ross, Kristin. *Fast Cars, Clean Bodies: Decolonization and the Reordering of French Culture.* Cambridge, Mass.: MIT Press, 1998.

Sadler, Simon. *The Situationist City.* Cambridge, Mass.: MIT Press, 1999.

Vinatzer, Astrid. "The House of Unease: Habitation in Michelangelo Antonioni." *Abitare* 367 (Nov. 1997): 136–38.

NOTES ON CONTRIBUTORS

Giulia Barrera holds a Ph.D. in African history from Northwestern University and works as an archivist for the Publications Division of the Italian State Archives Administration. Her publications include works on archival issues and on Italian colonialism in Eritrea, with special focus on issues of gender and race.

Giorgio Bertellini is a fellow at the Michigan Society of Fellows at the University of Michigan, where he is also Visiting Assistant Professor in the Program of Film and Video Studies. Author of a monograph on Bosnian director Emir Kusturica (Il castoro, 1996), Bertellini has published extensively on film history and culture in numerous periodicals and anthologies. In 2000 he edited the first-ever special issue on early Italian cinema for *Film History*. He is currently working on a book about the film experience of Southern Italians living in Italy and New York City at the turn of the twentieth century.

Cecilia Boggio is completing her Ph.D. in comparative literature at the University of Southern California. She is writing a dissertation on epic space in the age of the emergence of cinema. She has published articles on Italian silent cinema and on early cinema as a mass medium.

Angelo Del Boca has worked as a journalist, essayist, and professor of Italian history at the University of Turin. He is the author of numerous important articles and books on Italian history. In books such as *Gli italiani in Africa orientale* (Mondadori, 1992) and *Una sconfitta dell'intelligenza: Italia e Somalia* (Laterza, 1993), Del Boca has made a seminal contribution to the study of Italian colonial history.

Nicola Labanca teaches contemporary history at the University of Siena. He is the author of *In marcia verso Adua* (Einaudi, 1993), *Storia dell'Italia coloniale* (Fenice 2000, 1994), and *Caporetto: Storia di una disfatta* (Giunti-Castermann, 1997), has edited several anthologies, and has written more than forty articles on Italian military history and postcolonial studies.

Cristina Lombardi-Diop teaches at the American University of Rome. She is the author of essays on D'Annunzio, Marinetti and futurist women, African migrant literatures in Italy, and Italian colonial literary and political culture. She is at work on a book on Italian colonial travelogues and novels written by Italian women in the period 1840–1940.

Patrizia Palumbo is assistant professor of Italian and French at Wagner College. She has written articles on medieval and contemporary Italian culture. This is her first edited volume. She is currently working on a manuscript dealing with medieval Italian exchanges with other cultures.

Robin Pickering-Iazzi is professor of Italian and comparative literature at the University of Wisconsin–Milwaukee. She is the author of *Politics of the Visible: Writing Women, Culture, and Fascism* (University of Minnesota Press, 1997) and has edited *Mothers of Invention: Women, Italian Fascism, and Culture* (University of Minnesota Press, 1995) and *Unspeakable Women: Selected Short Stories Written by Italian Women During Fascism* (Feminist Press of the City University of New York, 1993).

Karen Pinkus teaches at the University of Southern California. She is the author of *Bodily Regimes: Italian Advertising Under Fascism* (University of Minnesota Press, 1995) and of *The Montesi Scandal: The Death of Wilma Montesi and the Birth of the Paparazzi in Fellini's Rome* (University of Chicago Press, 2003).

Born and raised in Rome, *Lucia Re* studied at the University of Rome "La Sapienza" and at Smith College. She received her Ph.D. in comparative literature from Yale University and she is currently a professor of modern Italian literature and culture at UCLA. Her books include *Calvino and the Age of Neorealism: Fables of Estrangement* (Stanford University Press, 1990) and *Gender and the Avant-Garde in Italy* (University of California Press, forthcoming).

Cinzia Sartini-Blum is associate professor of Italian at the University of Iowa. She is author of *The Other Modernism: F. T. Marinetti's Futurist Fiction of Power* (University of California Press, 1996) and editor of *Futurism and the Avant-Garde* (special issue of the South Central Review, 1996). Her other publications include *Contemporary Italian Women Poets: A Bilingual Anthology* (in collaboration with Lara Trubowitz; Italica Press, 2001), a forthcoming translation of Carlo Michelstaedter's *Persuasione e rettorica* (in collaboration with Russell Valentino and David Depew), and various essays on futurism, fascist culture, and Ludovico Ariosto.

Barbara Sòrgoni holds an M.A. in social anthropology from Sussex University (U.K.) and a Ph.D. in cultural anthropology from IUO (Naples, Italy) and currently lectures on cultural anthropology at the Second University of Naples. She is author of *Parole e corpi: Antropologia, discorso giuridico e politiche sessuali interrazziali nella colonia Eritrea 1890–1941* (Liguori, 1998) and *Etnografia e colonialismo: L'Eritrea e l'Etiopia di Alberto Pollera* (Bollati Boringhieri, 2001).

INDEX

Text: 10/12 Baskerville
Display: Baskerville
Compositor: G&S Typesetters, Inc.
Printer and binder: Thomson-Shore, Inc.